An economic history of Britain since 1700, in three volumes by thirty-nine
eminent historians and economists, this book will succeed the first edition
of 'Floud and McCloskey' (published in 1981) as the leading textbook on
its subject. The text has a firm economic basis, but emphasises the
historical context and chronology and is written in straightforward and
jargon-free English. It will appeal particularly to first and second year
university students, but is also suitable for anyone interested in the
history of the British economy. Volume 1 covers the period 1700–1860,
that of Britain's rise to relative economic supremacy. Volume 2 discusses
the period 1860–1939, that of the height of British economic power and
of painful readjustment after 1914. Volume 3 considers the period since
1939, that of relative economic decline and of increasing involvement
with the European Community.

THE ECONOMIC HISTORY OF BRITAIN SINCE 1700

SECOND EDITION

Volume 3: 1939–1992

THE ECONOMIC HISTORY OF BRITAIN SINCE 1700

SECOND EDITION

Volume 3: 1939–1992

Edited by RODERICK FLOUD *and*
DONALD McCLOSKEY

CAMBRIDGE
UNIVERSITY PRESS

Published by the Press Syndicate of the University of Cambridge
The Pitt Building, Trumpington Street, Cambridge CB2 1RP
40 West 20th Street, New York, NY 10011–4211, USA
10 Stamford Road, Oakleigh, Melbourne 3166, Australia

First published 1981
Second edition 1994

Printed in Great Britain at the University Press, Cambridge

A catalogue record for this book is available from the British Library

Library of Congress cataloguing in publication data

The economic history of Britain since 1700/edited by Roderick Floud and
Donald McCloskey. – 2nd ed.
    p.   cm.
Includes bibliographical references and index.
Contents: v. 1. 1700–1860. v. 2. 1860–1939. 3. 1939–1992.
1. Great Britain – Economic conditions. I. Floud, Roderick. II. McCloskey,
Donald N.
HC254.5.E27 1993   330.941'07   93-20093

ISBN 0 521 41498 9 (v. 1) 0 521 41499 7 (v. 2)
ISBN 0 521 42520 4 (v. 1 pb) 0 521 42521 2 (v. 2 pb)
ISBN 0 521 41500 4 (v. 3) 0 521 42522 0 (v. 3 pb)

ISBN 0 521 41500 4 hardback
ISBN 0 521 42522 0 paperback

UP

To Lydia, Sarah, Daniel and Margaret

Contents

Figures

Tables

Contributors

STEPHEN BROADBERRY is Senior Lecturer in the Department of Economics, University of Warwick

SIR ALEXANDER CAIRNCROSS is Chancellor of the University of Glasgow

CHARLES FEINSTEIN is Chichele Professor of Economic History in the University of Oxford

RODERICK FLOUD is Provost of London Guildhall University

LESLIE HANNAH is Professor of Business History at the London School of Economics

PETER HOWLETT is Lecturer in Economic History at the London School of Economics

SUSAN HOWSON is Professor of Economics at the University of Toronto and Visiting Fellow, Wolfson College, Cambridge

PAUL JOHNSON is Lecturer in Social History at the London School of Economics

DONALD McCLOSKEY is Professor of Economics and of History at the University of Iowa

ROBERT MILLWARD is Professor of Economic History at the University of Manchester

BARRY SUPPLE is Director of the Leverhulme Trust and Emeritus Professor of Economics at the University of Cambridge

JIM TOMLINSON is Reader in Economic History at Brunel University

Introduction to first edition

Roderick Floud & Donald McCloskey

Economic history is an exciting subject, a subject full of problems and controversy. It is exciting because in economic history one is constantly forced to ask the question – why? Why were steam engines brought into use at a particular point during the industrial revolution? Why did so many millions brave great dangers to emigrate to the New World? Why were so many unemployed in the depression of the 1930s? Why do parents today have fewer children than parents 200 years ago? Economic history is not, therefore, a story – still less a chronological story, for most events in economic history cannot be neatly dated. Instead it is a list of questions; some can be answered, some cannot, but it is the search for answers, and for the best way to seek answers, which gives the subject both its justification and its interest. 'Economic history concerns the dullest part of human life. Sex, art, aberrant behaviour, politics, bloodshed – it is largely devoid of these' (Parker 1971). Yet it is concerned instead with how people live most of their lives, how many people are born and how they die, how they earn and how they spend, how they work and how they play.

At the same time, economic history can be hard, boring and frustrating, both to write and to learn. Simply because it is concerned with how people have commonly lived, and why they have commonly behaved in a particular way, it is often difficult to discover relevant evidence; people, certainly most people, do not record in great detail for posterity what they buy or what they do at work, nor even how many children they have. The historian has to reconstruct the details of such behaviour from scattered and ambiguous evidence, and his reconstruction can often only be imprecise; few of the statements made in this book are, for that reason, entirely free from the possibility of error, and many represent only guesses. They are the best guesses made, when the book was written, by economic historians expert in their subject, but guesses nonetheless. Indeed, part of the fascination of economic history, although also one of the main causes of the controversies which rumble on for years in the scholarly journals of the subject, lies in making new guesses, and in working out what the effect on our knowledge of the past might be if we made different, but still sensible, guesses about the interpretation of evidence.

Even when we know, at least approximately, whether people ate white or brown bread, or at what age they married, they are very unlikely to have recorded for posterity why they ate white bread when their parents ate brown, or why they married at twenty-seven when their parents married at twenty-four. Even if they did so, their records would be inconclusive, for two reasons: first, people are poor at self-analysis; second, the factor which they choose as 'the' reason why is usually one among many joint reasons. In any case, the economic historian's interest is not normally in the behaviour of individuals, except as exemplars of the behaviour of society, or large groups within society, as a whole. While a political historian can reasonably hope to understand something of the political history of the nineteenth century by studying the life and thoughts of Queen Victoria or of Abraham Lincoln, the economic historian knows that the behaviour of any one individual has very little or no effect upon, and may even be totally different from the observed behaviour of society as a whole. The fact that the marriage age in a parish is observed to have fallen from an average of twenty-seven in one generation to an average of twenty-four in the next does not show that all those who married did so at the age of twenty-four; nor, conversely, does the fact that two people married at twenty-nine invalidate the fact of the fall in the average.

The answer that we give to a question such as 'why did people marry at an earlier age than their parents' cannot therefore stem directly from the memories or writings of those who were doing the marrying. It can stem partly from such evidence, but only because such evidence helps to build up a set of the many possible reasons why people might have decided to marry earlier. This set of reasons, based partly on evidence from those who married and partly on the knowledge and common sense of the historian, is a necessary beginning to the task of explanation. Armed with it, the historian can begin to explore the evidence, and to see to what degree the behaviour which he observes fits best with one reason rather than another. He might begin, for example, with the belief that people are likely to marry if they are richer and can afford to set up house at an earlier age than their parents; if he finds after seeking for evidence of changes in income levels that on the contrary income levels fell at the same time as marriage became earlier, then that belief seems unlikely to be helpful, and another possible reason must be explored.

In other words, the historian uses evidence of the behaviour of individuals to help him to build up an expectation of how people might have behaved, against which he can contrast his observations of how they actually seem to have behaved. The expectation, or model as it is often called, is founded on assumptions about human behaviour, and therefore about the likely response of groups of individuals to changes in their circumstances. At its most simple, for example, the expectation might be that in general people buy less of a commodity as it becomes more expensive. The expectation may not always be correct for each individual, but it serves in general.

We need to have such expectations, or models, if we are to organise our thoughts and assumptions and apply them to the elucidation or solution of problems about what happened in history. If we do not, then we can only flounder in a mass of individual observations, unaware whether the individual behaviour which we observe is normal or aberrant. Models, therefore, cut through the diversity of experience and behaviour which we all know to characterise any human activity, and embody our judgement as to why people are likely to have behaved as they did.

If the models of historians are to be useful in analysing the past, then they must be carefully chosen. The economic and social historian deals in his work on past societies with subjects which are the concern of many analysts of contemporary society: economists, geographers, sociologists, political scientists. It is sensible for the historian to consider whether he may use their models to aid him in his work. In making the choice he must always be conscious that contemporary society is different from past society, and that a model may either have to be adapted to the requirements of historical analysis or, at the extreme, rejected as entirely inappropriate. But if the adaptation can be made then the historian is likely to gain greatly in his work from the insights of contemporary social scientists; these insights help him to expand and refine his model of the past.

These assertions are controversial. Not all historians accept that it is useful to apply models drawn from the social sciences to historical analysis. Not all, even today, would accept that the primary task of the historian is to explain; they would hold, instead, that description, the discovery of the record of what happened in the past, should be given pride of place. Most frequently, critics of the use of models and of the statistical methods which often accompany them claim that models cannot cope with the rich diversity of human behaviour in the past, that they simplify and therefore distort. Even mere statistical description – counting heads and calculating averages – has been attacked for dehumanising history and for replacing people by numbers.

Such attacks are based largely on misunderstanding. It is certainly true that models of human behaviour must simplify; indeed, that is their purpose, to enable the historian to concentrate on a restricted set of possible explanations for that behaviour, rather than being distracted by the diversity of individual deeds. It is also true that models concentrate on expectations of normal or average behaviour; again, this is deliberate and necessary if the normal is to be distinguished from the aberrant. The historian who uses models does not forget that diversity exists; indeed he makes use of that diversity, those different reactions to different circumstances, to help him to frame and then to improve his model. In some circumstances, no doubt, the diversity of the past may defeat the simplifying powers of the historian and the most complex of models, but such circumstances are no grounds for rejection of the use of models as a whole.

A more reasonable criticism of models and their application to history is that they are often themselves too simple, and that they embody unjustifiable assumptions about human behaviour. In later chapters of this book, for example, we make use of models which assume the existence of full employment, or of perfect mobility of labour; such models may lead to misleading results if such conditions do not obtain. Yet to criticise the use of one model in one set of circumstances does not show that all use of models is wrong. It shows simply that the historian, and the reader of this or any book, should be alert and critical and should not make silly errors; the same could be said of any scholarly work.

A third ground of criticism of the use of models and of statistical methods in history is better founded. Many social scientists use mathematical language to express their ideas and to formulate their models, while most historians, and even many social scientists, are not sufficiently familiar with mathematics to understand what is written. They do not appreciate that mathematics is often used merely as a shorthand, and are even less likely to appreciate that it is sometimes used merely to impress the unwary. Very reasonably, someone who does not understand may reject the ideas along with the language by which they are veiled, even though, in truth, the models can almost always be expressed in a language which is comprehensible to non-mathematicians.

This book has been written by economic and social historians who are expert in the use of models and of statistical methods in history, but are conscious of the fears, doubts and misunderstandings which such usage evokes. They wish to show that economic and social history is not diminished thereby but augmented, and that the results can be understood by anyone interested in historical problems. The economic and social history which they write, and which is discussed in this book, is sometimes called the 'new' economic and social history. The novelty of applying the methods of social science to history is by now about a quarter of a century old; it is often 'new' not so much in its aim nor even in its methods, but merely in the language which it uses. The results, however, are of great interest, and for this reason the authors have expressed their ideas in a language which any student of the subject can understand; where they have used a model or a statistical method which may be unfamiliar, it has been explained.

Together, the chapters in this book make up an economic history of England and Wales since 1700. The basic chronology and the evidence on which it is based are discussed, and the book as a whole provides a treatment of the most important themes in English social and economic history during the period of industrialisation and economic growth. Much has been left out, for the authors and editors have chosen to concentrate on the topics which are most problematical and yet where solutions to problems may be attainable. The book is divided into five overlapping chronological divisions, corresponding to the periods from 1700 to 1800, from 1780 to 1860, from 1860 to 1914, from 1900 to 1945, and from 1945 to the present day. Each division except the last begins with a general survey of the period, which is followed by a number of chapters which consider the main problems which have arisen in the historical interpretation of that period; each division except the first and last concludes with a chapter dealing with the social history of the period in relation to the economic changes which have been considered. The period since 1945 is treated as a whole in one, final, chapter. The book is divided into two volumes, with the break at 1860, although a number of chapters in both volumes bridge the break. Each volume has its own index and glossary, and its own bibliography; frequent references to sources and to further reading are given in the text, making use of the 'author–date' system of reference. In this system, books or articles are referred to in the text simply by the name of the author and the date of publication, for example (Keynes 1936); the bibliography is an alphabetical list of authors, with the date of publication immediately following the author's name. Thus (Keynes 1936) in the text has its counterpart as Keynes, J. M. 1936. *The General Theory of Employment, Interest and Money* in the bibliography.

The book has been planned and written by many hands. The Social Science Research Council of Great Britain generously made funds available both for an initial planning meeting and for a conference at which the first drafts of the chapters were discussed. The authors and editors are grateful to the SSRC for its generosity, and to Donald Coleman, Philip Cottrell, Jack Dowie, Malcolm Falkus, Jordan Goodman, Leslie Hannah, Max Hartwell, Brian Mitchell, Leslie Pressnell, John Wright and Tony Wrigley for attending the conference and making many helpful comments. Annabel Gregory, Alan Hergert, Nigel Lewis, and Ali Saad gave invaluable help in preparing the manuscript for publication.

Introduction to second edition

Roderick Floud & Donald McCloskey

The first edition, in 1981, had two volumes. This, the second, a dozen years later, has three. The change marks not only the expansion of the study of the last fifty years but also the acceleration of historical research on the British economy. From its beginnings in the late 1960s, with a thin, bright stream of predecessors back to the 1940s and before, the historical economics of Britain has flourished.

This edition, like the first, embodies a collaboration between British and North American authors which has been characteristic of the subject. Much of the underlying research, of which it is a synthesis, was first published in American journals such as *Explorations in Economic History* and the *Journal of Economic History*, as well as in the British *Economic History Review*. British and American economic historians have published their findings in those journals and, increasingly, in general interest journals of economics, reflecting a continuing interest among economists in the past of the first industrial nation. The British economy was the first to commercialise, industrialise, move to services and mature. Small wonder that economists have come to see Britain's history as a laboratory for economic science.

The materials used in that laboratory have become more varied during the 1980s. Two books in particular, each the product of years of research, have extended our knowledge of the fundamentals of the economy; Wrigley and Schofield (1981) have put *The Population History of England* on a firmer footing, while Matthews, Feinstein and Odling-Smee (1982) have given a magisterial account of *British Economic Growth*. But their work has been accompanied, on a lesser scale, by a host of economists and historians who have continued to explore both the central issues of economic history – growth, distribution, consumption – and the inter-connections between those issues and topics of social, demographic and other forms of historical enquiry.

These enquiries have often been controversial. A political emphasis on the role of markets which was common to Reagan's America and Thatcher's Britain in the 1980s led to studies of such diverse topics as child labour, education and inter-war unemployment. Monetarists tested the power of money to explain British experience. From the left, a generation of economically trained Marxists challenged the optimistic view of Victorian economic performance which had characterised the first generation of cliometricians. Research into the distribution of income, into the speed of Britain's growth and the alleged decline of the British economy and into demographic history and the history of nutrition, mortality and morbidity has given rise to fierce challenge.

These controversies are reflected in the pages which follow. There is no agreement on many topics in British economic history and it is right that differences should be exposed rather than glossed over. The 1980s have, however, seen much less controversy than in previous decades about the methods of enquiry; the role of economic theory, of statistics and computing, whose use in economic history had been challenged but which now underpins all the chapters in these volumes. Underpin is the right word, for there is much less explicit quantification and theorising than in the first edition; it is still there, but the authors feel less need to expose it and less need to parade technical expertise and technical language.

As with the first edition, the style of the book owes much to discussion between the authors at a conference at which first drafts were presented to a critical and constructive audience of the authors themselves and invited commentators. The commentators were Bernard Alford, Sue Bowden, Andrew Dilnot, Peter Mathias, Roger Middleton, Geoffrey Owen, George Peden, Peter Wardley, Katherine Watson, and Tony Wrigley; the authors and editors are grateful to all of them for their help. The conference was made possible by grants from the Economic and Social Research Council, from the British Academy and from Cambridge University Press and it benefited from the hospitality and the pleasant surroundings of St Catharine's College, Cambridge. The production of the book has been greatly aided by the enthusiasm of Richard Fisher and the copy-editing of Linda Randall, together with other staff of Cambridge University Press.

It is salutory to remember, in considering a book which is to a large extent about technical change, that the first editon was produced without the aid of word processors, fax machines or electronic mail. Twelve years later all have been used but the travails of editorship remain, together with our wish to acknowledge, in overcoming them, the support of our wives, Cynthia and Joanne, and of our children to whom this edition, like the first, is dedicated.

ATLANTIC

OCEAN

SHETLAND ISLANDS

North

ORKNEY
ISLANDS

SUTHERLAND

ROSS
AND
CROMARTY
Inverness
·Culloden

·Aberdeen

Sea

SCOTLAND

·Edinburgh
Glasgow
LOTHIANS

·Newcastle

LOWLANDS

BORDERS

NORTH-EAST

NORTHERN
ULSTER
IRELAND
·Belfast

NORTH-WEST

Irish Sea

Leeds Hull

CONNAUGHT

Manchester

·Liverpool

REPUBLIC

R. Boyne

·Dublin

Sheffield

LEINSTER

OF IRELAND

·Limerick

NORTH
WALES

EAST
MIDLANDS

WEST   EAST

MUNSTER

WALES

MIDLANDS
·Birmingham

ENGLAND

ANGLIA

St George's Channel

SOUTH WALES

HOME

SOUTH-EAST

COUNTIES

London

Thames
Estuary

Cardiff·
Bristol Channel
Bristol

SOUTH-WEST

·Southampton
·Portsmouth

0   50   100 150 km

0   50   100 miles

Plymouth

English Channel

ISLES of SCILLY

FRANCE

XXV

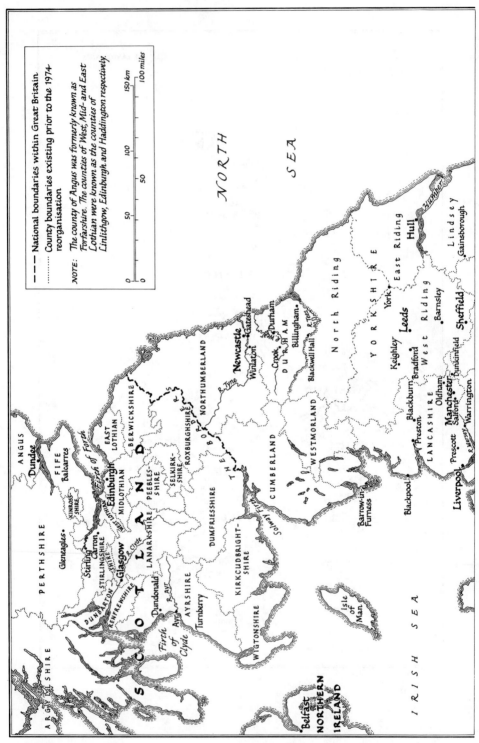

National boundaries within Great Britain.

.... County boundaries existing prior to the 1974 reorganisation

NOTE: The county of Angus was formerly known as Forfarshire. The counties of West, Mid- and East Lothian were known as the counties of Linlithgow, Edinburgh and Haddington respectively.

150 km

100 miles

NORTH SEA

IRISH SEA

SCOTLAND

ENGLAND

NORTHERN IRELAND

Belfast

Isle of Man

ARGYLLSHIRE

PERTHSHIRE

ANGUS
Dundee

FIFE
Balcarres

KINROSS-SHIRE

Gleneagles

Stirling
Carron
STIRLINGSHIRE
DUNBARTONSHIRE
RENFREWSHIRE

Glasgow

LANARKSHIRE

Dundonald
AYRSHIRE
Turnberry

WIGTONSHIRE

KIRKCUDBRIGHT-SHIRE

DUMFRIESSHIRE

Edinburgh
WEST LOTHIAN
MIDLOTHIAN
EAST LOTHIAN

PEEBLES-SHIRE

SELKIRK-SHIRE

ROXBURGHSHIRE

BERWICKSHIRE

NORTHUMBERLAND

THE BORDERS

Newcastle
Gateshead
Winlaton
R. Tyne

Crook
DURHAM
Durham
Billingham
Blackwell Hall

CUMBERLAND

WESTMORLAND

Barrow-in-Furness

North Riding

YORKSHIRE
York
East Riding
Hull
Humber

Lindsey
Gainsborough

Keighley
Bradford
Leeds
West Riding
Barnsley
Sheffield

LANCASHIRE
Blackpool
Preston
Blackburn
Oldham
Manchester
Salford
Dunkinfield
Liverpool
Prescot
Warrington
R. Mersey

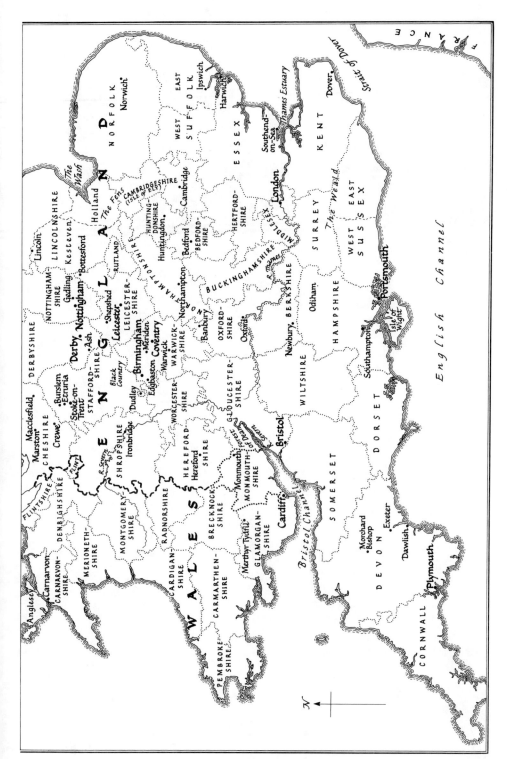

1   The wartime economy, 1939–1945

Peter Howlett

Introduction

During the Second World War, as it moved from a peacetime footing to
one of full-scale war mobilisation, Britain was transformed from a
predominantly free market economy into a centrally managed economy.
The transformation is shown in Table 1.1: expenditure on war-related
activities increased from a mere 7 per cent in 1938 to 53 per cent by 1941
and peaked at 55 per cent in 1943, at which time it totalled £4,512 million.
This increase was achieved through substantial negative non-war capital
formation and by severely curtailing the growth in the consumption of
non-war goods and services; in 1938 the latter had stood at £4,090 million
but, despite the rapid wartime growth of the economy, it had reached only
£4,526 million by 1943 and its share of net national expenditure had fallen
by 32 percentage points. The greater involvement of the state in the
economy is also clearly demonstrated by Table 1.1: government expenditure rose dramatically; as early as 1940 the government accounted
for more than half of the net national expenditure. This transformation
was almost entirely due to its increased expenditure on war.

This chapter will examine several issues related to the war economy.
Why did the role of the state increase? How did the war affect GDP and
productivity and how did Britain perform relative to other combatant
nations. What changes did the war cause in the broad industrial structure
of the economy? What were the constraints under which the wartime
economy operated and how did it deal with them? Did the war have any
impact on the long-term growth of the British economy?

Free market versus planning in the wartime economy

Why was the wartime transformation from a predominantly free market
economy to a centrally managed economy necessary? To answer this
question one must consider the nature of the free market economy. The

1

Table 1.1. *The distribution of net national expenditure, 1938–44* (%)

Year	Consumption	War	Non-war investment	Government
1938	87	7	5	16
1939	83	15	2	25
1940	71	44	−15	51
1941	62	53	−15	61
1942	59	52	−11	60
1943	55	55	−11	64
1944	56	53	−10	62

Note: national expenditure is the sum of expenditure on consumption, war and non-war capital formation. Government expenditure is the sum of government expenditure on non-war current services (part of consumption) and government war expenditure (part of war).
Source: Combined Committee on Non-Food Consumption (1945: 144).

abstract neoclassical free market economy is characterised by perfectly mobile factors of production, fully informed and rational economic agents, and market clearing. Its essence is that pure competition between self-interested economic agents will, through the operation of the price mechanism, not only lead to the full employment of all resources but also ensure that those resources are employed efficiently. If for any reason the economy is in a state of disequilibrium then the unfettered forces of the free market will cause a return to the desired full employment equilibrium.

Of course, the British economy in 1939 was not a pure free market economy: labour and capital did not move freely; tariffs, employer cartels and trade unions all hindered the operation of the price mechanism; and markets did not clear, as the mass unemployment of the period testifies. However, the inter-war economy did, in essence, resemble a free market economy more closely than a planned economy. The war was to change this. There were many reasons for the abandonment of the free market economy but the three most important were: the fear of inflation; the adjustment time, that is the length of time it takes for an economy to adjust to a new set of economic conditions (an important consideration in a system where there is a need for a sudden increase in certain outputs and inputs); and the system of rewards and penalties. The problems which these posed could only jointly be solved by government intervention.

War and inflation are common bedfellows. The reasons for this can be explained in simple terms: the advent of war will lead to an increase in the demand for munitions and at the same time raw materials may become scarce and thus prices will rise; this might be due to the loss of external supplies, such as imported iron ore, or simply because of the pressures of internal wartime mobilisation, which may reveal, for example, shortages of skilled labour. At the same time the civilian sector of the economy may well be contracting, in order to release resources for the war effort, reducing the amount of consumption goods available just as money incomes increase because of the increased demand for labour. This adds to the inflationary burden. Although inflation may provide the government with a short-term windfall, by providing a stimulus to output and increasing revenue via the inflation tax, it also increases the cost to the government of buying goods and services and may also cause political and social problems which can possibly result in open dissent. Thus, in order to ease the financial burden of the war and to appease the populace the government is forced to take action to control inflation; how this was actually done in wartime Britain is discussed below.

The second reason why a neoclassical free market economy model is inappropriate is the weakness of the model in its time specification (Eatwell and Robinson 1973: 161–5). In the context of a war economy, the adjustment time – the time it takes for the economy to adjust from a peacetime economy to a wartime economy – is crucial. It is not possible to wait for the unspecified length of time – a month? a year? ten years? longer? – which it would take for a free market system to adjust properly to the new demands. To take an extreme case, it may be envisaged that if Britain had failed to produce a sufficient quantity of fighter aircraft in the space of a few months in mid-1940, it might have lost the war. The neoclassical free market model cannot explain the vast and rapid movements of resources and labour that occur in the war economy; nor would it have achieved such a readjustment within the time horizon called for, even if it had been allowed to try. Such a readjustment can only occur through the central direction of the economy (Robinson 1951: 34).

The third reason why the state is likely to become more directly involved in the economy in wartime stems from the reliance of the price mechanism on rewards and penalties. In wartime producers want higher rewards than in peacetime both because of the low current consumable output (a result of the increasing proportion devoted to war) and because of the uncertainty surrounding future, post-war, output. Higher rewards for the producers inevitably means higher prices, and thus, *ceteris paribus*, lower living standards for the consumers. As producers are few and consumers are many, this is potentially a recipe for revolution; at best it can demoralise the workforce and adversely affect production. In order to prevent such a situation developing, and to gain the support of the many which is an implicit necessity for victory, the government must be seen to support and enforce a reasonable degree of equality; this led, for example, to the measures adopted by the British government in both World Wars to control profits and to ration goods.

Problems concerning inflation, adjustment time and the rewards and penalties system therefore make it inevitable that the role of the government in the wartime economy will grow. Why does this invalidate the neoclassical free market economy model? In an economy where the government is dominant, such as that of Britain in the Second World War, the causal mechanism operates from society as a whole, as represented by the state, to the firm and from the firm to the individual. This is the exact opposite to the situation in the free market system. Efficiency in the latter is ensured because the allocation is first sorted out at the individual (or micro-economic) level and then aggregated to derive the state (or macro-economic) level. The free market system works because no individual, or group of individuals, is able to dominate any other individual, or group of individuals: all economic units are 'price-takers'. In a war economy, by contrast, the state is not interested so much in the needs of the individual as in the needs of the state; indeed, in wartime the state may interfere even with the choice of individuals about whether to work or not, where to work and what sort of work they will perform. The state would argue that in the long run the two needs are identical but in the short run they may conflict. The needs of the state are largely decided, in war, by exogenous factors, that is by strategic conditions which create demands that must be met if the state is to survive, even if this means creating disequilibrium in the economy; indeed, this is often unavoidable.

The war economy

Wartime trends in national income

Table 1.2 charts the wartime performance of the British economy in terms of real GDP (at factor cost) and two measures of productivity. The productivity measures are measures of labour productivity only since capital data for the war period are extremely sketchy; for example, the gross domestic capital formation figures given in the relevant national income statistics were not based on any actual returns but were in fact merely a residual and, since this was the first time such statistics had been produced, there is considerable doubt about their reliability (Mars 1952). The lack of capital data and the widespread use of rationing and fixed price contracts makes the use of standard productivity measures, such as total factor productivity or the translog or cost function approaches, inappropriate. A simple labour productivity measure cannot capture such

Table 1.2. *Real GDP (at 1938 factor cost) and related measures, UK, 1938–46 (1939 = 100)*

Year	GDP (1)	GDP per head (2)	GDP per person employed (3)
1938	96	97	100
1939	100	100	100
1940	116	116	112
1941	124	123	115
1942	125	124	112
1943	127	125	114
1944	121	119	109
1945	113	110	104
1946	112	109	108

Note: total employed labour force includes the armed forces but excludes ex-members of the armed forces on release but not yet in employment.
Source: calculated from Feinstein (1972: Tables 16, 121, 126).

effects as changes in product quality or labour intensity nor is it possible to quantify the impact of warfare itself, through air raids, blackouts and the forced dispersal of industry; it is therefore highly probable that such a measure will understate the actual changes in wartime productivity (Elliot 1976: 53, 67).

GDP grew rapidly in this period, peaking in 1943 at a level 27 per cent higher than in 1939; this equates to an average annual rate of growth between those two dates of 6.2 per cent. Given the burden of paying for the war, the growth in real output was a crucial ingredient in the war effort, supplying more than half of the necessary domestic finance for war expenditure (Harrison 1988: 185). In Table 1.2, column two reflects the production of the whole economy per head of population and shows that productivity, like production, peaked, on this measure, in 1943. Indeed, the movements it illustrates reflect the general trend of wartime production very well: the cautious build-up of the 'Phoney War' period, in which civilian and military demands still competed against each other in the market for resources, was followed by the rapid expansion of 1940–1 and the transition to a truly managed economy; finally there was the 1943 peak and subsequent decline, reflecting the D-Day demands, the increased American supplies and the reaching of the labour mobilisation limits.

Column two is not, however, a good indicator of industrial labour productivity because it says nothing about the proportion of the population involved in actual production. The more usual measure of overall productivity, GDP per head of the employed labour force, is presented in column three. The employed labour force grew faster than the actual population because of the decrease in unemployment and the greater absorption of female workers. In the Second World War the mobilisation of women was impressive: the female participation rate rose from 30 per cent in mid-1939 to a peak of 45.3 per cent in September 1943 (Ince 1946: 33). The mobilisation was necessary because of the vast numbers of men absorbed by the Armed Forces, some of whom came from the ranks of the unemployed but the majority of whom were drawn from industry and who had to be replaced: as early as mid-1941, 95 per cent of men of working age had been mobilised for the war effort (Ince 1946: 33) (see also below). The major difference between columns two and three is the fact that in column three the peak in productivity comes in 1941 and not 1943. This is consistent with the claim by Postan that in 'the history of war production the eighteen months between the summer of 1940 and the end of 1941 – the period when Britain stood alone – were the period of great achievement' (Postan 1952: 45). This trend possibly reflects the fact that after 1941 increases in the labour force were achieved by absorbing untrained labour; it also undoubtedly reflects the fall in the capital–labour ratio.

Ideally the raw GDP per employee figures should be adjusted for the changes in the average amount of hours worked but unfortunately the data that are available are too crude to give meaningful results. Nevertheless what evidence we do have suggests that the average hours worked in industry increased during the war: from 47.7 hours in 1938 to a peak of 52.9 hours in 1943 for manual male workers and from 43.5 hours to 45.9 hours for manual female workers over the same period (Department of Employment and Productivity 1971: 104). These official figures probably underestimate the increase in the average amount of hours worked because, at the end of 1941, the government advised the Select Committee on National Expenditure that the average working week for men should not exceed sixty hours and for women fifty-five hours; this implies that the actual hours worked were greater than these guide-lines which were themselves higher than the officially recorded figures for both 1938 and 1943. The official concern to limit the hours worked was the result of reports from the Central Statistical Office which indicated that absenteeism increased with the number of hours worked (Parker 1957: 445). The conclusion from this must be that, if the GDP per employee figures were adjusted to take account of the actual amount of hours worked, then the average annual growth rate of labour productivity that they imply (2.5 per cent for the period 1938 to 1943) would be reduced, possibly by a substantial margin.

Column three also hides some important factors bearing on productivity: for example, there was a dilution of labour throughout the war and, although Postan has claimed that it could have been carried out more effectively, it probably helped to improve productivity levels in those cases where the skill barrier was an artificial one which merely hid restrictive practices (Postan 1952: 152; Matthews *et al*. 1982: 114). On the other hand, there was a real shortage of skilled labour and this must have acted as a break on productivity, a situation not helped by the slow utilisation of training facilities (Postan 1952: 96–8; Ministry of Labour and National Service 1947: 348–9). The figures on the employed labour force also largely ignore the input of the following groups of workers: prisoners-of-war, of whom 224,000 were working in the economy by mid-1945 (mainly in agriculture and navvying); Irish labour; voluntary workers, mainly female, who numbered 1 million at their peak; males over the age of sixty-four and females over the age of fifty-nine, who again probably numbered over 1 million at their peak; part-time female workers, whose numbers rose from 380,000 in June 1942 to 900,000 a year later and who almost certainly contributed more effort than the half-worker the official statistics equated them to; and, finally, full-time workers (such as bank workers) who did part-time work in the munitions industries outside their normal working hours (Ministry of Labour and National Service 1947: 54–68). It is not possible quantitatively to assess the impact of such labour on wartime labour productivity but it was undoubtedly great.

Having discussed the wartime GDP and productivity performance of the UK, the standard procedure would be now to compare it to that of other combatant nations to try and place it in a more objective context. Indeed, this is what will be done below (where it will also be contrasted with the performance of the UK economy in the First World War) but it is far from clear that this is an entirely objective exercise. The assessment of comparative economic performances over long periods of time does have a strong theoretical justification, in that the achievement of most socio-economic goals relies on having the resources to meet them and, in the long run, this means achieving sustainable economic growth. However, such comparisons made over short periods of time have a less sound foundation: any economy could, in theory, achieve rapid growth over a short period of time simply by mobilising all its available resources. This does not mean that such growth is viable over a longer period, as the economic growth record of the Soviet Union amply demonstrates (Ofer 1987). The desire for such a mobilisation will normally come from political leaders but the ability to achieve it will depend on its acceptance by the population, and possibly also by the suppliers of external capital, and on the existing economic infrastructure. The fact that an economy is at war does not

Table 1.3. *Real GNP of the main combatants, 1938–45 (1939 = 100)*

Year	UK	USA	USSR[a]	Germany
1938	97	93	94	91
1939	100	100	100	100
1940	115	109	109	100
1941	122	125	88	102
1942	122	139	62	105
1943	125	153	72	116
1944	118	165	87	—
1945	110	163	86	—

[a] USSR figures are for net national product.
Sources: UK from Feinstein (1972: Table 16), at 1938 factor cost; USA from US Bureau of the Census (1960: Figures 1–5), at 1929 market prices; USSR from Harrison (1988: 185), at 1937 factor cost; Germany from Klein (1959: 257), at 1939 market prices.

change these constraints or choices; it simply means that the social utility function may change so that, for example, the population is more willing to endure a postponement of present consumption.

In the Second World War the growth of each individual economy was governed by political, strategic and social considerations which may have called, at least initially, for different responses. In Germany, for example, the Blitzkrieg strategy was designed so that the civilian economy remained as insulated as possible from the war whereas in Britain, by contrast, it was decided at an early stage that the war could only be won by transforming the peacetime economy into a fully fledged war economy. The prior expectation in any comparison should therefore be that, given that the UK was mobilising all necessary resources for war whereas Germany was taking a more relaxed approach, the UK would achieve a higher rate of growth than Germany; simply because the UK achieved a higher rate of growth than Germany between 1939 and 1943 does not necessarily mean it was more successful (Milward 1977: 54).

Table 1.3 provides some evidence of the comparative performance of different economies during the war in terms of their real national product. It shows that the UK did very well and was only surpassed by the powerhouse of the US economy which expanded by more than 60 per cent in the space of five years. Reservations could be made to this favourable conclusion particularly as far as the USSR is concerned since the dominant factor in its wartime economic performance was its initial loss of territory (and hence resources) in 1941 as a result of the successful launch of

Table 1.4. *Real output and government expenditure in the UK: a comparison between the First and Second World Wars* (*at constant 1938 prices*)

Year	GDP (1)	GDP per head (2)	GDP per person employed (3)	Government expenditure as % of GNP (4)
1913	100	100	100	8
1917	115	113	109	37
1919	101	99	97	17
1938	100	100	100	14
1943	133	129	114	54
1946	116	112	108	25

Note: government expenditure is defined as public authorities' expenditure on goods and services in current prices and is expressed as a percentage of GNP at factor cost.
Source: calculated from Feinstein (1972: Tables 8–9, 15–16, 121–2, 126).

Operation Barbarossa by the Germans and the subsequent regaining of territory after 1942 (Ranki 1988: 314–31).

The outstanding comparative study of the economies of the Second World War is that by Milward (1977) but since he harbours doubts like those expressed above he avoids the normal quantitative comparisons and one must turn to Harrison (1988) to get these. Harrison is specifically concerned with the degree of resource mobilisation within the wartime economies of the UK, the USA, the USSR and Germany. In deriving his results on mobilisation, Harrison provides a meticulous and logical guide through the quagmire represented by the existing but diverse statistics. The previous comparisons had many problems: some were basic ones, such as Carroll comparing UK net national product at factor cost to US gross national product at market prices, and others more technical, such as the problem of double-counting, whereby Lend-Lease supplies were counted both by the supplier (the USA) and the receiver (the UK and the USSR) in their war expenditure. Harrison addressed these and other problems to derive as consistent a series as possible of monetary estimates for the four economies. He defines two measures of wartime mobilisation: the first, which he calls *national utilisation*, is an attempt to measure national priorities and encompasses all resources supplied to the war effort of a country irrespective of its origin; the second, which he calls *domestic mobilisation*, measures the domestic finance of resources supplied to the war effort of a country irrespective of utilisation. His conclusion is that whilst in *national utilisation* terms the UK allocated more resources to the war effort than the USA the situation was reversed in terms of *domestic mobilisation* (Harrison 1988: 183–4).

Table 1.4 offers a comparison of the performance of the UK economy in the First and Second World Wars: 1917 and 1943 were chosen as the respective years of peak production whilst the other years represent the last full years of peace before and after the periods of conflict. In terms of GDP the wartime expansion was much greater in the Second World War, with a peak 33 per cent higher than the last full year of peace, compared to a 15 per cent expansion in the First World War (the equivalent average annual rates of growth being 5.9 per cent and 3.6 per cent); the contraction from the peak to the first post-war year of peace was also slower in the Second World War. The two measures of productivity, GDP per head and per employed person, also reflect a better performance in the Second World War but the greater expansion of the labour force in the later conflict brings the figures for GDP per employed person much closer together (between 1913 and 1917 the average annual rate of increase in GDP per employed person was 2.2 per cent compared to 2.7 per cent for 1938 to 1943). Finally, column four offers a view of the relative centralisation, in terms of government expenditure as a percentage of GNP; it reinforces the widely accepted view that the First World War was a more laissez-faire affair although even in this conflict government expenditure rose substantially to reach 37 per cent of GNP by 1917.

Industry in wartime

In terms of national expenditure, therefore, the war sector expanded and the consumption sector contracted: this section considers how this process affected different industries. The most obvious feature of wartime industrial policy was the deliberate decision to reduce the production of consumer goods in order to release raw materials, labour and capital for the munitions industries. This was achieved by controlling both demand and supply: demand was controlled through various means such as rationing (see below) whilst supply was controlled through import restrictions and the Limitation of Supply Orders which set a quantity ceiling (which was progressively reduced) on what wholesalers could sell. Once quantity ceilings were imposed the state was then able to concentrate the production of particular industries in selected firms, known as nucleus firms. The idea was that the designated nucleus firm would absorb other firms in the industry in some manner; it could, for example, buy all of their raw material ration, take on their machinery or even buy the whole firm outright (Allen 1951). The process started in earnest in mid-1941 and, in terms of reducing the production in certain consumer industries, was very successful: for example, between 1939 and 1943 paper production fell by 51 per cent, cotton yarn production fell by 35 per cent and the gross value of activity in the building and civil engineering industry fell, in real terms, by 45 per cent (Central Statistical Office 1951: 123, 126, 207; Kohan 1952: 426, 488); over the same period employment in industries such as cotton spinning and weaving, woollen and worsted and silk and rayon fell by a third whilst the declines were even sharper in industries such as hosiery, lace, furniture and upholstery (Hargreaves and Gowing 1952: 641).

The contraction of the civilian sector was matched by a massive expansion in the war sector, ample evidence of which is provided in the tables on munitions production in the official *Statistical Digest of the War* (Central Statistical Office 1951: 111–34). To give just a flavour of this expansion: between 1939 and 1943 the annual production of light anti-aircraft guns increased from a mere 30 to 5,570; mortar production jumped from 2,822 to 17,121; .303 rifle production went from 34,416 to almost one million; tank production increased from 969 to 7,476; the number of heavy bombers built went from zero to 4,615; light bomber and fighter production increased from 2,403 to 11,103; and the tonnage of naval ships produced increased more than sixfold. An index of the total munitions output of the UK was actually compiled during the war by Austin Robinson, who was then working in the Ministry of Production, and this has been recently reworked by Harrison. The Harrison revised index (1941 first quarter = 100) suggests that munitions output increased fourfold between the outbreak of the war and the last quarter of 1941 and that it had more than doubled again when it reached its peak in the first quarter of 1944 (Harrison 1990: 665). This expansion looks even more impressive when it is realised that it was carried out against a background of almost constant modification of existing armaments which continually disrupted the production process: Milward cites the example of the Spitfire, whose design underwent over 1,000 technical modifications during the war (Milward 1977: 192). There were also other war-related problems, such as air raids and the forced relocation of industry to less vulnerable areas, which prevented munitions production from scaling even greater heights.

The agricultural sector was also very important to Britain's wartime success: it increased the supply and variety of domestically produced food which reduced food imports and thus released valuable shipping space for other vital imports. The net calorie output of British agriculture increased by over 90 per cent between 1938/9 and 1943/4, and the calorific reliance on imports was cut by 75 per cent (Milward 1977: 245–55; Hammond

1951: 394). To achieve these results the government had provided farmers with price incentives which resulted in farmers increasing their income greatly; they benefited far more than any other group from the war (Milward 1977: 285–6). The increased prices of food products were not, however, passed on to the consumers, who were protected by government subsidies. The subsidy of agriculture by the government, a process that obviously interferes with the efficient operation of the free market, was an important change that extended into the post-war world and was not abolished until Britain joined the EEC and the national subsidy was replaced by supra-national subsidies (Milward 1977: 285).

Despite this seemingly impressive performance, the industrial record of the war economy has been attacked by Barnett (1986). His main thesis is that the British grossly exaggerated their wartime achievements (ignoring, for example, the invaluable assistance of American Lend-Lease) and thus created the welfare state on a weak foundation, on an economy whose industrial performance was poor in several key areas. The first thing to note about the Barnett thesis is that it is not really concerned with the performance of the economy during the war at all but is about what Barnett sees as the long-term structural problems of the British economy: thus, he does not consider how the British economy in this period compared with previous periods nor whether the relative disadvantage that he identifies between the British and the German and American economies increased or decreased during the war years. An interesting contrast is to compare Barnett's very pessimistic assessment of the wartime performance of the British aircraft industry with the much more positive picture presented by Overy in his truly comparative study (Barnett 1986: 143–58; Overy 1980: 168–71).

Further, Barnett is primarily interested in demonstrating the poor productivity performance of the British economy during the war relative to other nations (particularly Germany and the USA); he argues that the war offers an excellent opportunity to assess the productivity performance because during this period the economy was pushed to its limits. This argument, however, ignores a fundamental problem: the most important concern of the government during the war was not productivity; its foremost concern was simply with increasing the output of those goods deemed necessary by the strategic demands facing the country within time horizons which were strategically determined. In terms of labour productivity this meant that as long as the numerator increased (to meet the production target) there was little concern, at least initially, as to what was happening to the denominator. This is not to argue that Barnett is wrong – there were industrial problems in many wartime industries, notably coal and shipbuilding – and indeed he provides much interesting information on the wartime performance of certain key industries, but merely to warn the unwary that his agenda and that of the wartime government were not the same and that discussion of wartime industrial productivity (both at a national and an international level) is still in its infancy.

The constraints of the war economy

Discussions of the British economy in the Second World War always consider the constraints which it faced, the limits that were imposed on its mobilisation: Robinson, in his influential article on the war economy, identified five major constraints – gold and foreign currency reserves, materials, manpower, shipping and capacity (Robinson 1951: 37). The emphasis on the scarcity of resources available to the economy during the war makes it somehow appear a unique situation; it is all too easy, therefore, to view the war economy as operating in a vacuum, sealed off from the 'normal' peacetime economy. Such a view is misleading on two grounds. First, on a practical historical level it is crucial not to divorce the wartime economy from the peacetime economy as it existed at the end of the 1930s since many of the constraints that the former operated under were largely determined by the latter. Second, on a more theoretical level it is important to remember that all economies at all times operate under constraints; if resources were not scarce there would be no need to study economics or economic history.

What made the wartime economy different was that the discussion of the constraints that always face an economy was made far more explicit within the government machinery itself. This partly reflected the fact that many academic economists had been drafted into the government as advisers and they imposed their technical language and knowledge on the debates (Booth and Coats 1980). It also reflected the fact that the nature of the war meant that strategic decisions had to be translated into production decisions within relatively short time horizons and thus the opportunity costs of the available production choices were made very clear. It meant also that wartime planners had to be aware of where and when potential bottlenecks in the system would occur and what were the limits of mobilisation.

Initially the government was concerned with the financial constraints, both internal and external, which it faced but this was soon replaced with worries about the physical constraints facing the economy; thus, the running of the war moved from relying on financial controls to physical controls. This section therefore begins by examining the financial constraints (particularly focussing on the evolving role of the wartime budget and the importance of the Lend-Lease arrangement) and then considers the major physical constraint which faced the economy, that of labour; there is also a short discussion of the role of capital.

Budgetary policy

The government was faced with two related problems in terms of its budgetary policy: how to pay for the war and how to dampen the inflationary pressures in the economy. It was important to tackle the latter for social and political as well as economic reasons: in the First World War both Britain and Germany had experienced serious social disruption as a result of the distorting effects of wartime inflation, which had changed both income distribution and the rewards system (Milward 1977: 106).

The way forward was pointed out by Keynes in a series of articles in *The Times* and in his subsequent pamphlet *How to Pay for the War* (Keynes 1940). Keynes argued that the traditional method of assessing potential government revenue by the Treasury, which worked on the principle of 'what the tax-payer could bear', started at the wrong end. He felt that the Treasury should first calculate national income (including its main components) in order to judge the war potential of the economy as a whole. Then it could calculate the level of taxation (and forced savings) which would bring about the level of transfer of national income from tax-payers to the government which was necessary to stop inflation (Pollard 1983: 212). To explain the problem of inflation Keynes referred to the notion of an 'inflationary gap' (that is, a gap between aggregate demand and aggregate supply). The inflationary gap was inevitable given wartime pressures, which would ensure that aggregate demand would rise just as the amount of consumer goods available would fall (as the consumer goods industries were deliberately reduced in size in order to release resources for war production). If the government did not intervene the potential gap between demand and supply would be closed automatically by an inflationary rise. In order to prevent such inflation the government, according to Keynes, should mop up the potential excess demand (thereby closing the potential inflationary gap) through taxation and forced savings (Sayers 1983: 112).

The proposals of Keynes initially faced opposition from two sources. The Treasury opposed Keynes because it believed that there was some 'natural flow' of voluntary savings and it felt that if the level of forced savings called for by Keynes (as a supplement to taxation) exceeded the natural level it would cause inflation rather than prevent it; nor was the Treasury impressed by the figures quoted by Keynes. The Labour Party also opposed what it saw as the increased taxation of the working classes;

even the attempt by Keynes to try and soften the blow by arguing that wartime taxation should be treated as deferred pay that would be repaid after the war did not convince them (Booth 1989: 63; Peden 1985: 132–3). However, the paralysis of the Treasury in the face of wartime inflation (coupled with the shock of military defeat in the spring of 1940 and the subsequent change in government) paved the way for the adoption of Keynes' main proposals; indeed, Keynes himself was co-opted to work in the Treasury in June 1940.

The turning point was the budget presented on 7 April 1941 by the Chancellor of the Exchequer, Kingsley Wood. Before the war budgetary policy was largely conducted in terms of financing government expenditure and attempting to achieve a balanced budget; however, the 1941 budget transformed the annual budget speech into 'a comprehensive survey of the national economy' and price and income stabilisation became explicit concerns (Sayers 1983: 108). It introduced two innovations: the economic theory that informed it – that is, the explicit introduction of Keynesianism – and the underlying national income accounting framework which it used (Feinstein 1983: 12–13). The budget also tried to strike a balance between being seen to promote social justice and ensuring that there remained adequate economic incentives (Sayers 1983: 110).

A crucial and innovative aspect of the 1941 budget was that it was conceived in national income terms and was accompanied by a White Paper setting out the official estimates of national income and expenditure (HMSO 1941). This was the result of the work of two young economists, James Meade and Richard Stone, who were working in the Cabinet Office at the time: Meade produced the initial double-entry framework for the national income accounts and Stone played the major role in filling in the numbers (Stone 1951; Booth 1989: 66). As well as the White Paper they also produced a paper for the *Economic Journal* which set out their conceptual framework (Meade and Stone: 1941). Not surprisingly, their estimates of national income were in many ways still rudimentary (with many of the items calculated as residuals) but their work has been described as 'a revolutionary departure in British official statistics' (Booth 1989: 67); it was to have an impact beyond the British economy and beyond 1945. Despite the importance of the national income accounts, however, they were not used in the actual planning of the war effort; this was done almost entirely in terms of physical resources (Robinson 1951: 40).

The budget itself proposed a two-pronged attack on inflation: taxation and forced savings were to be used to tackle the problem of demand-pull inflation and cost of living subsidies were to be used against cost-push inflation (it was hoped that stabilising the cost of living index would lead to moderation in wage settlements because of the widespread indexation). The two-pronged attack was necessary since rapid wage inflation would defeat the attempt to mop up excess demand through taxation; if the inflationary gap was not closed by the government, it would be difficult to prevent wage inflation: the two were really the different sides of the same economic coin (Sayers 1983: 107, 113).

It was estimated that there was a potential inflationary gap of approximately £500 million. Kingsley Wood hoped to close half the gap, £200–300 million, by increasing personal savings (that is, by promoting a policy of forced savings). This was to be achieved by a series of measures: suspending various investment opportunities; putting pressure on the clearing banks to turn all their available resources (that is, idle balances) over to the government; restricting bank advances intended for use for capital construction; and making attractive offers to savers through government bonds. The decreased availability of consumption goods also helped this process as it restricted even the opportunity to consume above a certain level.

The remaining part of the inflationary gap, £250 million, was to be closed through taxation. In the budget all forms of taxation were increased: the standard rate of income tax went up from 8s 6d to 10s 0d in the pound (that is, from 42.5 per cent to 50 per cent); personal allowances were reduced; purchase tax was increased on a broad front; the excess profits tax (a tax intended to stop wartime profiteering by, at least theoretically, taxing profits that were in excess of peacetime levels) was increased from 60 per cent to 100 per cent. These anti-inflationary measures would thus also help to pay for the war by raising government revenue (Sayers 1983: 112–13). The approach outlined in the 1941 budget was refined throughout the war: in September 1943 the Pay As You Earn (PAYE) scheme was introduced which made tax collection easier and more efficient; purchase tax was developed as a weapon to restrict and influence consumption (Pollard 1983: 213).

The success of the strategy of increasing taxation and forced savings is clearly shown in Table 1.5. Direct taxation was increased substantially during the war: it more than doubled between 1939 and 1941 and almost doubled again between 1941 and 1945. This increase was achieved by tripling income tax receipts and by introducing the excess profits tax, which at its height brought in £482 million (equivalent to a quarter of total direct taxation). Receipts from indirect taxation also tripled, although most of the increase had already occurred by 1942. Forced savings are measured in the table by public borrowing. This saw a massive expansion in the first year of the war, increasing almost fourfold, before almost doubling again between 1940 and 1943. Within public borrowing, small savings and net

Table 1.5. *Taxation and public borrowing, 1939–45 (in £m)*

	1939	1940	1941	1942	1943	1944	1945
Indirect taxation	465	676	1,000	1,137	1,233	1,239	1,211
Direct taxation	515	706	1,143	1,426	1,819	2,023	2,054
of which –							
income tax and surtax	410	551	741	921	1,184	1,353	1,426
excess profits tax	0	44	211	318	453	482	440
Public borrowing at home	352	1,550	2,553	2,576	2,972	2,792	2,442
of which –							
small savings	62	466	602	600	719	702	668
other public issues (net)	10	567	1,031	1,047	1,059	896	1,176

Source: Sayers (1956: 493–4).

other public issues became more important: in 1939 they had accounted for only 20 per cent of public borrowing but by 1945 that figure had leapt to 76 per cent.

The subsidy of key items in the cost of living index also appeared to be successful in its aim of restraining wages as labour mobilisation reached its limits. The cost of living index had increased sharply between 1939 and 1941 but thereafter remained fairly steady; this led to a deceleration in the rate of increase of the average weekly wage, from 10 per cent in 1940 to only 4 per cent in 1943 (Central Statistical Office 1951: 205). A major feature of this success was the massive growth of food subsidies: in 1939–40 the net cost of food subsidies borne by the Ministry of Food was £13 million but by the end of the war that figure had leapt to £162 million, a more than twelvefold increase (Hammond 1951: 398; Nash 1951). Two things should be borne in mind in evaluating the success of the policy. First, the manipulation of the official cost of living index did not eliminate inflation but merely disguised it (Peden 1985: 130–1). Second, factors such as the increased availability of overtime and the dilution of jobs that had been deemed skilled and semi-skilled meant that average earnings increased faster than wages (Department of Employment and Productivity 1971: 99).

Taxation, forced savings and stabilisation of the cost of living index were not considered enough to close the inflationary gap: in particular it was felt that if taxation was too heavy it could, even in wartime, adversely affect incentives and that it might also fail to curb consumption if people responded by drawing on their savings (Reddaway 1951: 182). Even if consumption was reduced there was no guarantee that the consumption of specific key goods, such as petrol and sugar, would be cut. Thus, the rationing of particular goods (which had been introduced as early as 1940) was gradually extended: by the end of the war about one third of all consumer goods and services were rationed. Of the exceptions to rationing the most important were bread, potatoes, fish and fresh vegetables (whose prices were strictly controlled) and tobacco and alcohol (whose exemption helped to boost morale and provided the Treasury with a lucrative source of revenue).

Two different types of rationing schemes were operated: a coupon scheme which covered most basic food-stuffs and which gave every consumer a minimum fixed weekly quantity of the foods covered, and a points scheme which was more flexible in that coupon points could be 'spent' at the preference of the consumer on a limited number of goods (Booth 1985). This system of rationing operated far more effectively in Britain than schemes tried in other combatant nations. This was mainly due to the panoply of controls, backed up by both financial and legal resources, which ensured that there was a strict supervision of both production and distribution; but it also reflects the fact that the control of materials and food-stuffs is simplified in an island economy which imports a high percentage of such goods (Mills and Rockoff 1987). Further, the relatively small size of the black market in wartime Britain, whilst reflecting the successful system of controls which had been evolved, also demonstrated the acceptance by the majority of the population that the system of penalties and rewards that their wartime rulers had imposed was basically fair. Rationing could not be imposed in a vacuum. It was recognised that the conduct of the war in the civilian sphere had to reflect what the civilian populace regarded as fair under the circumstances: they were willing to make sacrifices as long as those sacrifices were borne equally, that they were seen to be borne equally, which meant that the rationing rules had to be easily comprehensible, and that the penalties for those abusing the system were swift and severe (Smithies 1984: 64–84).

External policy and Lend-Lease

The Treasury initially believed that the war could be financed through the sale of gold and foreign exchange and higher exports; hence the war began with what, in retrospect, seems to be a ludicrous export drive which only served to add a further strain on the resources of the fledgling war economy. As the cost of the war exploded and Ministers and officials realised the folly of the export policy, the latter's high economic priority was dropped (Sayers 1956: 267). This accelerated the decline in exports that had already occurred: in volume terms exports fell by 71 per cent between 1938 and 1943 and export earnings were cut in half; at the same time the cost of imports rose by a third, even though the volume of imports fell (Central Statistical Office 1951: 162). In terms of the external account the result of these changes was dramatic: external liabilities more than doubled between December 1939 and December 1941, by mid-1940 assets in North America were being sold off cheaply in a desperate attempt to pay for American goods, and by the beginning of 1941 hard currency reserves had been exhausted (Sayers 1956: 438–64). The situation was rescued when, in March 1941, the so-called Lend-Lease Act was passed by the American government: this effectively gave Britain, and the USSR, free access to the amazing power-house of the US war economy. The Lend-Lease agreements removed all existing restrictions on purchases in the USA and, crucially, deferred the payment for American goods and services until after the war.

The total net value of US Lend-Lease aid to all countries during the war was $43.6 billion of which the UK, excluding the empire, received $27 billion (62 per cent) and the USSR $11 billion (25 per cent) (Allen 1946: 250, 258). Aid for the UK was also provided by the empire, notably by Canada which supplied the UK with $Canadian 1.2 billion of Mutual Aid during the war and more or less wrote this off after the war (Milward 1977: 351). The UK did provide reciprocal aid to the US which amounted to $5.7 billion, leaving the net US contribution at $21 billion, but even so the contribution of the American economy to the UK war effort cannot be underestimated: in Britain Lend-Lease took an enormous burden off the productive shoulders of the country with US supplies being equivalent to UK wartime production of, for example, 104 per cent for tanks, 24 per cent for combat aircraft, 60 per cent for landing craft and ships, 67 per cent for small arms ammunition, and so on (Postan 1952: 247); in total US Lend-Lease aid supplied 17 per cent of all British empire munitions during the war (Allen 1946: 268). This helped to ease many of the constraints on the British economy, particularly that of labour.

The evaluation of Lend-Lease has, however, been a fertile ground for disagreement: on one side are those who agree with the words of Prime Minister Churchill that Lend-Lease was 'the most unsordid act in the history of any nation' (Churchill 1949: 503); on the other side are those who saw it as a hard-nosed business deal by the Americans which would reflate the American economy and denude their greatest potential rival of any real economic power in the post-war world.

The latter view was expounded by no less a figure than Keynes. He was very much involved in Lend-Lease discussions with the Americans and was under no illusion about the supposed generosity of the Lend-Lease programme: he claimed that the US government 'was very careful to take every possible precaution to see that the British were as near as possible bankrupt before any assistance was given' and that they operated the programme with the aim of 'leaving the British at the end of the war ... hopelessly insolvent' (quoted in Salant 1980: 1059). This cynical view of how the US perceived Lend-Lease even finds support among contemporary American historians (Vatter 1985: 30–1). The almost indecent swiftness with which the US ended the Lend-Lease arrangement (it was promptly terminated one minute into the first day of official peace) offers some support to this view since it left Britain with an immediate bill for $650 million just at the time it was facing a dollar crisis (Cairncross 1985: 4–10).

A slightly more favourable stance could be that the Americans were simply being too inflexible in how they viewed Lend-Lease. Allen, for example, has argued that the Allies engaged in a form of international division of labour during the war with a greater mobilisation of troops by Britain, the USSR, Australia and India compensated by a greater provision of munitions by the US and Canada (Allen 1946: 247–9). If this were true then it could be argued that in evaluating the cost of Lend-Lease this should be taken into account: 'it could surely be argued, for example, that in those cases where British tank crews had used American tanks it would make at least as much sense to charge the US for the crew as the UK for the tank. But this was not the view taken in the US' (Milward 1977: 351). Another factor that should be taken into account was that it was largely orders from the UK and France that enabled the US to expand its pre-war capacity and thus created the strong base from which it was to launch its war effort. Allen, in fact, has claimed that the post-war settlement of Lend-Lease actually took all such factors into account because the Americans effectively wrote off about $20 billion of the outstanding debit although the counter argument would be that it was not the sum of the Lend-Lease credit itself that was important but the conditions attached to it and the strength it gave to the US bargaining position in the post-war world (Allen 1946: 246).

Whatever the long-term impact of Lend-Lease, there is no doubting its short-term benefits for the UK economy, as Table 1.6 demonstrates; Sayers believes that the total debit noted in Table 1.6 may be an overestimate, because 'to some extent the pricing of lend-lease goods was too high for purposes of comparing economic efforts', possibly by as much as £1.6 million (Sayers 1956: 499). Over the period of the war as a whole only 41 per cent of the external debits were financed by credits which left a large gap to be filled. The shortfall was made up in many ways, including capital disinvestment and drawing on the gold and dollar reserves, but the two most important means were increasing overseas liabilities and the US Lend-Lease scheme. The importance of Lend-Lease (which was the dominant component of net US grants) can be seen by comparing 1941 and

Table 1.6. *The financing of the UK external debit, 1940–5*

Year	External debit (£m) (1)	Credits (2)	As a percentage of (1)		
			Net US grants (3)	Liability accumulation (4)	Other (5)
1940	1·5	47	0	13	40
1941	1·9	42	16	32	11
1942	2·6	35	38	19	8
1943	3·6	42	56	19	−17
1944	4·2	40	57	17	−14
1945	2·8	43	36	25	−4
Total	16·6	41	40	20	−1

Note: the external debit is the sum of imports plus shipping plus government overseas expenditure (minus munitions). The current account credits include exports, reciprocal aid, other governments' expenditure in the UK, shipping and errors and omissions. Other includes other net grants, sale of investments, requisitioning of balances of gold and dollars and net drawings on gold and reserves.
Source: Sayers (1956: 499).

1942. In 1941 the accumulation of overseas liabilities helped to finance almost one third of the external debits and was threatening to get out of hand. By 1942, however, its importance as a source of financing for the debit had almost halved as US Lend-Lease came on stream properly. By 1943 more than half of the debit was being effectively paid for by Lend-Lease aid. Thus, Lend-Lease eased the pressure on the UK to accelerate its rate of accumulation of overseas liabilities; although by the end of the war such liabilities had still increased massively – from £0.5 billion in June 1939 to £3.4 billion by June 1945 (Sayers 1956: 497).

Labour as a constraint

Policy makers in Britain in the Second World War believed that manpower was the ultimate constraint on the performance of the wartime economy and from the end of 1942 onwards (when it seemed that the limits of labour mobilisation were being reached) the most important planning tool was the manpower budget (Robinson 1951: 48–55). The first manpower budget of the war was produced at the end of 1940 by the Manpower Requirements Committee. This was a comprehensive survey but it did not tackle the central problem of the allocation of manpower

Table 1.7. *The distribution of the working population (WP) of Great Britain, 1939–45 (at June each year)*

	1939	1940	1941	1942	1943	1944	1945
WP (in 000)							
Total	19,473	20,676	21,332	22,056	22,285	22,008	21,649
Male	14,476	15,104	15,222	15,141	15,032	14,901	14,881
Female	4,997	5,572	6,110	6,915	7,253	7,107	6,768
WP (as % of total)							
Female	26	27	29	31	33	32	31
Unemployed	6	3	1	...	...	...	...
Armed Forces	2	11	16	19	21	23	24
Civil defence	...	2	2	2	1	1	1
Civil employment	92	84	81	79	77	76	75
of which							
Group I	16	17	20	23	23	23	20
Group II	27	25	26	25	25	25	26
Group III	49	41	36	32	28	28	29

... = negligible (less than 0·5%).
Note: for the definition of Groups I, II and III, see text.
Source: calculated from Central Statistical Office (1951: 8).

between the production programmes of different government departments – indeed this was not tackled until the so-called First Manpower Budget of December 1942 – and its data were not always reliable. That it did not examine allocation is not too surprising as the bottlenecks in the economy at the time were raw materials, machine tools and skilled labour, and not the general supply of labour (Gowing 1972: 149–51, 157–9). The voracious appetite of the Armed Forces for manpower, however, meant that labour mobilisation on a massive scale was required to satisfy it and that the scarcity of labour would eventually spread from the specific to the general.

The dramatic expansion of the Armed Forces is the most significant trend shown in Table 1.7: the Armed Forces comprised 477,000 men before the outbreak of war but the number rose rapidly with the onset of hostilities and by mid-1944 had exceeded 4,500,000 (at which time there were also 467,000 women in the Auxiliary and Nursing Services) (Ince 1946: 38). The expansion was made possible by drawing on two main sources: decreasing unemployment (which was well over 1 million at the beginning of the war) and withdrawing labour from civil employment. However, the troops needed to be supplied with weapons, clothed and fed and so the withdrawals from civil employment had to be, at least partly, replaced. This was done by expanding the size of the working population:

it rose from 19,473,000 in 1939 to a peak of 22,285,000 in 1943 (a rise of 14 per cent). About one fifth of the increase was due to natural population increase (Milward 1977: 218) but by far the most important factor was the increase in the number of women absorbed into the labour force: 80 per cent of the expansion of the working population was the result of the increased participation ratio of women.

The increased participation of women in employment during the war was a phenomenon replicated in other combatant nations although the actual scale and timing of the expansion differed across countries (Rupp 1978: 185–6; Saunders 1946: 18). In Britain women who had not previously been part of the officially defined working population were mobilised on a massive scale, both to replace the men who had been absorbed into the Armed Forces and to meet the growing appetite of the munitions industries. Initially unemployment among women had actually risen (by 12,000 in the first year of the war), possibly because the dislocation of the economy as it moved to a war footing meant that there was a mismatch between women coming on to the labour market and the actual jobs available. By mid-1941, however, over one million women not previously in the labour market had been mobilised; this despite the fact that compulsory registration for women did not begin until April of that year (Ince 1946: 36–7). By 1943 women accounted for 34 per cent of the total insured workforce in engineering (compared to only 10 per cent in 1939), 52 per cent in the chemical industry (27 per cent) and 46 per cent in miscellaneous metals industries (34 per cent) (Summerfield 1984: 199).

The net result of these changes in terms of the distribution of civil employment is shown in Table 1.7. Wartime planners categorised civil employment into three groups: Group I industries were those concerned with munitions production, including metals, engineering, aircraft production, shipbuilding and chemicals; Group II industries were those deemed to be 'other essential industries' such as agriculture, mining, transportation and the utilities; Group III industries were those deemed 'less essential' and included textiles, building and services. There was an expansion in the Group I industries, which by mid-1943 were employing more than 5 million workers. The level of employment in Group II industries remained relatively stable at approximately 5.5 million. Employment in Group III industries contracted severely, falling from over 9 million workers at the beginning of the war to a mere 6 million by mid-1944, with employment in the textile industries alone falling by 41 per cent (Ince 1946: 42–5; Central Statistical Office 1951: 24). The signs that the economy was reaching the limits of possible labour mobilisation had been clear since 1942: from Table 1.7 it can be seen that the number of women in the working population increased by 13.2 per cent in 1942 but by only

4.9 per cent in 1943 and thereafter the numbers actually decreased; by 1942 the other main source for increasing the employed labour force, the well of unemployment, had also run dry. Indeed, the contraction of the Group III industries was so severe that by 1944 it was felt that it had reached its limit and Table 1.7 implies that the expansion of the Armed Forces after that date was solely at the expense of the munitions industries.

The enormous expansion and redistribution of the working population was achieved through a system of legislative measures and administrative controls (Ince 1946: 18–27). In particular, the Schedule of Reserved Occupations and the Essential Work Orders were used to control the supply and movement of labour; at a local level the Employment Exchanges played a crucial role in matching demand and supply. However, although the state gave itself wide powers of labour compulsion they used these powers with great care and avoided recourse to them whenever and wherever possible (Robinson 1951: 51).

This reluctance to be heavy-handed, and to rely as much as possible on voluntarism and cooperation, partly reflected the desires of the Minister of Labour, Ernest Bevin who, prior to his appointment in the coalition government, had been the outstanding trade union leader in the country (Bullock 1967). It also, though, reflected the general awareness within government of the need to avoid industrial unrest which might adversely affect production programmes. Trade union leaders and workers in general were not blinded by patriotism to the need to protect and improve their jobs, environment and wages. Indeed, the war saw an expansion in trade union membership (from 6 million in 1938 to 7.9 million in 1945), and strikes, despite their wartime illegality, were more numerous between 1940 and 1945 than in the whole of the 1930s, although the average days lost per strike during the war was about a quarter of that lost during the 1930s (Department of Employment and Productivity 1971: 395–6). In order to appease labour and to compensate it for the pressures of wartime work, the government actively encouraged improvements in the working environment and in the social care of workers (Milward 1977: 241) and it tackled the potential menace of inflationary wage demands by providing huge cost of living subsidies (see above).

Capital as a constraint

Although there is no study that shows clearly how, in quantitative terms, the manpower constraint affected potential wartime production, it was widely accepted by contemporaries and is widely accepted by economic historians that it was the most important limitation placed on the war economy. A similar consensus exists that capital, on the whole, was not a constraint (Milward 1977: 229). In fact, as was seen in Table 1.1, current production of war goods and services was expanded partly by capital disinvestment: in effect, some future consumption (that is, investment) was foregone in order to increase current consumption. An alternative view of expenditure on war production was put forward by Kuznets who argued that since the ultimate aim of war production is to 'sustain or augment the capacity of the nation's economy to produce goods in the future' it should be classified as investment (Kuznets 1945: viii).

Capital investment in wartime is perceived as extremely risky: at one level there is the very real risk that your newly acquired plant or machinery may be destroyed by the enemy; and in terms of financial planning it is virtually impossible to determine if the investment will show a positive return. Thus, what new investment did occur during the war was mostly financed by the state, which tended to base its decisions not on monetary considerations but on the availability of other resources, particularly manpower (Robinson 1951: 53–5). Given the role of the state in wartime capital investment it is not surprising to find that such investment was geared towards meeting the military priorities which primarily meant expanding the capacity to produce finished armaments (Harrison 1988: 188).

These trends are borne out by the figures for gross domestic fixed capital formation, which fell in both absolute and relative terms during the war: between 1939 and 1943 gross domestic fixed capital formation dropped from £530 million to £170 million (at 1938 prices), or by approximately two-thirds; in current prices its share of GNP at factor cost shrank from 11.4 per cent in 1938 to a mere 3.3 per cent in 1944 (Feinstein 1972: Tables 9, 89). The fall in capital formation combined with both the massive labour mobilisation and the surge in output to produce decreases in both the capital–labour ratio and the capital–output ratio, by respectively 13.1 per cent and 20 per cent (Feinstein 1972: Table 52).

Another significant feature of wartime capital formation was the shift in its composition and, in particular, the reversal in the position of buildings relative to plant and machinery: in 1939 buildings had accounted for more than half the gross domestic fixed capital formation whilst plant and machinery accounted for about one third; in the following year it was plant and machinery that accounted for more than half and buildings which accounted for only a third (Feinstein 1972: Table 86). This partly reflected the need to expand the output of specialist machine tools and other items vital to the war effort (for example, alloy steel capacity had to be increased); indeed, in the first year of the war one of the major bottlenecks in production was the supply of drop forgings. The squeezing of civilian house building was one obvious way to reallocate investment resources in favour of war production and it was a method which the German war economy also adopted (Overy 1988: 622).

Long-term impact

In the three volumes that comprise this book all contributions except one are concerned with relatively long periods of time: typically eighty or more years in volume 1; fifty years in those chapters in volume 2 which deal with the pre-1914 period and twenty years for those concerned with the inter-war period; forty years in this volume; the one exception is this chapter, which deals with a mere six years. The natural question is: why study such a short period of time? There are two obvious, but not necessarily mutually exclusive, answers: first, these six years of war were an economic aberration and that alone requires them to be treated as a distinct event; second, the war brought about changes in the economy that had important consequences for the post-war world. In this final section it is the second question that will be addressed. However, for the economic historian there is a serious causal problem in trying to assess the consequences of the war.

In economic history the primary concern is with causality: did event A cause event B to happen? Often, given the complexity of economic forces and/or the paucity of much historical data, it is only possible to demonstrate that A was a necessary but not sufficient condition for B to occur. Assessing the long-term impact of the war implies trying to show that the war itself was a necessary condition for A to occur and that A then helped to cause B; or, to put it another way, that without the war A would not have happened and therefore B would not have occurred. The problem is that the war itself is not, in these terms, an event; it is merely a period of years during which many different events occur. It is possible that if event A occurred during the war it was not the result of the war *per se* but the culmination of a process that had started before the war, so that A occurred by chance in the years of war or, possibly, that the war acted as a catalyst for A and that if there had been no war A would simply have taken longer to occur. Thus, in historical terms the assessment of the long-term consequences of the war will, in many cases, be a messy and possibly unsatisfactory task; this may well explain why so few economic historians have undertaken it – the exceptions being Milward and Broadberry (Milward 1984a, 1977: 329–65; Broadberry 1988).

Milward lists a whole series of consequences of the war for the British economy including: permanent increases in capacity and labour training as a result of the need to increase armaments production; general improvements in both labour and capital productivity; the decline in domestic service employment and in the textile industry; the temporary reversal of the decline in the manufacturing sector and the rise of the service sector (Milward 1984a: 30–1, 38, 1977: 62, 185–7, 221, 230–3). In most of these cases, however, the causal link between the war and the permanent change that is detected is not fully analysed and so it is not proven that the war was a necessary condition for each change to occur. To illustrate the problem further let us consider consequences of the war that are discussed by three other contributors to this volume: the creation of the welfare state; the post-war settlement; Keynesian demand management policies.

It is generally agreed that one of the most influential reports published during the war was the Beveridge Report, published in 1942, which mapped out the future welfare state (see ch. 10). Its aim was to take all the existing *ad hoc* social insurance schemes and to gather them into one overall scheme which would provide cover for every crisis in life, from maternity grants to funeral grants, from the cradle to the grave. It also aimed to provide a national minimum income in the form of National Assistance. Perhaps even more important than the scheme itself were the three assumptions upon which the Beveridge Report rested: family allowances would be paid for all children; a National Health Service would be set up; full employment would be guaranteed by the state. The Report was later followed by a series of White Papers that laid down the foundations of the welfare state: in February 1944 the National Health Service; in May, full employment; in September, National Insurance; in March 1945, housing. The other important building block of the new post-war state was the Education Act of 1944. These developments are considered in more depth in chapter 10 but the creation of the welfare state is not seen as a process that was initiated, or indeed ended, by the war. Instead, it is argued that the wartime developments were the result of a process whose origins preceded the war by a great many years and that the process which they initiated was refined for many years after the war.

The so-called post-war settlement has also often been viewed as a consequence of the Second World War. The post-war settlement is broadly defined as the consensus that emerged in the post-war period between trade unionists, industry and the government, a consensus that had its origins in the growth of tripartite organisations, both formal and informal, during the war. In simple terms the basis of this consensus was the willingness of trade unionists to restrain real wage growth in exchange for a full employment pledge by the government. In terms of employment the result was impressive: 'from 1920 until 1940 unemployment never fell below 1 million; from 1945 until 1975 it never, except for a few weeks, rose above it' (Cairncross 1981: 371). The post-war settlement is discussed more fully in chapter 7, contrasting the positive outcome of full employment with its more negative corollary of overmanning, restrictive practices and low productivity. As argued there, however, in many ways the post-war settlement was not simply a consequence of the war but a continuation of restrictive practices, by both employers and trade unionists, that had evolved in the 1930s; indeed, its precedents could be even traced back to the First World War.

Chapters 2 and 9 touch implicitly at several points on the debate about the 'Keynesian Revolution' although they do not tackle the question of its timing and, in particular, whether it was caused by the war. The ogre of chronic excess demand stalked the British economy in the early years of the war and threatened to gorge itself in a manner that would have led to a chaos greater than that of the First World War. That such chaos did not descend on the economy was largely due to the adoption of Keynesian budgetary policy, resting on the bed-rock of the new national income accounts (see above). Indeed, Booth regards the 1941 budget as a 'critical stage in the absorption of Keynesian analysis by Whitehall' although he qualifies this by pointing out that it had been adopted in a simplified world in which imports and both internal and external capital use was severely controlled by the state (Booth 1989: 68–9). Even so, despite the 1941 budget there was still resistance at the heart of the Treasury to Keynesian budgetary policy (especially applied in peacetime) and intellectual support for the more orthodox Treasury approach of the 1930s (Peden 1983; Booth 1989: 70–2).

Indeed, it can be argued that post-war economic policy was not Keynesian-based in that it did not follow through the premises of *The General Theory* (Keynes 1936) and that the advance was merely to use the Keynesian framework for developing the national income accounts in order to help the government to control inflation (the main fear of the Treasury in wartime); once peace returned it was not used to maintain full employment – the main impetus behind *The General Theory* – but was used to maintain the orthodox Treasury goal of a balanced budget and in particular to stabilise the balance of payments. Even if one accepts that there was a 'Keynesian Revolution' the question of timing remains and here there are many answers: the war is an obvious candidate for the timing of the shift in policy direction but Booth has argued that the real turning point was 1947; more recently both Tomlinson and Rollings have also pushed the decisive point into the post-war period (Booth 1983; Rollings 1985; ch. 9); Sayers, on the other hand, argues that the 1941 budgetary policy was not radical but a logical development from earlier measures and Booth himself has suggested, on a different but related front, that the wartime measures of control over domestic and external money markets were mainly extensions of measures introduced in the 1930s

(Sayers 1983: 108; Booth 1989: 47). Thus, in all three cases – that of the welfare state, the post-war settlement and the Keynesian Revolution – it is far from clear that the war was a necessary condition, although it undoubtedly acted at least as a catalyst for the first two.

The most obvious cost of the Second World War was the massive loss of human life: throughout the world probably 40 million people died as a result of the war, including 17 million Russians, 6 million Germans, 6 million Poles, more than 2.5 million Chinese and 2.4 million Japanese. In these terms the British casualties of 360,000 were relatively light, although another 250,000 casualties were suffered by the Commonwealth (Milward 1977: 211; Broadberry 1988: 31). Because the UK had a high pre-war level of national income per head, however, its aggregate human capital loss, at least in monetary terms, was higher, although still far less than the loss suffered by Germany or Russia (Broadberry 1988: 30–1). Although the destruction of the human capital stock during the war is obvious, its long term impact on economic growth is more difficult to assess beyond the fact that it clearly changed the age structure of the population. Indeed, the demographic impact of wars in general is far from clear and, as Milward says, the 'only recurrent demographic phenomenon relating to all or most wars over a long period is the fact that war kills many people' (Milward 1977: 209); further, the actual impact on any individual economy will be critically dependent on the production function which it faces after the war.

If consideration moves away from people to machines, there is a perverse logic which implies that war is good for economic growth because it encourages inventions and innovations which have positive long-term 'spin-off' effects. On this simple criterion the Second World War was indeed a boon for mankind: the wartime work done on the long-range bomber and the jet engine laid the basis for the post-war development of long-distance passenger aircraft; the loss of vital raw material supplies due to wartime disruption led to the development of synthetic oil and rubber; there were numerous advances in the fields of medicine and chemicals during the war (including penicillin, synthetic quinine and DDT); radar, atomic energy and many new metal fabrication methods also saw their first applications during the war (Milward 1977: 169–207; Vatter 1985: 146).

However, the crucial question is whether such developments would have occurred without the impetus of war. Milward concludes that the pro-war case is far from proven; he even argues against the idea that at the very least the war acted as a catalyst for such inventions and innovations by pointing out that non-war-related activities were denied funds, thus preventing other potential developments (Milward 1977: 175, 180). Investment projects were undertaken during the war which would not have been considered during peacetime by any company, because they would not have shown a positive return in conventional terms; this is not an argument for war but for government intervention to force the pace of technological change.

The war was partly financed by reducing the capital stock: the loss of internal and external capital during the war was the equivalent of 25 per cent of the pre-war national wealth whilst the loss of assets due to warfare has been calculated by Maddison at 3 per cent (Broadberry 1988: 31; Milward 1977: 333). The implications of this loss were at times very serious. Between 1939 and 1947 British merchant fleet tonnage fell by 17 per cent while the USA was able to expand its fleet threefold in terms of gross tonnage; indeed it was the only major merchant shipping nation not to suffer a decline over this period and was able to gain ascendancy over Britain in this important area (Milward 1977: 346).

In terms of the destruction of physical capital the loss suffered by the defeated powers was greater than that suffered by Britain. Despite this, Germany and Japan, not Britain, were to be the miracles of the post-war world; this has led some to claim that their success was built on the fact that the destruction of their physical capital was so great that it meant that they had to build their economies from scratch in the post-war period and thus invested in the latest technology, giving them a capital stock that was to be younger and more productive than that of Britain. Broadberry has dismissed this folk view of the post-war success of Germany and Japan by citing the studies of Rostas and the Anglo-American Council on Productivity which implied that it was not the age of machinery but its utilisation and the utilisation of 'best-practice techniques' that explained the productivity gap between the UK and the USA; Denison, in his study of post-war economic growth did not find the decrease in the age of capital to be a significant factor (Broadberry 1988: 32).

Indeed, Broadberry, in trying to explain the differences in post-war performances by reference to the impact of the war, has suggested that the Olson theory of institutional sclerosis may be of more significance (Broadberry 1988: 34–5; ch. 7). The Olson thesis is that over time certain groups (such as unions or employer cartels) emerge to gain some form of monopoly power in the economy and therefore, in pursuing their own vested interests, contribute to a long-run deceleration of economic growth; over time, the economy becomes sclerotic (Olson 1982). The argument is usually applied to the national economy and war can be seen in a positive light if it helps to sweep away the institutional structures that are contributing to the economic sclerosis (as, it is argued, the Second World War did in Japan and Germany but not in the UK or the USA).

Perhaps the most important effect of the war, in terms of institutional sclerosis, was not, however, on the nation state but on the international arena. The post-war international settlement aimed to replace the chaotic and protectionist stage of the 1930s with a more ordered and freer environment via such new structures as the Bretton Woods system, the International Monetary Fund, the World Bank and the General Agreement on Tariffs and Trade (Vatter 1985: 157–69). Within Europe the European Common Market, and all its attendant bodies, were to rise from the ashes of destruction, lay the foundations for rapid recovery from the war and create a new and powerful economic bloc (Milward 1984a: 59–75, 1977: 329–65). It was against this background that the UK, and the world economy, experienced a prolonged post-war boom that lasted for approximately twenty-five years and has been likened by some to an economic 'golden age' and it was in the encouragement of international cooperation (and in showing the dangers of isolationism and nationalism) that the war was to have its most important long-term impact.

2 Economic policy and performance, 1945–1964

Sir Alexander Cairncross

Introduction

The purpose of this and the following chapter is to provide a sketch of developments over the entire period at the macro-economic level. These chapters do not enter in detail into a discussion of the forces influencing growth, inflation, employment and the balance of payments in the longer term since these are all discussed in other chapters but, instead, will trace the changes taking place chronologically, dwelling on those episodes when a crisis interrupted the trend.

The role of the state

First, however, some picture is needed of the changes at work in the post-war world, both within the domestic economy and in the international environment. One such change was the increase in the responsibilities falling on the state. In the Second World War as in the First, the state had taken control over the entire economy, acting as 'the sole consumer of the products of the economic system' (Devons 1950: 3) even to deciding what should be left for civilian consumption. Something of this expanded role continued after the war and there was much talk then and later of central economic planning. What emerged, however, was a managed rather than a planned economy. Governments attempted to steer the economy towards specific objectives such as full employment, stable prices, faster growth and greater equality. In the pursuit of these objectives, reliance was placed on demand management through monetary and fiscal policy while intervention on the side of supply was more spasmodic and on a narrower front.

Demand management was initially conceived as a means of freeing the economy from unemployment. But for nearly thirty years after the war it was mainly used to check rather than to stimulate demand and was used, moreover, in fairly small doses. The world economy, after a few anxious years of reconstruction, proved to be unexpectedly buoyant and to suffer from excess rather than deficient demand. Unemployment remained at a low level and economic growth was at a record pace. The more persistent problem was inflation; and demand management was incapable of serving the two conflicting aims of preventing inflation and maintaining demand at a level consistent with full employment. From the middle 1970s priority passed to control of inflation, demand management was under a cloud, and unemployment was allowed to rise to levels not seen since the 1930s.

The retreat from demand management was combined with a reaction against state intervention and a greater willingness to trust to market forces. There was also a disposition to attack earlier economic management as misguided in its pursuit of illusions and for lavishing public money on the creation of a welfare state to the neglect of industrial reconstruction (chs. 9 and 10 below). Where the Labour government in 1945 had spent much of its time bringing large sections of the economy into public ownership, the Conservative government in the 1980s set about restoring as much as it could to the private sector. Between 1960 and 1980 successive governments had sought to transform British industry by tax concessions, subsidies, a national economic plan, restructuring through government agencies and industrial policy in different guises. These efforts had not had much success and by 1990 had almost entirely ceased.

One influence behind these efforts on the part of government was the sense that British industry was somehow in decline and failing to keep pace with its continental competitors (see also ch. 11 below). Productivity might be improving more rapidly in Britain than ever before but in other countries it was improving still faster, and in some countries much faster. One measure of the inadequacies of British industry was taken to be the declining share of British exports in world trade and the increasing penetration of the British market by imported manufactures. By the 1980s Britain had become a net importer of manufactures and there was an uneasy feeling that as North Sea oil declined the shortcomings of British industry would be revealed in a formidable balance of payments deficit.

Although the 1980s, in Britain as elsewhere, saw a swing away from some forms of reliance on the state, it continued to exercise a powerful influence on the economy. It still disposed of as high a proportion of the nation's purchasing power in 1988 as forty years previously – indeed, a rather higher proportion than in 1948. An appreciably higher proportion than in 1978 was taken in taxes, social security contributions and rates (local government taxes); 36.7 per cent was taken in 1988, compared with 35.2 per cent in 1948 and 33.5 per cent in 1978. Much of the increase in public expenditure was in social security payments of all kinds – transfers from a group of payers to a group of beneficiaries with some overlap between the two. But expenditure on goods and services, including health, education and defence, rose just as fast: fiftyfold in forty years before correcting for inflation or about three and a half times in real terms.

The state certainly retained the power to tax and spend. But did it retain the kind of control over the economy it had possessed in 1945 or 1950? In two separate ways, control weakened progressively. The process began with a gradual abandonment of forms of control inherited from wartime. The last to go was exchange control in 1979. Other instruments of policy introduced in post-war years were also discarded: hire purchase restrictions, investment allowances, the selective employment tax, the regional employment premium and many others. By the late 1980s the range of policy instruments had narrowed steadily until it seemed as if economic policy was almost exclusively dependent on variations in bank rate – much as it had been before 1913.

The international environment

Economic management was further restricted by international developments. These included deliberate acts of policy such as joining the European Community and accepting the closer economic integration with Europe that accompanied it. Britain had at first hesitated to join the Community partly because it might limit the free exercise of British ideas of economic management and partly because Britain's wider links with the Commonwealth and with continents outside Europe made it lean towards world-wide rather than European institutions. But in the late 1950s and 1960s fear of being debarred from the rapidly expanding European markets, together with the beginnings of a change in the pattern of British trade in favour of those markets, disposed the government to accept the obligations of membership although it was not until 1973 that it was able to join.

More important was a change in the international environment binding economies more firmly together through the freer flow of trade and capital. In the post-war period differences in policy aims between the leading industrial countries did not prevent an increasing similarity in experience in the face of common economic problems. In a country so deeply embedded in the international economy as was Britain, but forming a smaller and smaller part of the aggregate, policy has been increasingly constrained and performance increasingly affected by what is happening elsewhere. The power to pursue an independent economic policy with any hope of success has been greatly reduced. Integration and convergence leave little room for independent economic management. So long as the international environment remains benign this need give little cause for concern; but if the world encounters a persistent depression, it may be difficult to devise effective instruments of international policy to take the place of the national instruments no longer in use.

For most of the post-war period the international environment was extremely favourable. An initial imbalance between North America and the rest of the world, expressing itself in a dollar shortage, was gradually overcome as production recovered in countries ravaged by war. As their trade with one another grew, European countries found less need to turn to North America as the sole available source of supply. The recovery was assisted by the relaxation of trade restrictions by international agreement and an expansion in world trade even more rapid than the growth in world output. A steadily expanding world market not only contributed to greater productive efficiency but eased the difficulty of regaining balance when a country's international accounts moved into deficit. In continental Europe, where output had fallen far below potential at the end of the war, markets expanded particularly rapidly, giving a momentum to intra-European trade that encouraged aspirations to closer economic integration.

Recovery both in production and in trade was greatly assisted by international collaboration under the leadership of the United States and by the financial assistance furnished under the Marshall Plan. The fears that the war would be followed, as in 1921–2, by a disastrous international slump, gave way as recovery proceeded and the danger of a series of balance of payments crises, as one country after another ran out of dollars, was dissipated by Marshall Aid. Although a mild depression in the United States in 1949 produced a devaluation of the pound and a realignment of most other currencies, some such adjustment could be viewed as an inevitable constituent of the process of post-war recovery; world trade continued to expand and the dollar shortage grew less acute.

There were fresh alarms after the outbreak of war in Korea in 1950 and the dislocation associated with rearmament. But from the early 1950s until the first oil shock in 1973 the world enjoyed a kind of Golden Age in which expansion continued remarkably smoothly. Between 1953 and 1963 world income grew at 3.7 per cent per annum and world trade at 6.5 per cent per annum. In the next ten years expansion was even more rapid with an annual growth in world income of 5.2 per cent and of world trade by 8.9 per cent (Maddison 1982). The growth in the aggregates concealed, however, some jolts at the country level and the transition from wartime controls to unrestricted trade that accompanied the growth was far from smooth and very protracted.

The expansion in world trade, for example, was boosted by the return to international markets of countries like Germany and Japan, keen competitors of the United Kingdom. Their success was of assistance to the countries trading with them but contributed to the balance of payments problems of the United Kingdom and in course of time produced a fresh imbalance in international trade, with Germany and Japan replacing the United States as persistent creditors.

Post-war balance of payments problems

Throughout the post-war period, up to the late 1970s when North Sea oil came on stream, the United Kingdom was in constant balance of payments difficulties. Right from the start in 1945 there was a continued struggle to balance the international accounts, a struggle that conditioned domestic economic policy and tended to dominate the activities of government. There was a foreign exchange crisis in 1947, 1949 and almost every second year from then until 1961.

The fluctuations in the British balance of payments on current account and in the drain of gold and dollars from the reserves in the early post-war years are shown in Figure 2.1. The balance of payments began in deficit, moved into deeper deficit in 1947 and then improved sharply in 1948. After the devaluation of 1949 there was a further improvement to a surplus of £300 million in 1950 – a surplus only once exceeded in the next twenty years. The outbreak of war in Korea in the middle of 1950, however, sent the balance of payments into equally heavy deficit as rearmament in Britain put pressure on domestic resources and rearmament abroad drove up commodity prices and inflated Britain's import bill (Cairncross 1985: ch. 8). Thereafter there was a small surplus, except in 1955, throughout the 1950s. The gold and dollar deficit fluctuated even more widely. Like the current account deficit it reached a peak in 1947, fell heavily in the next two years and was remarkably favourable in 1950 before deteriorating again in 1951.

The burden imposed by rearmament in 1950–2 on the balance of payments is a reminder of the contribution of the public sector throughout the post-war period to the difficulty of establishing external balance. Britain's responsibilities in all parts of the world made it necessary to incur substantial military expenditure in Germany, Palestine, Egypt, Malaysia and other countries long after the war was over.

The current account deficit was aggravated in the early post-war years by a swing in the terms of trade against the United Kingdom. A rise in American prices after decontrol in 1947 helped to raise the cost of British imports by well over 20 per cent. Although exports also rose steeply in price, there was an adverse shift in the terms of trade of 7 per cent. There was little change in the next three years but in 1951, as rearmament drove up commodity prices all over the world, there was a further adverse shift of about 11 per cent. These shifts were reversed in the 1950s, the terms of

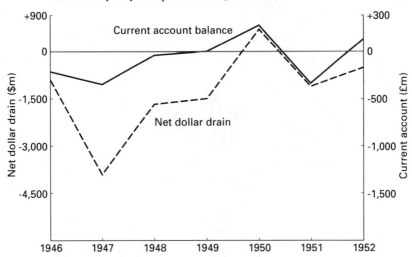

Figure 2.1 The balance of payments on current account and the net dollar drain, 1946–52

trade returning to their 1945/6 level by 1958; but, coming in the middle of the transition from war to peace, they constituted a heavy additional burden in that transition.

As will be seen from Figure 2.2, the move from a current account deficit in 1945 to a small surplus in 1952 involved a growth in exports from 30 per cent of their 1938 volume in 1945 to over 160 per cent in 1952 while imports were held throughout below their pre-war volume. It was an adjustment that, once accomplished, did not need to be repeated and paved the way for a more relaxed treatment of consumer needs in the 1950s. In the five years 1945–50 the rise in net exports absorbed more than the increment in output over those years while in the 1950s imports rose faster than exports, yielding a net addition to the increment in output.

The dollar shortage and inconvertibility

The post-war balance of payments problem was aggravated by the debts incurred in wartime and by the inconvertibility of currencies into dollars – the so-called 'dollar shortage'. In the course of the war Britain had run up a cumulative deficit in the balance on current account of £10,000 million, casting that burden on other countries. Half of the necessary finance had been supplied by the United States under Lend-Lease arrangements and the rest had had to be found by borrowing in sterling or by selling foreign investments. The resulting debts consisted largely of short-term liabilities to foreign banks and official holders in the form of

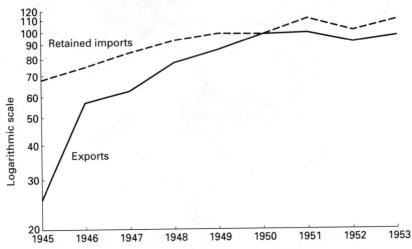

Figure 2.2 The volume of exports and retained imports, 1945–53[a]
(1950 = 100)

[a] The estimates for 1945–7 are on the basis of 1938 weights.
Source: Annual Abstract of Statistics 1953.

sterling deposits in London. Of these sterling balances, which overhung the balance of payments far into the future, a large part represented debts to poor countries like Egypt and India in which heavy military expenditures had been incurred.

Before the war, sterling's use as an international currency had led to foreign deposits in London of some £500 million and these had been matched by reserves of gold and dollars to a similar amount. By 1945 sterling balances had mounted to nearly £3,500 million while the reserves had increased only to £600 million. No other belligerent had incurred debts of this kind or on this scale. It has been estimated that the net change on capital account in the six years of war, including external indebtedness and the run-down in domestic capital through depreciation and bomb damage, left the country no richer than in 1914, thirty years earlier (Matthews *et al.* 1982).

The dollar problem did not become acute until 1947, when recovery was well under way in most European countries. North America had become the one intact source of food, materials and equipment on which the rest of the world sought to draw, leaving America in surplus with almost every other country. Immediately after the war the United States had poured out dollars through the UN Relief and Rehabilitation Administration (UNRRA), foreign loans and in other ways. But by 1947 the outflow had fallen off and countries were having to draw on their reserves at an unsustainable rate. It was this international imbalance and the difficulty of settling accounts with the United States that created the dollar shortage.

One consequence for Britain of the dollar shortage was that it made sterling less acceptable than dollars in all international transactions and diminished the incentive to hold sterling as a reliable international currency. This reduced Britain's freedom of manoeuvre in settlements with other countries. A more important consequence was the collapse of triangular or multilateral settlements that had enabled Britain before the war to earn dollars through surpluses with one set of countries and to apply them to meeting a deficit with North America and other countries which required payment in dollars. The surpluses yielded only inconvertible, 'soft' currency and the excess of exports to the countries concerned was derided as 'unrequited'. It became necessary to divert exports to dollar markets in an effort to reduce the dollar deficit. But such diversion was not easy when competition in dollar markets was far more severe and prices much lower than in markets elsewhere. Moreover the disproportion between exports and imports in trade with North America, with imports in 1946 six times as great as exports, made any advance towards a balancing of accounts unlikely to get very far.

The outlook for the balance of payments in 1945 was gloomy. As Attlee told the House of Commons in August 1945, outgoings on imported supplies of food and materials, together with military expenditure abroad, were running at an annual rate of £2,000 million whereas earnings from exports were bringing in only £350 million a year, supplemented by a further £450 million from other (invisible) earnings. The deficit might be cut to £750 million in 1946 but was likely to continue for several years. Official forecasts put the total deficit in the three years 1946–8 at £1250 million. The published estimates at the time came very close to this total but later calculations yield a total less than half as large.

The US loan agreement

The prospects for the balance of payments led the Labour government, shortly after taking office in the summer of 1945 to enter into negotiations for a large grant or, failing that, a loan from the United States. The negotiations, led by Keynes, were lengthy and unhappy. Agreement was finally reached in December to borrow $3,750 million at a rate of interest of 2 per cent. Repayment was to be spread over fifty years from 1951 to 2001, the annual instalment of interest and capital working out at $140 million (Pressnell 1986). The loan was not approved by Congress until July 1946, after a change in America's attitude to the USSR and revaluation of the British connection. By that time it had been supplemented by a loan from the Canadian government of $1,250 million bringing the total to $5,000 million. The terms of the American loan included a condition which the British government accepted with great reluctance: sterling was to be made convertible one year after the loan agreement came into operation.

It had been expected that there would be a transitional period of at least three years before countries were required to fulfil the international obligations assumed at Bretton Woods; but three years proved far too short and the hope of convertibility of sterling within a year was completely unrealistic. There was too much sterling around the world and too great a temptation to convert it into dollars if allowed. When convertibility was introduced in July 1947 it lasted for only five weeks before it had to be suspended. The reserves were pouring away in mid-August at $1 billion a month. At the end of the year the drain on the reserves totalled over $4 billion and the American credit was nearly exhausted.

Much of the drain on the reserves reflected a deficit on current account initially estimated at £675 million and now put at £381 million. The rest, £643 million, represents an outflow of capital on a colossal scale in spite of the restrictions imposed by exchange control on capital movements. Some of this – perhaps £300 million – reflected drawings on the dollar pool to meet the deficits of sterling area countries, and some corresponded to drawings from sterling balances. But there was also some outflow of capital for investment in the sterling area, some movement of commercial credit (leads and lags) that put pressure on the capital account, and some encashment for dollars of sterling held outside the sterling area (Cairncross 1985: ch. 6).

1947 proved to be an exceptional year. It had opened with a fuel crisis in February which interrupted industrial production and checked the expansion of exports (Robertson 1987). On the other hand, imports increased from the low level to which they had been restricted in 1946 by a world food shortage and delays in delivery. There was also a poor harvest in 1947 which put more pressure on imports as also did the need to build up stocks as output expanded. On the other hand, the first hint of the Marshall Plan at the beginning of May held out the prospect of some alleviation of the dollar shortage. By 1948, when Marshall Aid began, the position had been transformed. Exports had soared to over 50 per cent above the pre-war level, the current account was in balance and thanks to Marshall Aid the reserves had ceased to fall.

The dollar shortage, however, continued and with it the dollar drain. Like other countries, the United Kingdom was still obliged to limit dollar outgoings by discriminating against imports from the United States. The multilateral, non-discriminatory trade which was sought by the United States, and to which Britain was pledged, could not be introduced in the absence of convertibility and convertibility was ruled out by the dollar shortage. Distinguished American economists then and later argued that all that was necessary to get rid of the dollar shortage was a devaluation of European currencies and an elimination of budget deficits (Kindleberger 1987: 65). But how far exchange rates would have had to fall and how much unemployment and impoverishment would have been required before balance was achieved was little considered.

Devaluation in 1947 would have been premature: by 1949, however, the situation had changed. The problem was no longer to bring exports and imports into balance but to get rid of the dollar deficit. For this purpose devaluation was indispensable as a means of making British (and continental) supplies more competitive both in dollar markets and at home. A relatively mild and short depression in the United States in 1949 produced a fresh exchange crisis as falling sales of rubber, tin and other commodities in America reduced dollar earnings and lowered the reserves to danger point. The Chancellor, Stafford Cripps, was brought reluctantly to accept the need for devaluation in September 1949; and the devaluation of sterling against the dollar by 30 per cent was the signal for a general realignment of currencies which reduced the trade-weighted devaluation of sterling to about 9 per cent (Cairncross and Eichengreen 1983). After some initial uncertainty the pound strengthened and in 1950 the reserves increased rapidly – so rapidly that at the end of the year the United States put an end to Marshall Aid to the United Kingdom.

1950 was a turning point in more ways than one. It saw the launch of the Schumann Plan in May and the first moves towards the creation of the European Community. In June war broke out in Korea and the fears of Russian intentions which this generated led to an effort of rearmament that produced yet another exchange crisis in 1951–2. In July came the establishment of the European Payments Union – a regional clearing union that served for the next eight years as a halfway house to convertibility.

The European Payments Union

The last of these had its origin in efforts to introduce some elasticity into the bilateral trading arrangements that had grown up since the war. European countries had sought to maintain strict control over their imports through quotas, licences and other devices and had entered into bilateral agreements aiming at an approximate balance with each of their trading partners, sweetened by a limited provision of credit to cover an excess in either direction. These credit lines grew year by year in a network of payments agreements. By the end of 1947 the total amount of credit available in the agreements had reached over $1,500 million and intra-European trade was sustained at a level equal to 60 per cent of its pre-war volume (Cairncross 1985: 288). But the bilateralism of the agreements made them increasingly restrictive as production recovered; and although they were designed to keep the use of gold and dollars to a minimum, it was never possible to carry on trade outside the dollar area without any settlements in gold and dollars. Efforts were made to relax the restrictions and find some way of introducing more elasticity through some element of multilateralism (Tew 1965: chs. 8–10).

These efforts fructified in a liberalisation of trade in 1949–50 following agreement on united action to liberalise a stated proportion of trade by members of the OEEC (Organisation for European Economic Co-operation – the organisation created in 1948 of countries in receipt of Marshall Aid). Two successive intra-European payments agreements were reached in 1948 and 1949, also under the auspices of the OEEC. Then in the summer of 1950 it was agreed to establish the European Payments Union. Each country's bilateral surpluses and deficits would all be added together by the EPU and the net surplus or deficit would be estimated monthly on a cumulative basis, i.e. the net position would represent the outcome of all surpluses and deficits since the scheme began. So long as cumulative surpluses and deficits amounted to less than 20 per cent of a country's quota these were settled by a credit to or from the EPU. Beyond that point creditors received 50 per cent of the excess in gold and extended the remaining 50 per cent in credit up to the limit of their quota. It rested with the Managing Board how surpluses in excess of quota were to be settled. Debtors had to meet a rising proportion of their cumulative deficit in gold, with settlements in excess of quota entirely in gold (Kaplan and Schleiminger 1989: 93).

The United Kingdom entered the Union with some hesitation, fearing that the new payments system would limit the use of sterling as an international currency. The Bank of England was reluctant to abandon the payments agreements it had reached, all of which provided for settlement in sterling. The British government would also have liked to limit more severely the use of gold and dollars in international settlements while creditor countries like Belgium wanted just the opposite. There were also times when the United Kingdom contemplated torpedoing the EPU by making a unilateral dash for full convertibility. However, nothing came of these plans and the scheme lasted until France and Germany joined with Britain in ushering in full convertibility of European currencies at the end of 1958.

Rearmament

The rearmament that began in the autumn of 1950 was responsible for a third balance of payments crisis in the winter of 1951–2. Early in 1951 the reserves were rising so strongly that serious consideration was given to a revaluation of the pound. But it was soon clear that the increase in the reserves reflected high export prices and export earnings in the countries of the sterling area and that much of the addition to the reserves was balanced by corresponding liabilities in the form of sterling balances in London. As the rearmament boom proceeded, these balances were drawn on by their owners with a consequent decline in the reserves. The increased pressure resulting from rearmament steepened the decline. But perhaps the most serious source of difficulty was the sharp change in the terms of trade, mentioned earlier. The crisis owed at least as much to rearmament abroad, with its impact on commodity prices, as to rearmament at home, with its curtailment of resources to meet consumer demand from domestic production.

While the British government did not hesitate to join the United States in embarking on rearmament and giving a clear lead to NATO, it asked for reassurance from America that it could count on help in dealing with any balance of payments difficulties. On this footing, but without any formal assurance of the aid required, it agreed to add £800 million (in addition to £200 million already authorised) to its defence programme over the next three years. As the situation in Korea became more desperate the total was increased by £200 million in September; in January, after China had entered the war, the programme was increased again by £1,100 million to a total of £4,700. This implied a diversion to defence, when there was little or no slack in the economy, of about 650,000 workers. It also implied a fourfold increase in defence production by the metal and engineering industries.

It was almost inevitable that the programme would stretch out over a longer period and this undoubtedly occurred with defence production. Rearmament as a whole seems to have reached its peak in 1952, still about 30 per cent below the peak planned at the beginning of 1951. This implied an increase above the pre-Korea level of spending of about two-thirds, with a larger increase of between two and three times in defence production in the metal and engineering industries. While rearmament represented a burdensome diversion of resources to military purposes and contributed to a slowing down of the export drive, what did more harm was the shift in the terms of trade and the exchange crisis that it precipitated (Cairncross 1985: ch. 8).

The crisis is best illustrated by the change in the gold and dollar balance from a surplus of $371 million in the first quarter of 1951 to a deficit of $937 million in the last. A deficit with other members of the EPU had also reached alarming proportions and by March 1952 any further deficit would be payable entirely in gold and dollars. In the first two months of 1952 there was a further loss from the reserves of over $500 million. It was also anticipated that the defence aid of $300 million from the United States which was due by the end of June would now be limited to $125 million. The Chancellor told his colleagues in January that the reserves were likely to fall by June to $1,400 million – the level at which the pound was devalued in 1949.

Robot

The Conservative government which took office in October 1951 made import cuts in November and January, and raised Bank Rate from 2 per cent (where it had remained since 1932 with a brief interruption in 1939) to 2.5 per cent. It also secured agreement from members of the Commonwealth at a conference in January to take action to eliminate by the second half of 1952 a sterling area deficit with the non-sterling world that had amounted in the second half of 1951 to £750 million.

Treasury officials had little expectation that this would be accomplished and predicted an early confidence crisis. In conjunction with the Bank of England, they prepared a plan labelled Robot, on the basis that it would be impossible to maintain the existing parity for lack of reserves and that it would be better to float at once before the reserves ran out rather than wait and lose control. Floating was to be combined with immediate convertibility (for non-residents only) and with the funding or blocking of nearly all sterling balances except 20 per cent of the balances held by members of the sterling area (Cairncross 1985: ch. 9; MacDougall 1987).

These proposals were to be rushed through for inclusion in the budget on 4 March. They were accepted by the Chancellor and first discussed by a small group of Ministers on 20 February. At a second meeting of Ministers two days later Lord Cherwell (Paymaster-General) was alone in voicing outright opposition to the plan.

There then began a bitter controversy which continued long after the Cabinet failed to give its approval to the scheme at meetings on 28–9 February. The opposition was led by Lord Cherwell and Sir Arthur Salter (Minister of State in the Treasury). The Foreign Secretary, Sir Anthony Eden, also came down against the scheme. The proposals, it was argued, breached many of the IMF articles, would have put an end to the EPU and were unlikely to be welcome to countries holding their reserves in sterling.

They would do nothing in the short run to close the gap between imports and exports and would encourage countries to discriminate against the United Kingdom as soon as its currency became convertible. There were fears also that employment would suffer, inflation accelerate and the sterling area break up.

The Chancellor (Rab Butler) admitted many of these disadvantages but claimed that a floating rate would automatically put an end to the dollar drain. Ever since they came into office the Conservatives had been anxious to 'free the pound' and were in principle in favour of floating and of convertibility. They were therefore attracted to a plan that incorporated the first and went a long way towards the second. The Chancellor also argued that the alternative would be found very unpalatable since it would include an increase in interest rates, a substantial reduction in food subsidies, further cuts in imports and in the defence programme, the suspension of depreciation allowances and other restrictive measures.

The controversy rested on a diagnosis of the prospects for the balance of payments and the reserves which turned out to be mistaken. The Treasury urged on 24 February that 'at the level to which the reserves are certain to fall … it will be impossible in any event to maintain a fixed rate'. But in fact confidence in sterling revived in March, perhaps because the budget did *not* include the Robot plan. An inventory recession checked imports and the balance of payments moved into surplus with the non-sterling world both in the United Kingdom and in the rest of the sterling area. The drain ceased completely by the end of March and never resumed. The reserves, instead of falling to $600–1,250 million, had climbed by the end of the year to $1,850 million.

A further attempt was made to get agreement to the scheme in June but this failed. Thereafter the scheme was drastically amended to become 'the collective approach to convertibility' and submitted first to a Commonwealth Economic Conference in December and later, in the spring of 1953, to the United States government (Cairncross and Watts 1989: 308). The progress to convertibility after Robot is discussed below.

The Schumann Plan

At the end of the war the victorious allies had sought to ensure that Germany would not again wage aggressive war against them. The French felt particular anxiety to delay German recovery while they rebuilt their own strength. The United States, on the other hand, came increasingly to the conclusion that Europe was unlikely to become self-supporting without a revival of Germany's contribution to the European economy. The conflict between these two positions came to a head with the Marshall

Plan. The French, under the influence of Monnet, recognised that their position had become untenable and swung round to a view, more congenial to the Americans, of tying Germany to France within a European framework. It was this strategy that underlay the Schumann Plan in 1950.

There had already been much discussion, in which the British participated, of a European customs union and other moves towards closer integration. But the United Kingdom, although anxious to assist in European recovery and in encouraging freer trade between European countries, did not wish to be too closely tied to its European neighbours. It had spent the war planning world-wide, not European institutions, conducted three-quarters of its trade with other continents, and was bound to the Commonwealth by ties to which there was no European counterpart. It was also afraid that, in its shattered state, Europe might be a drag on its recovery, not a source of future strength. Above all, it was anxious to be left to manage its own affairs, confident that it would make a better job of economic management if it retained its freedom of action.

The French, aware of British susceptibilities, had framed the Schumann Plan for a European Coal and Steel Community with no expectation of British participation (Milward 1984b). Britain hesitated to offer unconditional acceptance, as demanded by the French, of a plan that was still extremely vague; the government was unwilling to accord powers of decision over its industries to a supranational body. Officials, however, submitted a sympathetic report, acknowledging the need for international action, and Ministers on 4 July approved in principle a scheme for the integration of the coal and steel industries of western Europe provided the Council of Ministers retained a veto. The scheme, however, was not submitted to other governments, perhaps because it was thought that the French government was deeply divided and that there might be an opportunity for Britain to make proposals later. No such opportunity arose and the Coal and Steel Community came into existence without British participation.

Domestic economic policy after 1945

During the war the economy had been mobilised through extensive government controls, with a thoroughness more commonly associated with Communist planning. Many of these controls were carried into the post-war years and only gradually abandoned. The controls were a way of dealing with shortages instead of leaving a rise in price to bring supply and demand into balance. They made it possible to ensure a supply to what were judged to be priority needs and were thought also to ensure that each consumer had no more than his 'fair share'. Since most controls arose out of some disruption of supply and it was reasonable to expect a gradual easing of shortages as reconversion proceeded, controls could be assumed to be transitional, lasting only as long as the apparent shortage. The totality of controls, however, could be looked at differently: instead of an overall shortage of supply they might signify an excess of demand and a state of suppressed inflation.

Excess demand, however, was congenial to a government committed to securing full employment; and controls had their uses as instruments of government planning. It was not until Dalton's last budget of November 1947 that a serious attempt was made to reduce the pressure of demand by means of a budget surplus. Even so, the pressure remained intense and unemployment, already below 2 per cent in 1948, continued to fall until the mild depression of 1952.

The controls in use were of five main types: price control, consumer rationing, control of investment, allocation of raw materials and import restrictions (Dow 1964: ch. 6; Cairncross 1985: ch. 12).

Price control covered about half of consumer spending and was tightest over rationed goods and commodities that could be specified with precision. There was little relaxation of control until 1949–50 when some items were removed, but after an effort to reimpose and tighten controls in the Korean War, they were nearly all abandoned in 1952–3, the exceptions including house rents, coal and rail and bus fares. On the whole, price control seems to have been effective in keeping prices more or less in line with costs.

Consumer rationing took various forms: entitlements to specific quantities of rationed items; points rationing of clothing, furniture, canned goods, etc.; and limitations of spending, e.g. on holidays abroad and house repairs. Of total consumer spending never more than one third, and from 1949 never more than one eighth was covered. Bread and potatoes, which were never rationed in wartime, were rationed after the war, bread for two years from July 1946 and potatoes in the winter of 1947–8. Fats, butter, bacon, cheese and meat were not derationed until 1954. After 1950, however, rationing did not prevent food consumption per head rising above the pre-war level. Since most rationed food was imported, the government was able to exercise effective control and there was little evidence of a black market.

Control of investment was less effective, especially in the period before 1948 when there was an enormous overissue of building licences. The shortage of building materials, however, gave the government power to influence the pattern of investment through allocations of steel and timber. It could put pressure on engineering firms to meet specific requirements or increase their exports. It could also set limits to the amount of timber used per house built. Building could be permitted more freely in the development areas and restricted more severely in areas short of labour.

Raw material allocations not only provided a means of controlling investment but could be used to influence industrial production and the volume of exports. Car manufacturers could be required to export a stated proportion – at one time three-quarters – of their output. Nearly all materials except coal and steel were imported by the government or under licence from the government and at the end of the war nearly all were subject to allocation. Derestriction spread from one material to another but was halted in the Korean War when, for example, the allocation of steel was reintroduced. By 1954, however, the only items still under allocation were coal and tin-plate.

Many of the controls were used to improve the balance of payments, by thinning out the use of imports, particularly imports paid for in dollars, and by exerting pressure for more exports, or exports to dollar markets. Import control served this purpose more directly. It allowed the government to switch to non-dollar sources of supply at higher cost, to engage in bulk purchase of imports on long-term contracts and to enter into bilateral deals with other governments. In a balance of payments crisis, import control could be used to make cuts, sometimes, as in 1949 and 1951, in association with other sterling area countries and always with the aim of reducing dollar expenditure.

At first nearly all the import trade was in government hands and all other trade required a government licence. There was then a gradual move back to private trading. When OEEC embarked on its programme of liberalisation in 1949 a rising proportion of private trade was freed from control so long as it was with non-dollar countries. By 1950 this proportion had reached 50 per cent (about a quarter of total imports) and was still increasing. The process then went into reverse for a time when import cuts amounting in all to £600 million were made between November 1951 and March 1952 but, when the crisis was over, liberalisation was resumed in 1953. After 1952 no further use was made of import controls to deal with an exchange crisis and the proportion of trade free from restrictions, already 50 per cent in 1953, continued to increase.

In addition to these controls there was a vestigial control over labour. The government had hesitated in wartime to make use of its powers to direct labour and abandoned most of its powers over labour recruitment in December 1945, preferring to rely on persuading applicants for jobs at the Labour Exchanges to take the work to which it attached most importance. In addition to this system of so-called 'first preferences' the government could also provide inducements such as better rations, deferment of call-up, more housing in designated areas, special training facilities, etc.; and it could allow, or promote, immigration to particular industries (for example from Eire or refugee camps in Europe). The only industries in which wartime powers were retained – and retained only until the beginning of 1950 – were coal mining, agriculture and building and civil engineering.

Some Ministers were by no means happy to see the abandonment of direct controls. In 1950 Gaitskell, backed by Douglas Jay, defended the use of controls as 'the distinguishing feature of British socialist planning' and argued for the retention of those that contributed to full employment, external balance and a fair distribution of income. Without controls it would not be possible to maintain an even pressure of demand throughout the economy and keep down unemployment; the more external trade was free of control, the more difficult it would be to plan domestic economic activity; and if it was left to the price mechanism to settle who obtained scarce goods, 'fair shares' would go by the board (Rollings 1992).

Economic controls rested on emergency powers that expired at the end of 1950. The Labour government contemplated taking statutory powers to perpetuate the controls it thought necessary for planning purposes in an 'Economic Planning and Full Employment Bill'. But after long debate the bill was dropped in February 1951 and the use of direct controls continued to rest on emergency powers.

What took the place of direct controls was demand management, i.e. the use of financial controls (fiscal and monetary policy) to influence the pressure of demand on resources. This did not mean that all attempts to influence or control supply were simultaneously abandoned or that the horizon of policy contracted to the budgetary year ahead. It was rather, as Cripps put it, that the budget was now recognised as 'the most powerful instrument for influencing economic policy which is available to the government' (Cairncross 1985: 332).

This was not the doctrine of the White Paper on *Employment Policy* in 1944, which had studiously avoided references to budgetary policy. Nor was it how Keynes had seen demand management: he hoped to stabilise employment by stabilising investment and to make use of a separate capital budget without resort to deficits in the current budget. So far as Ministers had any views on economic management, they thought in terms of a manpower budget such as had been used in wartime and they left economic policy to the Lord President of the Council (Herbert Morrison) while financial policy was to be the separate domain of the Treasury under the Chancellor of the Exchequer, Hugh Dalton. The White Paper had provided only the vaguest sketch of how 'a high and stable level of employment' was to be achieved but recommended reliance on the economic staff in the Cabinet Office, who had been the main source of economic advice in wartime. It was only when Cripps took charge of economic policy in 1947 and added the Treasury to his responsibilities in November of that year that a unified approach to economic management became possible.

The Economic Section of the Treasury had meanwhile developed the technique of national income forecasting and prepared regular economic surveys analysing the problems facing the economy and making recommendations for dealing with it. The early surveys remained unpublished and when the first did appear in 1947 it had been written partly by Cripps himself and partly by 'Otto' Clarke in the Treasury (Cairncross and Watts 1989). From 1948, however, the version published was normally drafted by the Economic Section. Advice to the Chancellor on his budget was offered by a Budget Committee in the Treasury of which the Director of the Economic Section was a member; and it was his advice that normally shaped the budget judgement i.e. the judgement as to the amount of purchasing power that the government should seek to withdraw or release in the budget in order to preserve a steady pressure of demand. In general, however, the variations that were made in either direction were never more after 1947 than about £150 million when the national income was near £10,000 million.

The budget itself moved from heavy deficit at the end of the war to a substantial surplus in 1948–50 with a negative borrowing requirement. As personal savings had fallen virtually to zero in those years the contribution of the government was an indispensable element in sustaining domestic investment without running into external deficit and borrowing abroad. With rearmament the government again became a borrower, partly to finance investment in the nationalised industries, and it remained a borrower for nearly two decades until the budgets of Roy Jenkins as Chancellor of the Exchequer in 1968–9. On the other hand, personal saving began to recover after 1948 and the ratio of savings to personal income after tax rose fairly steadily over the next three decades.

Monetary policy played a subordinate part. Dalton sought to bring down interest rates, beginning with a cut to 1 per cent in the rate on Treasury bills in November 1945 and aiming to reduce the long-term rate to 2.5 per cent. He succeeded in driving the price of Consols up to £99 in October 1946 largely by getting official holders to move into longer-dated securities. The public then became net sellers of gilt-edged, this produced an expansion in the money supply and the City took fright. The bond market weakened in successive crises in 1947 and by the spring of 1948 gilt-edged had fallen in eighteen months by 25 per cent. Cripps as Chancellor of the Exchequer contented himself with using surplus funds to redeem short-term debt and for two years from 1948 to 1950, until the onset of rearmament, was able to stop the growth in the money supply. With Bank Rate fixed at 2 per cent monetary policy remained passive and had little

Table 2.1. *UK economic indicators, 1938–52*

	GDP (1948 = 100)	Manufacturing production (1948 = 100)	Unemployment (000s)	(%)	Consumer prices (% increase)	Current balance of payments (£m)
1938	89·3	82·8	1,414	—	1·5	
1945	100·6	—	(130)	—	2·9	
1946	99·7	86·7	(400)	(1·8)	3·1	−230
1947	97·2	91·7	(300)	(1·4)	7·1	−381
1948	100·0	100·0	(300)	(1·4)	6·2	26
1949	103·1	106·4	283	1·3	2·3	−1
1950	106·5	113·5	298	1·4	2·6	307
1951	110·3	118·1	207	1·0	9·4	−369
1952	110·2	114·2	336	1·6	6·1	163

Sources: Col. 1: Feinstein (1972: Table 5). 1938 GDP at 1948 factor cost; 1945–8 GDP at 1938 factor cost; 1949–52 GDP at 1958 factor cost.
Col. 2: London and Cambridge Economic Service *Key Statistics*. Re-based from 1958 to 1948.
Col. 3: wholly unemployed in UK in June of each year as given in Department of Employment and Productivity (1971: Tables 162 and 165). Percentages include 'temporarily stopped'. Figure for 1938 is for insured persons unemployed.
Col. 4: Feinstein (1972: Table 61).
Col. 5: *Economic Trends Annual Supplement* 1990.

independent influence on economic activity until the change of government in October 1951 (Dow 1964; Howson 1991).

Production between 1945 and 1952 was not constrained by demand; indeed in 1947 it could be said to have suffered from excess demand. Cuts in the investment programme in the autumn resulted in work proceeding more rapidly and facilitated a volume of investment greater than the original total. What did limit production was the shortage of materials and labour and the bottlenecks in capacity. These were particularly acute in 1946–7 but eased in 1948–51 when labour productivity improved by about 3 per cent annually. By 1951 manufacturing production was some 36 per cent above the level in 1946, unemployment was down to 1.0 per cent and consumer prices had risen by over 30 per cent (Table 2.1).

Nationalisation

Although full employment took priority over other aims, the Labour government attached special importance to the nationalisation of the country's basic industries. Starting in 1946 with the Bank of England, which was already a semi-public body, they took into public ownership the coal, gas and electricity industries and most of the transport and communications sector: rail and canal transport, long-distance road haulage, civil aviation and telecommunications. What caused more controversy than any of these was the decision to nationalise the steel industry – the only manufacturing industry included. The decision was taken in the middle of the convertibility crisis in 1947 at a time when the Labour government most needed the united support of the country. It was not until February 1951 that the necessary legislation was completed.

The nationalisation measures added nearly 2.5 million workers to the public sector and brought within it a much higher proportion of the investment programme, all the industries concerned being highly capital-intensive. How the industries were to be run remained obscure. They were instructed to cover their costs, taking one year with another; but on what principles they should fix prices or undertake investment, and what their relations should be with Ministers, was left open for debate (Chester 1975 and ch. 6 below).

The welfare state

The public sector was further extended by a comprehensive scheme for improving the social services proposed by Sir William Beveridge in his wartime report on *Social Insurance and Allied Services*. This aimed at a rationalisation of the various social services which had developed before the war, linking them together in a national system of benefits covering sickness, unemployment, retirement, maternity, death and other contingencies. The cost of these benefits was to be met from national insurance contributions which would also meet a small part of the cost of the National Health Service, the remainder falling on the tax payer. The coalition government in the war had accepted the National Health Service in principle and had passed the 1944 Education Act which laid the basis for modern secondary education. But the creation of the Health Service and the raising of the school-leaving age to fifteen were both the work of the Labour government.

These various developments – in the social services, health and education – have been dubbed the welfare state (ch. 10 below). The creation of the welfare state has been attacked as a frittering away, on the 'New Jerusalem' of the Beveridge Plan, of resources needed for the reconstruction of British industry (Barnett 1986). This seems doubly mistaken. There was not much that the British government could do to reconstruct British industry, especially when the urgent need was to eliminate the dollar deficit. As for the additional expenditure on the social services, this was not the main burden on the Exchequer after the war. Never less than £750 million a year was spent annually on defence after 1945 (and over £1,400 million in 1952–3). The food subsidies reached nearly £500 million in 1949 and cost more than any of the social services. Total expenditure on the social services, including education, health, housing, pensions and unemployment benefit, had risen to about £1,500 million by 1950 compared with a pre-war total of about £1,000 million in terms of post-war prices. Much of the £1,500 million, however, did not fall on the tax payer but on the (contributory) National Insurance Fund which, in the early 1950s, was running an annual *surplus* of nearly £600 million.

It is true, however, that the rising cost of the National Health Service created some alarm in the Treasury in the later years of the Labour government. First Cripps and then Gaitskell proposed the introduction of health charges. The proposal was successfully resisted by the Minister of Health, Aneurin Bevan, who had been the architect of the National Health Service and was determined that it should remain free. It was when Gaitskell proposed to introduce a charge on false teeth and spectacles to raise £13 million in his 1951 budget that Bevan resigned, although he made more play in his letter of resignation with his opposition to the increase in the rearmament programme. He was joined by Harold Wilson and John Freeman and these resignations, together with the death of Ernest Bevin and the loss of Stafford Cripps, contributed to the downfall of the Labour government six months later.

Domestic economic policy, 1951–64

After the exchange crisis in the spring of 1952, the 1950s proved to be much less eventful than the years immediately after the war. Difficulties with the balance of payments continued, particularly in 1955, but were never as severe as they had been earlier. The more awkward difficulty was the failure to add to the reserves, which fell in four of the six years between 1951 and 1956 and were at about the same level at the end of 1959 as they had been at the end of 1946; they were already then thought to be inadequate.

The growing concern of the decade was not so much the balance of payments or the reserves as inflation; these concerns came to a head in 1957 when the Chancellor, Thorneycroft, brought about the first 'stop' for purely domestic reasons. There was also, towards the end of the decade, a growing awareness that continental countries were enjoying greater economic success than the United Kingdom. People began to look to the government to take measures to ensure steadier and faster growth, in place of what was derided as 'stop–go', and pointed to the example of French indicative planning as a model for Britain to imitate. First the Conservative government in the early 1960s and then in 1964 the newly elected Labour government embraced the idea of national economic planning as a means to faster growth.

The Conservatives in 1951 had held very different ideas. The similarity of outlook with their predecessors in office, expressed in the term 'Butskellism', did have some substance. They retained a belief in economic management and in the need to maintain a high level of employment, continued many of the controls that were still in use, and refrained from attacking the welfare state and undoing Labour's nationalisation measures (steel and road haulage excepted). But there were some major differences of emphasis. They reacted in 1951 against anything savouring of planning and sought to eliminate economic forecasts from government publications. They took a very different view of monetary policy, reviving the use of Bank Rate after Gaitskell had repeatedly refused to raise it above 2 per cent, and accepted the advice of the Bank of England much more readily than had the Labour government. They were also drawn to the idea of market freedom and, when they took office, talked of 'freeing the pound' (letting it float) and making it convertible within a short time. Once controls were removed they were unwilling to revive them: hire purchase restrictions were the unique exception. Long before they left office, virtually all wartime controls except exchange control had been removed.

Their thirteen years in power began with a crisis in 1951–2 and ended with a crisis in 1964. In their first twelve months industrial production fell in the earliest post-war recession, the textile industries being particularly hard hit. By the last quarter of 1952, however, production was beginning to recover. It expanded steadily over the next two years in spite of fears that a recession in America at the end of 1953 would spread to Europe. These fears coincided with doubts in 1953 that anything would take the place of housing and defence in both absorbing the slack accumulated in 1951–2 and putting renewed pressure on the economy, investment in housing having risen by over 50 per cent between 1951 and 1953 (Cairncross and Watts 1989: 262–3).

Such fears proved to be groundless. Consumption was rising strongly and manufacturing investment, which had increased by about one third since 1948 but had shown little sign of expanding further, was just about to experience a boom and to grow by over 50 per cent in the next four years. So far from slackening after 1953, the pressure on the economy grew in each successive year; unemployment by the autumn of 1955 had fallen below 200,000, to the lowest level reached in post-war years.

The events of 1953–5 demonstrated how imperfect was the under-standing of demand management among officials and how limited was the commitment to it of Ministers. The Inland Revenue, for example, were expecting a deficit in the 1954–5 budget of £53 million and in the 1955–6 budget of perhaps £300 million, basing themselves on a gloomy but out-of-date national income forecast that predicted a sharp fall in activity (associated with an American depression) and hence also a fall in tax revenue. The predicted deficits alarmed the Budget Committee which was at first inclined to press, not for lower taxes as employment considerations would have suggested, but for higher ones in order to restore budget balance. It ended by recommending a standstill budget and Butler, the Chancellor of the Exchequer, insisted on showing a small surplus of £10 million in his budget estimate. At the end of the financial year the surplus turned out to be £433 million (Roberthall, 1991: 8; Cairncross and Watts 1989: 263).

This was by no means the only occasion on which Ministers showed distrust of orthodox demand management. In 1955, with a general election lying ahead, the Chancellor decided to 'give away' half of what was now expected to be a substantial budget surplus. In this he was backed by the Budget Committee of officials who recommended a reduction in the income tax by 6d (2.5p) in spite of the mounting pressure on the economy and the weak state of the balance of payments. The Committee did, however, suggest 'a further tightening of credit policy' and in the budget speech the Chancellor (R. A. Butler) indicated his reliance on 'the resources of a flexible monetary policy' (a phrase thought up by his economic adviser, Sir Robert Hall). The combination of tax reductions in order to strengthen incentives with a tighter monetary policy is one that has been favoured by Conservatives on more recent occasions and with equal lack of success.

The boom continued unchecked into the summer and before the end of July the Treasury concluded that an autumn budget was likely to be necessary. The need for such a budget became increasingly urgent in the summer months and Butler even urged (without success) the recall of Parliament. At the end of October, he introduced his last budget, raising purchase and profits taxes and cutting building programmes.

In the meantime there had been a growing conflict between the Bank of England and the Treasury (Cairncross and Watts 1989: 222). The Treasury was concerned at the continuing rise in bank advances while the Governor of the Bank was equally concerned at the absence of cuts in government expenditure. The clearing banks were busy selling investments to obtain finance for the increase in their advances and the Bank seemed to assume that so long as it held down the money supply it had done all that was required. Nearly half the increase in advances was to the nationalised industries which could not sell their bonds as they had planned because of the depression in the stock market (which in turn reflected the rise in Bank

Rate and the sales of bank investments, as well as strikes and other factors). The banks had no wish to deprive the private sector of credit when the public sector was borrowing more, even if the borrowing was for officially approved programmes. With the agreement of the Governor and to the fury of the Treasury they told the Gas and Electricity Boards to keep within their overdraft limits (Cairncross 1987: 15).

For the first time ever, Treasury and clearing bank representatives met at the Bank of England and the banks agreed to restrict credit, even to the point of causing bankruptcies, if they could point to an official statement by the Chancellor (Roberthall 1991: 43). By the end of July the Chancellor had received agreement to his request for 'a positive and significant reduction' in bank advances. But although the banks kept their promise and bank advances fell heavily, there was little easing in the pressure on resources. The rise in output slowed down in 1956 but the labour market did not ease much until the second half of the year. Even in 1957 unemployment was at no time as high as it had been in 1953.

In January 1956, with Macmillan at the Exchequer, further efforts were made to check the strong inflationary pressure. Cuts were made in public investment, defence spending and the civil service and hire purchase restrictions were introduced. Macmillan was also successful, as Butler had not been, in securing agreement to the reduction in stages of the subsidies on bread and milk. As pressure eased there was an increasing acceptance that there must be no return to the overload on the economy of the previous two years. The Treasury also began to urge a target for the balance of payments of a surplus of £350 million, assuming, rather too readily, that this could be converted into an equivalent increase in the reserves, when its achievement might instead require increased lending or foreign investment.

In the autumn came the Suez crisis, a bombshell to the civil service, which had no inkling of what was planned, and a threat to the balance of payments. The crisis passed, however, without much effect on the economy. What it did affect was opinion in Whitehall and the City. The abandonment of a military operation half-way through, largely under pressure from the United States, was a revelation of the weakness and vulnerability of the economy. The Governor of the Bank (Cobbold), who was in the habit of demanding cuts in public expenditure at intervals, called for 'dramatic, far-reaching and convincing measures' by which he meant a large budget surplus with no increase in taxation. Macmillan, now Prime Minister, and Thorneycroft, the new Chancellor, held similar views. Both Macmillan and Cobbold wanted to balance the budget and to wipe out the government's borrowing requirement. There were also anxieties over balance of payments prospects and the rise in prices although the balance of payments was in substantial surplus and the rise in prices had slowed down. The government was also under attack for what were regarded as inflationary wage settlements and was accused by the press of having 'given up the fight against inflation'. Inflationary expectations exprcsscd themselves in a depressed market for gilt-edged securities, a build-up in bank liquidity and an outflow of capital through the gaps in exchange control in Kuwait and Hong Kong.

It was against this background that Thorneycroft took deflationary action in September 1957. He had prevailed on the Prime Minister to issue a directive to Ministers in August limiting current civil expenditure in 1958–9 to the level in 1957–8. He had also warned his colleagues not to add to public investment programmes pending an autumn review. Advised by Lionel Robbins, the Chancellor then prepared a statement, released on 19 September, blaming inflation on the money supply and announcing a standstill for the next two years on government expenditure, current and capital. He had received Cabinet approval for a 5 per cent cut in bank advances which, however, the banks refused to make and which the Bank of England refused to enforce by the issue of a directive. The Chancellor then found himself without power under the 1946 Bank of England Act either to oblige the Bank to issue a directive or to dismiss the Governor as he proposed (Roberthall 1991: 127). His statement on 19 September was coupled with an increase in Bank Rate to 7 per cent after further disagreement between the Bank and the Treasury over the size of the increase. This provision was added at a late stage as a result of currency speculation in advance of the IMF meeting in September and was not part of the deflationary package (Holmans MS).

The September measures represented the first attempt by a post-war Chancellor to give priority over full employment to the fight against inflation. Whether the Cabinet fully shared the Chancellor's ideas must be very doubtful (Dow 1964: 102). Thorneycroft and Macmillan wanted to put an end to wage pressure on the price level by allowing unemployment to rise to 2–3 per cent. They talked in terms of controlling the money supply but in fact what Thorneycroft wanted to limit was money GDP through ceilings on expenditure, i.e. through demand management, though for a novel purpose.

In January 1958, when the limits were not accepted to the letter by Cabinet, Thorneycroft resigned along with two of his Junior Ministers, Nigel Birch and Enoch Powell. The Estimates for 1958–9 had risen by £175 million above the Estimates for 1957–8 and the most Cabinet was prepared to accept was a reduction in the gap to about £50 million. Economic activity, however, was already beginning to slacken after over two years of governmental restraint and unemployment had begun to increase. As it continued to rise in 1958, but before it had reached even 2 per cent, the Cabinet took fright. No action was taken in the 1958 budget while major wage claims were still under negotiation; but Bank Rate was brought down to 4 per cent in five stages from March to November and from June onwards a number of reflationary measures were introduced, notably a relaxation of hire purchase restrictions in September.

At the end of 1958 the Chancellor (Amory) thought that 'enough had been done for the time being' by way of stimulus, and indeed unemployment was already near its peak of 500,000 (seasonally adjusted). Nonetheless the budget in April 1959 was highly expansionary, with tax concessions of £360 million, plus a release of £70 million in post-war credits and additions to public expenditure. A violent upswing followed, with output growing in 1959 by more than 6 per cent and unemployment falling over the next two years to 320,000 or 1.3 per cent, the level from which it started in September 1957. This seemed to bring the economy to the limits of its potential since output in 1960 virtually ceased to expand and the balance of payments which had been in record surplus in 1958 moved into increasing deficit in 1960.

Meanwhile there had been much debate over how the economic system really worked. It had seemed to many in 1952 that monetary policy in the form of higher interest rates was successful in slowing down production and prices. By 1955 that judgement was questioned and reliance was placed instead on a credit squeeze. When that, too, seemed slow to take effect, a Bank/Treasury committee of officials prepared a joint report on monetary control. This considered, and rejected, the use of a prescribed liquidity ratio or alternatively an advances ratio (Cairncross and Watts 1989: 224–5). A second report on credit control was prepared after the September 1957 measures by a joint working party to which the distinguished economist Lionel Robbins was added. Against strong opposition from the Bank, this favoured a prescribed liquidity ratio and a scheme which later took shape as one for special deposits, that is the deposit by the clearing banks with the Bank of England of a proportion of their deposits without payment of interest (Roberthall 1991: 250).

By this time the Bank of England had proposed, early in 1957, an enquiry into the working of the monetary system and in April the Chancellor announced the appointment of a committee under Lord Radcliffe. The Radcliffe Committee Report, when it appeared in the summer of 1959, aroused considerable controversy. It was attacked for belittling the importance of monetary policy and for laying emphasis on liquidity when there was no way of measuring this, rather than on the stock of money which could be measured without difficulty. The Report attributed a limited role in the finance of economic activity to bank credit and regarded money as no more than the most important of a wide range of liquid assets. What chiefly upset the critics, however, was the Report's insistence on the variability of the velocity of circulation which the monetarists of later years treated as stable and its warning not to expect too much from the control of money. The main consequences of the Report lay less in the adoption of specific recommendations for policy than in a major improvement in financial statistics and information, closer working relations between the Bank and the Treasury, and a continuing debate over the role of monetary policy in which ideas very different from those of the Radcliffe Report received increasing attention.

The early 1960s

The last five years of Conservative government, before Labour took over in 1964, saw two more 'stops', both associated with balance of payments difficulties. World trade in 1960 grew more slowly and the British share of it continued to fall, as it had done throughout the previous decade. There was no increase in British exports and output for the domestic market was also little changed. Demand grew instead for imported goods, manufactured imports rising by a third in one year, possibly because, with convertibility after 1958, restrictions surviving from earlier years were at last removed. The resulting deficit in the balance of payments was offset in 1960 by an inflow of short-term funds in response to attractive rates of interest. Then in the first half of 1961 exports improved while imports fell slightly so that the current account deficit virtually ceased. On the other hand, currency speculation was stimulated by a revaluation of the deutschmark and the Dutch guilder and funds began to flow out again, drawing nearly £500 million from the reserves in the first six months. Fears of a continuing outflow and forecasts of increasing pressure in 1962 caused the government to take deflationary measures in July 1961.

The measures taken included several novel elements. One was the first use of the tax regulator introduced in the April budget. This allowed the Chancellor to raise or lower indirect taxation across the board by up to 10 per cent between budgets and so to collect or release about £200 million in revenue. There had been a second regulator empowering the Chancellor to impose a pay-roll tax of up to 4s (20p) a week on all employees through national insurance contributions but this was soon abandoned. A second novelty was a call for a 'pause' in wage increases in the private sector and its imposition for the next six months in the public sector. Finally, the Chancellor proposed joint planning arrangements with representatives of employers and workers in the interests of faster economic growth. It was proposed to set up a National Economic Development Council (NEDC), served by a staff of officials independent of government and constituting the National Economic Development Office (NEDO).

Of these three measures, the first continued in use long after 1961 and proved a useful additional instrument of demand management. The second had a limited life but was a first step towards a more considered incomes policy. The third reflected increased pressure to embark on national economic planning on the French model. Although indicative planning ceased when the National Plan was dropped in 1966, the NEDC and NEDO continued in operation until 1992 and provided an opportunity for a regular exchange of views between the government and both sides of industry.

The course of the 1961–4 cycle was not unlike that of 1957–61. The measures of July 1961 were followed by a depression that caused a good deal of alarm but proved to be comparatively mild. It had been expected that production would recover in 1962 with a rapid expansion in exports but in fact exports fell in the later part of the year and the check to manufacturing activity was intensified early in 1963 by very severe weather. In February 1963, at the height of the freezing weather, unemployment reached just under 4.5 per cent, the highest level since the war.

Reflation was again belated and overdone. A new Chancellor (Maudling) had been appointed in July 1962 and was reluctant to make changes in policy too soon. Bank Rate, however, had been lowered to 4 per cent by April 1962 and special deposits were reduced in stages beginning in June. So also were hire purchase deposits on all goods except cars. A second round was postponed until October and November when post-war credits (a remnant of government borrowing during the war) were released, public investment expanded and a large cut was made in the purchase tax on cars. By far the most powerful stimulus, however, was made in the 1963 budget, partly under the influence of the peak in unemployment in February. Tax concessions amounting to £460 million in a full year were made, including the abolition of Schedule A taxation on housing and the introduction of 'free' (at whatever rate businesses chose) depreciation in the development areas.

It is likely that the underlying trend in activity was already beginning to rise. The effect of the tax concessions was to produce a fresh spurt in output, with an 11 per cent increase in industrial production in fifteen months from the last quarter of 1962 to the first quarter of 1964. But at that point the needle seemed to stick. Although later figures tell a rather different story, the published index of industrial production showed no change for the first nine months of 1964, until the general election in October. The balance of payments, on the other hand, which had been expected to move from surplus in 1962 and 1963 into a small deficit in 1964 sank quarter by quarter until by October the deficit on current and long-term capital account was expected to reach £800 million. In terms of its call on the reserves, which were not much over £2,000 million, this was a horrendous total. It could be argued, however, that half the total was on capital account so that at least other assets were acquired in compensation for the reserves surrendered. Even so, the thirteen years of Conservative government ended on a note of uncertainty as to the competitive position of British industry at the current rate of exchange.

The early days of incomes policy

From the White Paper on *Employment Policy* of 1944 onwards it was recognised that the size of wage settlements exercised an independent influence on inflation which might be susceptible to persuasion and the pressure of public opinion. In the early post-war years Labour Ministers were particularly concerned over the need to limit the pace at which money wages increased (Figure 2.3). In 1948 they induced the Trades Union Congress (TUC) to agree to a standstill in wages and to prolong it after the devaluation of 1949, provided prices did not rise by more than 5 per cent. In this they could claim considerable success, since in spite of the intense pressure on resources weekly wage rates rose by no more than 2 per cent in the year to October 1949 and by less than 1 per cent in the year following.

The Conservative government had even greater cause to be concerned about inflation after a 9.4 per cent rise in consumer prices during 1951 (Table 2.2) but it showed no sympathy at first with the idea of incomes policy and made little effort until well into the 1950s to bring home to the public the danger of wage inflation. It was not until 1956 that they issued *The Economic Implications of Full Employment*, a pamphlet that had been in preparation for years, arguing the need for stability in wages and prices as a prerequisite of full employment. In the same year Macmillan entered into talks with employers and employed, hoping to persuade them to hold prices and wages steady. But there was no clear statement of policy backed by a sustained political campaign; there was bickering between employers in the private and public sectors; and the unions withheld support. In 1957 the government fell back on deflation as the one sure remedy after some short-term success in getting employers to hold to a 'price plateau'. By this time wage earners in each industry felt entitled to an annual increase in wages in what became known as the wage-round; wage-push was recognised as a long-term problem in its own right that might or might not interact with excess demand (Dow 1964: 99, 402 n. 3).

The next attempt to influence wage settlements was the appointment in July 1957 of a Council for Prices, Productivity and Incomes (COPPI). This

Table 2.2. *UK economic indicators, 1951–64*

	GDP (1955 = 100)	Manufacturing production (1955 = 100)	Unemployment (%)	Consumer prices (% increase)	Current balance of payments (£m)
1951	88·4	85·8	1·3	9·4	−369
1952	89·2	83·0	2·2	6·1	163
1953	92·6	88·1	1·8	2·0	145
1954	96·6	94·1	1·5	1·9	117
1955	100·0	100·0	1·2	3·5	−155
1956	101·4	99·6	1·3	4·6	208
1957	103·2	101·8	1·6	3·4	233
1958	103·0	100·5	2·2	2·7	350
1959	107·2	106·5	2·3	0·6	164
1960	113·1	115·2	1·7	0·9	−237
1961	116·1	115·4	1·6	3·0	35
1962	117·7	115·9	2·1	3·8	143
1963	122·5	120·6	2·6	1·3	114
1964	129·3	130·1	1·7	2·9	−372

Sources: Col. 1: *Economic Trends Annual Supplement* 1990: Table 1. GDP at 1985 factor cost, average estimate re-based to 1955.
Col. 2: London and Cambridge Economic Service *Key Statistics*. Re-based from 1958 to 1955.
Col. 3: London and Cambridge Economic Service *Key Statistics*. Registered unemployed in UK. Monthly average as given in Department of Employment and Productivity (1971: Table 165).
Col. 4: Feinstein (1972: Table 61).
Col. 5: *Economic Trends Annual Supplement* 1990.

was originally intended to include representatives of employers and employed but the unions refused to cooperate and it ended up with three independent members including one economist, at first Sir Dennis Robertson. The first report of the Council, which spoke of Thorneycroft's 1957 measures as 'justified and long overdue', and advocated falling, not rising, prices, antagonised the unions and although three further reports were issued, the unions withheld support and the Council was finally wound up in July 1961. As a means of rallying opinion behind anti-inflationary measures, it had had little success.

This was less true of Selwyn Lloyd's 'pay pause' in the middle of 1961. From then on, incomes policy in one form or another was very much in the public eye and a long succession of measures tried to give effect to the idea of voluntary agreement to a slowdown. These measures had only begun

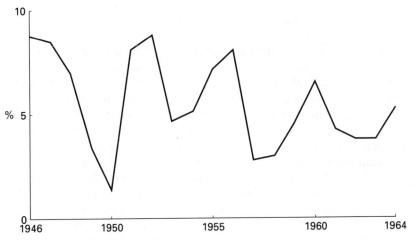

Figure 2.3 The annual increase in hourly wage rates, 1946–64

when the Conservatives lost office. But they had run through several experiments in their last three years: a pay pause, broken by a settlement in December on wages in electricity generation; a National Incomes Commission, boycotted by the trade unions, that lasted only two years and heard only four cases; and an unsuccessful effort by Maudling to reach agreement on a target for wage increases in parallel with the 4 per cent target for economic growth already set by Selwyn Lloyd. While none of these came to anything they brought incomes policy to the centre of the political stage where it remained throughout the next six years of Labour rule.

External economic policy after 1952

British trade in the 1950s had to face increasing competition from other countries as their economies emerged from post-war reconstruction. In 1948 British exports of manufactures had formed 29 per cent of a rapidly expanding volume of world trade; by 1960 the proportion had fallen to a little over 16 per cent and was still declining. The growth in exports had slowed down to an average of under 2 per cent a year and British industry was losing competitive advantage as export prices outdistanced those of other countries. A change had also begun in the relative importance of different export markets, with the proportion of British exports sold in the rapidly expanding markets of western Europe rising from 26 to 29 per cent of the total while the proportion sold in sterling area countries declined over the decade from 47 to 39 per cent. The current account showed on the average a small surplus, barely enough, thanks to a return of the terms of trade to a more normal level, to balance net exports of capital without adding to reserves.

Apart from the dwindling competitiveness of British exports, the main concerns of external economic policy were to re-establish convertibility and to find some alternative to joining the European Economic Community. After the abandonment of the Robot plan, modified proposals were put forward for a 'collective approach' to convertibility in conjunction with the main European countries. The proposals were still for a floating pound and for non-resident convertibility only but, instead of blocking sterling balances, the plan envisaged negotiations with the United States for a substantial supplementation of the reserves. It was decided to tackle the United States before going to the Europeans, who were kept in the dark until after a visit to the United States in the spring of 1953 by Eden and Butler. The United States, however, thought the plan 'premature' and could offer no support while the Europeans, when at last consulted, wanted neither floating nor convertibility, preferring to stick to the EPU and to continue the discrimination against non-European countries that it permitted.

In March 1954 the Bank of England arranged to unify all non-dollar transactions in sterling by non-residents within a single transferable account area, with a regular market in transferable sterling at a fluctuating rate, a little below the official rate. In January 1955 it sought approval from the government for official intervention in the market to bring the two rates together and let them fluctuate within a wider spread between $2.70 and $2.90. This was tantamount to *de facto* convertibility by another route, although this was disputed by the Governor since it involved no legal obligation to merge the two rates. In spite of opposition from the Treasury, the Cabinet gave its agreement on 24 February 1955 to market intervention but not to a wider spread in the official rate. Sterling was henceforth convertible at a small discount.

The Bank continued to press for a widening of the spread but the Chancellor decided that such an arrangement was unlikely to be given international acceptance. When the impression gained ground in banking circles that the Bank had had its way and secured agreement to convertibility at a floating rate, the Chancellor was obliged to deny in July 1955 any intention of floating or widening the spread and to repeat the denial more emphatically at the IMF meeting in Istanbul in September. Thus an important element of the 'collective approach' disappeared; and when convertibility finally came in December 1958 it was at a fixed rate and with an unchanged spread (Cairncross and Watts 1989: ch. 18).

Relations with Europe

As the Marshall Plan drew to an end, the idea of closer European integration continued to attract support. After the Schumann Plan and the formation of the European Coal and Steel Community (ECSC), negotiations continued, first for a European Defence Community until the plan collapsed in 1953, and then for a common market.

No British Minister attended the preliminary discussions at Messina in 1955 or the later negotiations in Brussels when agreement was reached on a customs union. Once it became clear that the negotiations would succeed, Britain put forward a plan for a free trade area which would include the six members of the ECSC as a single unit and the other members of OEEC as individual countries. The plan was confined to manufactures, leaving arrangements to cover agriculture to be made separately; each country would be free to maintain its own tariffs. The reason for these provisions lay in Britain's desire to continue freedom of entry for Commonwealth food-stuffs and to avoid having to surmount tariffs on its exports of manufactures. The plan was primarily intended to prevent a strict division of Europe between the members and non-members of what became the European Economic Community (EEC).

The plan was advanced shortly before the signature in February 1957 of the Treaty of Rome establishing the EEC. A committee of OEEC Ministers under Reginald Maudling engaged in negotiations on the plan throughout 1957 and 1958 and received support for it from the Council of OEEC in October 1957. In November 1958, however, the French announced their rejection of the plan. There was a feeling that Britain was asking for the best of both worlds in retaining the Commonwealth preferential system while seeking the benefits of the European preferential system; and the French hesitated to expose their economic system to competition simultaneously from Germany and the United Kingdom. The retention of low tariffs on raw materials by some countries in competition with other countries with higher tariffs raised further problems.

At bottom there was a fundamental difference of approach. The aims of British policy were primarily economic, not political. Britain sought an economic association for its own sake, rather than as a step towards ultimate political union. During and after the war it had sought to found international rather than European institutions and it hesitated to join a community from which the United States and the Commonwealth were excluded. The OEEC, later the OECD, was more in keeping with its vision of European cooperation than the more far-reaching obligations of the EEC. Even in 1960, a year before the first British bid to join the Community, there was no indication of British willingness to abandon

Commonwealth free entry, or tariff autonomy, or its own system of agricultural protection, as membership was almost certain to require.

The first reaction to the breakdown of free trade area negotiations was the signature of a convention in Stockholm in November 1959 with six other non-Community members for the establishment of a European Free Trade Area (EFTA) along the lines of the original British proposal. All tariffs on manufactured goods were to be removed over the next ten years in step with the removal of tariffs on trade within the EEC. In this way, and with reciprocal action by the Six, an effort was made so to arrange tariff reductions by the two groups that discrimination in trade between them was kept to a minimum.

Within a few months of signing the EFTA Convention the Prime Minister (Harold Macmillan) decided that Britain ought to apply for membership of the EEC and in the course of 1960 an official committee, dominated by the Foreign Office and the Treasury rather than by the Board of Trade, endorsed this conclusion. After taking soundings in the Commonwealth, EFTA and the United States, Macmillan felt sufficient confidence to make an application and negotiations under Edward Heath began in the autumn of 1961. The negotiations made slow progress on the major problems of agriculture and trade with the Commonwealth and little agreement had been reached when General de Gaulle issued a veto in January 1963.

3   Economic policy and performance, 1964–1990

Sir Alexander Cairncross

Introduction

The twenty-six years between 1964 and 1990 fall into three contrasting periods: a period of comparatively rapid growth up to 1973; a period of low growth from then until 1982, terminating in an actual fall in output in the last three years of the period; and a period of gradual recovery from 1982 onwards, developing in 1987–8 into an unmistakable boom.

The first period, 1964–73

The first nine years are now looked back to as the concluding phase of the so-called golden age, in which there was never any serious and continuing departure from full employment (Blackaby 1978; Cairncross and Cairncross 1992). The period began and ended with a year of crisis in which the pressure of demand was intense, unemployment abnormally low and the balance of payments in heavy deficit. Elements of crisis persisted almost throughout. This did not, however, prevent growing prosperity and an expansion in output (and consequently in income) per worker faster than in any post-war period of equal length.

The increase in output in those nine years (as measured by GDP at constant prices) amounted to 31 per cent. This compared with 29 per cent over the previous nine years from 1955 to 1964 and 7 per cent over the following nine years from 1973 to 1982. Employment from 1964 to 1973 changed very little in total so that output per worker rose to much the same extent as output, the rate of increase averaging 3 per cent per annum. Weekly earnings in real terms at the end of the nine years were not far short of one third higher than at the beginning. The rise in nominal earnings was very much larger, for they more than doubled, but the increase in money wages inevitably pushed up prices and brought the rise in real earnings into close accord with the movement in output per worker.

The rise in prices marked the onset of the acceleration in inflation that was to plague the second period. Retail prices rose at an average of 5.7 per cent per annum but between the first six years and the last three the rate of increase nearly doubled. It was not until the very end of the period that the fastest increase was recorded. By that time the prices of primary commodities were rising fast all over the world, the increase in dollar terms reaching 60 per cent between the beginning and end of 1973. It was at that point, too, that the first oil shock took place and oil prices were raised fourfold. The legacy of the first period thus included an awkward dose of accelerating inflation.

In the labour market there was initially an intense shortage of labour which became, if anything, more intense until the first half of 1966 when unemployment was down to 300,000. At that point deflationary measures pushed the total up to 500,000 and for the next four years it fluctuated between 500,000 and 600,000. In 1971 the total rose sharply towards 900,000 but the rise was checked and reversed early in 1972 and at the end of 1973 unemployment was again at about 500,000, a level never since regained. Employment followed a similar course, rising at first to a peak in the first half of 1966, falling fairly steeply over the next year and then more gradually until, as with unemployment, there was a sharper check in 1971. By the end of 1971 employment had fallen in six years by 1.0 million from the peak of 25.4 million in 1965; but two years later it had made up 800,000 of the drop and was at a level not exceeded (except briefly in 1974) until the end of 1978.

The fluctuations in employment fell almost exclusively on manufacturing (Figure 3.1). The post-war peak in manufacturing employment was reached in the first half of 1966 when a fall began that has continued more or less ever since. By the middle of 1972 the reduction from the peak had reached 800,000 and accounted for virtually the whole of the drop in employment over the previous six years. Employment in other occupations, accounting for about two-thirds of the workforce, fell off remarkably little. The contrast, moreover, between the two groups of occupations was not confined to the first period but held good in the later periods as well.

During much of the period after 1964 policy was dominated by the state of the balance of payments. The deficit on current account in 1964, now estimated at £372 million, was the highest since the immediate post-war period. Because of capital movements, the deficit requiring official finance from the reserves and borrowing from other monetary authorities was much larger, totalling £695 million (Figure 3.2). A large drain from the reserves continued for four more years, not just until devaluation in 1967 but on an even greater scale in the year following devaluation when £1,410 million had to be found to cover official settlements.

From 1969 to 1971 the pressure eased. The debts incurred earlier to the IMF and other monetary authorities were greatly reduced and large

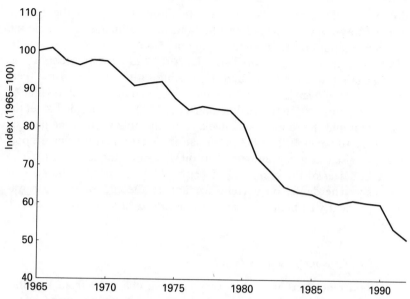

Figure 3.1 Employment in manufacturing, 1965–90 (mid-year) (employment in June 1965 8·9 million)

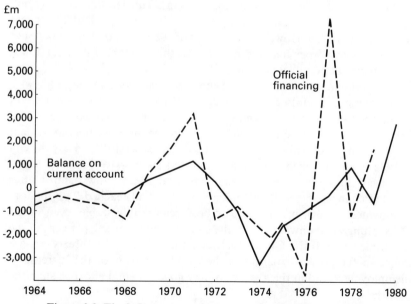

Figure 3.2 The balance on current account and official finance provided, 1964–80

additions were made to the reserves. In those three years the current account moved into growing surplus and as confidence in the pound recovered capital flowed in on an expanding scale.

But the recovery was short-lived. By 1972 the current account was moving again towards deficit, funds were being withdrawn again and there was a balance of over £1 billion to be met from reserves and borrowing. As the pressure mounted in the second quarter of 1972 it was decided to let the pound float and the rate of exchange against the dollar fell in the next six months by 10 per cent. In 1973 the situation deteriorated further. Import prices had risen steeply even before the oil shock and the terms of trade in the final quarter of the year were 15 per cent less favourable than a year previously. The deficit on current account by the end of the year was running at nearly £2 billion a year, with the effects of higher oil prices still to register.

The second period, 1973–82

The second nine years were of a very different character from the first. Inflation became the principal source of anxiety, reaching a record rate in the mid-1970s and rising alarmingly again at the end of the decade. At the highest point in the summer of 1975, retail prices were rising at 27 per cent per annum (using a year-on-year comparison). This fell to between 7 and 8 per cent in 1978 but accelerated again in 1979–80 to a peak of 22 per cent in the spring of 1980. However, by the end of 1982 inflation had sunk to not much more than 5 per cent and it looked at that point as if it might at last be coming under control (Figure 3.3).

The employment record of those nine years was an unhappy one, with unemployment mounting steadily up to 1977. There was then a slight respite for two years to the end of 1979 when unemployment stood at a little over 1 million. But in the next eighteen months unemployment doubled and continued to rise for another five years until 1986. By the end of 1982 it had reached 2.7 million and had risen sixfold in nine years. Indeed as the figures stood at the time, and not as now defined after repeated changes in the 1980s, unemployment had reached 2.95 million. Employment, which had previously been remarkably stable, even in the 1970s, plunged downwards from the end of 1979 by over 7 per cent in the next three years to the lowest level since the 1950s. Those three years are unique in the post-war period in the speed and scale of the increase in unemployment and in the absence of any governmental effort to stem the increase.

As in the first period, the brunt of the reduction in employment fell on manufacturing. Between the end of 1979 and the end of 1982 employment

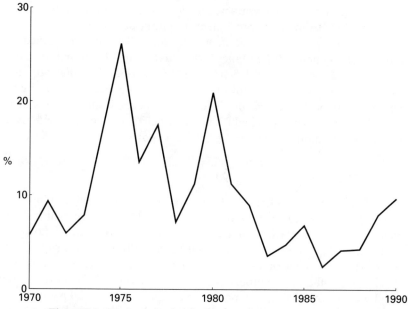

Figure 3.3 The increase in retail prices (June–June), 1970–90

in manufacturing fell by over 20 per cent from 7 million to 5.5 million (Figure 3.1). Since the total reduction in employment was from 25.5 million to 23.6, i.e. by 1.9 million, it is clear that only a relatively small fall took place in other occupations, one of less than 2 per cent. Earlier, in the six years between 1973 and 1979, the changes in employment were much smaller; manufacturing employment fell by about 800,000 and other employment rose by about 1,150,000 so that again the contrast was very marked.

These changes in employment and unemployment were accompanied by a marked slowing down in the growth of output. As we have seen, the rise in output in nine years was no more than 7 per cent. Output per worker suffered a similar check. From a rate of growth of 3.0 per cent per annum in the first period there was a drop to 1.3 per cent per annum in the second. In consequence, there was far less room for an improvement in real wages and living standards.

The rise in earnings over this period was dramatic in monetary terms but almost negligible in real terms. In the first six years, while earnings went up by 151 per cent, retail prices rose by 139 per cent, yielding a net improvement in real earnings of 5 per cent. In the next three years the rise in earnings was 47 per cent and the rise in retail prices 44 per cent, leaving a gain in real terms of 2 per cent. The improvement in earnings in real terms of 7 per cent over the nine years was in close accord with the improvement in output but below the improvement in output per head.

The second period was one in which North Sea oil transformed the balance of payments. It had taken a devaluation in 1967 to put an end to the run of current account deficits in the first period. A similar but more powerful effect was exerted towards the end of the second period by the development of North Sea oil. The current account surplus was at its highest in 1981 when it reached £7 billion as deflation combined with rising oil supplies to limit imports and maintain exports.

The third period, 1982–90

In the final period from 1982 to 1990 growth was resumed and employment, after a further fall to 1983, gradually regained the level from which it had fallen after 1979, reaching a fresh peak in 1990. As before, however, manufacturing employment continued to fall, although at a slower rate after 1983 while other employment expanded comparatively rapidly. While in 1964 manufacturing employed about 35 per cent of the workforce in employment, by 1990 the proportion had fallen to under 20 per cent.

Unemployment was at first little affected by rising employment and continued to grow until late in 1986. It took the boom of 1987–8 to make substantial inroads into the unemployment total, which had reached well over 3 million, but by the spring of 1990 it had been cut by almost one half and stood briefly at 1.6 million, before beginning to climb rapidly again.

With rising unemployment there was a rapid growth in output from the low level of 1982. The growth rate to 1989 averaged 3.4 per cent per annum – higher than in any previous period of equal length. This in part reflected the recovery in employment; output per head, or labour productivity increased at 2.7 per cent per annum, somewhat lower than in 1964–73 but higher than in 1955–64.

For nearly the whole of the final period inflation remained in single figures, falling to under 4 per cent at one point in 1983 and to under 3 per cent for part of 1986 but rising again in 1989–90 to over 10 per cent. The average rate of increase in the retail price index over the eight years 1982–90 was 5.7 per cent – a moderate increase in relation to what went before in 1973–82 but no different from the rate between 1964 and 1973. Money earnings, as usual, rose faster than prices: over this period by a little over 20 per cent. Once again this tallied almost exactly with the growth in output per worker.

The boom which developed at the end of the period did more than raise output and prices. As consumers borrowed and spent more freely, imports were sucked in on a large scale. Exports rose only half as fast as imports and the balance of payments moved rapidly into the red. In 1989 it was again, as it had been in 1964, in record deficit.

Policy objectives and results, 1964–73

Faster growth

The Conservative government that lost office to Labour in mid-October 1964 had hoped to achieve a breakthrough to a faster rate of growth by sustaining the pressure of demand instead of putting a stop to expansion once a balance of payments crisis developed. For this purpose it had declared its willingness to draw on the reserves or borrow abroad. It sought also to guard against a cost inflation through an incomes policy.

The idea that the pressure of demand had much to do with the underlying rate of growth in productivity never seemed very plausible and the power of incomes policy to hold back wage increases in a boom was also very doubtful, even if the TUC could bring itself to cooperate with a Conservative government in an election year. In the event, demand was allowed to outgrow capacity and overflow on to imports, throwing the balance of payments into heavy deficit. At the same time the government's efforts to achieve agreement on a workable incomes policy had little effect.

The expansion in demand in 1963 had been faster than was realised at the time. Even so, some check to the expansion was clearly necessary. When the 1964 budget was introduced, taxes on drink and tobacco were raised to bring in an additional £100 million in 1964–5 but it was soon evident that this was insufficient. No further restrictive measures were taken, however, partly because by mid-summer it looked as if production had ceased to expand (the index of production remained unchanged from January to September).

Unemployment continued to fall and vacancies to increase, while the trade balance remained in heavy deficit. Forecasts of the deficit on current and long-term capital accounts mounted from £200 million in the spring to £700–800 million in the autumn but pressure on the pound became acute only after the October election when a Labour government was returned. The pressure reached crisis proportions in November and for the next four years the Labour government wrestled with constant balance of payments difficulties (Beckerman 1972).

These difficulties had had no part in the thinking of the government before it took office. Their programme was directed to the restructuring of British industry by long-term measures to improve its efficiency. A National Plan was to be prepared by a new Department of Economic Affairs, which would be responsible for economic policy, while the Treasury was to confine itself to matters of finance – a division which had been attempted in 1945 and abandoned once Cripps became Chancellor. Two new taxes – a corporation tax and a capital gains tax – were to be introduced. There was also to be an incomes policy with an agreed norm for wage increases.

The balance of payments

The immediate problem faced by the government, however, was the balance of payments deficit and distrust in sterling. A drain on the reserves, on a scale difficult to sustain, reflected both the deficit and the distrust. The traditional cure for a deficit was a dose of deflation but this the government would not contemplate. Alternatively it might have devalued but decided not to. This left three possibilities: borrowing, import quotas and a surcharge on imports. Borrowing was necessary in any event to cover the deficit but could not put an end to it. Neither could import quotas nor a surcharge unless retained indefinitely. The government settled on a surcharge of 15 per cent on manufactured imports although this was in contravention of international obligations. After sharp attacks by EFTA countries it announced its intention of reducing the surcharge 'in a matter of months'. The surcharge was reduced to 10 per cent in April 1965 and removed in November 1966 after an existence of only two years (Blackaby 1978).

The pressure on sterling after 1964 did not derive from the current account so much as from capital movements and speculation in both spot and forward markets. In the four years 1964–7 the cumulative deficit on current account was no more than £600 million, whereas the government had to find nearly £2,300 million to meet the drain on the reserves (Figure 3.2). For this purpose it had to borrow heavily and repeatedly from foreign monetary authorities and the IMF. It tried in many different ways to reduce outgoings in foreign exchange but it was unsuccessful in restoring confidence in sterling until well after devaluation in 1967, when the current account was eventually brought into surplus.

In its relations with financial markets, the government got off to a bad start. Markets had assumed that the decision to defend the parity would be supported by restrictive measures but the budget introduced on 11 November was thought to be expansionary because it added to public expenditure. There was then a palpable delay, indicative of hesitation, in countering market reactions by putting up Bank Rate to 7 per cent and a run on the pound began which fell away only when the Governor of the Bank of England raised £3 billion from other central banks. In June 1965 a second run developed and the government responded by a number of cuts in July in its investment programmes. The Prime Minister kept pointing to this and other measures as if they added up to severe deflation but it was only too apparent that unemployment was still falling and production still expanding well into 1966.

A third speculative attack took place in the summer of 1966 and led to a tightening of monetary policy in the middle of July when Bank Rate was increased to 7 per cent. For the first time, devaluation was discussed in Cabinet, with some Ministers in favour of devaluing or floating the pound, but the vote went in favour of holding the rate. Next day, on 20 July, deflationary measures were announced that produced what was virtually a stop on the old pattern. Having refused initially to choose between devaluation and deflation the government now found itself obliged to choose deflation and was soon to have to devalue as well.

For a time confidence in the pound recovered. Short-term funds flowed back and by the spring of 1967 nearly all that had been borrowed from other central banks had been repaid. From May onwards, however, the situation deteriorated. Markets abroad were less buoyant, exports began to decline, the current account moved into deficit and the inflow of funds ceased. The outlook by the autumn was for an aggravation over the winter months of the downward trend, with no obvious sources of recovery on the horizon. Quite apart from strikes and rumours, it was becoming clear well before November that there was no escape from devaluation. A decision was taken on 13 November to move from $2.80 to $2.40 to the £1 and the decision was announced five days later on 18 November. The delay, occasioned by the lengthy consultations that preceded the announcement, allowed speculators to make large profits from the change in parity. There was a heavy loss of £356 million on the forward transactions in which the Bank of England had engaged as a means of relieving the pressure on the spot rate for sterling (Cairncross and Eichengreen 1983).

Devaluation did not put an end to the pressure on sterling. On the contrary, it was resumed almost immediately and intensified in 1968 in spite of what was recognised to be the most deflationary budget since the war. The pressure reflected a succession of influences: at first doubts over the adequacy of the measures accompanying devaluation; then in March 1968 a speculative rush into gold; and in November, expectations of a revaluation of the deutschmark. The current account was slow in improving but by the second half of 1968 it was not far off balance and for three and a half years from the beginning of 1969 remained in appreciable surplus. It was not until 1972 that there was any renewal of balance of payments difficulties.

In its struggles to maintain the parity the government relied principally on borrowing. It also hoped, as described below, to stabilise wages and prices through an incomes policy and to improve the competitive position of British industry by an interventionist industrial policy under the National Plan. There was a withdrawal from military positions 'east of Suez', with a corresponding abandonment of British pretensions to the status of a great power, in order to save foreign exchange. In addition, exchange control was tightened in various ways, of which one of the most significant was the requirement to surrender 25 per cent of the investment currency obtained on the repatriation of portfolio investment outside the sterling area (the investment currency used in such transactions being dealt in at a premium and segregated from official dealings in foreign exchange) (Tew 1978b).

Incomes policy

The Labour government had hoped to reduce the danger of inflation through an incomes policy agreed with the TUC. A 'statement of intent' was signed by representatives of employers and employed in December 1964 and a National Board for Prices and Incomes (NBPI) was set up early in 1965. The statement was vague on the mechanics of the policy and linked it with the National Plan, attempting, as indeed the Conservatives had done, to put wage restraint in the context of economic growth. The main departures from earlier policy were that it covered prices as well as wages, that the NBPI was conceived of as a permanent institution, and that it could make recommendations for the improvement of productivity in firms and industries as well as on wages and prices. The NBPI had no statutory powers and, as with the National Incomes Commission abolished by the Labour government, the relatively small number of cases referred to it were of wage settlements already made (Blackaby 1978).

Although the TUC had agreed to a norm of 3.5 per cent, hourly wage rates in the first year of the Labour government rose by nearly 8 per cent and hourly earnings by nearly 10 per cent. The TUC remained opposed to any form of statutory intervention but agreed, under pressure, to an 'early warning' system under which all impending claims were notified to the TUC and examined by a special TUC vetting committee. This committee, which unlike the NBPI considered all claims, had a month to comment on them but had no power to require action on the basis of its comments. It continued in operation from October 1965 until January 1970.

Neither the vetting committee nor the NBPI (which tended to act as a kind of national management consultant) had much effect on the rise in wages in 1965–6. Towards the end of May 1966 the National Union of Seamen called a strike for a 17 per cent increase in pay and, although the strike was settled on 1 July on the terms recommended by a Court of Inquiry, it helped to precipitate a balance of payments crisis and forced the government to take further action on wages. As part of the package introduced on 20 July, the government included a six-month freeze on wages, prices and dividends, to be followed by six months of 'severe restraint'. The freeze was given the reluctant endorsement, first of the General Council of the TUC and then of the annual Congress and there were few attempts to infringe it. For the first six months no increase took place in the index of weekly wages and in June 1967 it stood only 2 per cent above the pre-freeze level.

For the period following that of 'severe restraint' the government envisaged a return to voluntary arrangements with no norm and all increases justified against criteria similar to those set out in 1965 (or, for that matter, 1962). The government took powers to impose a standstill for one month on claims under examination and a further delay of up to six months on claims referred to the NBPI. But from the middle of 1967 settlements had little relationship to White Paper criteria or to the ceiling of 3 per cent on claims satisfying these criteria. The only exception was to have been for higher productivity but this clause merely encouraged bogus productivity deals. By 1969 the government had switched its attention to unofficial strikes (without being able to pass legislation against them) and was proposing to abandon its powers over prices and incomes at the end of the year. As incomes policy expired, wage settlements reached double figures (Table 3.1).

Less intervention and more rapid inflation

The Conservative government which took office in June 1970 shared the hopes of both its predecessors, Conservative and Labour, that it would transform the economy and achieve faster growth. But it aimed to do so by reducing government intervention in the economy in the belief that this would make for greater efficiency. It also disclaimed any interest in incomes policy and wound up the NBPI.

It proved impossible to hold to this position. Although there was a healthy surplus in the balance of payments, industrial production was flat and unemployment mounted slowly. This did not prevent an accelerating rise in wages and prices to which the government could not avoid reacting in the public sector (including the nationalised industries) however much it tried to disengage from wage claims in the private sector. Since it took a close interest in the amount conceded in wage settlements in the public sector and aimed to make each successive settlement lower than the one before, it came increasingly into confrontation with the unions. The government was also in conflict with the unions over its labour legislation, to which they were deeply opposed. They declined to register under the

Table 3.1. *UK economic indicators, 1964–90*

	Index of GDP at 1985 prices	Broad money (M4 in £b)[a]	PSBR (£b)	Treasury bill yield (%)	Weekly wages (% increase)[b]
1964	64·9	16·0	1·0	6·74	4·8
1965	66·8	17·7	1·2	5·60	4·3
1966	68·1	18·8	0·9	6·64	4·8
1967	69·6	21·3	1·8	7·62	3·7
1968	72·6	22·9	1·3	6·90	6·6
1969	74·4	24·1	−0·5	7·80	5·3
1970	75·9	27·0	−0·1	6·93	9·9
1971	77·2	31·6	1·3	4·46	12·9
1972	79·4	39·1	2·0	8·48	13·8
1973	85·2	47·6	4·1	12·82	13·7
1974	83·9	52·8	6·5	11·30	19·8
1975	83·2	58·2	10·2	10·93	29·5
1976	85·4	64·7	8·9	13·98	19·3
1977	87·6	74·2	5·4	6·39	6·6
1978	90·2	85·3	8·3	11·91	14·1
1979	92·7	97·4	12·6	16·49	15·0
			....		
1980	90·7	114·1	11·8	13·58	18·0
1981	89·7	137·9	10·6	15·39	10·1
1982	91·3	154·8	5·0	9·96	6·6
					....
1983	94·6	175·4	11·6	9·04	8·3
1984	96·2	199·4	10·3	9·33	6·1
	....				
1985	100·0	225·6	7·4	11·49	8·3
1986	103·6	261·5	2·5	10·94	7·9
1987	108·1	304·0	−1·4	8·38	7·8
1988	112·7	357·5	−11·9	12·91	8·7
		....			
1989	114·7	424·5	−9·3	(14·48)	9·1
1990	115·3	473·4	−2·0	(13·06)	9·7

.... = changed definition of series.

[a] Broad money: end of year.

[b] Weekly wages: wage rates 1964–82; earnings 1983–90.

Sources: Economic Trends Annual Supplement 1990: for Col. 1 to 1985, Cols. 2 and 4 to 1988; Col. 3 to 1979. Later figures from *National Institute Economic Review*. Col. 5 from *Economic Trends Annual Supplement* 1979 to 1981 and *National Institute Economic Review* from 1980.

Industrial Relations Act or to allow their members to serve on the National Industrial Relations Court and Commission on Industrial Relations set up under the Act.

More moderate wage awards in the public sector in 1971 were not accompanied by similar moderation in the private sector. The rise in prices did slow down, in part because of the agreement of many leading members of the Confederation of British Industries (CBI) to avoid raising prices for twelve months or to hold any increase to a 5 per cent maximum. The nationalised industries were required to follow suit but could do so only with the help of increased subsidies.

The government's policy broke down over a dispute with the miners which led in January 1972 to the first national coal strike since 1926. A state of emergency was declared in February and most of British industry was put on to a three-day week. After seven weeks the strike was eventually called off on the basis of a settlement that raised pay by 17–20 per cent and included concessions negotiated with the Prime Minister (Heath) himself.

In his 1971 budget the Chancellor (Barber) had cited the level of pay settlements as a reason for refraining from more expansionary measures. But when unemployment rose unexpectedly fast to over 900,000 at the beginning of 1972, without much slowing down in inflation, he changed his tune. He took reflationary action in November and December 1971 by announcing plans for additional public expenditure and the repayment of all outstanding post-war credits. Then in the March budget tax cuts were made that aimed at (and achieved) a growth in output by 5 per cent per annum and a fall in unemployment to 500,000. What was not appreciated was that such a target implied a very tight labour market – much higher than the same figure ten years previously.

Forecasters uniformly underestimated the pace of the expansion that followed. The National Institute and the London Business School forecast respectively increases of 6.2 and 7.2 per cent in GDP between 1971 and the first half of 1973; the actual increase was over 10 per cent. It was not foreseen that in 1972–3 all the main industrial countries would be simultaneously in boom and that primary produce would be rising rapidly in price. Some writers lay stress also on monetary factors: in September 1971 Bank Rate was reduced to 5 per cent and ceilings on bank lending removed, with the result that bank advances rose steeply. That this played a part in the expansion in demand in 1972–3 is clear enough. But its contribution to the acceleration in inflation in 1974–5, when more obvious influences were at work, is questionable.

Other important departures in policy were made in 1972. Industrial policy was modified to help the development areas, rescue 'lame ducks' and extend free depreciation to the whole of the country. In June, when the pound came under pressure, it was allowed to float downwards (it had been revalued upwards to $2.60 to the £1 under the Smithsonian agreement of December 1971). Controls were also imposed for the first time on capital investment in the sterling area and this effectively meant the end of the sterling area. At the end of 1972 a different association was born when the United Kingdom formally joined the European Community.

In a further reversal of policy the government entered into protracted negotiations with the unions which broke down in November 1972. A statutory ninety-day wages and prices freeze was introduced on 6 November and in January pay increases before the autumn of 1973 were limited to £1 a week plus 4 per cent of the employer's total wage bill. Stages I and II both followed the pattern set by the United States, as also did the creation of a Pay Board and Price Commission.

The next stage (Stage III) began in November 1973. Pay increases of up to 7 per cent were allowed, with various 'flexibility margins', plus flat rate increases of 40p per week for every 1 per cent by which the rise in the cost of living exceeded 7 per cent. This was the first time such a link between increases in pay and prices had formed part of incomes policy and it had disastrous consequences. Retail prices which had already risen by 9 per cent over the previous year rose by 48 per cent over the next two years and the threshold arrangement helped to accelerate the wage increase far above 7 per cent (Table 3.1).

In October 1973 an international oil crisis developed with the first sharp rise in oil prices and a cut in oil supplies. The mineworkers, after rejecting a 13 per cent pay offer, began an overtime ban on 12 November and the electric power engineers took industrial action in support of their pay claims (Blackaby 1978: 384). The government declared a state of emergency on 13 November and, a month later, a three-day week for the whole economy from 1 January 1974. After a ballot on 4 February, a coal strike was called to begin six days later and on 7 February the Prime Minister called a general election on the issue of 'Who governs Britain?' The Conservatives lost the election by a narrow margin and the claims of the mineworkers were conceded in one of the first acts of the incoming Labour government.

Anti-inflation policies had thus had little success. Wages and prices were rising fast, output (quite apart from the three-day week) was beginning to fall and unemployment to rise, and the balance of payments was moving into record deficit (Figure 3.2). Everything seemed to be going wrong at once.

Policy objectives and results, 1973–82

The first period had ended in one of the greatest booms of the century. It was not confined to the United Kingdom but was international in scope and produced a rise in commodity prices unparalleled since the Korean War in 1950–1. During 1973 the price of exports from primary producers (measured in dollars) increased by over 60 per cent and at the end of the year the export price of oil quadrupled between September and January. United Kingdom import prices inevitably reflected these changes, rising by 55 per cent between the first quarter of 1973 and the first quarter of 1974. In a country spending a third of its income on imports such a rise was bound to have a powerful inflationary effect. It took some time to work through to domestic prices and was at first damped by the government's incomes policy and by the relative inertia of wage and other costs. In 1973 the rise in retail prices was under 10 per cent; but in 1974 it was 20 per cent and still accelerating. In the meantime the rise in wage rates, which in the 1960s had been at under 5 per cent per annum, was gathering speed and had already reached 28 per cent by the end of 1974. Inflation was at a rate unprecedented in peacetime and was very alarming (Figure 3.3).

The sources of inflation

In the initial stages, the main cause of the inflation lay outside the United Kingdom, as is evident from the simultaneous rise in prices in other countries. But it was aggravated by domestic factors and was more pronounced in Britain than elsewhere. In December 1974, for example, consumer prices had risen in the previous twelve months by 19.5 per cent in the United Kingdom as against 14.2 per cent on average in members of the OECD.

Three reasons can be offered for this divergence. The first is the depreciation of sterling after it was allowed to float in June 1972 (Figure 3.4). There was a further sharp drop of 10 per cent in the dollar rate in the second half of 1972, but taking the two years 1973 and 1974 together there was little or no depreciation over that time. A second interpretation sees the rise in prices in 1974 as a delayed response to the expansion in the money supply two years previously (Table 3.1). This purports, however, to explain the whole of the rise in prices when what is at issue is the divergence from the rate of inflation elsewhere; there can be little doubt that most of the inflation was international in character. How far monetary factors were the root causes of world inflation and how far they merely reflected it is a matter of controversy but most economists would be sceptical of

Figure 3.4 The effective exchange rate, 1971–90 (average of Q2 and
Q3)

explanations of international booms and oil shocks in terms of earlier
monetary expansion.

What stands out is the third reason, the dominant role of wage increases.
The Labour government, when it took office in March 1974, continued the
threshold arrangement made by its predecessor; before the system came to
an end eleven successive increases in pay had been triggered from May to
December 1974. In spite of a 'social contract' concluded with the TUC to
replace the Conservative statutory wage policy, wages in the second half of
1974 outstripped the rise in prices by a large margin, rising in six months
by over 16 per cent compared with a rise in retail prices of only 8 per cent.
In 1975, wages continued to rise rapidly in the first six months while the rise
in retail prices accelerated to a rate of over 26 per cent per annum in the
summer. Thereafter, however, inflation slackened off progressively until
the year-on-year rise in retail prices was under 8 per cent in the middle of
1978 (Artis and Cobham 1991; Britton 1991).

How was it that inflation was checked after rising so dramatically in 1974–5? An important contributory factor was the behaviour of international prices. The surge in commodity prices had more or less spent itself by the spring of 1974, and after wobbling between May and November they fell by about 20 per cent in the ensuing year while foodstuffs exported by primary producers fell by a third. British import prices, by contrast, rose through 1975 but there was a distinct check to the earlier rate of increase that helped to keep down the cost of living and moderate wage claims.

A more obvious influence was the rise in unemployment. This had risen slowly in 1974 from the low point at the end of 1973 but in 1975 the pace quickened (Figure 3.5). In 1974 it had risen by about 100,000; in 1975 the increase was 500,000 and was still in progress. Vacancies had fallen by two-thirds to the lowest total on record. Even if wage claims showed little response to a raising of the level of unemployment, workers might well hesitate to submit still higher claims while their mates were being sacked and bankruptcies were on the increase.

A third factor was a tightening of monetary policy and efforts to slow the growth of public expenditure. Bank Rate had been raised progressively from 9.75 per cent in April 1975 to 12 per cent in October and the growth in the money stock (as measured by £M3) fell to one third of what it had been in 1973. These moves were designed to check the growth of demand, when output and demand were already falling. So far as they had that effect they operated partly through the rise in unemployment just discussed but also through the direct operation on prices of an abatement of demand pressure.

The difficulties of the Labour government came to a head in 1976 (Dell 1991). At the beginning of the year there seemed some prospect of a gradual improvement in the economic situation. Production was recovering all over the world from the depression of the previous year. The balance of payments deficit had been cut in half and continued to improve. North Sea oil was about to flow. Exports were expected to increase at 9 per cent per annum. Domestically, too, the outlook was good. The rate of inflation was falling and might be in single figures by the end of the year. The rise in unemployment had slowed down and vacancies were increasing. The growth in the money supply was being contained.

By the middle of the year, however, it was necessary to obtain a standby credit of $5.3 billion from European central banks on a promise to repay in December. Repayment, as the central banks had foreseen, required recourse to the IMF on terms acceptable to the IMF. So, by December the government was involved in a long wrangle over the cuts in public expenditure and other measures that would satisfy the IMF. Agreement

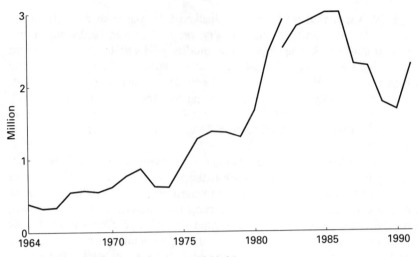

Figure 3.5 Unemployment, 1964–91

was finally reached on cuts of £1 billion in 1977–8 plus the sale of £500 million of British Petroleum shares and an additional £1 billion in cuts in the following year. These may seem modest in relation to a budget of £63 billion but they were additional to cuts which had been made earlier. At the end of the financial year it turned out that expenditure in 1976–7 was already more than £3 billion short of estimates. Cuts on the scale the IMF insisted on had therefore been made before the discussion with them began (and hence two years ahead of time) without anyone knowing. They resulted, not from Cabinet decisions, but mainly from the caution of a miscellany of spending authorities faced with cash limits of which they had no previous experience (Burk and Cairncross 1992: 183–6).

The sterling balances

The crisis that obliged the government to turn to the IMF had begun in March when there had been some talk of allowing the exchange rate to fall as a means of improving competitiveness; financial markets believed the government to be meditating action in pursuance of this. By chance a foreign holder of sterling (alleged to be the Nigerian government) had simultaneously decided to withdraw some of its large sterling balances held in London. Its sales of sterling were misinterpreted as sales by the Bank of England on government instructions. The result was heavy speculation against the pound and further withdrawals. In the second quarter of the year over £900 million held in London as the reserves of central banks were withdrawn and the total amount of foreign exchange that the authorities had to supply to the market was not far short of £2,000 million. It was this drain of foreign exchange that made it necessary to seek help from other central banks; and it was the continuation of the drain, but on a much more limited scale, that ruled out repayment of the loan except via fresh borrowing from the IMF.

In earlier years arrangements had been made to deal with the problem of sterling balances either through the use of swap facilities with European central banks, to cope with fluctuations in these balances or, after the devaluation of 1967, through a medium-term facility of $2 billion arranged by the Bank for International Settlements (BIS) enabling the United Kingdom to offer a dollar-value guarantee to sterling area countries on most of their official holdings of sterling. The swap arrangements ceased in 1971 and the facility was replaced in September 1973 by a six-month unilateral guarantee which lapsed in March 1974 (Tew 1978: 351–2).

Under what may have seemed an alternative arrangement the national-ised industries and other public bodies were encouraged, starting in 1973, to borrow abroad instead of in sterling, this 'foreign currency borrowing' being guaranteed by the government against changes in the exchange rate. By the end of 1976 the foreign debt incurred in this way (including borrowing by the government) was over £5 billion and in 1976 alone £1.7 billion was borrowed.

In 1976 the government sought to re-establish a safety-net for the remaining sterling balances but encountered strong opposition until agreement was reached with the IMF. Thereafter negotiations conducted by the Governor of the Bank of England issued in a fresh agreement. Long before this – before even the agreement with the IMF – the withdrawal of funds had begun to give way to an inflow. This persisted throughout 1977, when £9.5 billion was added to the reserves. Fearful of the inflationary consequences of a continuing inflow of funds, the government felt obliged to abandon offsetting arrangements and to let the exchange rate appreciate. Thus began the rise which was to carry the pound from $1.55 in 1976 to a peak of $2.43 in 1981 (Figure 3.4).

After 1976 the outlook for a time was brighter. Inflation fell slowly to about 8 per cent for most of 1978 and unemployment, after rising a little in 1977 fell back again in 1978. The balance of payments continued to improve and moved into surplus in 1978. But in the course of 1978 the domestic situation again began to deteriorate. Interest rates rose from April onwards; the rise in wage rates which had slowed down in 1977 accelerated again in 1978 (Table 3.1). The government's hopes of holding to a 5 per cent norm encountered strong resentment at the prolonged restraint on wages and the slow improvement of real wages which in four years had averaged less than 1 per cent per annum. A 'winter of discontent' followed in which even grave-diggers went on strike. By May, when a general election returned a Conservative government, inflation was again in double figures and wage rates had increased by 13 per cent in twelve months.

Disengagement

The aims of the Conservative government which took office in May 1979 were somewhat similar to the initial aims of the Heath government in 1970. They wished to disengage the state from much of its intervention in the economy, to reduce public expenditure and cut taxation and to rely on market forces to steer the economy in the right direction. In contrast to the Heath administration, however, the Thatcher government was not deflected from these aims either by rising unemployment or by initial difficulties in containing public expenditure. On the contrary, as time went on, it took stronger action to disengage. For example, it seems originally to have contemplated only a modest amount of privatisation of state-owned industries and made no reference to the idea in its election manifesto. But when privatisation proved to have popular appeal it assumed increasing prominence in the government's programme.

The government also claimed to be able to control inflation through the use of monetary policy. It repudiated any formal incomes policy and treated the budget as ancillary to monetary policy rather than as the prime instrument of demand management. But control of the money supply could be exercised only through variations in interest rates since there was no direct control over the monetary base, no direct control over bank lending, and no intention of relying on requests to the banks such as were used in the 1940s and 1950s (Britton 1991).

Inflation and the exchange rate

The first actions of the government had raised, not lowered, wages and prices. In an effort to shift some of the burden of taxation to indirect from direct taxation the government increased VAT from rates of 8 and 12.5 per cent to 15 per cent. It also accepted pay awards in the public sector that were based on comparability but were likely to have inflationary repercussions. A second oil shock later in the year reinforced these influences. A year after the government took office, retail prices were up by 22 per cent.

The balance of payments had meanwhile moved into slight deficit in spite of the contribution of North Sea oil, but in comparison with other currencies sterling looked relatively strong. It was not external weakness but fear of inflation that caused the government to raise Bank Rate (now called Minimum Lending Rate) first to 14 per cent in June, then to 17 per cent in November. The exchange rate, already at a level of over $2 to the £1 at the beginning of 1979, now appreciated much more rapidly as North Sea oil supplies increased and had reached the fantastic rate of $2.43 to the £1 by January 1981. Thus while the domestic value of the £1 fell, the external value rose.

From the point of view of the impact of this appreciation on the competitive position of British industry the more significant change was in the effective rate of exchange against a basket of currencies (Figure 3.4). Between the first quarter of 1979 and January 1981 the effective rate rose by 25 per cent. So violent a change, combined with the abnormally high interest rates which were driving the pound up and submitting industry to a fierce credit squeeze, had disastrous effects on output and employment, particularly in British manufacturing (Keegan 1984). Employment fell by over a million or 15 per cent in the two years to June 1981 and did not recover when the exchange rate fell again from January 1981 onwards. Between 1979 and 1981 manufacturing output, too, fell by 15 per cent. It is true that exports continued to expand and that imports actually fell in 1980. But the pressure on profit margins was intense and the squeeze was intensified by the high cost of credit.

By the end of 1982 the strong deflationary pressure exerted by the combination of dear money and a high rate of exchange had been relaxed. The Treasury bill rate was under 10 per cent (Table 3.1) and the effective rate of exchange was lower than it had been at the change of government in 1979. But in the aftermath of the deflation unemployment was nearly 3 million and still climbing while employment had yet to reach its lowest point. Inflation had fallen dramatically to about 5 per cent. This reflected deflationary forces abroad as much as in the United Kingdom. Un-employment in OECD countries, which had averaged 5 per cent in 1979, now averaged nearly 9 per cent; and the dollar index of commodity prices for exports from developing countries had fallen by a quarter since October 1980. Whether because of rising unemployment or falling commodity prices, weekly wages were rising at a much slower pace: instead of the 18 per cent increase in 1980 the rise in 1982 was under 7 per cent (Table 3.1).

Monetary and financial strategy

Meanwhile, what of the government's monetary and financial policy? A Medium-Term Financial Strategy was announced in the 1980 budget; it showed declining targets for monetary expansion year by year and a progressive reduction in public expenditure, designed to reduce the borrowing requirement and to hold down interest rates. Monetary targets were never very successful and ultimately rather meaningless. By the end of 1982 the money supply had risen in three years by nearly 60 per cent and the targets seemed to be devised to fit the increase in the stock of money rather than the other way round (Table 3.1). Public expenditure was a different matter and was indeed compressed even while unemployment was increasing rapidly (Pliatzky 1984; Britton 1991).

In those early years of Conservative government, when output began by falling by nearly 6 per cent in the first two years and had recovered only 2.4 per cent eighteen months later, the main contractionary element was investment, both fixed investment and stockbuilding, and it was in those also that recovery began. Consumer spending hardly changed between 1979 and 1981; exports, apart from a fall in 1981, also changed little; expenditure on goods and services by public authorities continued to increase. It was investment, and particularly investment in stocks, that took the brunt of the depression, and it was employment in manufacturing that suffered most of the loss of jobs.

Policy objectives and results, 1982–90

The final period, from 1982 onwards, can be dealt with more briefly. Similar policies were pursued throughout and until the boom of 1988–9 the economy departed very little from a consistent trend. In each year from 1982 output increased and from 1983 employment, too, grew year by year.

The balance of payments

While most of the trends in the economy were favourable there were some disturbing signs. First of all, the balance of payments deteriorated after 1981 in every year except 1985. After 1986, with oil exports past their peak, it was in increasingly heavy deficit. There is some uncertainty, it is true, about the interpretation to be put on the balancing item, which may conceal some invisible income, but the trend in the trade balance from a deficit of £3 billion in 1985 to one of £23 billion in 1989 was all too plain. One consequence of this trend was a decline in the effective exchange rate throughout the period to 40 per cent below the level in 1982 (Figure 3.4). A second consequence was a sharp rise in the share of imports in the domestic market, the ratio to GDP increasing to 32 per cent in 1989 from 27 per cent in 1982. The share of imports of manufactures in the British market rose over the same period from 10.7 to over 15 per cent. Exports also increased but much more slowly; in the early 1980s, but not after 1987, they maintained their share of world trade in manufactures. A third consequence was that, once a large gap developed in the balance of payments requiring finance from abroad, the government had no option but to maintain high rates of interest (in comparison with those in foreign financial centres). By the end of 1988 Bank Rate was at 13 per cent and by the end of 1989 at 15 per cent (Table 3.1).

Savings and spending

A second disturbing trend was a fall in the net savings ratio. From 11.6 per cent of personal disposable income in 1982 – well below the ratio in the late 1970s – it fell progressively to 4.3 per cent in 1988 before showing any signs of recovering. The fall took the form of a marked increase in consumer indebtedness, much of it mortgage debt. Mortgage borrowing from building societies and consumer credit both doubled between 1984 and 1988; bank lending to persons (including lending on mortgage) trebled over the same four years and bank lending to companies rose between five and sixfold. Since the increase in bank lending is roughly equal to the increase in bank money, it was surprising that no action was taken to limit the rate of increase by a government which associated inflation so closely with the quantity of money. The government indeed was inclined to argue either that it was unnecessary to control consumer credit or that efforts to control it would prove ineffective. This too was surprising if it was considered necessary and possible to control the money supply, which is the counterpart of bank debt.

A possible explanation lies in the role of consumer spending in pulling the economy out of the depression into which it fell in 1980–1. Since the government was determined to apply no stimulus itself, and kept applying the brake to public expenditure, while the balance of payments was contractionary, some other element in demand had to expand if recovery was ever to take place. The initial stimulus came from the rebound in stockbuilding: de-stocking ceased in 1982. Private fixed investment also turned round in that year and increased steadily thereafter. But this recovery and its continuation rested heavily on the expansion of the home market for consumer goods. From the low point in 1981 to the top of the boom in 1988 consumer spending rose by one third while GDP rose by less than a quarter. Of the increase in GDP of £67.4 billion (at 1985 prices) consumer spending accounted for £64.4 billion. Of course, part of this spending disappeared into imports and the rising external deficit and provided no stimulus. It is also true that fixed investment rose much faster than consumer spending from the low point in 1981. But the central fact in the recovery process was first, the steadiness of consumer spending when the economy was contracting and second, the debt incurred by consumers and (partly in consequence) by the economy as a whole in the later phases.

Structural change

What were the major structural changes during these twenty-five years?

Decline of manufacturing

The decline in the manufacturing sector, which has already been mentioned and is discussed further in chapter 5 below, was most apparent in terms of unemployment which fell gradually from a peak in the winter of 1965–6 at an average rate of a little over 1 per cent per year up to 1979. Thereafter the fall was for a time very much faster and in the ten years to 1989 amounted to 2 million or 28 per cent.

In the early stages of the run-down it was taken as one more sign of the uncompetitiveness of British industry and associated with the fall in Britain's share of world trade in manufactures. In the course of the 1970s it was still regarded as unique to Britain and was labelled 'deindustriali-sation' (Blackaby 1979b). Some observers at the end of the decade explained the continuing fall as a natural corollary of the development of North Sea oil, which furnished exports no longer required from manu-facturing (Forsyth and Kay 1980). But the sharp contraction by well over a million in manufacturing employment in 1979–81 had a much more obvious explanation in the deflationary pressure in those years. Exports of manufactures fell by 5 per cent in volume but imports fell by 3 per cent so that the net change was small in relation to a 16 per cent fall in employment. In any event, with the ending of exchange control in 1979 the development of North Sea oil was just as likely to be accompanied by large capital exports, leaving the need for a net excess of manufactures more or less unaffected.

It became increasingly apparent that the manufacturing sector was in decline in most industrial countries. As consumers became more affluent their spending patterns, which had made room earlier in the post-war period for increasing expenditure on consumer durables, were now modified so as to permit a higher proportion of the work to be done outside the factory. No doubt North Sea oil has also played a long-term part in the case of the United Kingdom. After 1986 a growing external deficit suggested that the fall in manufacturing employment had gone too far to be consistent with a balanced current account, especially with oil production falling off. But a relative decline in manufacturing is part of a world-wide trend.

*International integration and the decline of national economic
management*

In common with other countries, the British economy is becoming more
and more closely integrated into the world economy and, more particularly, into the European economy. One way of measuring this is simply
to compare the ratio of imports and exports to gross domestic product at
the beginning and end of the period. In 1964 imports of goods and services
made up 20.4 per cent of GDP and exports of goods and services 18.6 per
cent. By 1988 these proportions had become 27.1 and 23.5 per cent
respectively. Similarly, the change in the direction of British trade can be
illustrated by the rise in the proportion that is within the European
Community. As the membership of the Community has been enlarged
since 1964 the comparison is best made in relation to the six original
members; unfortunately it has also to be confined to commodity trade. In
the case of imports the increase in the proportion, from a time in 1964 when
the United Kingdom was not a member to 1989 when it was, has been from
16.5 to 43.7 per cent in the case of imports and from 20.4 to 44.6 per cent
in the case of exports. If one goes further back the same trend is already
apparent although rather less steep.

This change was not simply the result of joining the Community. Much
of the change had already taken place before Britain became a member in
1973. In 1972, for example, imports from the Six had already increased
from 16.5 per cent to 24.5 per cent in eight years; for exports the increase
was from 20.4 to 30.1 per cent. The fact is that in the post-war period it has
been trade between manufacturing countries that has grown fastest, partly
because the prosperity of these countries has grown fastest. Even the
original members of the Community found their trade with one another
growing faster than trade with other countries well before the Treaty of
Rome in 1957. Indeed it would be hard to date the Treaty from the trade
statistics of the participants.

Integration was not just a matter of closer trading relations. It affected
all aspects of economic activity and, more than anything else, the
movement of funds. The greater mobility of capital had important
repercussions. It made largely futile the efforts to control capital
movements to which so much importance had been attached at Bretton
Woods. It also threw doubt on the power of any one country to pursue a
truly independent monetary policy when it was so easy to lend or borrow
abroad (Wass 1978; Middleton 1988). In the years after 1964 the Labour
government had buttressed the exchange rate by tightening exchange
control; by 1979 exchange control had been removed, in part at least
because it had become ineffective. Interest rates in different countries

tended increasingly to move in step with one another and Finance Ministers met regularly to consult and sometimes collaborate with their opposite numbers in the Group of Seven and other bodies.

The decline of national economic management, which was implied by integration, was carried further by the progressive abandonment of the instruments it required. Long before control over capital movements ceased, direct intervention to control the balance of trade had been given up except in the case of imports from developing countries. With that exception, there were no import quotas, no surcharges such as had been imposed in 1964, no import deposits as in 1968. There was no exchange control. Control over domestic activity had also shrunk. Hire purchase restrictions, on which so much reliance had been placed in the 1950s and 1960s, had not been revived since the mid-1970s. The tax regulator introduced by Selwyn Lloyd in 1961 had passed out of use. The use of the budget itself as an instrument of demand management had almost been forgotten. Incomes policy had vanished. Almost the only remaining instrument of national economic management was the short-term interest rate and even that was at the mercy of the forces of integration. Meanwhile the instruments of international management remained woefully inadequate.

Regional development

A great deal of effort in this period went into efforts to promote a more even development of the different regions of the country. One symptom of uneven development was the variation in unemployment rates which registered differences in the pressure of demand from region to region. These ratios maintained a remarkable constancy in their relationships to one another throughout the period (with some exceptions noted below). This does not imply a similar constancy in the employment pattern, as might be supposed, since the impact of additional job opportunities in any region tended to reduce the outflow of labour to other regions rather than the relative proportion remaining unemployed. Scotland, for example, had either the highest or the second highest rate of unemployment throughout the period in spite of North Sea oil, a more powerful influence on employment than anything that successive governments did. Government policy could, and did, affect the development of the regions suffering most heavily from depression; but it did so by operating on outmigration rather than on unemployment.

Some regions did, however, improve their relative position while others lost ground. The most striking improvements were in the south-west, Wales and East Anglia. The south-west, with a higher than average unemployment rate in 1965 and 1974, had fallen well below the average in 1989; Wales, which had one of the highest rates in 1965, was fairly close to the average in 1989; East Anglia, from a middling position in 1965, had the lowest unemployment rate of any region in 1989. On the other hand, the west midlands had changed dramatically from having the lowest un- employment rate in 1965 to just below the average in 1989. Yorkshire and Humberside suffered a comparable change for the worse. The northern region, which was already relatively depressed in 1965, was second only to Northern Ireland in 1989. Northern Ireland was alone in having a rate that remained almost throughout at more than double the national average.

Conclusion

In the years after the end of the Second World War, economic and social change was more rapid than ever before. The national income grew roughly 2.5 times between 1945 and 1990 and earnings in real terms grew, if anything, even more rapidly. Household income gained additionally from the higher proportion of women in paid jobs. The standard of living of the average family in 1990 was far above where it had been in the 1930s.

Production increased in every decade and in nearly every year: fastest in the 1960s when GDP rose by one third and slowest in the 1970s when the increase was less than one fifth. On the other hand, the fastest rise in consumer spending was in the 1980s, when it was comparable with the increase in GDP, and slowest again in the 1970s. Productivity, for most of the period, grew more slowly than on the Continent; but whereas continental rates of productivity growth slowed down decade by decade, the British rate maintained a comparatively steady pace which, at the end of the period, was for the first time as high, if not higher, than in the rest of the European Community.

Three major economic evils – inflation, unemployment and balance of payments difficulties – beset the economy at one time or another during the period and none of them had been disposed of at the end. Inflation never ceased: it reached a peak of over 20 per cent in the mid-1970s and in 1979–80 but, even when it was at its lowest, inflationary impulses were still at work. In the inter-war years there had been periods of falling prices and little net change in twenty years. After 1945 there was no year in which consumer prices fell; and in the best five-year period, 1957–61, the average annual increase in retail prices was 2.3 per cent – enough to halve the value of money in thirty years. With unemployment, experience was even more disconcerting. For a generation the problem appeared to have vanished. Except in bad weather unemployment never exceeded 600,000 before 1970. But after 1970 it was never as low except briefly in the boom of 1973–4. By the 1980s, unemployment was at levels never seen since the 1930s and in each successive boom from the middle 1960s onwards it ceased to fall at a progressively higher turning-point. Employment had at first been only too full, and the economy was overloaded. But by the end of the period the very idea of full employment seemed illusory and even Keynes' view that 5 per cent was a reasonable level to aim for would have seemed highly optimistic.

The balance of payments problem, too, persisted but took a different shape. In 1945 it had been a question of rebuilding exports and shouldering debts. When that problem was disposed of, there had been a need to face keener competition as war-ravaged countries like Germany and Japan re-entered world markets, to remain competitive in spite of wage inflation and managerial limitations, and to change the pattern of British trade so as to enlarge the share of exports going to the highly competitive markets of North America and Europe. These adjustments were not made easily or without a prolonged decline in the value of sterling. When they were in progress the exploitation of North Sea oil provided easement for a decade. But by 1990 the balance of payments problem had returned in the form of a large deficit and the supply of North Sea oil had passed its peak.

This coincided with a movement of opinion in favour of a European central bank and a common currency. It might seem that under these conditions balance of payments difficulties would disappear. As we learned long ago, however, what makes balance of payments difficulties disappear when exchange rates cannot be altered is a general impoverishment and rising unemployment. It remains to be seen whether the problem yields in the 1990s to improved competitive power or whether it imposes additional constraints on employment and economic expansion.

4 Success and failure: British economic growth since 1948

Charles Feinstein

Introduction

Britain's economic performance since the Second World War falls broadly into two main phases, the first of which was considerably more successful than the second. In the 'golden age' from 1951 until 1973 both real output and output per worker increased at an appreciably more rapid pace than anything previously achieved since at least the mid-nineteenth century, perhaps earlier. This period was also notable for two other much-desired features: a remarkably low level of unemployment and a very modest rate of increase in both prices and money wages. Only the balance of payments position was consistently unsatisfactory. Even though there was generally a surplus on current account it was too small and too uncertain to prevent recurrent crises over fears that sterling would be devalued, as it finally was in 1967.

In the subsequent period, from 1973 until 1988, there was a significant deterioration in macro-economic performance. Real output and productivity grew more slowly, there was a steep rise in unemployment, and an acceleration in the rate of increase of prices and wages. The balance of payments worsened, and from 1973 to 1979 there was a deficit on current account. There was then a brief respite while the benefits of North Sea oil and gas provided a large boost which restored the balance of payments surplus. By the end of the 1980s this windfall gain was largely exhausted, and the current account moved back into deficit. 1988 is taken as the end of the final phase because it is the most recent year in which the economy was close to full capacity, and it is thus broadly comparable with earlier cyclical peaks. Since then the country has been in prolonged and deep recession.

Given this contrast between the two phases, it might be expected that the early post-war decades would be seen as a time of proud achievement, and that criticism would focus on the years after 1973. In fact the reverse has more often been true, and a common note in recent commentaries on the twenty-five years after 1948 has been one of criticism and recrimination. It

95

was predictable that the Thatcher administration should have actively disparaged the record of past governments, Conservative included, in order first to strengthen the case for its own policy innovations, and then to claim greater success for their results. But adverse comment on the earlier decades was frequently expressed before this by writers of very different economic and political persuasion. To take one example, the substantial survey of economic policy by the National Institute of Economic and Social Research began its appraisal of the period 1960 to 1974 by stating: 'It is generally accepted that the performance of the British economy during this period was relatively poor as measured by the standard criteria normally used for assessing economic success or failure' (Blackaby 1978: 619).

The principal reason for this pessimistic assessment of the early post-war decades is clear. Even though Britain achieved a marked improvement by her own historical standards, her main competitors made even greater progress. During the 'long boom' that lasted from the end of the Second World War until the early 1970s, almost all Britain's rivals attained even higher rates of growth of output and productivity, and most also enjoyed high levels of employment and low rates of increase in prices and wages. When the war ended Britain was regarded as a major world power, second only to the United States in measures of economic superiority such as income and consumption per head of population, or output per worker. However, in the course of the 1950s and 1960s the faster growth of her rivals, notably in western Europe and Japan, enabled them to close the gap, and a growing number of countries moved ahead. This sense of being surpassed and overtaken inevitably generated strong feelings of dis-satisfaction among British policy makers, politicians and the public.

The first objective of this chapter is to provide a broad overview of these aspects of Britain's economic performance in successive post-war periods. This is done in the following section, which amplifies these introductory remarks by summarising the main features of the historical record. The two main post-war periods are set in context by comparison both with each other and with earlier periods. Where appropriate, shorter cycles and sub-phases are also examined.

The chapter's second objective is to suggest possible explanations for three of the dominant questions posed by Britain's record of economic growth in the post-war period. First, what were the major factors which made possible Britain's improvement in the golden age by comparison with earlier periods? Secondly, what is the explanation for the deterioration in Britain's performance after 1973? Finally, why were most other advanced countries able to do so much better than Britain during the golden age?

The post-war period in historical perspective

The assessment of British economic performance since the war begins by examining a number of the individual criteria by which it might be judged. It is important to remember that these should not be viewed in isolation. There are critical links between different criteria, both as a result of market forces (for example, between the level of domestic activity and movements in prices and wages determined in the private sector) and also because of the impact of government policies. Different policy objectives may not be mutually consistent, so that, for example, policies designed to curb inflation may have adverse side effects on the growth of output and productivity. Some of these possible interconnections are taken up in the discussion of explanations for the observed trends later in the chapter.

Output, productivity, and consumption

The most general measure of economic performance is the growth of output. Material goods and services are wanted for private consumption, for investment in machinery and other capital assets, for public services (such as health and education), for military and other spending by the government, and for exports. The ability of an economy to satisfy these ever-expanding demands is an important index of its progress. However, additional output can almost always be produced simply by using more inputs, and it is also necessary to evaluate the efficiency with which inputs are utilised. For this purpose it is desirable to examine the trends in an appropriate measure of productivity, and labour productivity (output per worker) provides a widely accepted measure of economic efficiency.

Estimates for these two series are given in Table 4.1 for various periods from 1856 to 1988. The figures in columns (1) and (3) are for the whole economy (as measured by GDP), and those in columns (2) and (4) for the manufacturing sector. Each period begins and ends with a cyclical peak, and thus growth is measured between broadly comparable years.

The first column of Table 4.1 shows that in the initial post-war period, 1951–73, the economy was expanding at a rate of 3 per cent per annum. This is significantly more rapid than the rate of just under 2 per cent per annum previously achieved in the late Victorian and Edwardian period from 1856 to 1913, and again in the inter-war years. It is also more rapid than the subsequent period from 1973 to 1988, when overall growth fell back to its pre-Second World War norm of about 2 per cent per annum. For manufacturing output (column 2) the initial post-war growth rate was also about 3 per cent per annum. Again this was more rapid than the pre-1913 rate, but about the same as the rate in the inter-war period, indicating

Table 4.1. *Growth of output and productivity, 1856–1988 (annual percentage growth rates)*

	Output GDP Manufacturing		Output per worker GDP Manufacturing	
	(1)	(2)	(3)	(4)
Main peacetime phases				
1856–82	1·9	2·5	1·1	1·6
1882–1913	1·8	1·9	0·8	1·0
1924–37	2·3	3·3	1·1	2·2
1951–73	3·0	3·1	2·7	3·0
1973–88	1·9	0·2	1·7	2·8
Post-war sub-phases				
1951–64	3·0	3·2	2·5	2·5
1964–73	3·0	3·0	3·0	3·8
1973–9	1·5	−0·7	1·3	0·7
1979–88	2·1	0·8	2·0	4·2

Sources: Feinstein (1972); *Economic Trends Annual Supplement* 1992.

that the improvement in overall growth shown in column (1) was the result of an acceleration in the growth of other sectors, notably services. After 1973, however, the manufacturing sector collapsed dramatically, and although there was some recovery in the 1980s, output in 1988 was virtually the same as it had been in 1973. On this first criterion of the rate of expansion of output, the comparative success of the performance in 1951–73 is thus very striking.

It should also be noted that growth in this period was not only more rapid, it was also more stable. The amplitude of cyclical fluctuations in output and exports was milder than in earlier periods, particularly if comparison is made with the exceptionally disturbed period between the wars. In the post-war years economists debated whether the business cycle was obsolete; and periods of recession were those when there was a slowdown in the rate of growth of output, not – as in the past – an actual fall.

Turning to the second criterion, GDP per worker, given in column (3) of Table 4.1, the standard achieved in 1951–73 exceeds that in earlier periods by an even larger margin than for output. It is also notable that there was an improvement within this period, from 2.5 per cent per annum in 1951–64 to 3 per cent in 1964–73. After 1973 productivity growth dropped back to 1.7 per cent per annum, with an especially poor performance from

Table 4.2. *Growth of personal consumption, 1856–1988 (annual percentage growth rates)*

	Consumption	
	Total (1)	Per head (2)
Main peacetime phases		
1856–82	2·2	1·3
1882–1913	1·7	0·9
1924–37	1·9	1·5
1951–73	3·0	2·4
1973–88	2·5	2·4
Post-war sub-phases		
1951–64	3·0	2·4
1964–73	3·0	2·5
1973–9	1·3	1·3
1979–88	3·3	3·1

Sources: Feinstein (1972); *Economic Trends Annual Supplement* 1992.

1973 to 1979. There was some recovery during the final period 1979 to 1988, but the peak growth rates of the initial post-war period were not regained.

The record for productivity in the manufacturing sector is very similar. In the main phases shown in the upper panel of Table 4.1 the period 1951–73 again holds the record, but in this case the margin of superiority over the following period is very slight. This reflects the exceptional character of the final sub-phase, 1979–88, shown in the lower panel. Output was expanding in these years, although only very slowly, but there was a dramatic collapse in manufacturing employment, and a consequent acceleration in productivity growth to record levels.

The ultimate purpose of economic growth may be regarded as the supply of goods and services for personal consumption. For this reason the previous indicators are supplemented in Table 4.2 by corresponding estimates of the volume of personal consumption, in total and per head of the population. Here again the most notable feature is the extent to which improvements in the post-war years have outpaced those in earlier periods. For consumption per head, the average annual growth rate since 1951 has been 2.4 per cent, compared with a much slower pace of 1.5 per cent in the inter-war period and even lower rates of improvement prior to 1913. This improvement reflects both the more rapid growth of the total supply of goods and services available for consumption, and a slowing down in the rate of increase in population.

The rate of growth of total consumption slipped back after 1973, from 3.0 to 2.5 per cent per annum (column (1)), but because the growth of population also declined by 0.5 percentage points there was no reduction in the growth of per capita consumption. It will, however, be noted that in the final part of this period, 1979–88, consumption increased at 3.3 per cent per annum whereas the corresponding expansion of GDP shown in Table 4.1 was only 2.1 per cent. This disparity was only possible because imports of goods and services increased much more rapidly than exports, taking the balance of payments on current account from a modest surplus in 1980 to an exceptionally large deficit in 1988. Deficits on this scale could only be sustained as long as foreigners were prepared to finance them by acquiring British assets, and could not be regarded as a secure platform for long-run economic prosperity.

Unemployment and inflation

In 1944 the wartime coalition government published its famous pledge accepting responsibility for 'the maintenance of a high and stable level of employment after the war' (UK 1944). The success with which both Labour and Conservative governments for a time achieved this objective is evident in Table 4.3. For more than two decades from 1952 to 1973 the average number out of work was as low as 460,000, less than 2 per cent of the total workforce. The data for this period are not exactly comparable with those for earlier or later periods, but the contrasts are so great that these minor statistical discrepancies can be safely ignored. Both in the inter-war years and after 1973 the number of men and women unable to find work averaged over 2 million, about four times as large as in the golden age. In the 1980s unemployment soared even higher, to almost 3 million, over 10 per cent of the workforce. The superior accomplishment of the 1950s and 1960s is thus overwhelming.

The next aspect of policy and performance to be considered is inflation. It is measured here by the rate of change of prices and earnings (see columns (1) and (2) of Table 4.4). Before the Second World War prices show no appreciable long-run change, either over the pre-1913 period as a whole, or over the inter-war years. Money earnings crept forwards at about 1 per cent per annum before 1913, and were broadly steady between 1924 and 1937. In the post-war period this degree of long-term stability proved no longer to be attainable, and inflation came increasingly to be seen as a major source of anxiety. The rate of increase of prices accelerated to 4.6 per cent per annum in 1951–73, and the corresponding figure for

Table 4.3. *Unemployment, 1857–1988[a]*

	Average number (000s) (1)	Per cent of total labour force (2)
Main peacetime phases		
1857–82	540	3·9
1883–1913	840	4·8
1925–37	2,210	10·3
1952–73	460	1·8
1974–88	2,150	7·9
Post-war sub-phases		
1952–64	380	1·5
1965–73	580	2·3
1974–9	1,150	4·4
1980–8	2,810	10·3

[a] The figures are averages over the cycles, beginning in the first year after the peak and ending at the peak.
Sources: Feinstein (1972); *Economic Trends Annual Supplement* 1992.

earnings was 7.5 per cent. This was cause for serious concern by the standards of the past, although it may be regarded as relatively satisfactory in comparison with what was to follow.

As the lower panel of Table 4.4 shows, the rate of increase of both prices and earnings was falling between 1951–5 and 1960–4. The break in trend came at the end of the 1960s, and for 1968–73 the average annual rate of increase shot up to 8 per cent for prices and over 11 per cent for earnings. In 1973–9 these rates accelerated even faster, to around 16 per cent per annum. The inflationary pressures were subsequently curbed to some degree, but the average rate of increase for 1979–88 was still over 7 per cent per annum for prices and 10 per cent for wages. By the 1970s inflation had seemingly become endemic in the British economy, and this development was to have major consequences both for the future conduct of economic policy – notably with respect to the desired level of activity and employment – and for economic performance.

The balance of payments

The final aspect of macro-economic performance that figured prominently in the concerns of post-war policy makers and commentators was the balance of payments on current account. The aim of policy was to achieve a sufficient surplus to enable the authorities both to build up Britain's

Table 4.4. *Growth of prices and earnings, 1856–1988 (annual percentage growth rates)*

	Gross domestic product prices (1)	Average weekly earnings[a] (2)
Main peacetime phases		
1856–82	−0·1	1·0
1882–1913	0·3	0·9
1924–37	−0·6	0·2
1951–73	4·6	7·5
1973–88	10·6	12·4
Post-war cycles		
1951–5	4·2	7·5
1955–60	3·5	5·4
1960–4	3·1	5·2
1964–8	3·5	6·3
1968–73	8·1	11·4
1973–9	15·9	16·1
1979–88	7·3	10·0

[a] Before 1963 covers only manual workers in selected industries; after 1963 covers all employees.
Sources: Feinstein (1972); *Economic Trends Annual Supplement* 1992; Department of Employment, *Gazette*.

meagre reserves of gold and foreign currency, and to cover a limited outflow of foreign investment. In practice this proved not to be possible for most of the period. The historical picture is given by Table 4.5. The respective contributions in successive periods of visible trade, services and transfers, and net property income from abroad are shown in columns (1) to (3), and the sum of these items, the net balance on current account (also equivalent to net foreign investment), is given in column (4). All the estimates are shown as percentages of GDP to eliminate the effect of changing price levels.

The pre-1913 years show a persistently large current account surplus, equivalent to about 5 per cent of GDP. This surplus both made possible, and was sustained by, the high level of capital export which was such a marked feature of Britain's international economic relations in this period. In the 1920s the current account surplus was reduced to only 2 per cent of GDP, and by the 1930s it was in deficit.

The position was somewhat better after the Second World War, with a sufficient improvement in the balance of visible trade to compensate for a

Table 4.5. *Ratio of the balance of payments on current account to GDP, 1855–1988 (average of annual percentages)*

	Goods (net) (1)	Services and transfers (net) (2)	Income from abroad (net) (3)	Balance on current account (4)
Main peacetime phases				
1855–73	−3·0	4·7	2·8	4·5
1874–90	−5·5	5·1	5·4	5·0
1891–1913	−6·1	4·3	6·8	5·0
1921–9	−5·1	2·2	5·1	2·2
1930–8	−6·0	0·9	4·2	−0·9
1952–64	−0·9	0·2	1·3	0·6
1965–73	−1·0	0·6	1·3	0·9
1974–9	−3·1	1·1	0·9	−1·1
1980–8	−1·4	0·9	1·0	0·5

Sources: Matthews *et al.* (1982); *Economic Trends Annual Supplement* 1992.

sharp fall in interest, profits and dividends from abroad. As a result, the current account was in surplus for most of the post-war period, but the performance was nevertheless unsatisfactory in two key respects. First, the average surplus was very small, and was generally too low to meet the requirements noted above. Secondly, and more crucially, it was not sustained over the course of the business cycle. Typically, the current account was in surplus only when the economy was operating at a low level of activity relative to its potential. As soon as the economy moved closer towards full utilisation of its capacity, the current account moved towards deficit, as additional imports were sucked in and exports were diverted to supply the booming home market.

The recurrent fear of actual and prospective deficits, together with speculation against the pound triggered by other factors, meant that there were repeated sterling crises, during which the currency was sold heavily by foreign holders and – if they could – by British residents. Until the move to a system of floating exchange rates in the early 1970s the value of the pound was fixed in accordance with the procedures agreed at Bretton Woods, with a rate against the dollar of $2.80 held from the devaluation of 1949 until 1967. With a fixed rate, the authorities were forced to respond to these attacks on sterling in other ways. They did so partly by seeking temporary relief in the form of loans from the International Monetary Fund and foreign banks, partly by reining back the level of domestic activity. This latter policy was designed to relieve the pressure on the balance of payments by reducing imports and encouraging exports, and was the basis of the infamous stop–go cycles. It is sometimes suggested that these cycles were responsible for Britain's inability to grow as rapidly as her competitors, but – as argued in the final section below – it would be more accurate to see the slower growth of productivity as the source of the underlying weakness in Britain's balance of payments position. The stop–go cycles were the result, not the cause, of relatively poor economic performance.

The golden age, 1951–73

1951 to 1973 has been described as a 'golden age' because during these years the world economy enjoyed a period of exceptional growth and prosperity. Both the developed countries of the OECD and the developing nations of the Third World shared in, and contributed to, an unprecedented expansion in output and trade. As has been shown, Britain also participated in this long boom with a dramatic improvement in performance by her own historical standards. What made this possible?

To answer this question it is helpful to distinguish three sets of determinants. First, the supply of the primary factors of production, labour and capital. These exercise a strong influence on the growth of output both directly, as the proximate sources of growth; and indirectly, through their impact on productivity. Secondly, it is necessary to consider the demand-side effects, and in particular the exogenous influences on demand stemming from Britain's international economic transactions. Thirdly, there are exogenous influences on the trends in productivity, such as technological innovations, and these constitute an independent contribution to the growth of output. The full story is inevitably more complex than this simple listing of separate factors indicates. In particular, there are important links running in both directions between each of the three sets of determinants, and between them and the growth of output and productivity. To take one example, additions to the stock of capital affect both demand and output, and both of these in turn affect investment in new capital.

Inputs of labour and capital

To take labour first, the data show that between 1951 and 1973 the supply measured in person-hours was actually declining, not expanding. A variety of factors were responsible for this, the most important of which was the progressive reduction in the length of the actual working week for those in full-time employment, from an average of 45.6 hours in 1951 to 41.4 in

1973 (Matthews *et al.* 1982: 566). Given the choice, it appeared that British workers preferred more leisure to higher incomes. This was reinforced by a rise in the extent of part-time work, particularly among women. With a steady extension of entitlement to paid holidays, there was also a downward trend in the number of weeks worked per year.

Did this decline in the supply of labour represent a constraint on economic growth? If one could assume that output per worker was unaffected by the scarcity of labour, then it would seem plausible to conclude that growth was restricted by shortages of labour in this era of full employment. The implicit counter-factual proposition – that Britain could have grown more rapidly if there had been a more elastic supply of labour – gains support from the fact that this was the case in other countries which enjoyed more rapid growth in this period (Kindleberger 1967).

It may, however, be inappropriate to assume that scarcity of labour had no impact on productivity. It is more probable that labour scarcity would have encouraged firms to raise their investment in fixed assets in order to substitute capital for labour, and this would have had a beneficial influence on productivity. In addition, though this was almost certainly a much weaker tendency, if labour scarcity helped to enhance actual and perceived job security, there may have been some diminution in traditional forms of resistance to productivity growth exercised by trade unions and workers anxious to protect employment in the face of technological innovations. On balance, it is likely that these productivity offsets would have been insufficient to compensate for the constraining effects of the diminishing supply of labour. The conclusion, therefore, is that Britain was able to raise its performance in this period despite this limitation.

The second factor of production to be considered is capital. The expansion of the stock of capital was indeed exceptionally vigorous over this period. In particular, there was an impressive spurt in capital accumulation in industry and commerce. In this critical sector the annual average rate of growth of fixed capital accelerated from little more than 1 per cent in the inter-war period to 4 per cent in 1951–73. There was a much smaller advance in the growth of capital for utilities, transport and social services; and for dwellings the post-war rate actually fell below the pace achieved during the housing boom of the inter-war period (Matthews *et al.* 1982: 332). The overall result for total domestic fixed capital was a post-war rate of increase of over 3 per cent per annum, compared to the previous long-term rate of about 2 per cent.

The very rapid post-war advance in the stock of industrial and commercial capital can be attributed to three main factors: the greater degree of business confidence engendered by the expectation of continued full employment; the more rapid growth of output and the consequent necessity for greater additions to capacity; and the need – noted above – to compensate for the shortage of labour. These forces were reinforced by favourable tax concessions for manufacturing investment.

This historically high rate of capital formation made an important contribution to economic growth through two distinct mechanisms. First, there was the direct effect of the expansion of productive capacity, and the cumulative benefits of the incorporation of the latest technical advances in the new capital, particularly in the industrial and commercial sector. Secondly, there was the Keynesian effect of a powerful boost to demand created by the role of capital formation as a component of aggregate demand. The resulting high level of demand in turn served as an indirect stimulus to the growth of productivity. Before looking more closely at this aspect of the growth process it is necessary to consider other possible influences on the level and growth of demand.

Demand: government policy and international transactions

Demand for the goods and services a country can supply plays a vital role in determining the pace and character of its economic growth. Two aspects are especially relevant. One is the *rate of growth* of demand. This will be important if, as some economists have suggested (see especially Kaldor 1966), the rate of growth of productivity in the crucial manufacturing sector is directly dependent on the rate of growth of output. This relationship, also known as Verdoorn's Law, postulates the existence of dynamic economies of scale. In theory, these could arise if, for example, rapid expansion of demand encouraged faster introduction of the most modern technology; or, if it encouraged management and labour to act in ways more favourable to faster productivity growth.

In fact, however, although such connections appear plausible in abstract, they do not help to explain the post-war performance in Britain. There was a marked acceleration in the rate of growth of productivity in 1951–73 even though the rate of growth of manufacturing output was no higher than in the inter-war period (compare columns (1) and (3) of Table 4.1). As the same table shows, there was also a sharp improvement in the rate of increase of productivity in manufacturing between the two parts of the post-war period, 1951–64 and 1964–73, without any corresponding acceleration in output. (Outside the golden age the relationship again fails in 1979–88 when record productivity growth occurred together with particularly slow growth of output.)

The other demand-side influence on productivity growth which needs to be considered is the *level* of actual demand relative to the potential productive capacity of the economy. As was seen above (Table 4.3), the long boom from 1951 to 1973 was characterised by the achievement of full employment, and thus by a uniquely high level of demand. This helped to increase business confidence, and so promoted higher levels of investment and more rapid growth of output and productivity than in previous periods. It is also probable that high demand stimulated productivity growth in other ways, for example by creating more openings for new entrepreneurs, and by creating a favourable environment for the introduction of much-needed changes in workshop practices. It may also have had some unfavourable effects if, for example (as argued by Paish 1970), it created a 'soft' environment in which inefficient firms and lazy workers could survive. However, the evidence suggests that, on balance, the effects of high demand during the long boom were beneficial and help to explain the acceleration in the growth of productivity.

It remains to examine the sources of this high level of demand relative to productive capacity. To a large extent it was determined by forces internal to the economy ('supply creates its own demand'), and analysis of the underlying causes leads back to other determinants of economic growth, in particular the high level of capital accumulation described earlier. It is, however, necessary to consider the specific impact of the government policy of demand management. In addition, independent external forces play a part in shaping demand, and these are especially significant for an economy like Britain's in which there are numerous and substantial transactions with the rest of the world on both current and capital account.

Throughout the golden age, British governments were actively engaged in demand management and it might be thought that these policies made a significant contribution to the high level of demand. They probably were important, but only indirectly. To the extent that awareness of, and belief in, the commitment to full employment helped to sustain business confidence, this strengthened the willingness to invest which has already been identified as an important factor. However, the government did not make a more direct contribution to the level of demand by spending more than it was raising in taxation. It is true that fiscal adjustments, intended to raise or lower the pressure of demand, were made with great regularity. But these always took the form of increasing or reducing the size of the government's surplus; at no stage did the budget actually move into deficit. Throughout this period there was always a substantial positive level of net government savings, and thus fiscal policy was probably always to some degree deflationary (Matthews *et al.* 1982: 140–1 and 309–13).

Turning to the post-war external position, there are two conflicting features which must be emphasised, one positive, the other negative. The positive forces helped Britain's exports of goods and services to grow more rapidly than at any time since the mid-nineteenth century. The average annual rate of growth was 4.3 per cent for 1951–73, compared to 3.6 per cent in 1856–73 and 2.6 per cent in 1873–1913. During the Great Depression of the inter-war period the volume of British exports had actually declined, so that the contrast with the immediately preceding period is even more striking. However, this post-war acceleration in exports was insufficient to prevent Britain's share of world exports of manufactures from declining continuously. It had been 22 per cent in 1937, and was indeed almost 25 per cent in 1950, when Germany and other potential competitors had not yet fully recovered from the disasters of the war. But by 1964 Britain's share had been reduced to 14 per cent, and by 1973 it was a mere 9 per cent. The positive effect of rapidly increasing exports is relevant to our present concern with the success achieved by Britain in the golden age. The negative aspects will be considered in the final section of the chapter, in the context of Britain's inability to match the performance of her competitors.

The foundation for this exceptionally rapid growth of British exports was the unusual buoyancy of world demand during the post-war golden age. This world boom was itself a result of several factors. These included the stabilising and liberalising effects of the international monetary system formulated at Bretton Woods; the encouragement to increased trade fostered by the reduction in tariff barriers under the auspices of GATT; and the enormous initial boost to growth during the recovery from the devastation and destruction of the Second World War. Exogenous world forces thus served to raise the level of demand in Britain by comparison with almost all earlier periods. This complemented and reinforced the domestic factors that were encouraging high rates of capital accumulation.

Productivity

Finally, there are two factors to be analysed which might have influenced the rate of growth of productivity, independently of the growth of labour and capital, and of the state of demand. The first is the impact of new technology. This is not easily measured, but it seems clear that, during this post-war period, Britain was able to take advantage of a substantial backlog of innovations – for example, in electricity supply, motor vehicles and steel making. These had emerged earlier in the century, mainly abroad, but for various reasons had not been fully exploited by Britain. Britain had ceased to hold the technological leadership of the world by the end of the nineteenth century, and the United States opened up a progressively larger productivity gap. This created tremendous possibilities for Britain to benefit from American progress in the form not only of innovative equipment and new products, but also of a wide variety of economic and social practices and institutions. The managerial structure of the large multi-divisional corporation is one such example which has received much emphasis (Chandler 1990). Little progress was made in the difficult circumstances of the inter-war period, but after the Second World War Britain was able to draw on this large pool of advanced technology and practice, and thus to boost productivity growth to a significant extent.

In addition, the pace of technological advance during and after the Second World War was exceptionally rapid and, as more countries joined the United States on the innovation frontier, the scope for borrowing from abroad increased still further. Sectors in which there were outstanding technological developments during this period included electrical engineering, electronics, aircraft production, synthetic chemicals and pharmaceuticals.

The second aspect to be considered in relation to productivity growth is the attitude of labour and the quality of management. There is no doubt that, in both respects, British performance left a great deal to be desired. Nevertheless, there does seem to be some indication that matters improved, at least to a modest degree. In particular, the post-war period saw increased efforts to extend educational openings, to recruit more professional management and to expand the role of the large modern corporation at the expense of small family firms.

To sum up, four principal factors have been identified to explain Britain's improved performance in 1951–73 relative to her own historical standards. These were inter-related in a cumulatively advantageous process. First, there was an historically high level of capital accumulation. This was both encouraged by, and itself contributed to, a high level of demand, and confidence that full employment would be sustained. Investment also generated a favourable cumulative interaction on the supply side. Increased capital formation added to productive capacity and so permitted more rapid growth of output; this expansion of output in turn called forth higher levels of capital accumulation.

Secondly, there was an exceptionally vigorous and persistent boom in world trade, and this enabled British exports to increase at an unusually rapid rate. This reinforced the high level of demand, and encouraged still higher levels of capital investment. Thirdly, the high level of demand created an economic climate which was, on balance, favourable to the rapid growth of productivity, independently of the increased supplies of capital. Finally, Britain was able to raise the technological level of her industry in terms of both equipment and products, and to improve her socio-economic institutions and practices, by borrowing on a large scale from more advanced countries, notably the United States.

The deterioration in performance after 1973

In terms of output and productivity growth the deterioration in Britain's economic performance occurred only after the exceptionally strong cyclical upswing which ended in 1973. But the underlying problems were evident well before then.

From price stability to inflation

The root of the trouble lay in the behaviour of prices and wages. As noted in the first part of the chapter, the rate of increase had been relatively restrained in the initial post-war period, and the trend was actually downwards over successive cycles until 1964 (see the lower panel of Table 4.4). But this pattern was reversed in the following cycle, and in 1968–73, when inflation broke through to new rates, the stability of the earlier period was fatally undermined.

The reasons for this are complex and controversial. One school of thought emphasised sociological and political factors which gave rise to more militant pressure from workers for higher wages. Their basic argument was that it was not until the mid-1960s that workers and their unions finally appreciated the increase in their bargaining power which full employment generated. Full realisation of their strength was delayed for so long because memories of the mass unemployment of the inter-war years were still powerful, and because working-class organisations were for many years reluctant to accept that capitalism was actually capable of providing sustained full employment. Gradually, however, there was a change in the generational composition of the working class and in their perception of their own strength. A significant argument in favour of this explanation is that the phenomenon was not confined to the United Kingdom. The 1960s witnessed similar wages explosions in many parts of the world, including such stalwarts of anti-inflation psychology as Germany and Switzerland, with the dramatic events of 1968 in France particularly prominent. This explanation for the genesis of the inflationary process is a prime example of what is sometimes referred to as 'cost-push' inflation. It is also distinguished by its emphasis on the historical discontinuity represented by the explosive character of the late 1960s pressure for higher wages (Goldthorpe and Hirsch 1978; Brown 1983: 155–61).

Supporters of the alternative hypothesis were dismissive of several aspects of this explanation. In their view economic forces were sufficient to explain what occurred. They were uncomfortable with abrupt disconti-nuities. They derided the notion that workers (or any other utility-maximising agents) could fail for almost two decades to take advantage of the bargaining opportunities available to them in a situation of full employment. Above all, the monetarists among them rejected the very idea of cost-push inflation, and held that the causes of inflation must always lie on the demand side, with either domestic or international conditions responsible for creating a situation of excess demand (Parkin and Sumner 1978).

Since government policies in the late 1960s were clearly deflationary, and unemployment was rising, it could not be argued that there was actually excess demand in Britain at the time of the initial explosion of prices and wages. In January 1968 the Chancellor, Roy Jenkins, had imposed a substantial cut in government expenditure, and followed this a few months later with what was 'perhaps the most formidable deflationary budget since the war' (Blackaby 1978: 46). These measures were designed to make room for the increase in exports expected to flow from the devaluation of November 1967. Interest rates were also raised, so that monetary policy was similarly deflationary at the critical time. In the world economy, liquidity was also extremely tight in these years. The principal subject of discussion in international monetary affairs was not excessive money supply and excess demand, but rather the debate inspired by Triffin's (1957) demonstration of the urgent need for policies to overcome an acute shortage of dollars.

More sophisticated exponents of the excess demand hypothesis have accepted this characterisation of the late 1960s. Their proposition was that demand-pull pressures had been building up for a number of years prior to this, because the authorities had attempted for socio-political motives to run the economy at a higher level of demand than was justified by the available productive capacity. As long as exchange rates remained fixed, this pressure could not be fully expressed in the movement of prices because firms could not afford to increase the price of tradable goods and services. Hence on this view it was the accumulated pressures of the early 1960s, before the deflationary turn in policy, which eventually forced the devaluation of 1967 and which were the true origins of the subsequent inflation (Ball and Burns 1976).

Although supporters of this view cannot accept the idea of a delayed response to full employment, they do suggest that there was a significant change during the 1960s in perceptions with respect to *expectations* of the future course of inflation. This was reflected in the capital market in the emergence in the mid-1960s of the 'reverse yield gap'. In normal circumstances the yield on ordinary shares exceeds that on gilt-edged securities because the former asset involves a greater degree of risk. However, once the capital market recognises the presence of inflation it requires a higher yield on gilts to compensate for the absence of any allowance for inflation in a fixed-interest security. A similar perception of inflation can be seen in the property market, in the belated move from fixed rents to leases with provision for periodic rent reviews. The last and most serious manifestation was in the labour market. As recognition of the pace of inflation developed, union negotiators understood that it was no longer adequate to bargain for an increase in money wages without regard to actual and prospective increases in prices. This allowance for *anticipated* inflation was increasingly built into wage demands, and as long as this prevailed it ensured the perpetuation of the inflationary process.

The socio-political and the economic factors are not mutually exclusive, and although their protagonists tended to see them as alternatives, it is possible that both forces contributed to the emergence of the inflationary situation. Whatever the initial cause, the explanation for subsequent developments is clear enough. A price-wage-price spiral ensued, and the situation was greatly exacerbated in the early 1970s by two further developments. The most obvious was the external shock of the first OPEC increase: the abrupt fourfold rise in oil prices in 1973. Greatly increased energy costs quickly fed through into higher prices for all goods and services, contributing strongly to the development of inflation in all industrialised countries. Its effect was still further amplified in Britain. At precisely the time when the impact of the oil shock was working through, Edward Heath's Conservative government had the misfortune to introduce an incomes policy under which wages would be permitted to rise in strict proportion to increases in the cost of living above a specified threshold. This built a strong cumulative effect into the inflationary spiral.

In 1968–73 GDP prices rose at over 8 per cent per annum, and this accelerated to 16 per cent per annum in 1973–9, including an alarming leap of 28 per cent in 1975. What made matters even worse was that this was accompanied by a slowdown in growth and a steep rise in unemployment (Tables 4.1 and 4.3). The traditional post-war concept of a trade-off between inflation and unemployment had broken down, and the ugly term 'stagflation' was coined to describe the new and unfortunate situation in which Britain now languished. It was little consolation that she was by no means alone in this predicament. For the major industrialised countries, GDP growth rates in 1973–9 were only half what they had been in the golden age; and there was a similar collapse to half the previous rate in productivity growth and in the volume of exports. In unhappy contrast, inflation accelerated from 4 to 10 per cent per annum, and the percentage of the labour force unemployed also rose sharply (Maddison 1991: 170–1).

These new tendencies reinforced each other, dragging the economies progressively further from the favourable conditions of the golden age. In particular, the downward trend in productivity limited the ability to provide increases in real wages at a time when workers' aspirations for more rapid gains were growing stronger. The potential conflict which this created could be resolved in two ways, neither satisfactory. One was to evade the issue by granting still higher increases in nominal wages, but in the end this simply aggravated the inflationary conditions. The other was to resist the process by introducing deflationary policies designed to reduce the pressure in the labour market. Although this might in the end curb inflation, it could only do so at the cost of slower growth and higher unemployment. Slower productivity growth also reduced profitability and discouraged investment, thus further weakening both demand and expansion of productive capacity.

The end of demand management

This deterioration in the state of the economy then interacted with, and was reinforced by, two emerging strands in economic analysis. Just as support for Keynes' analysis of the 1930s was strengthened by the prevailing conditions of mass unemployment, so in this period the appearance of stagflation added credibility to the criticisms of Keynesian-style demand management. On a theoretical level the rise of monetarism challenged the resort to fiscal policies as a means of stimulating real economic growth. On a more pragmatic level, increasing doubts were expressed about the practicalities of 'fine tuning'. The authorities, it was claimed, knew too little about either the true state of the economy or the effect of any actions they might take, and their intervention was at least as likely to be destabilising. The upshot was that confidence in the ability of government policy to sustain full employment was eroded just as the need for action to sustain a higher level of activity became more urgent.

The crucial break in policy occurred in 1975, while the Labour government was still in office. In April of that year the Chancellor, Denis Healey, acknowledged in his budget speech that unemployment was high and would probably continue to rise to a then unprecedented post-war level of around one million. He declared, nevertheless, that he did not intend to use the budget to reverse this trend:

the Budget judgment is conventionally seen as an estimation of the amount of demand which the Government should put into the economy or take out of it in order to achieve the optimum use of resources in the short term. For many reasons I do not propose to adopt that approach today ... I fully understand why I have been urged ... to treat unemployment as the central problem and to stimulate a further growth in home consumption ... so as to start getting the rate of unemployment down as fast as possible. I do not believe it would be wise to follow this advice today. (*Hansard*, vol. 890, 1975, col. 282)

With this decision the Chancellor broke with the essence of demand management as practised by all his predecessors since the war. This transformation was confirmed the following year when the Prime Minister, James Callaghan, made his famous remark to the Labour Party conference, repudiating previously held views that 'a nation could just spend its way out of recession ... by cutting taxes and boosting government spending' (*The Times*, 29 September 1976).

Subsequently, opposition to economic management was further strengthened by the rising political movement in favour of the free market, exemplified by Margaret Thatcher in Britain and Ronald Reagan in the United States. They claimed that government action to regulate the economy was both unnecessary and ineffectual; market economies were self-regulating and would operate most effectively with the minimum degree of intervention. With the election of the Conservative administration in 1979 the rejection of demand management in Britain was complete.

The end of the golden age

The combination of hostility to government intervention with stagflation in the real economy at home and abroad thus undermined the major props on which the success of the golden age had depended. Business confidence in the government's ability to sustain full employment was destroyed, and with it the basis for a high level of investment. The decline in the rate of growth of domestic fixed capital eroded the twin benefits that were earlier derived in the form of fast growth of productive capacity and a high level of demand.

The second major source of support for the golden age had been the buoyancy of world trade. This too was no longer sustained to the same extent. After 1973 the rate of growth of output declined sharply in all of Britain's major trading partners, and markets for British exports were seriously restricted. From 1979 the domestic policies of the new Conservative administration created still further difficulties for exporters. Seeking to give effect to their monetarist beliefs the government pursued a policy of tight money and high interest rates. This attracted foreign capital into Britain, and the value of the pound against the dollar appreciated by some 25 per cent: from $1.9 in 1978 to $2.4 in the second half of 1980. With the rise in the exchange rate to this level many manufacturers were simply unable to compete in export markets.

The golden age of rapid growth of output with full employment and (almost) stable prices was thus over. In its place came slower growth, rapidly rising prices and wages and a high level of unemployment. The nature of the underlying factors responsible for this transformation in both Britain and other developed countries is inevitably a controversial matter on which opinions differ. Numerous explanations have been mooted. One possibility, discussed more fully in the concluding section of this chapter, emphasises exhaustion of the scope for 'catch-up'. Others include diminishing returns to investment after the long boom; an exogenous decline in the pace of scientific and technological innovation; the damaging effects of the first and second OPEC oil-price shocks of 1973 and 1979; the breakdown of the international monetary arrangements sustained under American hegemony during the Bretton Woods era; a rise in the share of resources taken by the public sector; an irreversible shift in attitudes engendered by the success of past growth, for example in labour discipline and intensity of work under conditions of full employment; and the persistent adverse effects of the inflationary expectations discussed above, leading to a determination in many countries (especially during the 1980s those in the European Monetary System operating under the stern leadership of Germany), to 'squeeze inflation out of the system', whatever the cost in growth and unemployment (Denison 1980; Boltho 1982; Matthews 1982; Lindbeck 1983; Bruno and Sachs 1985; Englander and Mittlestaat 1988; Marglin and Schor 1990; Maddison 1991). Much more research is needed before the respective contributions of these and other factors to the slowdown can be adequately evaluated.

Britain's failure relative to her competitors

Two contradictory themes of the golden age have already been emphasised. On the one hand, Britain shared in its prosperity, and enjoyed an economic performance which was extremely good by her own historical standards. On the other, many of her competitors did considerably better. The steep decline in Britain's share of world exports (noted above) was a particularly vivid indicator of this competitive weakness. This left Britain with a deep sense of relative failure and of dissatisfaction with both economic performance and policy. The task of this final section is to analyse one possible explanation for this relative failure. In the light of the contrast between these two themes the question has to be posed as: 'Why did other countries do so well?', not 'Why did Britain do so badly?'

Vicious and virtuous circles

The relationship between Britain and her more successful rivals can usefully be set in the framework of the vicious (or virtuous) circles in export-led growth. As a result of slower productivity growth, Britain's prices and unit labour costs tended to rise more rapidly than those of her main competitors. This put Britain at a competitive disadvantage in international trade, reflected in a slower rate of growth of exports, and a rising propensity to import. The resulting trends had two important consequences. First, slower export growth and faster import growth translated directly into a slower rate of growth of output. Secondly, competitive weakness meant that Britain's trade was less profitable than that of her rivals.

Both these tendencies then further exacerbated Britain's relative weakness by acting as a constraint on the level and character of home investment. Slower growth of output reduced the need to increase capacity; lower profits reduced the funds with which new capital expenditure could be financed. (The go-slow policies adopted by the government in response to chronic balance of payments weakness may also have had some effect on domestic investment.) The vicious circle was thus completed. With more recent technological advances embodied in their larger and newer stocks of capital, the countries which were initially most successful strengthened their advantage. They were thus once again better placed to display superior productivity growth at the next round, and so to move still further ahead. Japan, Germany, France and Italy illustrate the growth achievement possible for those in the virtuous circle; Britain and the United States exemplify the problems of those unable to break out of the vicious circle.

This analysis helps to explain how more rapidly growing countries can sustain and even increase their advantage over a prolonged period. It does not, however, help to answer the crucial question of how the process got started. What initially allowed some countries to get into an orbit of cumulatively favourable expansion, while others found themselves hurtling round in a persistent cycle of inferior performance?

The list of explanations which has been advanced during the last forty years to explain Britain's failure to match her competitors is truly vast. It includes a divisive class system, an innate cultural hostility to industrialisation, the domination of government and industry by the financial interests of the City of London, lack of venture capital, excessive taxation, too much government spending, too little planning, insufficient expenditure on education and training, an adversarial two-party electoral system, restrictive labour practices and over-manning, incompetent managers and obstructive trade unions.

Some of these explanations seem more persuasive than others, but one strand of thought is common to all: there was something fundamentally wrong in the organisation and operation of Britain's economy and society. If only these flaws could be identified and eliminated, Britain would be able to race ahead in the company of the elite. The crucial assumption underlying all these diagnoses of Britain's deficiencies was that there was

Table 4.6. *Levels of GDP per worker, selected years, 1913–88*
(*level of USA at each date = 100*)

	1913 (1)	1948 (2)	1973 (3)	1988 (4)	1988 level (1948 = 100) (5)
USA	100	100	100	100	192
UK	78	61	66	76	242
Netherlands	69	52	78	79	292
Denmark	58	51	64	67	252
Sweden	43	51	69	74	277
Belgium	61	49	70	87	338
France	48	37	73	90	470
Germany	49	32	68	81	488
Italy	36	31	60	75	468
Japan	18	16	56	78	907

Source: Maddison (1991).

no *necessary* reason why output per worker should not have grown at 5 per cent or more in all countries, Britain included. Was this a valid assumption? The following section examines the case for believing that it was not; that, on the contrary, there was a fundamental difference between Britain and her rivals which no policy change could have eradicated.

Changing levels of economic development

There were two powerful forces operating to make the initial rate of growth more rapid in a number of other countries than it was *or could be* in Britain. The first was the greater scope for recovery from abnormally depressed levels at the end of the Second World War in those countries which had suffered most from wartime destruction and economic collapse. These wartime differences were superimposed on the second and more persistent factor, the historical disparities in level of economic development attained before the war.

A broad indication of the magnitude of these differences in 1948, and of their historical context, is given in Table 4.6 for ten of the major market economies. GDP per worker is taken as a proxy for the level of technological development, and the countries are listed in order of their standing in 1948 (shown in column 2). The level in each of the four given years is shown relative to that for the United States in that year. The consequence of the difference in wartime experience, superimposed on the pre-war position, is that by 1948 disparities between the nations were even greater than in 1913 (compare columns (1) and (2) of Table 4.6). In that year output per worker was 65 per cent higher in the USA than in UK; double that in the Netherlands, Sweden, Denmark and Belgium; roughly three times the level in France, Germany and Italy; and more than six times the Japanese level.

The post-war pattern of growth which flowed from this initial position is very striking: there is a remarkably strong inverse relationship between the initial level in 1948 and the pace of advance over the subsequent decades. The levels of GDP per worker achieved by the ten countries in 1973 and 1988 are shown in columns (3) and (4), and the extent of the growth between 1948 and 1988 is indicated in column (5).

The United States, starting with the highest level of output per worker, did not quite manage to double this in forty years (a miserable average growth rate of 1.6 per cent per annum). The United Kingdom, second in 1948, did only slightly better than this, with a growth rate of 2.2 per cent per annum. In contrast, Japan, starting in the most backward position, raised her standard almost ninefold (a vigorous 5.7 per cent per annum). All the other countries fall neatly into place between these extremes. The Netherlands, Denmark, Sweden and Belgium, ranked in the upper tier in 1948, achieve moderate increases in the range from 2.5 to 3.4 times the starting level (2.3 – 3.1 per cent per annum). In the lower tier France, Italy and Germany display far more vigorous expansion, rising almost fivefold (4 per cent per annum).

As a necessary consequence of this inverse relationship between levels and rates of growth there was a striking convergence towards the United States level of output per worker. By 1988 six of the other nine countries (including the United Kingdom) were bunched at 75–80 per cent of the United States level, Denmark was just below this, and France and Belgium had moved to about 90 per cent. In contrast to 1948 (or 1913) the differences both within the group of follower countries, and between them and the United States, were now comparatively modest.

Late starters and leaders

With this historical data as background, the explanation for the observed process of convergence can now be considered. The backwardness (or convergence) hypothesis linking initial levels and subsequent rates of growth is drawn from historical studies of the process of development (see, for example, Gerschenkron 1962; Abramovitz 1986; Maddison 1991). Obviously, backwardness does not automatically generate advance; modern economic growth cannot proceed until a backward country has managed to reach a certain minimum level of economic development, education, social cohesion, administrative efficiency and political stability. It is clear, however, that even the most backward countries covered in Table 4.6 had long since satisfied these basic criteria.

Latecomers who have advanced beyond the capability threshold have three powerful factors working to their advantage as they proceed to exploit the gap between their actual level of productivity and the potential level set for them by the superior achievement of the leading countries. These are (1) the effects of relative backwardness on attitudes and institutions; (2) the ability to borrow from the leaders; and (3) the possibility of transferring labour out of low-productivity sectors, especially agriculture.

The first advantage is that a backward or war-devastated economy embarks on the path to modern economic growth with an acute awareness of the need for reform and for sustained exertion. It knows that it starts far behind, and that it can only escape from its inferior status if it casts off old habits of thought and activity. This approach will be reflected in willingness to work harder for longer hours, and in acceptance of the necessity to sacrifice present consumption in order to make the additional investments essential for expansion and modernisation of the capital stock. Most important of all, it will create a more favourable environment for technological progress and facilitate the introduction of manning levels and workplace practices which will promote, not obstruct, productivity growth.

Given the inherited gap between the group of nations under consideration, these fundamental differences in attitude would have existed in 1948 even without the impact of the Second World War. But they were powerfully reinforced by the economic and psychological conditions which prevailed at the end of the war. Defeated countries approached the task of reconstruction with a great sense of urgency and determination, and little prospect of early benefits. Victorious countries – especially Britain – saw the outcome of the war as a triumph for which they could now expect to be rewarded. This difference in attitudes was reflected in expectations with respect to working hours, housing, welfare benefits and many other facets of socio-economic life.

Institutions were affected as much as individuals. In defeated countries, most government agencies, associations of employers, trade unions and professional societies had been discredited or destroyed; it was usually necessary to start afresh with new or substantially remodelled institutions. In contrast, in countries like Britain and the United States which were neither occupied nor defeated, old institutions survived unchanged, preserving the powers and practices which had accrued to them over centuries.

The second, and perhaps the most crucial, benefit of relative backwardness is that once development is under way late starters can borrow from more advanced nations. This ability to gain from the experience of those already on the technological frontier covers not only the diffusion of the most advanced physical equipment and machinery, but also a wide array of economic and social arrangements. These include, for example, property rights and legal practices, corporate structures and management hierarchies, banking systems and intermediate sources of finance, procedures for industrial relations and personnel management. A substantial process of adaptation will almost invariably be needed to fit the imported practices to the factor endowments and socio-economic circumstances of the borrowing country, and some may achieve this more successfully than others. Nevertheless, the benefits of this international diffusion of best-practice procedures and techniques represent a highly significant contribution to growth.

Finally, the third factor favouring the relatively backward countries is that they have a large proportion of their working population still engaged in agriculture, usually employing little capital and primitive farming methods, and with correspondingly low output per worker. Thus average productivity can be raised quite rapidly, by transferring labour to industry and other high-productivity branches of the modern economy. In addition, as long as surplus labour is freely available in agriculture (and related low-income sectors such as domestic service), this elastic supply of labour will permit rapid growth of labour inputs in the modern sector without immediately putting great pressure on wages and prices. The surplus-labour countries will thus enjoy a considerable advantage over those which have already completed this process of transition to an urbanised, industrialised economy.

Some implications of the backwardness hypothesis

The basic proposition of the backwardness/convergence hypothesis is thus that a very large part of the discrepancy in economic performance of the post-war years can be explained in terms of the lower level from which the fast-growing followers started their advance. The lower the starting point, the greater the opportunity to take advantage of the benefits of backwardness. On this view, comparable rates of growth were *not* attainable by Britain and the United States, precisely because they were already at a higher level of development in 1948. It was not realistic, therefore, to expect them to attain productivity growth rates of 5 per cent per annum, and their failure to do so during the golden age was neither reprehensible nor remediable.

No doubt some of the alternative explanations for Britain's relative decline should be incorporated into the analysis, and some improvement on the rates actually achieved would have been possible with alternative policies, but the margin was very much smaller than many commentators have suggested. Equally, the rapid rates achieved in Germany, Japan, France and Italy owed far more to their low starting point than to any special merits of their particular economic and social arrangements.

The hypothesis does not imply that differences between nations will come to an end at precisely the point at which the formerly backward countries catch up. Rapid growth develops its own momentum, both psychologically and in terms of the virtuous circle of economic relationships outlined above. This will carry a country forward for some time. By the same token, slow progress creates its own obstacles to reform, and a one-time leading country is likely to continue – and may even strengthen – patterns of behaviour which inhibit rapid growth, long after its leadership position has been eroded.

It is, however, an implication of the hypothesis that one-time leaders will ultimately respond to the changed circumstances and, in particular, to the increased threat to markets and jobs posed by the formerly backward economies. Established attitudes and ossified institutions will finally be recognised as barriers to progress, and will gradually be forced to make way for new and more effective arrangements. Once this happens the potential for growth swings in favour of such countries because they have moved to a position of relative backwardness where they can borrow from the new leaders. The process of convergence will be strengthened by converse forces at work in the countries which have forged ahead to arrive at last in the front rank. They will now feel entitled to relax their efforts and to claim more of the benefits of their economic advance in leisure and consumption. Their institutions will become more rigid and less well-adapted to the new circumstances.

The convergence hypothesis thus helps to explain three major features of the post-war period. First, it accounts for a significant part of the initial discrepancy in performance during the golden age. In 1948 the disparity between the main industrial countries was abnormally wide, and exceptionally high growth rates could be achieved by those countries which were best able to exploit the potential benefits of their backwardness. Conversely, much of the slower growth of Britain and other leading countries can be attributed to the absence of such possibilities.

Secondly, the gradual convergence towards a broadly uniform level of output per head is an important part of the explanation for the slowdown which occurred in all countries after 1973. The golden age was undermined by its own success. As levels of productivity and income increased in the formerly backward countries, their three major advantages were progressively eroded. The highly favourable attitudes for economic growth could not be sustained in the more prosperous conditions, there were fewer opportunities for borrowing from abroad and it was no longer possible to gain from massive transfers of labour from agriculture to the modern sector. In all the advanced industrial countries the rate of progress became increasingly dependent on pushing the technological frontier forward. In this situation the overall rate of growth was inevitably slower than it had been when a number of countries could race towards an already established frontier.

Finally, these concepts also help to explain the partial reversal of performance standards in 1979–88, when, for the first time since the war, productivity growth in the United Kingdom exceeded that in countries like Germany, France and Italy. To some extent these countries were suffering from the problems of adjustment to their new situation as the previous possibilities for rapid growth were exhausted. To some extent, Britain had by that stage accepted its status as a relatively backward country, and was beginning to respond to the advantages which this offered.

5   Industrial and commercial performance since 1950

Robert Millward

Those whom the Gods would destroy, they first raise on high

(Euripides)

Introduction

It is true, but unfortunate, that the industrial performance of a country is often taken as a measure of its global political standing. For Britain, so dominant industrially in the nineteenth century but no longer now a major political power, the link is inescapable. This was to be important in contemporary reaction to the events of the post-war period which saw a dramatic change from the position in 1950. Then, Britain was the world's leading car exporter, with 45 per cent of its labour force in manufacturing, accounting for one third of the manufacturing exports of the world's leading industrial countries, and with less than 20 per cent of its imports in the form of manufactures. By the mid-1980s over a half of its imports were manufactured goods, its manufactured exports accounted for less than 10 per cent of the world total, with a quarter of its labour force in manufacturing and British Leyland car exports accounted for some 2 per cent of the world's total car exports.

There are other important contrasts between 1950 and 1985. The world of one cinema for every 10,000 inhabitants, smoking chimneys and railways, wringers, waiters in pubs, grocery shops on every corner, local venues for summer holidays, Dickensian bank managers, was transformed to microwaves, diesel trains, videos, washing machines, oil exports, TV advertising, bank help for small businesses, self-service in garages, pubs and restaurants, not to mention an unprecedented rise in real incomes. It is an important strand of this chapter that the composition of Britain's industrial output, broadly defined, changed significantly whilst many still clung to the idealisation of manufacturing as the fundamental source of economic well-being.

The focus here is on that part of the private sector which produced goods and services entering foreign trade. In fact there are few 'tradables' not in the private sector (some transport, communication and government

123

services) and only a small part of the private sector was not involved in the production of tradables (construction and dwellings). This sector thus involved 'private production for trade', and the aim is to assess its development from the early 1950s to the mid-1980s in a long-term historical perspective.

For some the die had already been cast. The anti-industrial spirit which Wiener has seen pervading British society had its origin before the industrial revolution, but the 'cultural cordon sanitaire encircling... technology, industry, commerce' persisted through to the post-1945 period (Wiener 1985: ix). On a slightly different tack, but capturing readers with a similar colourful prose, Barnett (1986) saw the 1940s as a decisive period when a 'New Jerusalem' was planned placing false hope in a society cleansed of the selfish greed of Victorian capitalism. Part of the story is therefore concerned with the freedom for manoeuvre that existed in the post-1940s period. The analysis starts in the next section by looking closely at the debate about the shares of industry and commerce in the economy's resources and output. The record of industrial productivity is then examined and is followed by detailed case studies of motor vehicles and textiles. The role of education and science in industry warrants a separate section, and this is followed by an assessment of the links between the changing role of industrial unions and the slicing of the industrial cake as between wages and profits. Trends in the concentration and distribution of industry are then examined. In all of this the emphasis is on a *quantitative* assessment of industrial and commercial changes. The last section, however, considers government industrial policy, assessing what determined its direction and content and how effective it was.

The industrial base – disappearing or re-forming?

The performance of the industrial sector increasingly came during the period to preoccupy the attention of politicians, economists and journalists. Their concern had several dimensions. The pressure to keep up export levels in the immediate post-war years 1945–51 prompted assessments of comparative industrial productivity levels in different countries. During the late 1950s and early 1960s the faster growth of the continental European economies was becoming apparent, so that industrial productivity growth and its links with innovation and technical progress became central policy issues. Then, from the 1970s, a falling level of employment in manufacturing sparked off a fear of 'deindustrialisation' (Blackaby 1979b; Cairncross 1979; Thirlwall 1982; Kirby 1984a; Clare Group 1982). For some like Bacon and Eltis (1976) this was a product of excessive growth in the public sector squeezing resources out of the private sector. For others like Singh (1977) the issue was the role of manufacturing in exports and the prospect of exports being unable to support the volume of imports associated with a full employment level of income. There was also the underlying worry of what might be called the engineering lobby about the secular shift away from manufacturing, which was seen as the source of taxes for the public sector and the basis of all economic activity, services being mere froth.

Whilst there will always be some for whom manufacturing is *the* 'productive' element in the economy, the argument looks suspect when its implications are spelt out; that for example manufactured products like ice cream and tractors are intrinsically more important than transport facilities, banking, the training of civil engineers. Modern manufacturing is heavily reliant on inputs from other sectors. Growing specialisation in all economic life enhances the role of specialist intermediaries like insurance agents, transporters, telecommunicationers. But perhaps on purely pragmatic empirical grounds the industrial sector has lost out? In what sense did an imbalance develop?

The focus here is on that part of the economy occupied by private enterprise producing tradables. The definitions and measures of this, taken from British official statistics, will be activity in manufacturing, extractive industry (mining, minerals, agriculture, forestry, fishing) and commerce (the distributive trades, hotels, tourism, banking, insurance and other financial services). This means omitting any detailed discussion of activities like sea and air transport and telecommunications which enter foreign trade; since many of these activities were in public ownership in the post-war period they are covered in chapter 6. Construction and the 'dwellings' part of the personal sector are also left out but their direct involvement in foreign trade is minimal; on the other hand the measures usually include steel, oil and coal, which were not in the private sector for significant stretches of the post-war period. But with all these qualifications there is no doubt that the measure captures 'private production for trade'. Looked at as a whole the sector's production process involves output of capital goods and final consumption goods and inputs from two sources, the infrastructure and imports. It draws in particular on raw material and manufacturing imports and on the domestic infrastructure services some of which it pays for directly (electricity, railways) whilst in other cases it has access to a wide range of public services provided free at the point of consumption – roads, training, basic research, health services.

Given the concern about whether industry actually declined, it is useful to start with an absolute measure of the sector and of employment in particular, since this affected people directly and employees are voters. The

Table 5.1. *Employment in industry and commerce in the UK, 1951–85 (000s)*

	1951	1964	1973	1985
Manufacturing				
Food, drink and tobacco	834	829	754	626
Chemicals	483	509	427	347
Vehicles	1,028[a]	878	797	584
Engineering	1,878	2,422	2,123	1,525
Textiles, leather, clothing	1,881	1,455	1,079	545
Paper and printing	526	628	574	497
Other manufacturing	2,116	2,160	2,074	1,408
Sub-total	8,746	8,881	7,828	5,532
Extractive industry				
Agriculture etc.	772	538	434	339
Mining and minerals	860	659	363	249
Sub-total	1,632	1,197	797	588
Commerce				
Distribution, hotels etc.	2,162	2,986	3,538	4,471
Banking and insurance	440	630	1,058	1,971
Sub-total	2,602	3,616	4,596	6,442
Industry and commerce	12,980	13,693	13,221	12,562
Other sectors	7,990	9,664	9,441	8,904
Total employment in UK	20,970	23,357	22,662	21,466

[a] The 1951 figure for vehicles includes some 300–400,000 employees, working on the manufacture of parts and accessories or on repair work, who were allocated in the 1958 Standard Industrial Classification to other sectors.
Note: data refer to total employees (females and males, full time and part time) in employment in the UK. The 1951 data are on the 1948 Standard Industrial Classification, the 1964 data on the 1958 SIC, the 1973 data on the 1968 SIC and the 1985 data on the 1980 SIC.
Sources: Department of Employment and Productivity (1971: Table 132) for 1951 and 1964 data; *Annual Abstract of Statistics* 1975 for 1973 data and 1987 edition for 1985 data.

data in Table 5.1 represent similar points in the economic cycle. Though 1988 might have been better in this respect for the 1980s, the use of 1985 at least gives some reflection of the unusual severity of the 1980s recession (Feinstein and Matthews 1990: 79). Though subject also to significant problems of industrial reclassification, the data give a fair picture of the broad trends. Employment in industry and commerce actually rose to 13.7 million in 1964. It is true that it fell thereafter, to 12.6 million by 1985, but so also did total employment in the UK such that the share of industry and commerce remained at 58 per cent. This is hardly the stuff of deindustrialisation.

Some observers are more concerned with the composition of industry and commerce. Employment in manufacturing started declining in the early 1960s and the decline thereafter accelerated. By the early 1970s manufacturing had lost 10 per cent of the labour force of the early 1960s; by the mid-1980s it had lost a further 20 per cent and by this time employment in vehicles and textiles was but one third of the immediate post-war level. In contrast commerce was expanding, with employment doubling in the distributive trades and quadrupling in banking and insurance. Does this matter? Some like Bacon and Eltis (1976) thought that the growth of the public sector was squeezing resources away from industry. Clearly Table 5.1 does not support that case. In any case the rise in the public services as well as retail distribution, hotels and catering was largely associated with part-time employment, especially of females, whilst the fall in manufacturing has been that of full-time males; the public sector was not squeezing labour from industry.

Nor can it be simply presumed that manufacturing makes a bigger contribution to national output and exports. Consider mining and minerals where employment declined throughout the post-war years. The 1970s saw the development of North Sea oil, real output grew at 9.5 per cent per annum over the period 1973–85 and output per man-hour at 12.4 per cent, faster than any other sector in the economy (Millward 1988). Oil also came to account for some 20 per cent of exports of UK goods. Within commerce, financial services grew to nearly 20 per cent of the total UK export of services. In other words if the concern is with output and foreign trade, manufacturing has no necessary prior claim to our attention.

Nor is it the case that manufacturing necessarily sets the pace in entrepreneurial zeal or institutional innovation. To the story of Jack Cohen blending with the tea importer T. E. Stockwell to form Tesco can be added Marks, Spencer, Morgan Grenfell and many other outstanding entrepreneurs in commerce. In the emergence of large-scale modern corporations, manufacturing in no sense set the pattern. The railway companies headed the list of largest British public companies by market value in 1905 and 1935. Despite the subsequent decline in the railways, in 1985 manufacturing can still claim only nineteen of the fifty largest public limited companies. The others include British Petroleum and Britoil in extractive industry, British Telecom, Shell Transport, Cable and Wireless and P. and O. Steam Navigation in the infrastructure sector. Then there are four conglomerate and holding companies which are difficult to classify and finally the following in commerce (Wardley 1991):

Retailers	*Banks*	*Insurance*	*Other*
Tesco	Barclays	Prudential	Grand
Boots	National	Royal	Metropolitan
Marks &	Westminster	Guardian R. E.	Land
Spencer	Lloyds	Legal &	Securities
Sainsburys	Midland	General	Associated
Great		General	Dairies
Universal		Accident	
Stores		Sun Alliance	

The above also excludes those large enterprises in infrastructure still in public ownership in 1985; British Gas, the Electricity Boards, National Coal Board, British Rail, Water Authorities. Commerce and extraction therefore have every claim to be included with manufacturing in any assessment of the 'private industrial' sector of the economy.

The share of industry and commerce as a whole in the value of UK national output has declined in the post-war period. However its prices have risen slower than other sectors. Its share of real output, as Table 5.2 shows, has actually risen, consistently if not very steeply, from 67.6 per cent in 1951 to 68.9 per cent in 1973 and (on the new classification) from 58.1 per cent to 62.6 per cent during the 1973–85 period. Since its share of labour measured in man-hours has fallen since the 1960s, output per man-hour has risen faster than other sectors. In a broad sense there are two proximate sources of this rise. As Table 5.2 shows, the capital stock in industry and commerce was, by the 1980s, roughly the same fraction of the total stock in the economy (again allowing for classification changes) as it had been in the 1950s; this implies that the capital–labour ratio rose faster here than elsewhere. A second source, considered later in the chapter, is the efficiency with which capital and labour are used. In the meantime, it is worth noting that within industry and commerce the major decline in resources, and especially labour, in the 1950s was in coal mining; this was joined in the 1960s by manufacturing whose share of real output rose faster than the other sub-sectors. Commerce was expanding throughout the post-war period, perhaps not surprisingly since profit rates, as we shall see later, were consistently higher than in manufacturing. Taken in conjunction with the rise in oil production this ensured that, in the latest period 1973–85, industry and commerce continued to increase their share of UK output despite the severe fall in resources in manufacturing.

Thus the decline in employment in industry and commerce with which we started and the large decline in manufacturing's share has not prevented the share of the private production sector in real output from rising. What about its impact on the share of exports in UK output? This was a

Table 5.2. Shares of labour, capital and output in the UK economy, 1951–85 (%)

	Labour				Capital				Output			
	1951	1964	1973	1985	1951	1964	1973	1985	1951	1964	1973	1985
Manufacturing	35·1	36·1	34·7 (36·3)	27·4	23·8	25·5	22·8 (19·2)	16·5	34·6	37·0	38·2 (31·5)	24·9
Extractive industry	9·3	6·7	4·4 (3·5)	3·0	6·7	5·9	5·1 (2·3)a	4·4a	8·8	6·2	4·6 (4·7)	9·6
Commerce	23·4	24·5	25·4 (21·7)	27·9	9·7	10·5	11·4 (9·9)	14·2	24·2	25·2	26·1 (21·9)	28·1
Dwellings	—	—	—	—	28·9	26·6	27·9 (31·1)	30·7	3·9	3·5	3·5 (5·6)	5·9
Other	32·2	32·7	35·5 (38·5)	41·7	30·9	31·5	32·8 (37·5)a	34·2a	28·5	28·1	27·6 (36·3)	31·5
Total	100·0	100·0	100·0	100·0	100·0	100·0	100·0	100·0	100·0	100·0	100·0	100·0

a Coal mining and oil processing included with 'Other'.

Note: the 1951–73 figures are on the 1958 SIC. The 1985 figures and the bracketed 1973 figures are on 1980 SIC. Commerce includes 'miscellaneous services' for 1951–73. Labour is measured in man-hours, capital as gross capital stock at current replacement cost for 1951–73 and at 1980 replacement cost for 1985 and the bracketed figures for 1973. Output is gross domestic product after stock appreciation at 1958 prices for 1951–73 and at 1980 prices for 1985 and the bracketed figures for 1973.

Sources: Matthews et al. (1982: Table 8.1) and Millward (1988: Tables 1 and 4).

Table 5.3. *Composition of UK foreign trade, 1951–85 (% share of GNP at market prices)*

	Exports				Imports			
	1951	1964	1973	1985	1951	1964	1973	1985
Manufacturing								
Chemicals	1·3	1·2	1·7	2·6	0·4	0·7	1·1	1·8
Material-based manufactures	5·1	3·4	3·8	2·9	2·8	2·8	3·9	3·8
Machinery and transport								
equipment	7·4	5·5	6·7	6·9	0·8	1·4	4·2	7·2
Other manufacturing	1·1	1·0	1·4	2·2	0·2	0·8	1·6	2·7
Sub-total	14·9	11·1	13·6	14·6	4·2	5·7	10·8	15·5
Extractive industry								
Agriculture etc.[a]	2·1	1·9	2·2	2·6	12·6	8·1	6·5	4·6
Mining and minerals	0·8	0·4	0·5	4·7	1·8	1·5	2·2	2·8
Sub-total	2·9	2·3	2·7	7·3	14·4	9·6	8·7	7·4
Commerce								
Travel	0·4	0·6	1·0	1·5	0·4	0·8	0·9	1·4
Financial Services[b]	[b]	0·3	0·8	1·3	0	0	0	0
Other services	1·5[b]	1·4	1·8	2·1	0·8	0·9	1·0	1·3
Sub-total	1·9	2·3	3·6	4·9	1·2	1·7	1·9	2·7
Sea and air transport	2·9	2·5	3·4	1·7	2·0	2·2	3·5	1·8
Government	0·1	0·1	0·1	0·1	0·7	0·8	0·7	0·5
Total	22·6	18·3	23·3	28·6	22·6	20·0	25·6	27·9

[a] Includes 'other export goods'.
[b] Imports are small and included net with exports. For 1951 financial services are included with 'other services'.
Note: based in part on ratios between national income, total traded goods and total traded services from data in UK National Accounts, the source also of the breakdown within services. The breakdown between traded goods is based on the Standard International Trade Statistics Classification, which is different from the British SIC; the 1951 classification is slightly different from that for later years.
Sources: Annual Abstract of Statistics 1960, 1973, 1985, 1991 and *UK Balance of Payments* 1963, 1968, 1986.

particular concern of the Cambridge School who linked deindustri-
alisation in Britain to balance of payment problems; Singh (1977) in particular warned of the danger from the decline in manufacturing. Britain was deindustrialising in the sense that it was failing to produce enough manufactured exports to sustain the full employment volume of imports. The situation, however, is by no means clear-cut.

Table 5.3 provides a breakdown of the components of British foreign trade. The early post-war period saw Britain in a favourable position to

Table 5.4. *Growth of resources, output and productivity in industry and commerce, 1951–85 (average annual % growth rates)*

	1951–64	1964–73	1973–85
Manufacturing			
Labour	0·2	−1·6	−3·4
Capital	3·3	3·3	1·6
Output	3·2	3·0	−0·8
Total factor productivity	2·0	3·1	1·3
Extractive industry			
Labour	−2·5	−5·7	−2·3[a]
Capital	1·8	2·9	1·8[a]
Output	1·0	0·2	6·4[a]
Total factor productivity	2·5	3·1	6·7[a]
Commerce			
Labour	0·3	−0·7	1·1
Capital	3·7	6·0	5·8
Output	3·0	3·0	2·2
Total factor productivity	1·7	1·8	−1·1

[a] Includes gas, electricity and water.
Note: see Table 5.2 for definitions and coverage.
Sources: Matthews *et al.* (1982: Table 8.3) and Millward (1988: Table 5). The figures for mining etc. and commerce for 1973–85 were calculated from Millward (1988), supplemented by data from UK National Accounts 1983 on income from employment as a fraction of gross domestic product after deducting stock appreciation.

export as Japan, Germany, France, Italy and other European countries struggled to rebuild their productive capacity which had been destroyed in the war (Foreman-Peck 1991; Krause 1968). In the 1950s, Britain inevitably lost some ground. But, from the 1960s, not only did exports from industry and commerce in total account for a rising share of GDP but so also did manufacturing exports. On the other hand, Britain did suffer periodic balance of payments crises which reflected in part the rising fraction of national income spent on manufactured imports, especially machinery and transport equipment. By the 1980s the manufacturing trade balance was in deficit.

Singh (1977), Sargent (1979) and the Clare Group (1982) doubted that the gap could be met by services, in part because Britain was already dominant in certain key services. Nevertheless the export of commercial services, especially financial services and travel, has more than doubled its share of national output, offsetting in part the severe drop in earnings from sea and air transport. Moreover, imports of commercial services have not risen by the same amount. The other concern is that the relief provided by oil will be short-lived (cf. Whiteman 1985). The trade balance in extracted products has also, however, been affected by the declining relative importance of imported agricultural products and raw materials. The overall effect can be seen, in the last row of Table 5.3, as a net trading surplus in services which offsets the visible trade deficit (that is in manufacturing and extractive industries) at the beginning and end of the period but not in the middle.

Since these figures can be highly sensitive to the particular year chosen, it is useful to look at averages of the various sub-periods, however crude the data may be. Matthews et al. (1982) show that the visible trade balance averaged $(-)0.9$ per cent of GDP in the period 1952–64 and $(-)$ 1.0 per cent in 1964–73. The respective net balances on services were 0.2 per cent and 0.6 per cent; this was enough, given net property income from abroad of 1.3 per cent, to give a trade surplus on the current account of the balance of payments of 0.6 per cent of GDP in the first period and 0.9 per cent in the second (Matthews et al. 1982: 442). A similar calculation for the 1973–85 period yields a visible trade balance of $(-)1.5$ per cent, a service balance of 1.8 per cent, net property income of 0.8 per cent and hence a current account surplus of 1.0 per cent (see sources for Table 5.3). In summary, it is not clear that Britain's long-term industrial problems lie in the share of industry in UK output and employment or in the share of exports in UK output. It might lie in productivity growth.

Britain's Janus-faced industrial productivity record

The significance of levels and growth rates of industrial productivity lies in their implications for living standards, either indirectly via export prices and the volume of imports which this allows, or directly in the generation of real income per head from production for the home market. GDP per head, or output per man-hour to reflect work effort, is an appropriate index of productivity for the economy as a whole but it is inappropriate for particular sectors like industry and commerce, since their use of capital goods is an important ingredient of the contribution of the industrial sector to national GDP per head or per hour. This leads to the use by economists of 'total factor productivity' approaches, which measure productivity growth as the difference between output growth and the summed growth of labour and capital, weighted usually by their respective shares in income at the beginning of the period.

Britain's industrial productivity record measured in this way was, despite all the doom and gloom about industrial performance, outstanding by all historical standards in the period from the 1940s to the 1970s. During this period, the so-called golden age of full employment and the mixed economy, the growth in industrial output and especially industrial productivity was higher than in any period since the mid-nineteenth century (Matthews *et al.* 1982: 228–9). As can be seen in Table 5.4, output in manufacturing grew at about 3 per cent p.a., at roughly the same rate as in the inter-war period. Productivity growth, however, was faster than before; this is a difference from the output pattern which refutes, at least in a long-term perspective, the Kaldorian idea that output and productivity growth are highly correlated. Output per man-hour grew at 1.8 per cent p.a. in the inter-war period. In the 1950s it rose at 3.5 per cent p.a. and at 4.6 per cent p.a. for 1964–73, whilst total factor productivity grew at 2 per cent p.a. and 3.1 per cent p.a. respectively.

Overall total factor productivity growth in extractive industry in this period was slightly higher than manufacturing, which reflected in particular a large reduction in manpower in coal mining. Output and output per man-hour in commerce was expanding at about the same rate as the other sectors but this was at a cost in terms of capital inputs which, if properly measured – and there are some doubts about this as well as about the output measure – implied that total factor productivity was growing rather more slowly, at 1.7 per cent p.a. The very last period, 1973–85, was one in which all major industrialising countries slowed down. In the UK, nevertheless, employment in commerce rose. The recorded decline in productivity may be misleading, because some 50 per cent of capital formation in commerce was in assets leased out to other sectors (Feinstein and Matthews 1990: 90 fn. 5). This shift of resources to commerce is typical of recessions – it had happened in the inter-war period – with more people in disguised unemployment in parts of commerce. On a long-term basis there is still a case for claiming that UK industrial productivity growth in the post-war period was good by all historical standards.

But the other face of the productivity record is the comparison with other countries. It was the unfavourable record relative to other western industrialised countries, notwithstanding the historically outstanding absolute level of performance, which came to be the focus of attention. Table 5.5 shows that labour productivity grew in the 'business' sectors (industry, commerce, construction, gas, electricity, etc.) in the period 1960–73 at 4.6 per cent p.a. in Germany, 5.4 per cent in France and 9.4 per cent in Japan as compared to 3.5 per cent in the UK. This, it should be noted, was not a reflection of different rates of capital accumulation – that is of the UK having relatively cheaper labour and relatively more expensive capital. Investment was some 14.3 per cent of output for the UK economy as a whole in this period, a figure certainly lower than the comparable rates

Table 5.5. *International comparison of productivity growth in the business sector, 1960–88 (annual average % change)*

	Output per man-hour	Capital per man-hour[a]	Total factor productivity
UK			
1960–73	3·5	1·6	1·9
1973–88	2·2	0·9	1·3
France			
1960–73	5·4	1·5	3·9
1973–88	2·6	1·0	1·6
Germany			
1960–73	4·6	1·9	2·7
1973–88	2·5	1·3	1·2
Japan			
1960–73	9·4	3·0	6·4
1973–88	3·1	1·3	1·8
USA			
1960–73	2·8	1·0	1·8
1973–88	1·2	0·7	0·5

[a] Weighted by capital's share of base year income.

Notes and sources: the data in the first and third columns are taken from Crafts (1991a). They are OECD data covering industry, commerce, transport, communications, gas, electricity and water. TFP is the growth of output less the growth of labour and capital weighted by their respective shares of base year income in the base period. It follows that the difference between the growth rate of labour productivity and TFP is equal to the growth rate of the capital–labour ratio weighted by capital's share. Hence the figures in the middle column which are simply derived as the first column minus the third.

of 17.0 per cent in France and 17.6 per cent in Germany (Maddison 1991: 41). But the investment rate was rising faster in Britain; in manufacturing from 10.9 per cent in the early 1950s to 12.9 per cent by the early 1970s; in commerce from 7.1 per cent to 12.4 per cent and in extraction from 12.4 per cent to 21.9 per cent. The net result is reflected in the middle column of Table 5.5 showing the capital–labour ratio in the UK for 1960–73 growing at roughly the same rate as in France and Germany. The main difference was in total factor productivity which grew at 1.9 per cent p.a., significantly less than in other countries.

It is this productivity difference which essentially accounts for the UK's declining share of world trade. Relevant data are restricted to manufacturing. Table 5.6 shows that UK exports were some 26 per cent of the exports of other industrialised countries at the end of the inter-war period.

Table 5.6. *Trading performance of manufacturing sectors in industrialised countries, 1937–85*

	1937	1950	1964	1973	1985
UK exports as % of exports of other countries	25·7	36·1	14·3	9·8	8·2[a]
UK output as % of output of other countries	16·6	14·7	11·1	8·7	7·6[a]
UK exports as % of UK output	28·3	34·5	28·3	37·9	52·8[b]
Other countries' exports as % of output	17·2	13·2	20·6	32·1	46·4[a]

[a] These are estimates at current prices and exclude Switzerland. Similar current price calculations for 1973 yielded results close to those in Matthews *et al.* (1982). The small percentage difference was applied to the 1985 figures to yield the results quoted above.
[b] The figures from Matthews *et al.* (1982) in this role exclude, from the denominator, sales within the manufacturing sector. Their figure for 1973 of 37·9 per cent is therefore significantly different from the figure in *Annual Abstract of Statistics* 1984 of 20 per cent for exports as a percentage of sales (at current prices) and from the result of dividing exports by manufacturing GDP (53·2 per cent at current prices). For 1985 the corresponding current price figures are 30·0 per cent and 72·6 per cent; our estimate above of 52·8 per cent lies at a similar distance between the two as did the 37·9 per cent figure for 1973.
Sources: Matthews *et al.* (1982: 436–7). Other industrialised countries comprise US, Japan, France, Germany (West from 1950), Italy, Luxembourg, Netherlands, Sweden, Switzerland, Belgium, Canada. The last column was derived from OECD *Statistics of Foreign Trade* 1976, 1987; OECD *National Accounts* 1973–85 Paris 1985 and 1976–88 Paris 1990; *Annual Abstract of Statistics* 1984, 1991.

After benefiting in the 1940s from the handicaps of countries devastated by war, the UK share declined rapidly to only 8 per cent by 1985. Even this has to be put into perspective. Britain led the world in the nineteenth century when there was very little real competition. It dominated industrial production and trade but has now lost this dominance. What is perhaps surprising is that the process took so long. The simple increase in total world productive capacity inevitably led to a decline in the UK share of total output as the second row of Table 5.6 shows, albeit this was not as great a decline as in the export share. Moreover, the UK's propensity to export had not diminished in one respect. As the other rows in Table 5.6 show, the share of manufactured products which is exported has risen consistently from the early 1960s and in 1985 that share (more than 50 per cent) was still bigger than the average for all the other industrialised countries. Finally Table 5.7 shows that, whilst the level of labour productivity in UK manufacturing was exceeded in the USA by the turn of

Table 5.7. *International comparisons of productivity levels,
1938–86 (output per hour worked, UK = 100)*

	1938	1950	1960	1973	1986
France					
GDP	82	70	84	105	119
Manufacturing	56	64	81	113	126
Germany					
GDP	73	54	84	100	105
Manufacturing	76	74	105	133	137
Japan					
GDP	35	24	33	62	68
Manufacturing	n.a.	n.a.	n.a.	125[a]	175[b]
USA					
GDP	154	185	188	156	133
Manufacturing	197[c]	247	242	220	207

[a] 1975
[b] 1985
[c] 1937

Note: the manufacturing data refer to output by industry of origin.
Source: Crafts (1991a: 84).

the century, it was not exceeded in Germany until about 1960 and in France until the 1970s. Insofar as the measures of GDP in Table 5.7 pick up some of the contributions of extractive industry and commerce, the overtaking of UK industry may have been even later. The USA benefited enormously in this regard from two World Wars (Broadberry 1988). Tables 5.5 and 5.7 show that the UK has caught up on the USA since the Second World War. The final twist is the experience of the 1980s. Industrial growth was halted everywhere but, as Table 5.5 shows, the UK productivity record improved considerably relative to other countries. At the end of the 1980s some convergence of industrial productivity levels seemed possible.

In the post-1950 period as a whole, therefore, the UK had by historical standards a good record in productivity growth, but it continued to lose its old dominance of world trade. There were some signs at the end of the 1980s that the industrial productivity levels of the western industrialised countries were converging. The UK loss of export share was probably bigger than can be explained simply by the others catching up. Its share of world trade in manufacturing by the end of the 1980s was only one half that of Germany, Japan and USA, albeit not much different from France. Relative to the USA, which suffered little loss of productive capacity during the Second World War, it seems likely that part of the growth experience of the European countries and Japan took the form of catching up to the USA. The catch-up hypothesis, advanced by Abramovitz (1986), suggests that the imitation and transmission of ideas leads to an expectation that the growth in productivity of any country will be larger, the bigger is the gap with the productivity level of the leading country. Crafts (1991b) calculated that a large proportion of the labour productivity growth in Japan, Germany, Italy and France can be put down to catching up to the USA, at least in the period up to the 1970s. On this basis, the UK underperforms – its productivity growth was less than expected; in the 1980s, however, it did much better in this respect than all the leading industrialised countries except France. Two broad questions emerge from this. First, what accounts for the residual differences in industrial productivity growth in the UK relative to other countries – after allowing, that is, for catch-up factors? Second, in what particular ways did Britain lose out industrially to other countries; was there anything which could have been prevented? Two case studies will help.

Cotton textiles

Cotton had been declining for some time. Record export levels were experienced in 1913, but in the inter-war period the industry lost many of the cheaper cloth markets to Japan and India. After the Second World War the question was: how much of the rest could it hold on to? As late as 1937, UK cotton cloth exports were 30 per cent of world exports. By 1950, despite some favourable conditions immediately after the war, the share had fallen to 16 per cent; it collapsed to 3 per cent by 1968 (Singleton 1986: 96). What was the source of this and what could managers, unions and government have done about it?

One diagnosis is that Lancashire failed to keep pace with modern technology and that this was a product both of conservative family firms and of intransigent trade unions. The technology which yielded the highest output of yarn per man was that which used 'ring' spindles, whilst automatic weaving looms yielded the highest output of cloth per operative. By 1955 all looms in the USA were automatic, whilst only 12 per cent were in the UK. In spinning, 40 per cent of the world's 'mule' spindles, the 'old' technology, were to be found in the UK, which had only 10 per cent of the world's ring spindles.

Technologies which yield high levels of output per man are, however, not necessarily the most economic. Ring spinning was always a labour-saving measure in the USA, an important consideration for a country which was relatively poorly endowed with labour. The UK was relatively better endowed with labour supplies and very skilled ones at that.

Nevertheless Lazonick (1983, 1986) has argued that Britain failed to adopt the new technology early enough. The issues involved in changing the organisation of firms to accommodate rings and automatic looms transcend the factor scarcity thesis. On this argument the UK would have held on to some of the cheaper yarn and cloth markets and not lost out, as it did in the 1950s and 1960s, to western Europe and USA in the better quality markets.

There are two prongs to the Lazonick approach (see also vol. 2, ch. 4). First, he argues that the new technology required large capital investment and hence mass production. This required close links between marketing and production, specifically the development of integrated spinning and weaving together with a standardised and large volume cloth output. Such large enterprises needed well-developed managerial hierarchies which were characteristic of the large US corporations. Hannah (1976c) has in fact pointed to evidence, in business histories from the early twentieth century, that British companies, although large, were often slow to adapt their managerial and financial practices.

The second part of Lazonick's argument is that Lancashire had a very skilled labour force with strong unions. Ring spinning uses high-quality raw cotton and generates yarn with few breakages. The UK operatives were skilled at making good breakages and the mule put less strain on the cotton and thereby allowed the use of cheap varieties. Operatives were paid fixed piece rates, which effectively devolved much of the day-to-day managerial problem to the mill floor. The wage lists allowed for different working conditions and the strong unions prevented departure from these practices. The yarns which emerged were less suited to automated processes in weaving so that power looms remained and the unions limited the number of these per operative.

Since decisions on this technology date from the nineteenth century, the scope for manoeuvre by 1950 was limited. For Lazonick, the 'fundamental problem was an industry mired in its own highly competitive and vertically specialised structure lacking any internal forces to set in motion structural transformation' (Lazonick 1983: 218). Lancashire's early success with a highly competitive set of family firms had the consequence that firms were not willing to relinquish control by amalgamations; Table 5.8 shows how small firms still proliferated. Although the industry was in rapid decline, the smallest category of firms identified in the table accounted for a rising share of spindle and loom capacity. By 1955, vertically integrated concerns still accounted for only one third of total output (Singleton 1991: 215).

How far could the government have rectified this situation? There were two major pieces of legislation after the war, both concerned in part to promote the use of new equipment. The 1948 Cotton Spinning Industry

Table 5.8. *Size of firms in UK cotton textiles, 1939–65*

Firm size	1939		1958		1965	
	No. of firms	% total spindles or looms	No. of firms	% total spindles or looms	No. of firms	% total spindles or looms
Spinning (000 spindles)						
< 80	139	14·8	74	11·8	60	32·0
80–199	110	33·2	46	18·9	12	23·0
200 +	31	52·0	30	69·3	4	45·0
Total	280	100·0	150	100·0	76	100·0
Weaving (no. of looms)						
< 200	438	7·6	320	10·1	195	14·0
200–799	447	40·4	247	38·5	116	37·0
800 +	178	52·0	87	51·4	31	49·0
Total	1,063	100·0	654	100·0	342	100·0

Source: Singleton (1991: 213–14).

Act offered a 25 per cent subsidy to re-equipment provided that the firms combined into groups of at least 400,000 spindles, or 250,000 for integrated firms. Another re-equipment subsidy of 25 per cent was offered to all sectors in the 1959 Cotton Industry Act, which also provided compensation for employees. The response was poor. Only eight combines were established under the 1948 Act and only £2.6 million out of a possible £12 million subsidy was actually claimed. Investment of about £53.5 million was made under the aegis of the 1959 Act, but this was well short of the £80–90 million which the government had expected. Both Lazonick (1983) and Mottershead (1978) see government policy as weak in not providing sufficient inducements for organisational change and in particular incentives for integration.

Yet there is a slightly different perspective that can be placed on this picture of the post-war years. Some would argue that the UK had lost any special advantage it had in cotton textiles; in this case the issue was how best the industry could be run down. Perhaps a niche could have been found in fashion markets, as the Italians demonstrated. In this respect the poor links between marketing and production in Britain were certainly a disadvantage. Other developed countries survived in other ways. The USA industry in particular had survived, according to Singleton (1990), simply because it was protected. Ring spindles and automated looms were no guarantee, claimed the UK employers' group, the Cotton Board, of success against the fierce competition of Hong Kong, Japan and India. Nor were British trade unions uncooperative; new manning levels, following work measurement principles, were introduced in cardroom labour organisation; night shifts were introduced in ring spinning rooms and weaving mills (Singleton 1990: 134). For most people in the industry, government help was needed and they complained about the poor response to their pleas.

Matters were rather unusual after the war. Exports were vital for the economy and the UK was able to meet initial deficiencies in the capacity of more war-torn countries, with spinning profits rising substantially. Soldiers and munition workers, remembering the low wages and unemployment of the inter-war years, were reluctant to return to the mills. Investment expenditure per operative in the 1940s and 1950s was low, consistent with the weak response to the 1948 and 1959 equipment subsidy schemes. In the 1950s share prices in British industry as a whole trebled, but they did not move at all in cotton. The wage lists were old and shift working in the UK was not as widespread as elsewhere but the implication was that they were not worth changing. Survival depended on protection so Lancashire 'whinged' through its unions, its members of Parliament and the Cotton Board.

The government attempted to help the industry in the 1940s, mainly by improving the flow of labour into the industry for the export drive. But as trade picked up, post-war governments had higher priorities than Lancashire. Japan was allowed to protect its textile industry because the development of heavy industry was held back by the Allies. Tariffs against countries like India carried the danger of retaliation in British engineering exports. Thus protection emerged in the form of 'voluntary' agreements with India, Pakistan, Hong Kong. Singleton's analysis (1986) of the proximate source of decline suggests that rising imports were a problem only in the 1955–60 period. Prior to that it was declining exports which were the source of the major loss of employment, as other countries built up their capacity. Then in the 1960s it was domestic demand for yarn and cloth which occasioned further declines, in part because of the rise of knitted fabrics.

In fact, the 1960s saw major changes with the development of man-made fibres. This was the province of large companies like ICI, Courtaulds and Du Pont; Lazonick (1983, 1986) viewed success in this area as indicating the importance of the different institutional setting: mass production, vertical integration, managerial hierarchies. Courtaulds expanded by amalgamating whilst ICI acquired financial holdings in Viyella, which had interests in all sections of production, finishing, hosiery and clothing. In fact financial results in these areas were poor, indeed 'appalling' for ICI's textile division. The new entrepreneurs 'had planned to overhaul the

Table 5.9. *UK vehicle production, 1937–86*

	1937	1951	1960	1974	1986
UK total production (in 000s)					
Cars	390	476	1,354	1,534	1,019
Commercial vehicles	118	258	458	403	229
UK share of world production (%)					
Cars	8	8	11	7	4
Commercial vehicles	10	12	19	6	2
UK share of world exports (%)					
Cars	17	44	24	9	2
Commercial vehicles	9	30	26	11	2
Shares of UK car production (%)					
Ford	18	19	28	25	34
Vauxhall	10	9	11	10	16
Rootes/Chrysler/Peugeot	10	14	11	17	6
BMC/British Leyland	53	50	47	48	40
Others	9	8	3	0·1	5

Note: world production and exports relate to activities of major OECD producers: UK, France, Germany, Italy, Japan, USA. The data on commercial vehicles exclude tractors. In the final section of the table, the second column refers to 1950 rather than to 1951. *Sources:* Silberston 1958; Wilks 1990.

managerial practices of the cotton textile industry, but what they failed to realise was that the supposedly defeatist managers whom they displaced had a very well grounded understanding of the enormity of the problem facing Lancashire' (Singleton 1990: 146).

Motor vehicles

Up to the 1960s, British producers dominated the domestic and world markets for cars and commercial vehicles. The lack of significant competition from war-torn countries allowed the UK to become the world's leading exporter in the early 1950s, accounting in 1951, as Table 5.9 shows, for 44 per cent of world car exports and 30 per cent of commercial vehicle exports. Though those shares fell in the 1950s, vehicle production rose at 5 per cent p.a., the share of vehicles in UK national output increased and the UK's share of world car production reached 11 per cent in 1960. Car production continued to rise in the 1960s but shares of UK national output flattened off and the UK share of world production and exports plummeted. During the recessionary years from the late 1970s, car production fell by a third. In the meantime major changes were occurring on the import side. Imports of 'transport equipment and machinery' were only 2.4 per cent of UK total imports in 1951 but this figure rose consistently to 31 per cent by 1985 by which time they accounted for nearly a half of all manufactured imports. The 'balance of trade' in cars went into deficit in 1973, that in commercial vehicles in 1977 and the whole industry, including components, in 1982 (Wilks 1990: 159).

A central criticism of the UK car industry concerned its use of modern technology. It was not that British car firms did not use assembly lines early in their history nor introduce automatic transfer machines and body shops later. The criticism is that the UK was invariably behind USA and continental producers in the speed with which these techniques were introduced and developed. In 1955 vehicle output per worker in the USA was 2.5 times that in the UK. From the late 1950s until the early 1970s the Ford Motor Company in Britain, using American production and managerial methods, produced approximately twelve vehicles per employee per annum whilst the major UK firm, British Leyland and its predecessor the British Motor Corporation (established in 1951) managed only seven to eight vehicles per employee per annum (Tolliday, 1991: 87; Lewchuk 1986: 143).

But as in the case of cotton, production methods which yield high levels of output per man are not necessarily the most economic; labour productivity is only a 'partial' productivity measure. The capital–labour ratio was consistently lower in the UK and the output–capital ratio higher. In 1969 British Leyland had approximately £1,000 of fixed capital per employee whilst Ford and most continental producers averaged £3,000. Capital productivity was higher in the UK; it has been estimated that in 1958 Ford were producing less than 300,000 vehicles with the same value of net assets that the British Motor Corporation were using to produce 500,000 vehicles. Indeed the less capital-intensive method proved very profitable to British car firms, since low labour productivity was accompanied by low wages. US hourly wages were more than three times higher than British levels in 1956 (3.22 to be precise), 2.14 times in 1974 and 1.55 in 1980 (Lewchuk 1986: 156; Tolliday 1991: 87).

In this respect the UK system made perfectly good sense (Ackrill 1988). The more damaging criticism is that the production and marketing methods which underlay this strategy rendered the British car firms vulnerable to any upward pressure on wages and less able to take advantage of new production techniques that raised total factor productivity. This, it is suggested, lay at the heart of the loss of world market share in the 1970s.

This thesis as developed by Lewchuk (1986) contrasts two systems. The 'Detroit' system relied first of all on mass production with a limited range of models; Ford initially produced only one car, the T. Even by the mid-1950s there were still five major firms competing in the British market whilst a US market ten times the size supported only three major firms. Production involved strong direct control by management of a relatively unskilled labour force, paid local factory wages per day. Marketing was fully integrated with production with dealers linked to one car producer only.

The British system, in contrast, had relatively more car models and paid piece-work wages to a relatively skilled labour force which undertook several tasks. An agency system dominated vehicle distribution; dealers sold the product of a number of firms and were less open to the dictates of the producer. The strong central role of a skilled labour force had its origins in the use in the earliest UK vehicle factories of craft workers from the Amalgamated Society of Engineers or the UK Society of Coachmakers, both with strong union traditions. In the post-1945 period this power at shop-floor level was strengthened by the rise in importance of shop stewards.

The British system in effect devolved several managerial tasks to skilled labour who, in the British Motor Corporation for example, were responsible for chasing up stocks and supplies as well as organising less skilled workers. The piece wage system was a tight system but did not guarantee output levels. When, in the post-1945 period, unions were successful in raising wages, the low labour productivity system came under pressure. Lewchuk (1986) argues that the attempt to shift to a more capital-intensive system meant very considerable adjustments because of the traditionally low labour effort. Management was in any case not well equipped to meet the full requirements of mass production and marketing because its supervisory control had traditionally been weak. The moves early in the 1920s away from the Fordist route 'helped generate a series of institutional constraints which the industry found itself unable to overcome in the 1970s' (Lewchuk 1986: 151). He also puts a lot of weight, but rather unconvincingly, on the car industry's ready access to external finance. This was alleged to induce both easy entry for new firms in the early parts of the century and to inhibit later expansion because firms had to distribute high dividends, prompting the question: why could they not expand by using external finance?

How far could matters have been otherwise and what does this imply about the role of government and unions? In all UK car companies, the growth of the role of shop stewards was undermining the payment system as opportunities for bargaining grew on the shop floor. Up to the late 1960s, strikes were not a major problem but by the late 1960s the British car firms had identified the piece-work system as the principal cause of productivity problems and 'measured day work' was introduced. The British Leyland Motor Company was founded in 1968 but ran into difficulties in the early 1970s and requested government assistance in 1974. By this stage the idea of 'national champions' in modern science-based industry was popular. Following an investigation of the industry (the Ryder Report) the British government acquired British Leyland in 1975 and altogether invested £1,000 million by the end of the 1970s. The Ryder Report envisaged an ambitious reorganisation into four groups but this was later abandoned. The Chrysler company was also in difficulties and wanted to be taken over; it received £100 million in grants and loans. In effect government was simply responding, in recessionary times, to the prospect of a loss of 170,000 jobs in British Leyland whilst Chrysler was a large exporter operating at Linwood, a politically sensitive area (Sawyer 1991, 1992).

It is not clear, however, that the 'Detroit' system would have been, or indeed was, easily transplanted to Britain. US Ford was initially anti-union but, in order to get war contracts in the 1930s, took a different line and shifted dramatically to 100 per cent unionisation with the United Automobile Workers. By the 1940s Ford UK was having to deal with ten different unions. It was nevertheless able to exclude shop stewards from wage bargaining which took the form of a Joint Negotiating Committee (JNC) made up of the company's representatives and the union's general secretary. After several disputes in the 1950s and early 1960s, the national JNC management had to concede Ford's right to run its plants. The 1960s, however, saw great strains in shop-floor relations at both the Dagenham and Halewood plants; 1968–78 was a period of change during which Ford institutionalised shop-floor representation and relaxed its insistence on centralised control, ironically at the same time that British Leyland was attempting to move in the other direction. Indeed Tolliday (1991) has suggested that Ford's success lay as much in its *sales* of Ford cars as in its production in the UK of Ford cars. In contrast to the picture in Table 5.9, where Ford's share of UK production is seen to have fallen in the 1960s and 1970s and looks better than British Leyland only in the 1980s, Ford's share of new car registrations (including imported Ford cars) has risen fairly consistently from 27 per cent in 1955 to 31 per cent by 1982. Its success in this respect lies as much in being a multinational as in using Ford production methods.

Education, technology and industry: the engineer's tale

It has been established that the fastest growing parts of industry and commerce in the post-war period were financial services, the distributive trades, hotels and latterly oil production. Industrial productivity growth has been high by all historical standards, albeit flattening off in the recessionary years from the mid-1970s. This performance has not been as good as other industrial countries like Germany, France, Italy or Japan, in part because they were catching up on the erstwhile industrial leaders, the UK and the USA, and in part as they remedied the physical destruction of the war. The remaining differences in productivity levels and growth have partly arisen from a slower rate of technological advance in Britain, but the case studies show that the inheritance by the late nineteenth century of a skilled workforce rendered wholesale modernisation and mechanisation a less economic option for Britain in the twentieth century.

Having put manufacturing industry and mechanisation in their place, it is difficult, nevertheless, to deny that Britain has been slower to adopt new production techniques. In any case the epigram 'invented in Britain, developed in the USA and made in Japan' has grated on many a politician, engineer or science journalist conscious of Britain's past manufacturing prowess. The source of these deficiencies has often been sought in the inputs to invention and industrial innovation. Industry and commerce acquire these inputs in imperfect markets; scientific and engineering personnel are trained and developed in Britain in the state sector and the government's own research and development (R & D) and government-sponsored R & D are important ingredients of industrial technical progress. A widely accepted measure of innovative activity is the number of patents taken out in the USA, where patent statistics are well developed. Of the total of such manufacturing patents for ten major industrialised countries in 1975 (excluding USA) Japan accounted for 27.5 per cent, West Germany 25.8 per cent, UK only 13.2 per cent, France 10.2 per cent (Pavitt and Soete 1980: 40–1).

The significance of the R & D effort in the post-1950 period stems from three issues. First, whereas technical improvements of production in the nineteenth century could emanate from on the job activities, and Britain's skilled labour force was well placed for that to happen, increasingly in the twentieth century new products and new processes have stemmed from scientific laboratories, shifting the balance away from experience to formal training. Second, new products can rarely be imitated immediately so that foreign trade is built upon such technology gaps, fostered by clusters of innovations and large-scale economies in production; hence the pattern of international trade is characterised by product cycles as innovations are diffused. Comparative advantage then resides in the availability in industry of professional and skilled people working in all aspects of industrial management; hence the US exported not so much labour-intensive goods – the Leontief paradox – but human capital-intensive goods. Econometric studies examining US/UK productivity differences also point to a strong role for human capital (Caves 1980; Crafts 1990a; Bowden and Turner 1990).

This leads to the third point; the leading exporters in the post-1950 world were in the research-intensive industries – electronics, scientific instruments, aircraft, drugs, machinery, transport equipment, chemicals. In consumer goods like clothing, furniture and food, R & D is relatively unimportant; fashion is important and technical changes come more from capital goods suppliers. Similarly, in the production of basic materials like paper, metal products and glass the product is fairly standard, innovation comes in processes and again often stems from the equipment suppliers. It is in the sectors which produce capital goods and chemicals where R & D is the key; Pavitt and Soete (1980) showed that, for twenty-two OECD countries in 1974, exports per head were bigger within the various industries producing capital goods and chemicals the greater was innovation, measured by the number of US patents per head. It is here where Japan, Germany and Italy are catching up and overtaking the USA.

How then did the UK fit in to this new world? A common theme has been the deficient provision of training for science and engineering. The post-war period has been seen as an improvement over the past, but only a marginal one. In the classic period of the industrial revolution in Britain, 1780–1830, productivity changes took place without institutional research or trained manpower. Indeed for Wiener (1985) this period was something of an interlude in Britain's penchant for rural non-industrial activities. By the middle of the nineteenth century, the centre of educational excellence, the public schools and Oxbridge, eschewed professional or vocational teaching. A liberal education was best for leaders. For industrial activities, including management, it was experience that counted; the *Economist* in 1850 claimed 'the education which fits men to perform their duties in life is not to be got in school, but in the counting-house and the lawyer's office, in the shop or the factory' (quoted in Barnett 1985: 72). The late nineteenth century saw several advances: the extension of grants-in-aid for secondary education, the growth of the civic universities and in particular the 1899 Technical Instruction Act which allowed local authorities to levy rates for technical colleges. Part-time technical education did proliferate thereafter in the provinces. Even by 1910, however, Britain was generating yearly only 19,000 graduates, a figure which Germany had all but achieved in 1830. There was no equivalent of the Technische Hochschulen or the Polytechnique Grandes Ecoles. Sanderson (1988) amongst others has pointed in particular to the failure to cater for the working-class and non-academic teenager. Before and during the First World War, junior technical schools and continuation schools (rather like the Trade Continuation Schools in Germany) were popular but they got lost in the public spending cuts of the 1920s and in the rise of the grammar schools, whose educational syllabuses were largely imitations of the classic public schools.

The 1940s continued the poor record of provision for full-time technical training. Under the Butler Education Act of 1944 a major expansion of technical education was envisaged. In the event, 20 per cent of 11-year olds in the state system went to grammar schools, the rest – the 'failures' – went to secondary schools; only 2 per cent of pupils finished up in the new secondary technical schools. There were no national examinations for secondary education, apart from the General Certificate of Education designed for the purpose of selection for higher education. As a result, for much of the post-war period, some 45 per cent of pupils left school with no examination passes (Landymore 1985: 701). The major non-degree route was then into part-time further education programmes for Ordinary and Higher National Certificates and Diplomas. In fact the further education colleges did a mass of other work, including school-type courses. For non-degree technical courses, however, grants for student maintenance were discretionary, rather than mandatory as they were for degree courses. With apprenticeship schemes bearing some relation to an adult wage, the incentives for full-time intermediate vocational studies were not good.

The good signs were elsewhere (Albu 1980: 75). From the 1950s, the public schools moved sharply towards science and industry, so that by 1976/7 engineering was the most popular career choice (19 per cent) of their pupils. Higher education also had some promising signs. At the height of the Cold War in the early 1950s, with alarms over Russian technical prowess, plans were made for a major expansion of Imperial College in London, the Manchester College of Technology and the Royal Technical College Glasgow. Then in 1956, in a major White Paper on Technical Education, the spread of technical provision was reviewed and paved the way for the conversion of technical colleges to Colleges of Advanced Technology (CATS). In the 1960s, following the Robbins Report, came a major expansion of university science and engineering places while the CATS themselves became universities. At the same time the polytechnics emerged with the duty of providing vocationally orientated non-degree and degree courses for full-time and sandwich students; they were expected generally to concentrate on teaching and research more directly relevant to industry and commerce. In one respect there were gains in the increased number of graduates, manifest in the decline of the income differential for degree holders and the eventual emergence in the 1970s of graduate unemployment (Landymore 1985: 710). On the other hand the age participation rate for degree courses, as low as 10 per cent even by the early 1980s, lay well below most other industrial countries. Much expansion in the CATS and polytechnics was in arts and social studies, for which students showed a clear preference. By the early 1980s, it was still the case that two-thirds of the industrial workforce, against one third in Germany, had no vocational qualifications.

There is little doubt that the education system, for all its faults, was reflecting the use and demand for qualified people in industry. It appears to be the case that a shortage (in the form of a large number of unfilled vacancies) existed in the early 1950s and Peck (1968) recorded how the salaries of engineers and scientists moved significantly upwards relative to others in the late 1950s, a trend which continued to the 1960s. Indeed, as the first two rows in Table 5.10 show, the overall research effort in the UK in terms of numbers of scientists and engineers and research expenditure compared reasonably well by 1962 with the other major industrial powers, even though by 1978 its civil R & D spending per head had been caught up by France and comfortably surpassed by West Germany and Japan (Morris and Stout 1985: 879). However, even in 1962 the UK research effort was heavily biassed, as the rest of Table 5.10 shows, towards activities which reflected its vain ambitions to remain a major world political power. Britain devoted a larger share of its research and development expenditure to military and space expenditure than did any other country except the USA. Germany's low outlays in this area are indicative of similar patterns in Belgium, Japan, the Netherlands, Switzerland and Italy (Freeman 1979: 67). UK spending in 1962 on industrial research and development included virtually the same proportion on the aircraft industry as in the USA but significantly less than Germany in electrical machinery, instruments, vehicles, other machinery and chemicals. The predominance of UK activity in military and aircraft development was especially unfortunate. This was not a big area, and it was impossible for Britain effectively to compete with the USA; in addition, it fostered the ideal of 'pure engineering', led to big commercial mistakes like Concorde and creamed off the best of the scientists and engineers. In stark contrast, parts of mechanical engineering had hardly any graduate engineers at all before 1960 (Freeman 1979: 69; Caves 1968: 299; Davies and Caves 1987: 85).

A further striking feature of the way in which qualified manpower was used relates to the different kinds of manpower. In 1959, not only did the UK have a lower proportion of its qualified scientists and engineers in industry (42 per cent) than France (52 per cent), Belgium (54 per cent) and the USA (74 per cent), but engineers also accounted for a smaller share (54 per cent) of those industrial scientists and engineers than in France (67 per cent), the USA (71 per cent), Belgium (77 per cent) and the Netherlands (80 per cent). Peck, writing in the 1960s, recorded that in each British industry there were more technicians (i.e. non-graduate engineers and scientists)

Table 5.10. *International comparisons of research and development activity, 1959–62*

	USA	France	Germany	UK
Qualified scientists and engineers as % total employment 1959	1·7	0·8	1·3	1·0
R&D expenditure as % GNP 1962 (US = 100)	100	124	65	151
Military and space as % total R&D expenditure 1962	52	30	15	39
% distribution of 1962 industrial R&D expenditure				
Aircraft	36·3	27·7	0	35·4
Electrical machinery and instruments	25·5	25·7	33·8	24·0
Vehicles and other machinery	15·6	10·0	19·2	10·3
Chemicals	12·6	16·8	32·9	11·6
Other	10·0	19·8	14·1	18·7

Source: Peck (1968: 449); Freeman (1979: 67).

than professionals; in the USA it was the other way round, even though the ratio of technician earnings to professional earnings was the same in both countries. In effect Britain was a relatively low user of graduate engineers in industry. The low valuation of formal technical training in the mid-nineteenth century was still strongly held at the turn of the century. Success, as in cotton, did not appear to rely on formal training but rather on on-the-job training; where formal training was necessary, as in steel, it was provided (at Sheffield University for example) but this still did not prevent the UK losing out to German and American steel producers (Sanderson 1980: 41). Engineering became a Cinderella profession, leading Freeman to argue that

the few really good engineers tended to enter the public sector or the national laboratories or a few prestigious private firms ... In Germany in contrast the normal professional route to most senior management positions across a broad range of industry was through six years of full-time intensive engineering education. (Freeman 1979: 69–70)

Unfortunately for the graduate engineer, the traditional skilled labourer had been at least a credible substitute, as we have seen in cotton and motor vehicles and has been noted in detail for shipbuilding (Lorenz and Wilkinson 1986).

Business leadership, insofar as it attracted a social elite, was therefore dominated by graduates with a liberal arts education – as in the USA. There is at least a case for thinking that the social elite was more attracted to other areas of management and indeed other professions and occupations. Rubinstein's work on the nineteenth-century middle class suggests that, after an initial mushrooming of incomes in Lancashire, the main fortunes were to be made in commerce, government, services, indeed in the south-east and London. His evidence from the pupils of three leading public schools 1895–1900 (Harrow, Winchester, Rugby) suggests that fathers engaged in manufacturing and heavy industry were less numerous than fathers in finance and commerce. Sons of business fathers and non-business fathers alike tended to go into finance and commerce rather than manufacturing (Rubinstein 1988: 56–7).

Nor are these trends a function of the prevalence of family firms in manufacturing. Retailing and the City are extensively populated by family firms, yet these sectors have been amongst the fastest growers (Hannah 1989). In many manufacturing firms in Britain, a significant portion of managers came up from the shop floor, with few formal qualifications. Swords-Isherwood (1980) reports on samples of British managers taken in 1958, 1966, and 1976 which reflected a continuing prevalence of two groups of managers, one from a fee-paying school background and the other with little formal training; the university-trained business student or engineer was certainly not dominant. In sum, the biggest rewards both financially and socially in post-1950 Britain were not in manufacturing and not in engineering. This reflected in part the role which pure science had played in the war and the armaments industry. It was also a confirmation that the major growth points of the British economy were finance, insurance, accounting, communications, indeed services generally.

Profits and unions

The links between government, unions and employers were an important feature of the industrial landscape of Britain in the twentieth century. Before looking at the elements of that tripartism, which figured so much in government industrial policy, it is useful to examine what happened to the way in which the industrial cake was sliced up between profits and wages, and to consider the changing role of industrial unions.

An American economist observing the British industrial relations scene in the 1960s (Ulman 1968) was clearly conscious of public perceptions of the British worker and the trade union. In view of the accusation of bloody-mindedness of British labour, Ulman was at pains to point out that the desire of unionised wage earners to defend their conditions of employment was neither a post-1945 phenomenon nor uniquely British. He found that workplace rules were similar in similar industries in the USA and in the UK, reflecting market and technological conditions. Though profit rates were declining in British industry, he recorded that hours worked were declining less than in many other industrialised countries. Finally he found that although the fraction of the labour force in unions was significantly higher than in the USA, this was largely a product of greater union membership in the government and related service sectors of the economy.

Nonetheless, rates of profit in industry and commerce have declined in the post-war period. Gross profits before deducting depreciation, interest and tax were of the order of 10 per cent of the value of capital assets in manufacturing in the early 1950s and declined to 7 per cent by the mid-1980s. In commerce, the fall was from 19 per cent to 12 per cent; in extractive industry there was a slight tendency to decline, but in the late 1970s and 1980s profit rates shot up with the development of the oil sector.

How far these changes are due to union pressures, greater capital intensity or technological changes is not easy to discern. A measure of union pressure – albeit a flawed one – is the proportion of the labour force in unions. This has indeed risen over the post-war period but only slightly. In 1951, 46 per cent of the employed labour force was in unions; it was 45 per cent in 1957 and 45 per cent in 1967, but rose in the next decade to 57 per cent in 1979, falling thereafter to 50 per cent in 1985 (Richardson 1991: 420). Membership tended to rise and fall with the economic cycle and was higher in large firms. The more important feature of the post-war period, however, has been a significant diffusion of union membership. The 1950s saw the decline of many British staple industries which, coal and railways in particular, were traditional homes of union members. The offset was a spread of unionism to the service sector, to white-collar work and government.

The other major changes in this context were in the methods of wage negotiation and in the legal rights of unions. For much of the early post-war period benchmarks for wages and hours worked were set by multi-employer single industry collective bargaining. Increasingly, however, this came to be supplemented by less formal, local plant-based negotiation. Local shortages of labour could not be reflected in the national agreements. The low unemployment levels and tight labour markets of the 1940s and 1950s certainly encouraged these developments, which were accompanied by the rise in importance of shop stewards. The phenomenon of 'wage drift' became of increasing concern by the late 1950s and early 1960s.

Up to that time, there was no such thing as a government policy on industrial relations. Government left unions and employers to get on with collective bargaining (Brown 1991: 213). Despite impressions to the contrary, strikes were not a major problem. Richardson (1991) estimates that, on average for the whole of the 1947–85 period, less than 0.01 per cent of working time was lost through strikes in Britain. In most years 90 per cent of British workers were not involved in strikes though labour disputes did rise and fall with the economic cycle. Nevertheless unofficial strikes were growing by the late 1950s and 1960s. In conjunction with the general concern about wage drift and rising wage inflation, and a belief that restrictive labour practices lay behind Britain's productivity performance relative to other countries, this led to the setting up of the Donovan Commission in 1965; in the same year new requirements on employers were introduced through the Redundancy Payments Act.

The Donovan Commission drew attention to the growth of informal wage-bargaining procedures. The Labour government's White Paper *In Place of Strife*, which followed in 1967, envisaged major changes in the form of compulsory 'conciliation pauses' and ballots for strikes, whilst sanctions were to include imprisonment in extreme cases. Though many observers have subsequently felt that these proposals would not have had a major effect on industrial relations, they were in areas sensitive for unions and were seen as an assault on voluntarism; the government retreated (Wrigley 1991).

The following Conservative government under Edward Heath set out, in its 1971 Industrial Relations Act, a much more radical and comprehensive programme with the closed shop effectively made illegal, written collective agreements enforceable through a National Industrial Relations Court and unions liable for strike damages unless the correct procedures were followed. This provoked widespread opposition and evasion so that the Labour government's 1974 Act repealed the whole structure and reconstructed the traditional cornerstones of British unionism: immunity from damages and non-enforceability of collective agreements.

By this stage the major problems were no longer unofficial strikes in the private sector but rather major disputes in the public sector, including the National Coal Board. The final twist of the tail was the return in the 1980s to the overthrown Heath programme, with the Employment Acts of 1980 and 1982 and the Trades Union Act of 1984, which enforced secret ballots for strikes and the election of officials, imposed limits on closed shops and reduced legal immunities.

It is not easy to identify the quantitative impact of these changes on industry and commerce, in particular because of the problem of separating out the impact of the economic cycle. The large rise in unemployment in the 1980s, for example, renders difficult any assessment of the specific impact of that decade's labour legislation. Table 5.11 is an attempt to decompose the movements of the rate of profit into relevant components.

Table 5.11. *Income shares and the rate of profit in industry and commerce, 1935–85 (%)*

	1935–8	1952–5	1961–4	1969–73	1982–5
Manufacturing					
Gross profit share	27·8	32·8	29·4	21·9	25·1
Capital–output ratio	2·5	3·3	3·3	3·8	3·7
Rate of return	11·1	10·0	8·8	5·7	6·7
Extractive industry[a]					
Gross profit share	17·2	10·4	19·1	17·1	75·6[b]
Capital–output ratio	2·0	1·9	3·1	3·8	5·9[b]
Rate of return	8·4	5·5	6·2	4·5	12·7[b]
Commerce					
Gross profit share	39·3	34·3	31·4	30·9	33·0
Capital–output ratio	1·5	1·8	1·7	2·1	2·8
Rate of return	26·8	19·1	18·0	14·5	11·6

[a] Agriculture not included.
[b] Includes gas, electricity and water.
Notes and sources: the data for 1935–73 are from Matthews *et al.* (1982: 183–8) and relate to gross profits, gross domestic product, gross capital stock, all measured at current prices and after deducting stock appreciation but before deducting depreciation. The capital–output ratios were actually deduced from the two other figures. The data for 1982–5 are on the SIC 1980 and were derived from the 1986 National Income and Expenditure book. The capital–output ratio could only be calculated at 1980 prices and this was then applied to the gross profit share to obtain the figures on rates of return.

The first row for each sector shows the proportion of value added (net output) which took the form of profits; the remainder was income from employment and self-employment (including rent). The profit share of income defined in this way shows a secular tendency to decline from the 1930s in both manufacturing and commerce and then to turn up in the 1980s. This seems to reflect the strong bargaining strength of labour in the post-war era of full capacity output and tight labour markets, followed by the massive rise in unemployment in the 1980s. Extractive industry is dominated by coal mining up to the 1970s and shows no secular trend. The data for the later period from the mid-1970s unfortunately include gas, electricity and water where the profit share has been of the order of 45–55 per cent in the post-war period. There is little doubt, however, that the figure of 75 per cent for 1982–5 reflects also the high profits from oil exploration.

The rate of return on capital is related to the above shares by a simple identity: profits/net output multiplied by net output/capital stock equals profits/capital stock. The capital/output ratio shows a clear secular tendency to rise in each sector. For commerce, a rise occurs in almost every period, reflecting the shift to self-service in the distributive trades and computerisation in banking and insurance. In some respects this decline in capital productivity is overstated, since the new capital is not the same as the old and incorporates an element of technical progress. Either way, the result was a continuous decline in the rate of return on capital in commerce though, as was noted earlier, the capital stock estimates for the last period may be inflated, leading to an understatement of the recovery of the profit rate. On this basis the rise in capital intensity from the 1930s probably accounted, at least up to the 1970s, for a larger part of the decline in the rate of return on capital in commerce than did changes in the share of the income cake. In contrast, in manufacturing it is the profit share which explains a significant part of both the actual decline in the rate of return, especially in the 1950–73 period, and the subsequent rise in the 1980s. The rise and decline of labour power is seen in the rate of profit.

In the case of extractive industry the rise in the capital–output ratio in the last period in Table 5.11 disguises the fact that the capital–output ratio in gas, electricity and water (of the order of 13.0) is much higher than in oil production. Thus the rise in the rate of return in extractive industry from the advent of oil production reflects both a high profit share of income and a high capital productivity. Both oil production and commerce are the expanding elements in the whole industrial area. Table 5.11 reflects this fact. The rate of profit in commerce and in oil production exceeds that in mining and manufacturing throughout the post-war period.

The concentration and distribution of industry and government policy

Apart from praise for the legislation outlawing price fixing and related market collusion devices, there has been hardly a good word for government industrial policy in the post-war period (see also ch. 9). The civil service and politicians in power have, in various contexts, been described as in the pocket of the City, insular, unimaginative, elitist, insufficiently dirigiste, providing no encouragement to banks or anti-industrial (Wilks 1990; Wiener 1985; Gamble 1985, 1990; Hall 1986a, 1986b; Grant 1990, 1991).

The accusation that governments have not sufficiently explored alternative strategies seems in retrospect unfair. The strong drive towards social ownership of industry in the 1940s (ch. 6) was followed by decontrol and deregulation in the 1950s, the imitation of French planning in the 1960s, the imitation of Italian industrial practice in the 1970s and complete disengagement in the 1980s. The list of activities and interventions that would count as industrial policy include investment incentives, location of industry, monopolies and restrictive practice legislation, financial support, nationalisation and privatisation, undertaking basic research, disseminating technical information, promoting industrial training. Some of these have been simply the instruments for wider policy objectives like balance of payments stability (see ch. 10). What determined the direction and content of policy? How effective was it?

There is a view that little separates the industrial policies of Conservative governments from those of Labour governments. Whilst this view may have been appealing in the late 1950s and 1960s, when both parties were struggling to develop forms of industrial intervention in order to cope with Britain's apparent industrial backwardness, in retrospect there have been different styles. The approach of the Labour Party in the late 1940s, and latter parts of the 1960s and 1970s, was at the least one of suspicion of private ownership and its products; to them, the structure needed controlling and private investment supplemented. At the limit is Wilks' characterisation (1990) of the attitude of the left of the Labour Party to the car industry; the product is inegalitarian, it generates pollution, production is for profit rather than need and shop-floor work is dismal. The 1950s, under the Conservatives, were dominated by decontrol and the promotion of competition, the early 1970s by a clear, if unfulfilled, commitment to let industry get on with it and the 1980s by unabashed disengagement.

What perhaps more nearly approximates to a consensus was a joint commitment to the mixed economy. Once it had become clear, by the early 1950s, that social ownership of industry was not going to herald a collectivist society and that private education and health were unlikely to be foisted on the general public, both parties' attitude to manufacturing, extractive industry and commerce was one of manipulating the boundary, the direction and the structure rather than revolutionary change.

Government industrial policy is decided by politicians; in the post-war period this seemed to have two broad implications for industry. One stemmed from the way in which industrial policy might affect voting behaviour; the other arose from the 'great industrial power syndrome', the reluctance to accept that Britain was no longer in the comfortably dominant position of world industrial leader with few competitors.

The main economic factors which affected voting behaviour in the post-war period seem to have been employment and inflation. With low inflation in the early years, the commitment to full employment pervaded all aspects of industrial policy. Considerations related to industrial productivity were present but came to have more weight when inflation took off in the 1960s. The development of policy to improve industrial productivity was affected also by the image of a great industrial power. By the 1980s, employment had all but disappeared as a central issue, as the first-past-the-post electoral system permitted a minority government to win within highly regionalised patterns of unemployment (Gamble 1990: 90). The aim of the rest of this chapter is to examine how far this thesis accounts for the direction and content of industrial policy and to assess how effective policy was in terms of the objectives stated by its proponents.

During the 1950s demand management was the dominant tool of economic policy (see ch. 10); with full employment, there was little need to use industry as a vehicle for employment policies. The process of abolition of direct controls was temporarily halted by the Korean War but was largely completed by 1954, the exception being some key raw materials like coal, jute and scrap iron whilst controls on company borrowing and share issues continued to the end of the 1950s.

The major development in industrial policy, the control of monopolies and restrictive practices, had its origin in part in the employment objective. As Kirby (1984b: 95) suggests, the 1944 White Paper on employment expressed the concern that attempts to stimulate employment and aggregate demand might be frustrated by price rings and monopoly firms, who would absorb wage demands by raising prices, thereby reducing output and employment. Whereas concentration had flattened off in the 1930s and 1940s, price agreements had proliferated; they carried none of the advantages of economies of scale that might accrue to a monopoly firm. Some 25–30 per cent of manufacturing output in the 1930s was controlled by trade association price agreements, a figure that had risen to 50–60 per cent by the mid-1950s (Mercer 1991: 79).

The 1948 Monopolies and Restrictive Practices Act set up a Commission which considered references from the Board of Trade in relation to a specific practice or to a market where one third of goods were sold or bought by one firm. The procedure was determined by the desired results for employment and efficiency rather than on any a priori diagnosis of the ills of restrictive agreements. The Commission made twenty reports but only one order (on dental products) and it would appear that it was affected by the unofficial criteria used by the Board of Trade, namely that the absence of complaints proved sufficient for a reference not to be made. Mercer (1991) concluded that business pressure on the government had muffled the impact of the legislation.

The dissemination of information about restrictive agreements was, however, sufficient to lead to the establishment of a Restrictive Practices Court under the 1956 Restrictive Practices Act (Hall 1962). Like its predecessor the new Act focussed on desired results but touched on means by presuming that restrictive practices were against the public interest; it set out in so-called 'gateways' (unemployment, protection against physical damage, etc.) why restrictions might be in the public interest. Although the Act reflected an ambivalent attitude to restrictive practices in that it really presumed that only the abuse of market power was against the public interest, it proved successful. All price agreements had to be registered and any supposed benefits had to be 'substantial' to offset other detriments. Legal precedents were set and those waiting judgements could then anticipate the outcome. By 1963, 83 per cent of registered agreements had been changed or abandoned. The Court was shown to have teeth in rejecting the price agreement of the Yarn Spinners' Association not-withstanding pleas about unemployment in Lancashire. In general the Act had displayed the pervasive character of restrictive practices, finding only 1 per cent of agreements to be in the national interest. By 1978 the Court had received 478 references but in the event 436 had not been defended (Walshe 1991: 363).

During the 1960s concern grew about the practices which were not registered; a new Act in 1968 made registration a statutory duty and made information agreements also registrable. The Court proceedings could also be fairly costly, so that the new Act also gave the Secretary of State power to exempt from registration activities which were clearly not against the national interest (for example petrochemicals, where knowledge of competitors is important). In a sample of 159 agreements examined by Heath (1961) it transpired that price agreements were being phased out and replaced by information agreements. In 1964 resale price maintenance was abolished by an Act of that name. In general the attack on price fixing had helped shift company strategy to other ways of cooperation, including mergers.

Interest in merger activity accelerated as concentration in British industry rose from the late 1950s. The share of the largest 100 companies in manufacturing was 20 per cent in 1930, remained at the same level up to 1953 but rose to 41 per cent by 1970, remaining fairly static thereafter. The three largest firms in each manufacturing industry accounted on average for 26.3 per cent of employment in 1935; the figure was slightly higher in 1951 (29.3 per cent) and 1958 (32.4 per cent) and then rose steeply to 41.0 per cent by 1968 (Hannah 1976b: 165; Walshe 1991: 339–41). The causes of this increased concentration seem to have been mergers and acquisitions rather than increases in plant size; the 100 largest plant establishments accounted for 11 per cent of manufacturing net output in 1935, a figure that had not changed by 1962 (Walshe 1991: 341).

Firms were increasingly attempting to escape the legislative attacks on price fixing and the attack by the GATT, EFTA and EEC treaties on tariff protection, gaining economies for multi-plant operation in the area of finance and managerial specialisation. Channon's study (1973) of 100 large companies showed that only 13 per cent had a multi-division structure in 1950 but this rose to 30 per cent by 1960 and 72 per cent by 1970. Only 25 per cent were diversified in product markets in 1950 but this figure had risen to 45 per cent by 1960 and to 60 per cent by 1975. The Monopolies Commission was given only seven new references in the period 1958–64 and there was growing concern about the Board of Trade's tendency to seek voluntary assurances from companies, a practice only slightly more forceful than its earlier policy of gently showing the companies that they were not acting in a socially beneficial manner (Mercer 1991: 82).

The year 1965 therefore saw the Monopolies and Mergers Act under which the Board of Trade was again required to refer cases to a Monopolies and Mergers Commission under the one third of market rule; 'services' were now included as were mergers involving £10 million or more of assets or £5 million for any one of the companies involved. The only other major legislative changes were the 1973 Fair Trading Act, which changed the one third market rule to one quarter, and the 1980 Competition Act which empowered the Commission to investigate the nationalised industries. On the face of it, and in an open economy where foreign trade is an important source of competition, the policy could be judged effective. Of the 3 per cent of mergers which met the criteria in the period 1965–85 most were referred or abandoned, the latter option being reinforced by the City Code on Take-Overs and Mergers, established in 1967, which required that a merger offer must lapse if it is referred to the Commission. On the other hand, the authorities were under no obligation, in contrast to the rules governing restrictive trade practices, to refer a monopoly or merger to the Commission, and the companies did not need to prove that they were operating in the public interest. The Commission had to establish that a merger would (not 'might') operate against the public interest, defined in a much broader sense than the 'gateways' for price agreements. Over the period 1965–73 the Board of Trade considered 875 mergers and the Monopolies Commission 18. Only 6 were forbidden, with the Board of Trade still reliant in part on assurances from the companies. Of the 102 merger referrals over the whole period 1965–87, 68 were horizontal mergers of which 15 were abandoned and 23 found to be against the public interest, rather a small percentage given that in these cases there was an a priori case for referral. The evidence on mergers for the 1955–73 period is that profitability did not increase but rather declined, so that in contrast to the attack on price fixing, the UK approach has not been effective (Walshe 1991: 365–7; Graham 1972; Mottershead 1978).

Large companies were seen to contain the potential for scale economies and innovation, so that by the 1960s the restructuring aspect of industrial policy came actually to support mergers. Similarly, once it became clear in the 1950s that monopoly policy was likely to have a minute effect on employment, relative at least to the power of demand management, the employment objective in competition policy lost much of its force except for specific problem areas. Insofar as unemployment had a regional dimension there were other more powerful policies to hand. The experiences of the inter-war years suggested that attempts to shift labour out of the depressed regions were ineffective; emigration was a risky business and in any case left the old and infirm behind. The 1940 Barlow Report and the 1944 White Paper on employment provided a rationale for regional policy in casting the problem of congested and polluted cities as the other side of the coin to unemployment in depressed areas. Confidence in the use of location controls during the war led to their retention and the Distribution of Industry Act of 1945 together with the Town and Country Planning Act of 1947 empowered the government to designate Development Areas, grant loans and issue Industrial Development Certificates (IDCs) for all industrial buildings occupying more than 5,000 square feet in area. It was the regions occupied by the staple industries which continued to form the Development Areas, but because of the healthy demand for the products of the staple industries in the 1940s and 1950s as other countries struggled to restore and replace their war-torn capacity, regional policy was initially relatively quiescent. By the end of the 1950s severe international competition was emerging and the 1958/9 recession prompted renewed attention to the regions.

The incidence of severe regional unemployment had not changed much. The regions which were at the top of the unemployment lists in 1986 were the same as those in 1932 and included Scotland, South Wales, the north-west, parts of the midlands, west Yorkshire and the north-east. It was the decline in manufacturing employment which came to characterise the post-war incidence, with the north-west, Yorkshire/Humberside and the west midlands being badly affected, the last one a new problem area. All conurbations were losing out to smaller towns and rural areas such as East Anglia. Production and site costs in free-standing cities made them vulnerable to losses in manufacturing and the growing service sector. Aid became available over wider areas and the Local Employment Act of 1960 established a new list of Development Districts, inclusion in which required only that the Board of Trade judged that high unemployment existed or was imminent (Henderson 1962: 339). The major claim to success in this period was an agreement with the five major car companies to undertake substantial new projects in the scheduled areas, especially Merseyside.

But it was 1963–70 which saw the most prolonged and intensive attack on the regional problem. Policy increasingly focussed on 'mobile manufacturing plants'. The stick was the IDCs, which from 1966 were not needed in Development Areas, while the carrot was a subsidy to either capital or labour. Initial allowances on investment projects, which allowed accelerated depreciation for tax purposes and effectively a saving on interest charges, had been introduced in 1945. They had rather a chequered history, being doubled in 1949, abandoned in 1952, restored in 1953 and supplemented by conventional allowances in 1954 (effectively allowing more than 100 per cent of the value of an asset to count for tax purposes on depreciation). In fact during 1950–60 allowances were changed six times and in 1963 were supplemented by straight cash grants for investment. Moreover the old allowance and the new cash grants all had regional differentials. The investment grants were abandoned in 1970 and initial allowances became the main investment incentives. In addition to all the ups and downs, they do have the disadvantage of encouraging substitution of labour by capital and during 1967–76 a selective employment tax was introduced with a differential incidence which favoured manufacturing and the Development Districts.

Armstrong (1991) has argued that these policies as a package were successful. Immigrant firms accounted for two-thirds of new jobs in 1960–71. Only 13 per cent of the projects which were refused IDCs in 1958–71 were abandoned and 50 per cent were modified. By projecting what employment would have been in the absence of the measures, he established for the period 1963–81 that regional policy, if not the selective employment tax, led to 277,000 surviving new jobs in the assisted areas and gave a strong boost to manufacturing investment in the 1960s and early 1970s. The general departure in the 1970s from a high demand economy undermined any attempts thereafter to induce firms to move into the depressed areas. The 1979–81 recession all but eliminated the pool of mobile manufacturing plants and in the 1980s various policy instruments were abandoned; the spread of eligible assisted areas was reduced, IDCs ended in 1981, expenditure on regional policy quickly fell and the 100 per cent allowance system was dropped in 1984. The EEC influence came to the fore for regional policy; domestically, however, the high unemployment rate everywhere rendered regional moves more difficult.

Policy for industrial productivity

Inflation was moving towards the front of the voters' concern as early as the 1960s. Industrial productivity had therefore a short-term electoral attraction as well as a longer-term importance for the economy. There were many useful developments in the links between government and industry, even though the ones which attracted most attention and money tended to reflect either the great industrial power syndrome or the electoral consequences of lost jobs in sensitive areas or periods.

The policy on industrial productivity took the form of attempts to raise the level of investment and technological advance. Whether under Labour or Conservative governments, the broad approach was to improve the skills of the labour force and the dissemination of technical information, to facilitate channels of communication between industry and government as large actors on the economic stage and to restructure and develop firms and industries where this was not likely to emerge voluntarily in an approved way.

The initial thrust came at the end of the 1950s and early 1960s, after a decade of stop–go macro-economic policies and a realisation that the productivity growth gap with continental Europe could no longer be viewed as a temporary war-related phenomenon. The 1960s saw a shift to indicative planning, to new government agencies to foster industrial restructuring and to an attempt to develop strategies for technology. In only the first area could it be said that Conservatives and Labour were operating on the same lines. Formal tripartite discussions had been anticipated in the Development Councils set up under an Act of 1947 to placate some of the worries about the Anglo-US productivity gap (Tomlinson 1991). It was, however, criticism of planning for public expenditure, together with the advocacy, by a Federation of British Industries group, of the role of government statements about economic expectations, that started the ball rolling in a significant way towards the end of the 1950s. In 1961 the Chancellor of the Exchequer was talking of the need for establishing the conditions for realising faster economic growth. Analogies were being drawn with industrial planning in France. There, however, the planning machine was fully integrated with government and the planning process incorporated strong directive policies, such as those on capital issues.

The National Economic Development Council was set up as a tripartite body, with the task of consulting with industrial sectors to identify the obstacles and required policies to achieve a target growth rate of 4 per cent p.a. In 1962 Economic Development Committees were established for individual industries, to examine growth projects and to consider ways of improving performance. Although an influential Labour politician of the period, Crosland, was thinking on similar lines – not physical planning but breaking bottlenecks, encouraging investment – the Labour Party felt that it had to give what it saw as more teeth by establishing the Department of Economic Affairs, a new government department separate from the Treasury. The idea was to generate a self-fulfilling prophecy – to develop a consistent, coordinated set of projections and thereby create expectations in the private sector which would be realised. In practice the whole venture was discredited by not having enough instruments of policy available to achieve the 5.5 per cent p.a. export growth needed for the 4 per cent overall growth target. The plan itself had been rather hurriedly concocted with only a small sample of companies effectively involved (cf. Kirby 1991; Meadows 1978) and the only item which increased in line with the plan was government current expenditure. 1966 saw deflationary measures which swamped the whole process and the plan was formally abandoned in 1969.

An equally ambitious aim of the 1964–70 Labour government's general industrial policy was the pursuit of rationalisation through the Industrial Reconstruction Corporation (IRC), set up under an Act of 1966. It had pump priming funds of £150 million and its group of independent businessmen were expected to act as merger brokers. Size was seen as the key to industrial efficiency and unlikely to emerge voluntarily in a satisfactory form. This novel agency was however anxious not to be accused of back-door nationalisation; it operated on strictly commercial criteria and proceeded cautiously, its most significant achievement being the merger of the Leyland Motor Company and British Motor Holdings in 1968. Since the merger movement was well under way in any case, there was an element of pushing at an open door (Mottershead 1978). Many of the structural interventions of the 1960s were less planned. This included shipbuilding, where decline had implications for the balance of payments and regional policy; government finance had followed detailed investigations in 1961 and 1966.

But the major private sector industry under government scrutiny in this respect was the aircraft industry. Here was an area where governments proved reluctant to face up to Britain's decline as a world power and to the prospect that it ought to develop modest plans for both the purchase and production of aircraft. In the 1950s the government had taken the view that there were too many projects and too many firms. Concentration of production would allow the government to avoid the embarrassing decision which it had to face in choosing between projects. In 1958 British European Airlines needed a new jet engine and the government used this opportunity to exert pressure for amalgamations, a degree of intervention unknown for nationalised, let alone private industry. By 1959 the British Aircraft Corporation had been established as one firm alongside the Hawker Siddeley Group, Westland for helicopters, Rolls Royce and Bristol Siddeley (who merged in 1966) for aero engineering, leaving Short Brothers and Harland as the special Northern Ireland case. Rising costs and the increased use of guided weapons were forcing the pace and in 1960 the government announced all its orders would focus on these five groups.

Then in 1962 came the joint Franco-British decision to build Concorde

– from the fear of not having a 'first-class' aircraft industry, said a Ministry of Aviation witness. Costs do not appear to have been a decisive consideration and by 1970 it was being forecast that revenue would not cover the development costs. More generally, in 1971 the Department of Trade and Industry echoed the 1966 government's acceptance of the case for a 'substantial' aircraft industry. It explained to a House of Commons Select Committee that support for the aircraft industry benefited the balance of payments – even though there were, as indicated earlier, much better bets for that objective – and the maintenance of technological skills across the whole field of engineering; this was said despite the fact that there were hardly any professional engineers in major sectors of the mechanical engineering industry.

This was not simply a vote-catching exercise. The Conservatives during 1970–1 had moved to a substantial disengagement from industry; the IRC was abolished and investment grants replaced by allowances to avoid subsidising loss-making firms. The subsequent U-turn was set off by the bankruptcy of Rolls Royce and the financial difficulties of Upper Clyde Shipbuilders. The former was nationalised and given funds to develop a new jet engine; the new owner of Upper Clyde Shipbuilders was subsidised. The 1972 Industry Act involved extensive provision for selective financial assistance, even offering grants in exchange for state holdings. This Act and the support for shipbuilding essentially reinforced the commitment to full employment and the rescue of lame ducks, but behind Rolls Royce and especially Concorde lay the other main driving force, the great industrial power syndrome.

It was such claims for financial support that continued to flourish whilst other elements of industrial policy floundered. The third major element in the industrial policy of the 1960s was the promotion of technical progress. By the end of the 1950s, the unfilled vacancies in professional scientific and engineering posts, the uneven spread of research and development work across industry and the haphazard government support prompted the appointment of a Minister of Science in 1959, although defence was outside his ambit. In the 1960s the Labour Party took a lead in promising revolution through the 'white heat' of industrial technology which many subsequently viewed as sheer bluster. Coopey (1992), in contrast, argued that Prime Minister Wilson did have a strategy, which rejected Keynesian economics as having any relevance to industrial policy and saw the Robbins' expansion of higher education as yielding more scientists and engineers in the long run, whilst the large pool of resources and expertise in the military sector and government research establishments would constitute the short-run resource base.

Hence the Ministry of Technology was set up in 1964 to take control of much government research by absorbing the Department of Scientific and Industrial Research (established in the 1940s); Mintech also had ministerial responsibility for the Atomic Energy Authority and the National Research and Development Corporation (NRDC) (established in the late 1940s as a government pump primer for innovation). By merging with the Ministry of Aviation in 1967, it opened up the prospect of shifting resources from aviation to other industrial activities and Coopey claimed that it helped in the 10 per cent cut in R & D defence expenditure and the 20 per cent rise in civil R & D spending, with the government for the first time spending more on the latter than the former. Yet the Ministry had in the end little in the way of any tangible results that might commend it to future governments. A Computer Advisory Centre was set up in 1965 and finance was put into International Computers Ltd (ICL). Mintech also had sponsorship functions for telecommunications, electronics and machine tools. Although the Department of Trade and Industry continued several of these policies, a 1971 report of the government's think tank rejected the idea of a general technology policy and advocated that applied research and development should be done on a customer-contractor basis. Organisational changes seemed to predominate over any serious attempt to grapple with policy. Foreign multinationals, for example, were given a warm welcome in Britain in the 1950s and 1960s but there was no attempt to favour inward investment in technology-intensive sectors (Freeman 1987; Jones 1990: 209).

The attempt by governments to achieve restructuring of industry had not, however, finished, and the Conservative government's 1972 Industry Act with its provision for selective assistance heralded wider-scale intervention. The range of policies adopted by the Labour Party were thought by supporters to involve a coherent package, whereby the 'social contract' and industrial democracy would induce the trades unions to participate in industrial restructuring. In the early 1970s Labour Party thinking had turned to the Italian State Holding Company, providing regional assistance, as one model for restructuring. Tripartite planning agreements would be drawn up for each sector with financial assistance contingent on the completion of such agreements; for the top hundred companies the planning agreements were to be mandatory with a prospect in any case of them being taken into public ownership. The projected National Enterprise Board (NEB) would hold a portfolio of twenty or more leading firms, extending public ownership and participation in the planning agreement.

The Labour leadership, once in power, retreated from this degree of intervention. By the time of the White Paper of 1974 on *The Regeneration of British Industry* the planning agreements, the content of which had never been thought through in any detail, had become voluntary and bilateral as between companies and the Department of Industry, whilst the plans for public ownership were considerably pared down. Only two planning agreements were signed, one by the publicly owned National Coal Board, the other (under duress) by Chrysler.

The NEB was established under the Industry Act of 1975. It was tripartite in constitution and operated under fairly strict commercial and therefore limiting criteria. It had two roles in practice; one which was difficult to escape was acting as a hospital for lame ducks. By 1978 four of the eight companies which it took on board were doing well, one had been sold and the remaining three were in financial difficulties (Sawyer 1991, 1992). The three comprised Herbert and Cambridge Instruments Ltd, British Leyland, which had been brought into public ownership in 1975, and Rolls Royce; the latter two accounted by 1979 for £570 million of the £780 million invested by the NEB. The rescue of British Leyland, the sole British car manufacturer, stemmed from a political decision to save face and to save employment. Rather more credit has been given for NEB's use of its remaining resources. It had major shareholdings in ICL and Ferranti, founded INMOS to produce semi-conductors, NEXOS electronic office equipment, INSAC computer software, and in general, apart from BL, had to keep a low profile as had the IRC because of the fear of back-door nationalisation and now the inquiring eyes of the IMF.

Complementary to these developments was the Industrial Strategy White Paper of 1975 which returned to the modest aims of reducing import penetration and raising the production potential in key growth areas; this was to be done by improving the flow of information through the tripartite dialogues in NEDO and the newly established Sector Working Parties of which thirty-nine had been established by 1983. Selective assistance under the 1972 Industry Act was able to feed on information from the Sector Working Parties and continued to promote scientific and technological development in traditional engineering trades; the Products and Process Development Scheme was launched in 1977 to encourage the introduction of new and significantly improved product and process, and the Microprocessor Applications Project began in 1978. The effectiveness of all this lower level activity in promoting the flow of information has yet to be properly assessed.

So also has the area of financial help for small firms, which was prompted by the Bolton Committee of 1971, commending the competitive ability of small firms. Much of it continued into the Thatcher era, even though the volume of expenditure on industrial support was cut. The diffusion of information technology was given a high priority, substantial funds were provided under the 'Support and Innovation' scheme launched in 1981 and in the same year NRDC and NEB merged into the British Technology Group. There was no initial drop in funds for British Leyland and Rolls Royce. Indeed the final twist was that in the course of privatising them in 1984 (Jaguar), 1987 (Unipart and Trucks) and 1988 (Rover), equity of £680 million was advanced to the DAF company who took over Leyland Trucks and £409 million to British Aerospace when it took over Rover.

Conclusion

Industry and commerce's share of the UK labour force declined in the post-war period. However, partly because the sector maintained its share of the capital stock and partly because of increases in industrial efficiency, the share of output rose. In that sense, talk of deindustrialisation is misplaced. Manufacturing certainly declined and for some observers that was decisive. In part this was a by-product of the recessionary years from the mid-1970s but, more generally, manufacturing has no prior claim to attention in economic terms. Other sectors have been capable of raising productivity and generating exports of goods and services.

In fact industrial productivity growth up to the 1970s rose considerably above the growth rate of the inter-war period and attained levels unprecedented since the middle of the nineteenth century. Japan and the continental European countries grew faster partly because they were catching up on wartime destruction and in part because they were copying the progress of the old industrial leaders, the UK and the USA. That still leaves a gap to be explained, and many have pointed to Britain's slowness in adopting technologically advanced processes and products. However Britain was different from many other countries, especially the USA, in the highly skilled labour force which it inherited from being first in the field. Wholesale modernisation and mechanisation of plant was not always so economically attractive for Britain.

Observers were critical of the British educational system in its provision for technical training and its development of professional engineers. In fact the pattern of educational development was as much a product as a cause of the distinctive features of British industry. Much unacclaimed improvement in technical training and dissemination of technical knowledge took place in the post-war period.

The elements of government policy which attracted rather more attention were attempts to restore the fortunes of manufacturing, often because of politically damaging regional unemployment levels, and to prop up a defence programme of research and development and an aircraft industry suitable only for a great industrial power. In the meantime the parts of the private production sector which were expanding included, apart from the 1970s oil developments, communications, finance, insurance, tourism, accounting and other service activities. Earnings were higher than elsewhere and attracted workers, managers and professionals; profit rates were higher and attracted capital. These changes sat uneasily on the former workshop of the world and the adjustment process continues.

6   The economic consequences of the state ownership of industry, 1945–1990

Leslie Hannah

> Of forms of ownership let fools contest, What e'er is best managèd is best
> (M. V. Posner (1987), former Labour government economic adviser on
> nationalised industries, with apologies to Alexander Pope)

Introduction

The nineteenth century saw a few utopian socialist experiments, and Victorians uncontroversially resorted to municipal ownership in a wide range of public utilities. In the twentieth century, a remarkable series of political experiments with nationalisation has given applied economists and historians an even richer variety of material for investigation and encouraged systematic empirical investigation of the record of different systems of ownership. It is still not possible unequivocally to recommend a superior form of organisation on the basis of such studies but we are now as aware of the prospects of failure for state ownership and regulation as of the market failure emphasised by earlier generations of economists. Idealists of left and right now – as in the past – will continue to by-pass evidence from the reality of capitalism and socialism. Their utopian dreams may ultimately be conducive to human improvement: certainly such hopes have sustained utopians in the past. Practical men may, however, benefit from learning some of the lessons of twentieth-century experience as a discipline on their dreams.

That experience is, of course, rich and diverse. In the communist bloc, whole economies were transformed from semi-feudal or capitalist market economies to socialist planned economies, of many varieties. They shared the common characteristic that the material means of production were largely owned by the state and many basic allocative decisions were made centrally. By the end of the 1980s the economic inefficiency and political bankruptcy of such socio-political systems precipitated their widespread collapse.

Yet experience of state ownership has not been confined to the totalitarian socialist countries. Among the liberal democracies, there was a wide range of state ownership. There are considerable problems in

168

Table 6.1. *The share of state-owned enterprises in some OECD economies, c. 1980*

	% of output	% of employment
France (1982)	16·5	14·6
Austria (1978–9)	14·5	13·0
Italy (1982)	14·0	15·0
Sweden (1982)	—	10·5
UK (1978)	11·1	8·2
Australia (1970–4)	10·7	—
West Germany (1982)	10·7	7·8
Portugal (1976)	9·7	—
Spain (1979)	4·1	—
Netherlands (1971–3)	3·6	8·0
Canada (1970–4)	—	4·4
USA (1983)	1·3	1·8

Sources: Pathirane and Blades (1982: 271, 273) for Canada and Australia; Milanovic (1989: Tables 1.4 and 1.7) for the remainder.

measuring the size of the state-owned industry sector in different economies, not least because of the variations in national statistical definitions of these industries (Pathirane and Blades 1982). Nonetheless, it is clear that Britain did not have an unusually high degree of public ownership, by European standards, even at the peak of public ownership before the 1980s privatisation programme began.

Table 6.1 suggests, for example, that Britain should be placed well below France or Italy, and at about the same level as Germany in the degree of state ownership. This might seem surprising. West Germany's post-war denationalisations and espousal of the *Sozialmarktwirtschaft* are commonly supposed to have concentrated state interest in the market economy on welfare rather than state industry. But government ownership in Germany, outside long-standing cases such as the Bundesbahn and Bundespost, was often on a *Land* (state), rather than a federal, level. Technocratic espousal of mixed public and private control had long given legitimacy to government involvement (for example, in electricity supply) in Germany, but there were also new industrial investments (for example in the aircraft industry). Together these forces led to German levels of public enterprise quite comparable to those in Britain.

There is no simple relationship generally between the levels of public ownership shown in Table 6.1 and levels of development. The lowest share of public enterprise occurs in both the rich countries, for example the USA, and the poor ones, for example Spain. Equally post-war productivity growth performance appears to be uncorrelated with public enterprise: though the slower-growing countries are slightly more likely than the fast growers to appear in the bottom half of the table, Japan (which is not included) was the fastest growing yet had a small public sector near American levels. There is, then, no *prima facie* case to see the degree of commitment to state enterprise (as opposed to the *quality* of state enterprise and its alternatives) as a major determinant of the poor economic performance of industrialised democracies like Britain. Some of the current euphoria about the collapse of communism and the parallel contemporary vogue for privatisation might suggest otherwise, but the question of the performance of state-owned enterprises in Britain is worth approaching with an open mind.

Definitions

There is no generally agreed economic definition of state-owned enterprises. At its core are the statutory public corporations of the kind conventionally referred to in the UK as 'nationalised industries': enterprises such as the BBC or British Coal (formerly the National Coal Board). In common parlance, the sector also includes businesses like the Post Office, even when (before 1969) it was run as a civil service department rather than as a separate, publicly owned corporation. It seems sensible to include also those joint-stock companies – like the car manufacturer British Leyland (the Rover Group) between 1974 and 1988 – in which a majority of the voting shares were owned by the government. The economic essence of a 'nationalised' or 'public sector' enterprise is that it is owned (and usually, but not invariably, also controlled) by the state rather than by private interests.

How do such enterprises differ from the rest of the public sector? In essence, it is that their output is not provided free, as, for example, the tax-financed output of the National Health Service or state education largely is. Even in that respect, however, there is scope for ambiguity: water authorities once financed their activities from local taxation but then charged separately for water. It is not obvious that this change (as opposed to their recent privatisation) fundamentally altered their nature as state-owned, public utilities. Contrariwise, British municipal rented housing, though locally managed, was (substantially) financed by the Treasury and (substantially) paid for by the tenants. It thus operated in many respects like a state-owned industry rather than a free public service, and indeed dominated other industries in the size of its capital stock (and in its contribution to 1980s privatisation proceeds). Bishop and Kay (1988: 3)

Table 6.2. *The main UK state-owned industries and firms with their dates of nationalisation and privatisation*

Industry/firm	Date of nationalisation[a]	Date of privatisation[b]
Post Office (Royal Mail)	—	—
Royal Dockyards/British shipbuilders (warships)	—/1977	—
Nuclear Power	—	—
British Waterways	1948	—
Bank of England	1946	—
Coal	1947	—
BBC	1926	—
Railways	1948	—
London Transport	1933	—
Girobank	—	1990
Royal Ordnance Works	—	1986
Airports	—	1987
Amersham International	—	1982
Britoil/Enterprise Oil	—	from 1982
Telecoms	1912	1984
British Petroleum	1914	from 1979
National Electricity Grid	1927	1990
Airlines	1946	1987
Cable and Wireless	1947	from 1981
Electricity Generation	1948	1991
Scottish Electricity	1948	1991
Electricity Distribution	1948	1990
Road Haulage	1948	from 1953
Buses	1948	1986 (NBC)
Ports	1948	from 1983
Gas	1949	1986
Steel (1st)	1951	from 1953
Steel (2nd)	1967	1988
Rolls Royce	1971	1987
Water	1973	1989
Jaguar	1974	1984
British Leyland (Rover Group)	1974	1988
British Aerospace	1977	from 1981
British Shipbuilders	1977	from 1985

[a] The date of 'nationalisation' is usually that of vesting not of the decision to nationalise (e.g. steel in 1951 not 1949). Many industries (e.g. gas, water, electricity) had a substantial degree of public (mainly municipal) ownership prior to nationalisation. Where no date of nationalisation is given, the enterprises began in the public sector or had mixed ownership which was changed at various dates.
[b] The date of 'privatisation' is that when substantial assets were transferred to the private sector, whether by public issue, tender offer or other means. Sometimes not all the assets were transferred – e.g. the first steel privatisation which began in 1953 was substantially complete by 1955 but one of the big fourteen firms – Richard Thomas & Baldwin – was still in the public sector when the industry was renationalised in 1967. Only about half the nationalised road haulage lorries were sold after the 1953 Act, and the public sector declined consistently until its rump was sold off in the National Freight privatisation of 1982.

suggest that the 1 million houses sold since 1979 were valued at £20 billion and (because of the discounts offered) produced £15 billion: this dwarfed the largest privatisation up to the time they were writing, which was British Gas (yielding £5.4 billion). Yet conventional discussions of nationalised industries exclude housing. This is essentially a matter of convention not of logic. Table 6.2 shows the main industries which were at some time nationalised in Britain, and their dates of entering (and, where appropriate, later leaving) the public sector.

In what follows, a broad definition of state-owned enterprises is used. Some of the studies which are referred to are confined to public utilities like gas, electricity, railways and telecoms; sometimes water is excluded, but non-utilities like coal or steel and, more rarely, other manufacturing industries are often included.

Arguments for nationalisation

The 'core' of public utilities in the state-owned sector largely comprises industries that, despite being subject to the consumer disciplines of marketed output, have often been considered unsuitable for capitalist ownership. Many of the constituent elements in this core – telecommunications, railways, electricity, gas and water – were network natural monopolies in which the market lacked balanced incentives to invest in the optimal capacity, because of monopoly pricing problems. This led to profits or prices in these industries being regulated, even in countries like the USA, when they were in private hands. Moreover, when they were again recently privatised in Britain, they required varying degrees of public regulation.

Yet the rationale for public ownership has extended far wider than such network monopoly considerations. Industries such as coal, steel, oil, cars, aeroplanes, aero-engines and shipbuilding, which figure in Table 6.2, were far from being natural monopolies: indeed they were often subject to vigorous domestic and international competition. The motives for their nationalisation were varied and nebulous. The nationalisation of coal in 1947 was seen as a way of resolving the deep-rooted labour problems of the industry, though there was talk also of gaining economies of scale in operating coal mines (Supple 1987). Much was heard in the Labour Party of the need for the state to control the 'commanding heights' of the economy, for example in the context of the 1951 and 1967 nationalisations of steel. By the 1970s, politicians of both parties nationalised failing companies on the grounds that they were too 'important' to be allowed to go bankrupt in the face of international competition. The state, it was argued, must act as the residual source of new capital for such 'lame ducks'. The only common factor in nationalisation is that politicians wanted to nationalise.

State ownership usually implied state control, but there were exceptions. British Petroleum (BP) had majority state ownership from 1914 until recently, because Winston Churchill before the First World War felt that it was important to secure naval fuel supplies. The dominant government shareholding in BP outlived memories of this rationale, but British governments were passive shareholders and exercised no more effective control over it than over other oil companies; BP's recent privatisation thus had almost exclusively financial implications. Contrariwise, Keynes (1927), when asked whether the British clearing banks should be nationalised, replied (only half-jokingly) that they already were; and indeed (though they were never formally nationalised as their French equivalents were) they have been disapprovingly described by the right as mere adjuncts of the state's financial apparatus between the 1920s and the 1960s (Griffiths 1973). By the same token, in the 1950s politicians on the left somewhat ruefully reflected that they had more effective control over the (private enterprise) chairman of ICI than they had over Lord Citrine, the ex-trade unionist chairman of the (publicly owned) electricity authority (Crosland 1956).

More generally in the post-war period, the case of a country like Japan has been held to show that, even though the state may have had a small share in industrial *ownership*, the *control* of its Ministry of International Trade and Industry over the economy's development was considerable (Johnson 1982). Ownership is in fact only one of the levers influencing industrial corporations available to democratic governments. In some respects it may be weaker than the alternatives, which range from sticks (e.g. rationing key resources and legal compulsion) to carrots (e.g. government purchasing and subsidies). Ownership may in some circumstances be weaker than moral suasion based on coalitions of mutual interest and shared values, which were important levers with which governments influenced British clearing banks or Japanese and French industry in the post-war era. Problems of agency, information flow, and transactions costs, both in state ownership and in the many varieties of market-based, capitalist systems of decentralised decision making in firms, complicate the evaluation of the economic efficiency of alternative economic systems (see also vol. 2, ch. 15) This chapter is concerned only with the economic efficiency implications of state ownership per se, not with broader issues of government planning and control in capitalist or mixed economies.

Nationalisation before 1945

Labour's election victory in 1945 inaugurated the largest ever transfer of ownership between the state and private sectors in Britain measured by the number of employees transferred; the privatisations of 1979–91 were larger in the sense that they covered a wider range of industries, but the transferred firms then employed fewer people than their counterparts of 1945–51. After allowing for the firms that were already municipally owned, the 1945–51 nationalisation programme – which included coal, electricity, gas, transport, and iron and steel – increased public sector employment by 2 million (Chester 1975: 38), that is by more than 8 per cent of the contemporary workforce.

In the following decades, employment in the labour-intensive industries like coal and railways fell, but other industries were newly nationalised and capital-intensive sectors like electricity and telecommunications for a time boosted the share of national fixed capital formation in the public sector (Pryke 1971: 289). The share of the public enterprise sector in total employment again peaked in 1977 at 13 per cent of GDP (Brech 1985: 774), probably below what it had been in 1951.

The post-war state-owned industrial sector in Britain was not only quantitatively but also qualitatively different from what had gone before, though it is tempting to see earlier parallels and precursors. As Table 6.2 shows, some industries (like the Post Office) have always been state-owned, while other nationalised industries (like telecommunications, the BBC or the National Grid) date from the first three decades of this century. There was also significant municipal ownership in the local network monopolies of gas, electricity and water, dating back to the nineteenth century; as well as industrial civil service organisations such as the Royal Dockyards and Royal Ordnance factories, which were both among the dozen largest manufacturing employers at the beginning of the century (Shaw 1983).

A common factor in early public ownership had been a perception by politicians of market failure, often buttressed by early cases of regulatory failure. In gas and water, for example, the need to avoid wasteful duplication of mains led to mergers and monopolies, requiring public ownership or at least public supervision. In telegraphs a price cartel of competitors was clearly inefficient, so a Post Office take over was agreed in 1868, though merger and public regulation might have done just as well (Foreman-Peck 1989). In telephones inefficient attempts at regulated competition were replaced by a full Post Office take over in 1912. In electricity, a full state take over was avoided, but in 1926 the government decided on a new form of regulatory control of generation which compelled existing private and municipal generators to achieve economies of scale.

The unusual (but well-directed) reorganisation of electricity wholesaling by a new, state-controlled national grid company, the Central Electricity Board, reduced bulk electricity prices to a third of their former level within a decade (Hannah 1979).

The methods of public ownership adopted before 1945 were more varied than the reasons for intervention: they included civil service departments with direct ministerial control (telephones, telegraphs, munitions, mail), municipal ownership (gas, water and local electricity generation and distribution), and public corporations (the Central Electricity Board, the BBC, London Transport). The nearest precursors to the post-war nationalised industries were the industries under civil service departments, rather than the superficially similar public corporations. Before the war, in marked contrast to their general post-war experience, such public corporations had an unusual amount of freedom from government intervention.

Public sector business leaders before 1945 used their freedom to develop positive and successful corporate strategies with little ministerial interference. While contemporaries referred to nineteenth-century 'municipal socialism', it has been correctly pointed out that 'municipal capitalism' might have been a more accurate designation (Waller 1983). Much the same can be said of early nationalised corporations. For example, the Central Electricity Board raised its capital directly from the public, without using the Treasury guarantee, and paid its staff salaries well above civil service levels. Although its board members were appointed by a Minister, they could not be removed by him, and hence they routinely ignored ministerial requests for policy changes where there was no clear statutory authority for such direction. They lacked any strong motive to maximise profits, which (with their monopoly of grid transmission) would have been easy for them, though socially undesirable. Otherwise, however, their behaviour was indistinguishable from that of privately owned companies.

Most 'nationalisations' before 1945 had been undertaken by Conservative or Liberal governments; Labour's 1931 legislation which survived to create London Transport in 1933 was the exception. This perhaps explains why they were less politically controversial than later nationalisation initiatives. There were criticisms of public enterprise: Post Office control of the telephone system, for example, led to Treasury restriction of capital spending below economic levels and this retarded development. Yet by the 1930s a wide range of middle opinion accepted the public corporations as a legitimate and efficient solution to the problems of running many areas of the British economy, where the need for public control was perceived. 'Gas and water socialism' at the municipal level had also initially been equally uncontroversial, though the electoral success of Labour and the politicisation of the municipal trading debate at the local level had destroyed that early consensus by the beginning of the twentieth century. Conservative rhetoric against the much more far-reaching nationalisations of 1945–51 followed the new trend of polarised opposition rather than the 1930s consensus of middle opinion. Yet Conservative ministerial policies did not conform to the party's rhetoric, and it was not until the 1980s that extensive privatisation brought the limited British experiment with state 'socialism' virtually to an end.

The performance of nationalised industries

The diverse range of nationalised industries in the post-war period and the changing political and economic regimes created a very diverse range of performance. The industries' managerial development can be traced in corporate histories, notably of coal, London Transport, TV, railways and electricity (Ashworth 1986; Barker and Robbins 1974; Briggs 1979; Gourvish 1986; Hannah 1982). For our purposes, however, a summary record of achievement must suffice.

A major objective of nationalisation was the improvement of the efficiency of the industries. The improvements in labour productivity over the post-war decades (see Table 6.3) show some clear patterns. There were nationalised industries, such as the airlines or telecommunications, in which a high rate of technical progress underpinned consistently high rates of productivity increase. The room for such productivity gains in industries like buses or coal mining, or (at least before the advent of North Sea supplies) gas, was considerably less. Taking this diverse public sector as a whole, however, the labour productivity gains were particularly feeble in the 1950s, picked up to a peak in the 1960s, fell again in the 1970s and were revived in the 1980s. The labour productivity gains registered in the post-war decades were better than those achieved by the same industries (under more diverse ownership regimes) in the first half of the twentieth century (Foreman-Peck and Waterson 1985). Supporters of public enterprise might take comfort from this, seeing in it a justification of Labour Party hopes in 1945–51 that they were inaugurating a programme which would fundamentally transform the efficiency of a large sector of the economy. However, such a productivity spurt was registered after the war throughout the economy (ch. 4); indeed productivity growth was on average nearly half a percentage point higher in the (largely privately owned) manufacturing sector, so it is difficult to interpret the change as uniquely the consequence of nationalisation.

Labour productivity is, of course, affected by the capital intensity of

Table 6.3. *Labour productivity growth rates in the core nationalised industries, 1948–85*

Sector	1948–58 (%)	1958–68 (%)	1968–78 (%)	1978–85 (%)
Steel	—	—	−0·2	12·6[a]
Airlines	14·0	8·9	6·4	6·6[a]
Electricity	4·6	8·0	5·3	3·9
Gas	1·6	5·5	8·5	3·8
Road freight	0·8[a]	4·9	—	—
Coal	0·9	4·7	−0·7	4·4
Railways	0·3	4·3	0·8	3·9
Buses	−0·6	−1·4	−0·5	2·1
Post Office	—	—	−1·3	2·3
Telecoms	—	—	8·2	5·8[a]
Manufacturing[b]	1·9	3·7	2·7	3·0

[a] Data relate to slightly different years than indicated at head of column.
[b] 'Manufacturing' includes some publicly owned companies, particularly in the 1970s.
Sources: Pryke (1971: 104) for cols. 1 and 2; Molyneux and Thompson (1987: 57–9), for cols. 3 and 4.

Table 6.4. *Total factor productivity growth rates in the core nationalised industries, 1948–88*

Public enterprise sector	1948–58 (%)	1958–68 (%)	1968–78 (%)	1979–88 (%)
Steel	—	—	−2·5	12·9
Airlines	7·8	9·11[a]	5·5	—
Electricity	3·6	3·1	0·7	1·4
Gas	0·7	3·7	—	3·3
Coal	0·4	3·0	−1·4	2·9
Railways	—	2·4	−1·4	1·3
Post Office	—	—	—	3·7
Telecoms	—	—	—	2·4
Airports	—	—	—	1·6
Manufacturing[b]	1·5	2·4	1·7	2·6

[a] Data relate to slightly different years than indicated at head of column.
[b] Manufacturing includes some publicly owned industries, particularly in the 1970s; while in the 1980s some of the nationalised industries were privatised (see Table 6.2 for dates).
Sources: Pryke (1971: 112) for cols. 1 and 2; Molyneux and Thompson (1987: 57–9) for col. 3; Bishop and Kay (1988: 45) for col. 4.

production. It is not a very good indicator of efficiency in highly capital-intensive industries like electricity supply, or in industries like gas, which are highly dependent on natural resource discoveries and consequential changes in technology and capital intensity. A better, though less reliably measured, indicator of productivity changes is total factor productivity shown in Table 6.4. Taking into account the productivity of capital as well as labour, as this does, the performance of the electricity industry looks less impressive throughout than on the labour productivity indicator. However, the performance of steel after 1979 is just as impressive as on the labour productivity indicator: capital productivity clearly was increasing as rapidly as labour productivity in this industry. The 1980s recovery in public sector performance is especially marked; total factor productivity in the nationalised sector, as Mrs Thatcher directed it towards privatisation, again reached high levels.

There are no obvious general reasons for these variations in public sector performance between industries and over time. The explanation for them must be sought in specific historical changes.

1945–58

Nationalisation involved, in most cases, managerial reorganisation on an unprecedented scale, though little thought was given by politicians to the managerial problems which they created. The National Coal Board merged 800 mines: on formation it was the largest business unit in Europe, with a workforce of 716,500 men at its peak in 1948. The British Electricity Authority merged 550 firms, the new gas boards 1,000 and the road haulage merger as many as 3,800. Much smaller multi-firm mergers in the private sector had a uniform record of failure, except where there were effective core firms capable of absorbing the managerial shock (Hannah 1974). This condition was only satisfied in a minority of nationalised industries: in most cases they had to create new central organisations from scratch.

The newly nationalised industries initially attracted much ill-informed political criticism for being over-bureaucratic, but it is now clear it was rather a *lack* of administrative and managerial resources that fatally compromised their early productivity performance (Pryke 1971: 26–7). The task of replacing the 'invisible hand' of the private market by the 'visible hand' of corporate management under state control posed severe problems for a British economy which already had acute shortages of managerial skills (Chandler 1990). Some potential gains from centralised control were simply never achieved: coordination of transport, for example, was minimal in Britain, especially when compared with that achieved between bus, rail and air in the Federal Republic of Germany. Yet eventually the managerial resources to improve productivity in the core businesses were assembled. By the mid-1950s, recruitment and development of administrators (helped in some cases by their enthusiasm for the principle of public enterprise) created a capacity for organisation which had initially been lacking (though low public sector salaries remained a major barrier to recruitment of senior management).

This new managerial capacity developed with little political intervention to change its direction. On returning to office in 1951, the Conservatives denationalised steel and road haulage (reducing the managerial strains in the public sector somewhat) and they generally encouraged more decentralised management structures. In electricity, for example, two Scottish boards were hived off, and in England and Wales generation was separated from the distribution and sales activities of twelve, loosely federated, area electricity boards. Like their Labour predecessors, however, Conservative Ministers initially tended to leave the boards to act in the 'public interest' without closely defining what that meant.

The contemporary conception of the nature of public ownership did not differ very much from that advanced by R. H. Tawney (1919: 127), when advocating the nationalisation of coal. The advantages, he said,

are of a kind which a public and representative body, of its very nature, possesses, and which private ownership (whatever its other merits) cannot pretend to cultivate. Such a body can organise the problem of organising production and distribution as a whole, instead of piecemeal. It can wait, and need not snatch at an immediate profit at the cost of prejudicing the future of the industry. It can enlist on its side motives to which the private profit-maker (if he is aware of their existence) cannot appeal. It can put the welfare of human beings, worker and consumer, first.

Those who ran the industries were perfectly willing to accept this generous view that they represented the public interest. Yet it did not take politicians long to see the flaws in Tawney's rosy, but naive, image of public-spirited, managerial discretion. Given the nationalised industries' monopoly position, there was a strong temptation for managers to take out their monopoly profits in what economists have long recognised as the best way: a quiet life. At first, the formal constraints on management were few. They were expected to break even financially ('taking one year with another'), though initially post-war price controls and rationing left such objectives in the government's rather than the managers' hands. The boards were also generally required not to discriminate in pricing (not to show 'undue preference' was the phrase used), a directive which usually led to more uniform prices and an increase in uneconomic cross-subsidies (for example to rural electricity consumers and bus travellers).

There was some debate on whether prices should be raised – particularly in industries like coal and electricity where demand clearly outstripped supply – but governments and managers showed a reluctance to finance new investment by unpopular price rises. Governments increasingly realised that, although they controlled the 'commanding heights', they really had very little idea about what commands they should be issuing, or the strategic principles on which such commands might be based, nor the way that managers could be given an incentive to meet government objectives.

1958–68

The catalyst for change was the Treasury's fear that the public sector was 'crowding out' investment in the private sector (see chs. 4 and 9). Cheap capital from the Treasury, it was argued, set too easy a target rate of return for nationalised industry management, a rate well below that required by new private sector investments with equal risks. Thus, too much investment was being undertaken by the nationalised industries: there were, for example, substantial demands for new investment in railway electrification and an extensive nuclear power station programme.

The White Paper on the *Economic and Financial Objectives of the Nationalised Industries* (HM Treasury 1961) raised the target rate of return for the public corporations. In 1967 it was supplemented (HM Treasury 1967) by the rule that prices should be set at long-run marginal cost and new investments were to be subjected to discounted cash-flow analysis consistent with the target return. The problem of individual ministerial reluctance to accept such rules was to be overcome by cost-benefit analyses of any non-commercial responsibilities that Ministers explicitly imposed on the nationalised industries: if industries agreed to shoulder social responsibilities at ministerial behest, they would be paid a commercial subsidy for doing so.

This policy was bipartisan: Conservative and Labour ministers were less impressed by the economic theory of allocative efficiency behind these prescriptions than by the improved productivity performance they hoped the higher financial targets would squeeze out of management. (Economists frequently pointed out that an objective function with both a marginal cost pricing rule and a test rate of discount for new investment was overspecified if it also specified a target rate of return on overall capital. Politicians were unimpressed by this truth: they wanted targets as an incentive to productive efficiency.) Under the Labour government of 1964–70 such pressures for efficiency were made more explicit by the audits undertaken by the Prices and Incomes Board.

There were new managerial appointments from outside the industries to signal the need for policy changes. In 1961, Dr Beeching (formerly an ICI director) took over as chairman of the railways, with the task of closing down unprofitable branch lines and targeting investment more effectively. Total factor productivity in railways, which in the early 1960s fell below 1948 levels, was more than 50 per cent higher by the end of the decade (Gourvish 1986: 612). In electricity supply, Ronald Edwards (an economist) was brought in as chairman to force more economic pricing techniques on to the area electricity boards (Hannah 1982: 193–217).

Profitability in the economy generally declined markedly in the 1960s (Matthews *et al.* 1982: 188), but the nationalised industries did not follow this trend: profits rose with improved productivity. Richard Pryke (1971), the leading academic investigator of the industries at the time, could soon confidently state that productivity gains were more rapid than in the past, and than in the manufacturing sector. He concluded that, by the 1960s, the management problems of reorganisation had been largely overcome by the nationalised industries (Pryke 1971). The new methods of public sector management were, he thought, such as to guarantee the continuation of superior performance into the future.

1968–79

Tables 6.3 and 6.4 suggest Pryke was wrong. Ten years later he wrote a much more pessimistic book (Pryke 1981), reflecting the experience of the 1970s. The record was particularly bad in the steel industry (newly renationalised in 1967) and in the Post Office, but other sectors as different as coal and airlines also fell to their lowest recorded rates of productivity increase in recent history. Their financial performance also deteriorated, as both Conservative and Labour governments in the 1970s capped prices, in further attempts to 'control inflation' by caps on the public sector. Faced with economic depression, both parties also nationalised more firms, though Labour proved the more enthusiastic. A remarkably high proportion of these 'lame ducks' proved to be dead ducks, whose factories and workers ultimately faced closure and redundancy after a brief subsidised half-life in a terminal care hospice, not the intended convalescence and recovery. If the productivity measures in Tables 6.3 and 6.4 had included such cases as British Leyland, the Meriden motor cycle factory or British Shipbuilders, the record would have looked even worse. The core nationalised industries by 1975 required more than £1 billion in revenue support for losses, as well as borrowing an equivalent sum to finance their capital expenditure (Pryke 1981: 261). While in the 1960s the good labour relations which had developed in many nationalised industries yielded productivity gains and desirable structural adjustments (such as the controlled run-down of coal mining), by the 1970s labour practices became increasingly ossified and blocked required changes.

Critics pointed to the absence of accountability (by either nationalised industry managers or civil servants) as the root of the failure to achieve the objectives of the 1960s White Papers. Managers felt rather that they were *too* accountable to politicians, but often for the wrong things. In truth there were more fundamental problems behind the attempts to establish coherent pricing and investment rules and financial targets. Essentially the 1967 rules required the nationalised industries to behave *as if* they were private firms operating in competitive markets. There was a paradox here: politicians were bound to ask why, in this case, they were in the public sector at all. These questions became more persistent with the economic troubles of the 1970s, when politicians were searching for any lever to control 'stagflation', and intervened repeatedly in the management of the industries.

By the end of the 1970s, the consequences for morale and efficiency in the nationalised sector were clear, and a renewed attempt was belatedly made to re-establish financial control. The White Paper on *The Nationalised Industries* (HM Treasury 1978) implicitly recognised the impracticability of the 1967 rules, and made financial targets (rather than economic pricing and investment rules) again the centre-piece of government strategy (Heald 1980). By then, however, more radical solutions to the problem of public sector management were in contemplation.

1979–90

Mrs Thatcher's government, hesitantly in the first term to 1983, but with increasing confidence thereafter, privatised most of the nationalised sector. Between 1979 and 1990 some £33 billion was raised for the public purse by privatisations (*Economist* 1990b), roughly the same (after allowing for thirteenfold inflation) as the £2.64 billion which had been paid in compensation for the nationalisations of 1945–51. The government also substantially ran down employment in the industries which remained nationalised, and a few new infrastructure projects such as the Channel Tunnel were also private from the start. The result was a substantial transformation of the size and nature of the nationalised industry sector. Less than half a million employees now remain in the core nationalised industry sector: coal, railways and the Post Office. The privatisation policy was a radical new departure, which even right-wing think tanks did not dare seriously to contemplate a few years earlier (Papps 1975).

Yet the successful preparations for privatisation required immediate productivity gains. Thus, a paradoxical achievement of the Thatcher years was that, by conventional aggregate productivity measures at least, they represent the most successful post-war experiment in the state management of industry. Contrary to popular impression, the substantial productivity gains of the 1980s (see Tables 6.3 and 6.4) were mainly achieved while the industries were still state owned, and not *after* they were privatised (Bishop and Kay 1988). The threats and opportunities of privatisation no doubt played a part in this achievement, but it clearly had other components too: clear financial objectives were set for the nationalised industries, and the commitment to support cost-cutting (even when it meant painful redundancies in marginal constituencies) was fully accepted by politicians. Politicians and industry leaders interacted in a way which bore more resemblance to the 1960s (when there were also favourable productivity achievements) than it did to the 1970s. New managers – such as Ian MacGregor at British Coal and British Steel – were, as in the 1960s, brought in to impose policy reforms. The pressure for efficiency was also consistent and serious: it was publicly symbolised now by referrals to the Monopolies Commission (which had previously only investigated the private sector) rather than the decidedly un-Thatcherite (but otherwise similar) Prices and Incomes Board investigations of the 1960s.

The consequences for productivity of the revised policies in the new environment were remarkable. The British Steel Corporation's turn-round is one of the most impressive on record in any business in any country at any time. After nationalisation in 1968, the performance of the already weak British steel industry deteriorated further in relation to its continental competitors. In 1980/1 the Corporation made a loss of £1 billion on a turnover of £3 billion and was rapidly yielding its domestic markets to more efficient producers abroad. Yet, within several years, more than half the workforce were dispensed with and labour productivity more than doubled. By the late 1980s, British Steel overtook both US and German productivity levels for the first time since Britain's loss of leadership in the industry a century earlier (see also vol. 2, ch. 3). Before it was privatised, British Steel became the lowest-cost steel producer in the world, alongside POSCO of South Korea, having overtaken the USA, Japan and all its European rivals (Aylen 1988). In 1990/1, the privatised steel corporation was profitable and had a turnover of £5 billion.

Exceptional gains such as those in steel can hardly be repeated, but there are clearly substantial opportunities for further increases in productivity there and elsewhere. In many privatised firms – notably those in manufacturing industry – the determinants of success or failure are now in those areas (competition, market structure, human and physical capital formation) discussed elsewhere (vol. 2, ch. 15).

For much of the former public sector, in the network monopoly industries, competition nonetheless remained limited after privatisation: there the regulatory framework remained a continuing responsibility of the state and an important determinant of performance. Network monopolies are not, of course, entirely exempt from competitive pressures, and technological progress has probably increased such pressures in recent decades. The process has perhaps gone furthest in the case of the railways, whose prices (commuter lines in the congested south-east apart) are already constrained more by road and air competitors than by government regulation. The development of microwave transmission for long-distance telecommunications has also reduced the cost of building a network and bolstered the entry of Mercury as an effective competitor to British Telecom.

Regulatory changes have had a similar effect of increasing competition: in 1980, for example, inter-city bus routes were deregulated and urban buses (outside London) followed in 1986. Earlier privatisations shied away from demerger and competitive structures, even where these were possible (e.g. in gas). Incumbent managers were usually able to oppose liberalisation and deregulation before privatisation by threatening to delay or oppose the privatisation on which the government had firmly determined. After experiencing this several times, to a chorus of academic criticism, the government became more adventurous and the benefits of competition were more amply recognised in electricity privatisation. The largest generating company was split into three (the nuclear component remaining in the public sector), and the Scottish boards and new entrants were encouraged to expand in England and Wales. This was achieved by hiving off the National Grid Company from the privatised generating companies to create a network market for wholesale power supply to the distributing companies and individual large consumers. While not entirely satisfying the critics, this certainly opened up the possibility of real competition developing in power generation, where technical considerations did not require a monopoly to be preserved.

Some observers suggested that the cultural change to private ownership, where successful, was itself enough to improve performance (Leadbeater 1990), while others stressed that the gains would be sustained only where a more competitive structure had been implemented (Bishop and Kay 1988). Whichever view proves correct, the 1980s and early 1990s saw increased emphasis on the methods of regulation for the network monopoly industries, where competition remained an ineffective control on pricing and performance (Vickers and Yarrow 1988).

Debates on regulation had, of course, been vigorous in countries like the US, which long ago adopted regulated private enterprise as their preferred organisational form for network monopoly industries. The British legislation reflected some of the lessons of that experience. In particular, profit controls were perceived by US economists as introducing distortions similar to those that critics had identified in British nationalised industries. US utilities were, for example, accused of excessive use of capital, in the sense of using more capital-intensive technology than would be required by cost minimisation. Rate of return regulation encourages this because increased capital expenditure, even if it is not strictly necessary, permits the regulated company to declare higher profits (Averch and Johnson 1962; Stelser 1988). Regulatory failures are, it seems, as common as state ownership failures.

The regulatory formula adopted in Britain for the network monopolies of gas, telecoms, water and electricity thus emphasised price not profit limitation. It took the general form of limiting price rises to RPI-X, where RPI was the retail price index, and X was a fixed amount determined by the (somewhat arbitrary) view of each industry's underlying potential for efficiency improvement. This meant that, at least in the short and medium term, shareholders and managers in the private corporations gained the full benefit of any overall efficiency gains above the level implied by X, and thus had a strong performance incentive. Sceptics did, however, point to the fact that periodic re-setting of X introduces *de facto* profit controls: desirable to limit monopoly profits, but with undesirable incentive effects. In both gas and telecommunications the X target was raised in response partly to the success – and great profitability – of the privatised companies. X was initially set at 3 in telecoms, but was raised to 4.5 in 1988 and 6.25 in 1991 (though the latter partly reflected the inclusion of international calls within the price controls and the recognition that price reduction was more feasible there). In gas, the initial X of 2 was raised to 5 in 1991.

The regulators also pointed to difficulties created by the structure and conduct of their industries, and where necessary resorted to the Monopolies Commission to enforce their views. The problems of information, incentives and equity, already experienced by civil servants dealing with nationalised industries, will not easily be overcome by the new-style regulators of the privatised utilities.

Technology and productivity in the nationalised industries

This account of productivity gains by the nationalised industries has focussed on changes in managerial organisation and incentives, largely determined by their changing relationship with the government. Such an approach seems to fit the contrasting productivity experience of the industries, decade by decade, and the exceptionally good performance of particular sectors at particular times, for example, railways in the 1960s, or steel in the 1980s. The model of economic behaviour which seems best to fit what we have described is that which postulates a degree of 'X-inefficiency'. There is a certain managerial or organisational slack which leads to firms performing within their production possibility frontier unless they are prodded sharply to do better (Leibenstein 1966, 1976). High productivity is, however, more than a matter of organisational efficiency. It may have its roots in the development of human resources or in technical progress, rather than in a specific management strategy imposed by a strong industrialist or a systematic government efficiency campaign.

In the case of technological innovation, the underlying rate of productivity increase may be boosted by factors which have very little to do with the nationalised organisations running the industries. The great efficiency increases in gas in the 1970s and 1980s, for example, derived from the shift from the old coal gas technology to natural gas from the North Sea: although it required investment in reorganisation, it was essentially a gift from the North Sea oil explorers. The telecommunications industry has also been the beneficiary of forces mainly beyond its own control: modern microwave transmission and electronic switching technology were not pioneered by British Telecom; they were principally the result of a series of world-wide technical innovations.

Of course, technology is not simply something exogenous to the British economy: it is partly generated by research and development expenditure by British nationalised corporations and their suppliers, and partly imported from the international stock of technology generated in a variety of ways by a range of nations. The speed of adoption is vitally affected by the policy of the nationalised industries. By ordering its own rival, 'system X', rather than buying on the international market, British Telecom contrived to delay and reduce the benefits it derived from the new switching technology. Nationalisation seems generally to have reinforced such technological nationalism (the 'not invented here' syndrome). Where Britain attempted to go-it-alone, the results varied from the troublesome to the disastrous. The best example of the latter, imposing substantial social costs on the British economy, was the British nuclear power station programme. Britain's Magnox gas-cooled reactors, developed in the 1950s, were the first effective commercial nuclear power stations; by 1965 half of all the nuclear electricity generated in the world had been generated in Britain. With falling oil and coal prices, however, the pioneering technology proved uneconomic: most had been ordered with rash optimism after the 1956 Suez crisis created false expectations of imminent oil shortage. By the early 1960s American water-cooled reactors seemed to have a better chance of competing with cheap alternative fuels.

Nonetheless from 1965 the nationalised electricity industry was cajoled by the Labour government into buying a series of new (and, as it proved, either unworkable or excessively expensive) British advanced gas-cooled reactors. The first, Dungeness B, had to be substantially rebuilt, was two decades late in operation and cost three times as much in real terms as the initial contract price. British electricity consumers had not only to forego much of the benefit of cheap oil in the 1960s but also the promised cheap nuclear power in the 1970s and 1980s. Electricity was cheaper in Japan and Germany, whose smaller, private or mixed ownership electric utilities reacted quickly to minimise costs with a flexible array of oil, coal and nuclear capacity, or in France which bought American pressured water reactor designs and built a set of reactors more cheaply than Britain (though France's nationalised industry also over-reacted to its success and overordered reactors – thus eroding this advantage).

Attempts to provide broader seed-corn funding to new technologies have been cheaper, but generally they, too, have not typically been effective in the public sector. The state-owned National Enterprise Board, established by the Labour government in 1975, was correct in spotting high growth markets (e.g. microchips and electronic office equipment) but the offshoots it established to exploit them (INMOS, NEXOS) did not become effective competitors. The state was more successful in a few high technology industries (e.g. through shareholdings in Ferranti and Fairey) but these benefited from the rather special conditions of the defence industries, where the state itself generated a highly specialised demand. The nationalisation of Rolls Royce (between 1971 and 1987) enabled the state to finance the successful development of the company's organisational and technical capabilities, preserving its role as one of the three leading aero engine makers in the world, which the private sector had been unwilling to finance, following temporary financial difficulties unrelated to long-term viability. The National Coal Board also successfully supported British manufacturers who were at the forefront of innovation in mining technology (Kramer 1989). Such cases do not, however, appear to have been sufficiently numerous to offset the losses from state failures in attempting to promote technical change and increased efficiency.

Nationalisation and British economic performance

Did the nationalisation of large sectors of the British economy improve its overall performance – as was intended – or did nationalisation on balance intensify the problem of British economic decline? Such a question implies a counterfactual, and it is not easy to choose one, for few of the industries which were nationalised would have been likely to have retained their pre-nationalisation structure intact if they had not been nationalised. Some – as in the British-owned car industry – might not have existed at all, and the alternatives might or might not have satisfied consumer needs more efficiently.

Where new entry and competitive markets prevail, the 'survivor technique' is a reasonable approximation to answering the counterfactual historical question. For example, in the car industry, British demand is now met by a variety of commercial organisations: foreign subsidiaries inheriting much of the past structure (e.g. Ford), privatised British firms which were rescued from bankruptcy by temporary nationalisation (e.g. the Rover Group), imports from abroad (e.g. Volkswagen) and overseas subsidiaries operating on green field sites in Britain (e.g. Nissan). All have certain advantages, they compete in the same markets, and, if, after several decades of such competition, their market share does not decline, it seems reasonable to suppose that they provide consumer value. Yet there may be market distortions (e.g. government subsidies to Nissan for opening in a depressed area) which render the survivor test suspect. Moreover, the survival of the Rover Group tells us nothing about whether the cost of temporary subsidy under nationalisation outweighed the benefits derived. Clearly unemployment would have been much higher in cities like Oxford if the firm had been allowed to go bankrupt. Yet it seems highly likely that the subsidies (both direct in government handouts to the Rover Group's predecessors, and indirect though the higher prices 'conceded' by Japanese importers to British consumers in order to keep Rover alive) reduced British national income. Such exercises demand their own counterfactual analysis, and typically reveal the very large opportunity costs of intervention to preserve jobs.

However, to judge the broader merits of public ownership – as opposed to the myopia of politicians and their short-term objectives – from particularly bad 1970s cases is not appropriate. Attempts to make more general judgements have therefore concentrated on the other (very few) industries where both public and private enterprises have competed in the same markets and been broadly subject to the same constraints, as well as open to the same opportunities. Historically, municipal enterprise sometimes performed as well as or better than private enterprise (Foreman-Peck and Waterson 1985; Millward and Ward 1987). However, comparisons of the few cases in which dual-ownership structures remained by the early 1980s were less supportive of public enterprise (Pryke 1982). The nationalised British Airways was (until the 1980s) overmanned compared with the private British Caledonian. The Sealink cross-channel ferries operated by the British and French national railways were slower, less fuel-efficient and less profitable (especially when they fixed similar prices for

Table 6.5. *Comparative labour productivity in network monopolies, 1970–5*

Industry	Date	West German output per man/ UK output per man	US output per man/ UK output per man
Gas	1975	2·21	3·32
Electricity	1975	2·11	3·54
Water	1975	0·99	1·97
Railways	1970	1·08	3·95
Local bus/rail	1970	1·34	1·45
Post and telecom	1970/2	1·08	2·28–3·17

Source: Smith *et al.* (1982: 136, 145–6, 154–5).

their inferior services) than the private Townsend–Thoresen ferries. Appliances from the shops of the nationalised electricity boards were more expensive to the consumer but less profitable to the boards than from private chains like Currys. Moreover, where consumers had the choice of buying from nationalised or private enterprises, the market share of private enterprise was rising, except where subsidies or government favours kept the nationalised firms 'competitive'. In the few cases where such direct comparisons were possible (and consumers were, of course, making them all the time), public sector managers simply were not surviving the market test.

In the case of network monopolies, the problems of assessing the implications of nationalisation for economic welfare are more intractable. As such firms generally do not operate in competitive markets and are operated by one national or regional monopolist, their changing market share is not a relevant efficiency indicator: the British water industry's share of the world water market is largely the result of the demand for water within a circumscribed geographical area, not an indicator of its competitive prowess. In principle, it is possible to measure such industries' performance by the yardstick of direct international comparison, but here too there are difficulties, which historians (and public utility regulators) are only just beginning to confront.

By the 1970s, the British public utilities registered a level of productivity substantially inferior to that of public utilities in other comparable, OECD countries. Comparisons with West Germany and the United States are shown in Table 6.5, with productivity in gas and electricity, especially, being significantly higher in Germany and America. Some of these differences may be due to the quality of output: US trains are, for example, distinctly inferior to British and German trains, so the higher physical productivity shown in the table overstates the true difference. But more careful analyses of specific sectors (for example, allowing for capital as well as labour inputs or for differences in the quality of output) have found shortfalls of British performance similar to the range shown in the table (Foreman-Peck and Manning 1988; Forsyth *et al.* 1986).

Such differentials in performance were, however, also found in a very wide range of private sector industries, for example, in manufacturing. They may thus have been a reflection of general British economic failings, traceable to broader social or cultural factors, such as a tendency to underinvest in training and education. Nationalised or regulated industries had, it is true, a stronger incentive to invest in training than competitive firms, because they faced less of a threat from the poaching of skilled labour. Significantly, the nationalised industries had a good record in training expenditure, compared with the private sector. Generally, however, such achievements were not superior to those achieved by the same industries abroad, for many of these network monopolies were, of course, nationalised in Germany and regulated in the US.

The case for arguing that nationalisation, as such, has led to a deterioration in performance would be strengthened if it could be shown that countries which had nationalised their public utilities systematically performed at below-average levels. In Table 6.4, for example, the only slightly superior performance of German railways and telecoms to the UK may have been due to the nationalised corporations which in Germany ran them at that time. However, initial attempts by the OECD systematically to compare national telecom systems produced no decisive results except that size was not a major determinant of efficiency (*Economist* 1990a). The long-run record is equally inconclusive. Comparison of Table 6.4 with similar data for the period prior to nationalisation (Rostas 1948; Paige and Bombach 1959) is only currently possible for the US. As with manufacturing industries, the tendency in public utilities was for the US/UK gap to increase during the war and fall during the great post-war boom. Only in electricity among the major utilities was there a sign of substantial long-run deterioration of relative UK productivity performance after nationalisation. Some of this increased differential may, however, be due to the increasing degree of vertical integration chosen by the nationalised boards (e.g. expanding their labour-intensive electrical contracting and retailing) rather than a true decline in relative efficiency.

The determinants of international efficiency differences in regulated or nationalised utilities thus still present an analytical puzzle. Nonetheless, it remains plausible that it will be the forms of managerial incentive, the quality of monitoring and the nature of regulatory yardsticks which will play a large part in the ultimate explanation, rather than the nature of ownership, on which so much unproductive political discussion in the post-war era concentrated.

Allocative efficiency

The emphasis on productive efficiency and technological progress in earlier sections of this chapter ignores the central concern of much economic analysis with allocative efficiency: that is the question of whether the right outputs are being produced (and with the right combination of inputs). Some analysts have suggested that removing allocative inefficiencies is a less important source of welfare gains than productivity growth (Pryke 1971), but others have seen serious allocative inefficiencies (Molyneux and Thompson 1987: 75) and the 1960s White Papers were principally aimed at removing them. Government policy initiatives to improve allocative efficiency were successful in some areas: for example, in developing off-peak pricing of electricity to reflect the cost structure of the industry. This was possible because the chairman of the industry, the economist Sir Ronald Edwards, shared the objectives and implemented them in collaboration with managers and civil servants (Hannah 1982). The results he achieved were clearly earlier than and superior to those of US regulators of private electric utilities (Papps 1975: 52; Hannah 1990).

Too often, however, attempts by government departments to promote discussion of this kind with nationalised industries foundered on asymmetries of information between them and the boards, which made intervention ineffective. In telecommunications, for example, where long-distance calls were priced well above costs to cross-subsidise local calls, the resultant welfare losses were considerable (Ergas 1984). The most effective (though perhaps only partial) solution proved to be, not the 1967 public sector pricing rules which worked for electricity, but the 1983 licensing of a competitor, Mercury, which soon forced more economic pricing of British Telecom's long-distance calls.

There remained, however, many problems of allocative inefficiency in the regulated industries which may prove as intractable to even the most skilled regulator as they were to the departments formerly controlling state industries. There is, as yet, no compelling evidence that either the public sector or regulated private sector solutions are best at resolving allocative efficiency problems in the network monopolies.

Other objectives of nationalisation

It is sometimes argued that the nationalised industries should be judged not primarily by the standards of productive or allocative efficiency, but rather by their success in pursuing other objectives. A wide range of objectives has been proposed – ranging from the specific (better labour relations, a cleaner environment) to the general (equitable distribution of the just fruits of labour). Politicians were usually sensitive to the power of such objectives; but, where Ministers shared them, they (often reluctantly) were led to conclude that the objectives were practically attainable in alternative ways. If equality is defined as an objective, it may, for example, be better to give the poor more money than to nationalise industries which then give them more high-speed trains, telephones and nuclear power stations. Even if it is concluded that more of these things rather than more money were required, it can be more effective to subsidise private provision rather than to nationalise providers. Other objectives were often best pursued on a broad front rather than by setting an example in state-owned businesses. For example, if managers in general did not have powers to hire and fire at will, or to discriminate against blacks or women, it is difficult to see why that power should have been constrained in nationalised industries but not in the private sector. (In fact, general legislation was used to spread good practice which was often pioneered by nationalised industries.)

For purposes of macro-economic management, it was sometimes argued that the state needed to accelerate domestic investment or overseas borrowing by the nationalised industries. Yet it might have been cheaper or more effective to offer general tax incentives than to instruct nationalised industries to implement these changes directly. It was certainly easier for the government to do some things – for example, forcing nationalised electric utilities to buy uneconomic British coal or technologically inferior British turbo-alternators – than if they had been dealing with private sector enterprises, but this was largely because politicians did not wish the costs and effects of their policies to be transparent. It is reasonable, then, to suspect their motives. The original intention of Morrisonian socialists had been that Ministers should provide general guidance on objectives to the managers of the nationalised industries, abstaining from detailed intervention on operational matters. In practice the opposite happened: general guidance came through Treasury-inspired but politically insignificant White Papers, while ministerial enthusiasm propelled specific interventions to the forefront (House of Commons 1968). It is far from clear that such policies were in the long run successful in enabling the protected industries to create sustainable long-run competitive advantages, though they may have been temporarily effective in buying votes in marginal constituencies.

There developed, therefore, a wider appreciation that, while there may have been market failures which the state could intervene to correct, there was also a strong potential for state failures. It was, for example, simple for the initial advocates of nationalising electricity to suggest that private enterprise generators had only weak incentives not to pollute the environment, but the experience of eastern Europe (and, on a lesser scale, the nationalised Central Electricity Generating Board at home) showed that collective ownership was a less than perfect solution. Both public and private ownership required some form of regulation (or pricing) of pollution.

For the issue of public ownership to be strictly relevant to any political objective, a case logically had to be made that the objective could best be achieved by nationalisation rather than by alternative means. Yet arguments of this kind frequently rested on a confusion of logic or a misunderstanding of facts. The case was frequently advanced, for example, that subsidising railways would benefit the poor: yet empirical analysis showed that the beneficiaries of rail subsidies were those on above-average incomes: overwhelmingly the poor either travel by bus or not at all (Beesley et al. 1983; Pryke 1971: 428). The state is frequently the tool of powerful pressure groups other than the poor.

The argument that the very act of nationalisation directly equalised wealth distribution was equally flawed. If adequate compensation were paid, as it generally was in Britain (Chester 1975), then the distribution of wealth remained unaffected: the acquisition of the physical assets by the state was counterbalanced by the acquisition of financial assets (in the form of freely tradable compensation stock) by the private shareholders. Privatisation was encouraged by substantial discounts on the market value of the assets sold (Bishop and Kay 1988). It probably had a more complex impact than did nationalisation on the distribution of wealth, for example through the overlap of the populations of tax payers (who probably lost) and shareholders (who gained), though since both of these were concentrated in the middle of the wealth distribution it is far from clear that the effect was to increase inequality.

It is more difficult than it first appears to calculate whether the British state has been a net accumulator of wealth through nationalisation (Hills 1989). The role of both nationalisation and privatisation in the changes has probably been small, relative to the state's accumulation of housing assets and collective provision of pension savings in the post-war decades. Certainly it was taxation and borrowing, rather than nationalisation with compensation, which ultimately determined the extent of collective savings administered by the British state on behalf of its citizens.

Those who considered it desirable to change that policy were increasingly convinced by the evidence of post-war British experience that nationalisation no longer had as central a role in achieving their objectives as socialists had once believed. The Labour Party soon attached a low priority to the renationalisation of the privatised industries. Meanwhile, the Conservative Party gradually recognised the weaknesses of some of the excessively monopolistic structures created by its hurried privatisation programme. The interesting debates on the network monopolies now turned on the extent and nature of regulation, and to the prospects for introducing greater market competition in areas where regulation could be made redundant by better conceived structures and policies. The wisdom of this refocussing of political energies cannot seriously be questioned by the student of post-war experience.

7   Employment and unemployment

Stephen Broadberry

Introduction

For more than two decades after the Second World War, it was widely believed that the problem of unemployment had been banished for good, due to the Keynesian revolution (Stewart 1967). Unemployment rates of less than 2 per cent were regarded as normal. This complacency was shattered, however, by the rising trend of unemployment from the late 1960s, continuing through the 1970s. The dramatic surge in unemployment in the early 1980s raised unemployment above the 3 million total, not seen since the 1930s. Although unemployment fell back in the second half of the 1980s, it remains in the 1990s well above the level of the 1950s and 1960s.

This chapter will consider the conditions which underlay the post-war boom and the reasons for the emergence of a harsher economic climate in the 1970s and 1980s. It will also look beneath these macro-economic trends to build up a more micro-economic picture of the operation of the labour market in post-war Britain.

Labour market trends since the Second World War

The survey of the post-war British labour market begins by emphasising broad macro-economic trends in the labour force and employment, noting that unemployment is the difference between the two aggregates. It is impossible to discuss these macro-economic trends without mentioning divergent movements in their micro-economic component parts; this section therefore concludes with a survey of regional, industrial, occupational and demographic aspects of labour market trends.

The growth of the labour force

The definition of the labour force that will be used is: employees in employment plus the armed forces and self-employed plus the registered unemployed. The aggregate figures for the UK are plotted in Figure 7.1, and indicate a rising trend with fluctuations. Before discussing the post-

Figure 7.1 Employment and labour force, 1950–92
Source: see text.

1945 situation in detail, it is helpful to give an historical perspective by examining the broad trends in the labour force since the mid-nineteenth century, As Matthews *et al.* (1982: ch.3) show, the growth of the labour force since 1945 has been considerably slower than during the preceding century or so. This is due to changes in population growth, the age distribution of the population and age- and sex-specific participation rates. Although the birth rate fell significantly from about 1870, the death rate also fell sharply, so that there was only a small fall in the population growth rate before 1914. Between 1914 and 1945, however, the fertility decline was faster than the mortality decline, so that population growth slowed from about one per cent per annum to about 0.5. Nevertheless, the labour force continued to expand during the inter-war period as the proportion of children in the population fell, and female participation increased. After 1945, the fall in the birth rate ceased, the proportion of children in the population began to rise, and this, together with a rising proportion of elderly in the population, led to a substantial slowing down in the growth rate of the labour force, despite rising female participation.

Looking at the post-1945 position in more detail, there were three phases; a period of moderate growth in the labour force until 1966, followed by a period of stagnation until 1974, and finally a period of renewed growth from 1974. This final growth phase has been punctuated by a short period of decline during the sharp recession of 1980–3 which can be attributed to a 'discouraged worker' effect. These trends in the labour force can be related to demographic factors and participation rates (Figure 7.1).

During the period from the end of the Second World War to 1966, population growth occurred at a steady rate of about 0.5 per cent per annum, or 5.5 per cent per decade. Changes in the age distribution, with a rising proportion of children and the elderly, acted to depress the growth of the labour force. Although there was a positive effect from changes in age- and sex-specific participation rates, particularly with rising female participation, the growth of the labour force was slower than during the inter-war period, falling from a rate of 1.1 per cent per annum during 1931–9 to 0.6 per cent per annum during 1951–66 (Matthews *et al.* 1982: Tables 3.3 and 3.5).

For the period 1966–74, the stagnation in the labour force can be explained, on the demographic side, by falling population growth and by continued changes in the age distribution. The proportion of young and elderly in the population continued to rise. In addition, changes in the age- and sex-specific participation rates acted to reduce the growth of the labour force, principally due to a rapid extension of education among the fifteen to twenty-four age group.

For the period since 1974, there has been a recovery in the growth of the labour force, due to demographic factors, since trends in participation rates have continued to dampen labour force growth, because of extensions of educational and early retirement opportunities (Johnes and Taylor 1989: 283–90). On the demographic side the growth of the labour force has been accelerated by the effect on the age distribution of the post-war 'baby-boom'.

The stagnation in the labour force during 1981–3 can be explained by the 'discouraged worker' effect. In recessions, jobs are scarce and wages low, so that marginal workers become discouraged from seeking jobs and withdraw from the labour force in some way, such as continuing with education, retraining or retiring. Thus the labour force contracts in a recession. It is sometimes argued that there is an 'added worker' effect which works in the opposite direction. If primary or 'bread winner' workers are made redundant during the recession, household income may be maintained by secondary workers taking temporary jobs. However, the pro-cyclical movement of the labour force apparent from Figure 7.1 suggests that the discouraged worker effect has outweighed the added worker effect during the post-Second World War period.

Looking behind the aggregate figures, undoubtedly the major trend is the difference between female and male participation rates. For men there has been a downward trend in participation, with young men spending longer in education and older men retiring earlier (Hannah 1986). These trends are the result of rising income and greater social provision.

While male participation rates have been declining throughout the post-

1945 period, female participation has risen sharply, mainly due to a rise in participation by married women aged twenty-five to sixty-four. This represents an acceleration of a trend that began at the turn of the century, and it can be explained by a combination of supply and demand factors. On the supply side, there has been a fall in family size and substantial labour-saving technical progress in housework, which has given women more time to spend in the labour market. However, care is needed here, since rising incomes may also be expected to lead to an increased demand for leisure, which would tend to reduce women's participation rates. On the demand side, the shortage of labour during the two World Wars and in the post-war period increased job opportunities for women. Occupational and distributional shifts have also been towards jobs that have traditionally been held by women (Matthews *et al.* 1982: 59–60). However, it should be noted that if hours of work are taken into account, the rise in female participation has been of less quantitative significance for the growth of the labour force, since much of the rise has been concentrated in part-time work by married women.

Employment

Aggregate employment, defined here to include the armed forces and the self-employed, is plotted in Figure 7.1 along with the labour force. After an upward trend to 1966, employment fluctuated around the 25 million level until 1979, before taking a deep plunge during the recession 1980–3. After a sustained recovery during the 1980s, the 1966 peak level of employment was only surpassed in 1988.

As with the labour force, the aggregate trends mask significant differences between males and females. Both male and female employment rose steadily to the mid-1960s, while from this period male employment fell while female employment continued to rise. Only during the sharp recession from 1979 did female employment fall significantly. As already noted, there is another significant difference between male and female employment, with a much higher proportion of women working on a part-time basis.

There have also been significant changes in the distribution of employment between sectors, with an expansion of services at the expense of manufacturing. Matthews *et al.* (1982: 221–5) note, however, that the share of employment in manufacturing rose exceptionally across the Second World War, so that to some extent the reduction in manufacturing employment (in absolute as well as relative terms from 1966) can be seen as a return to pre-war normality. In fact, however, this shrinkage of manufacturing employment sparked off a huge debate on fears of deindustrialisation, suggesting that things have gone well beyond a return to normality (Blackaby 1978). Although the fall from a share of 34.5 per cent in 1973 to 31.3 per cent in 1979 could be seen in this light, the further fall to 23.0 per cent by 1989 suggests a major structural shift.

This sharp decline in manufacturing employment has been accompanied by a rise in service sector employment, particularly in two categories: (a) insurance, banking, financial and business services and (b) public, professional and scientific services. This is usually explained in terms of productivity growth differentials, with higher productivity growth in manufacturing reducing the demand for labour in that sector. However, care needs to be taken here, since convincing measures of output in many service industries are lacking and output is simply assumed to grow in line with employment. Hence, as Millward (1990) argues, the claim that productivity growth has been faster in manufacturing than in services is open to question. Demand shifts can also be used to explain structural shifts in employment patterns.

Another major change in post-war employment patterns is the sharp rise in the number of self-employed which has occurred during the 1980s. Between 1979 and 1988, the number of self-employed workers rose by over 1 million (Feinstein and Matthews 1990: 82). This can be explained as a result of the low demand for labour during the recession of the early 1980s, with laid-off workers setting up in business on their own.

One point worth noting is that, despite the stagnation of employment from the mid-1960s, the rate of change of the labour input, measured in terms of hours worked, has been roughly constant over the post-war period (Feinstein and Matthews 1990: 83–4). Although the growth of employment has stagnated, this has been offset by a less rapid reduction in hours worked per person.

Unemployment

The stock of unemployment is given by the difference between the labour force and employment. Since the Second World War, with the universal extension of the unemployment insurance system, a complete quantitative picture of unemployment exists across the entire economy. For earlier periods, however, it is necessary to infer the level of unemployment for the aggregate economy from information collected by trade unions and an unemployment insurance system of incomplete coverage. However, the picture of aggregate unemployment during the twentieth century that has been obtained from this information by Feinstein (1972) commands widespread acceptance, and is presented here in Figure 7.2.

Unemployment before the First World War is usually seen as highly

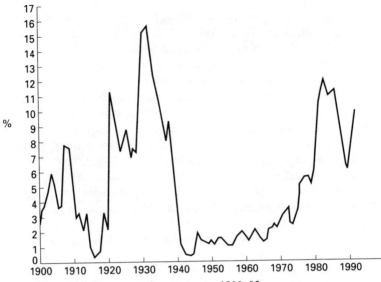

Figure 7.2 The unemployment rate, 1900–92

volatile, with large sectors of the economy subject to intermittent, casual employment conditions (Matthews 1968; Baines 1981). Equally clearly, there is general agreement that the inter-war period was characterised by an underlying high level of unemployment, with peak levels higher than anything seen before 1914 (Broadberry 1986; Garside 1990). With a return to full employment during the Second World War, the 1950s and 1960s were characterised by a very low and stable level of unemployment. It should be noted that it is this post-war boom which stands out as exceptional in an historical context, rather than the periods of high unemployment. During the 1970s and particularly the early 1980s, unemployment rose above 3 million, to levels on a par with those of the 1930s. Although unemployment has fallen substantially during the latter half of the 1980s, it remains in the early 1990s well above the level of the 1950s and 1960s.

It should be noted that there have been many changes in the official definition of unemployment during the 1980s. Nevertheless, the trends indicated by Figure 7.2 do clearly reflect the underlying trends. Furthermore, Feinstein and Matthews (1990) reject the claim that the official unemployment figures are now too low. Rather, the adjustments have brought the British figures into line with the standard (ILO/OECD) definition.

Turning to international comparisons, Table 7.1 presents estimates of unemployment rates based on OECD data, which have been standardised

Table 7.1. *International comparison of unemployment rates, 1950–90 (%)*

	1950	1955	1960	1965	1970	1975	1980	1985	1990
USA	5·3	4·4	5·5	4·5	4·8	8·3	7·0	7·1	5·2
Japan	1·8	2·4	1·7	1·2	1·1	1·9	2·0	2·6	2·3
Belgium	7·1	4·6	4·3	1·9	2·1	5·1	9·0	11·3	8·1
France	n.a.	n.a.	n.a.	1·7	2·4	4·1	6·3	10·2	9·6
Germany	10·2	4·3	1·0	0·5	0·8	1·6	3·1	7·2	5·6
Italy	12·2	10·5	5·5	5·3	5·3	5·8	7·4	10·1	10·9
Netherlands	2·0	1·3	1·2	0·8	1·4	6·3	4·9	10·6	8·3
Norway	2·7	2·5	2·5	1·8	1·6	2·3	1·7	2·6	4·9
Sweden	2·2	2·5	1·4	1·1	1·5	1·6	2·0	2·8	1·4
UK	2·9	1·9	2·9	2·5	3·1	3·9	7·4	11·2	6·9

Sources: OECD *Labour Force Statistics*, Quarterly Supplement; OECD *Main Economic Indicators*; Mitchell (1975, 1982, 1983).

Table 7.2. *Regional unemployment rates, 1929–88 (%)*

	1929	1937	1951	1964	1973	1979	1988
South-east	{4·5	5·4	0·9	1·0}	1·3	2·9	4·9
East Anglia					1·6	3·7	4·7
South-west	6·8	6·8	1·2	1·5	2·1	4·6	5·7
West midlands	{9·1	6·6}	0·4	0·9	1·7	4·7	8·2
East midlands			{0·7	1·1}	1·8	3·8	7·0
Yorkshire and Humberside		12·0			2·3	4·7	9·1
North-west	{12·6}	12·8	1·2	2·1	2·9	5·9	9·9
North		16·7	2·2	3·3	3·9	7·3	11·5
Wales	18·2	20·7	2·7	2·6	3·0	6·3	9·5
Scotland	11·0	14·0	2·5	3·6	3·8	6·8	10·9
Northern Ireland	13·8	21·7	6·1	6·6	4·9	9·7	15·7
United Kingdom	9·7	10·1	1·3	1·7	2·0	4·7	7·6

Sources: Beck (1951); Department of Employment and Productivity (1971); *Economic Trends*.

for cross-country comparison. If the figures in Table 7.1 give a rough guide to international differences in unemployment rates, a number of trends can be established. First, Britain's performance in the 1950s and 1960s can be seen as characterised by low and stable unemployment relative to many of the industrialised countries. Second, the rising trend of unemployment in Britain during the 1970s and early 1980s can be seen as part of a general trend affecting most of the major European economies. This upward trend, however, is much less clear in the USA and Japan, and also in the

Scandinavian economies. Third, the fall in unemployment in Britain during the second half of the 1980s was part of a general world-wide cyclical movement, although the scale of the recovery in Britain has been greater than in other countries.

These international and historical comparisons suggest that the key questions about post-war British unemployment are:

1. Why was unemployment so low during the 1950s and 1960s?
2. What caused unemployment to rise so sharply during the 1970s and early 1980s?
3. Why did the recovery of the late 1980s not lead to a restoration of the low unemployment levels of the early post-war period?

Before attempting to answer these questions, however, it is useful to complete the picture of the labour market by considering in more detail the micro-economic factors which underlay the aggregate trends outlined above.

Regional and industrial aspects

Table 7.2 presents unemployment rates by region for the years of peak activity since 1929. A number of trends can be observed. First, over the period as a whole there has been a clear divide between the relatively prosperous south or inner Britain, and the depressed north or outer Britain. Regions in the north, Wales and Scotland had unemployment rates well above the UK average during the 1930s, and this trend persisted through the post-war boom of the 1950s and 1960s, and into the high unemployment period of the 1970s and 1980s. Second, changes in the fortunes of particular regions can nevertheless be identified. The west midlands, for example, moved from a period of tremendous relative prosperity in the 1950s and 1960s to above average unemployment during the 1970s and 1980s. This change was largely connected with the rise and decline in the fortunes of the engineering industry, particularly motor vehicles (Rhys 1988; Armstrong and Taylor 1987). The continued importance of the north–south divide suggests that regional policy has not been a great success. This is particularly true since the rise in the relative importance of services as a source of employment might be expected to have lessened the dependence of a region on a small number of manufacturing industries, which caused such regional problems during the 1930s, when the old staple industries collapsed (Aldcroft 1984: 14; Garside 1990: chs. 8–9).

The dispersion of unemployment across industries has become more evenly spread during the post-war period. Between the wars, the unemployment rate in the old staples of coal mining, shipbuilding, cotton textiles and iron and steel was at times as much as seven or eight times as high as in the new industries such as chemicals, cars, aircraft, electricity and electrical engineering (Department of Employment and Productivity 1971: Table 164). In the post-war period, although the unemployment rate has generally been higher in manufacturing than in services, within the manufacturing sector unemployment has been fairly evenly spread. For example, in 1975, when the rate of unemployment for the economy as a whole was 4.7 per cent, the highest rate in manufacturing was 9.0 per cent for leather, leather goods and fur, and the lowest rate was 2.8 per cent for instrument engineering (Department of Employment *Employment Gazette* 1975).

Inflows, outflows and the characteristics of the unemployed

It is instructive to consider inflows and outflows from the stock of unemployed. Several points can be made here. First, inflows and outflows are of the same order of magnitude, about 300,000 to 400,000 each month (Department of Employment *Employment Gazette* 1990 December: 540). If inflows exceed outflows, the stock of unemployment rises. Second, these monthly flows are large in relation to the stock of unemployed, which was in 1990 about 1.5 million (Department of Employment *Employment Gazette* 1990 December: 518). Hence the stock of unemployed can change rapidly as inflows and outflows change. During the period of rising unemployment from the mid-1960s, inflows changed very little, with most of the rise in unemployment accounted for by a fall in outflows from the stock of unemployed (Cross 1982: 90). Similarly the fall in unemployment from the mid-1980s has been caused by a rise in outflows.

The high turnover rates quoted by Thomas (1988: 103) for the 1930s suggest that turnover has been much reduced in the post-war labour market. Since high levels of turnover are often interpreted as signs of a healthy labour market, ensuring efficient allocation of workers to jobs, this requires some comment. As Thomas argues, however, if rapid turnover is produced by intermittent spells of unemployment of a casual nature as in the inter-war period, it is hard to sustain the interpretation that the labour market is healthy. Reduced turnover can be seen instead as a healthy sign of decasualisation of the labour market.

An analysis of inflows and outflows helps to build up a picture of which groups of society have borne the burden of unemployment. In principle it is possible for a given stock of unemployment to be caused by a high inflow rate and low duration or by a low inflow rate and high duration. In the former case the burden of unemployment is evenly spread, while in the latter it is concentrated. For example, if the weekly inflow rate were 1 per cent of the labour force and the average duration of each spell of unemployment was four weeks, the measured unemployment rate in each week would be 4 per cent. If the inflow rate were only 0.25 per cent and the average duration was sixteen weeks, this would also result in the 4 per cent measured unemployment rate (Knight 1987: 32).

In post-war Britain, the burden of unemployment has not been shared equally. One dimension to this is occupational structure. The less skilled have a much larger probability of experiencing unemployment than the skilled. There is evidence to suggest that the position of semi-skilled and manual workers has deteriorated over the post-war period, particularly since the 1970s (Aldcroft 1984: 16).

Perhaps the most pronounced differences, however, are demographic. The different labour force and employment experiences of men and women have already been noted, so it is not surprising to find lower unemployment rates among women in the post-war period. This was also true between the wars (Beck 1951). This pattern of relatively low female unemployment remains true for all age groups. However, for both men and women, unemployment rates have varied considerably by age group. Prime age men and women have had lower unemployment rates than younger (under twenty-five) and older (over fifty-five) age groups. Youth unemployment (under twenty) was particularly serious during the 1970s and early 1980s, due to a cutback in recruitment during the recession and a rise in the cost of hiring young workers relative to the cost of hiring adults (Metcalf and Richardson 1984: 254). This relatively high youth unemployment during the 1970s and 1980s is in striking contrast with the situation during the 1930s, when juvenile unemployment was relatively low. Garside (1977) attributes this low juvenile unemployment of the 1930s to the relative cheapness of juvenile labour at the time, although Benjamin and Kochin (1979b) argue that it was a result of the unavailability of unemployment benefits for this group of workers.

The relatively high unemployment among older workers during the post-war period is a continuation of a trend which also existed during the inter-war period. This high rate of unemployment among older workers is caused by long duration rather than by any greater probability of job loss. This reflects a reluctance of firms to hire older workers, since many older workers are less flexible, more prone to illness and disability and likely to command a wage in excess of their declining productivity (Metcalf and Richardson 1984: 254–5).

The rising duration of unemployment in the 1970s and 1980s has seen a rise in the proportion of those unemployed for twelve months or more, as during the 1930s (Crafts 1987). This is of particular concern, since such a long spell of unemployment leads to loss of skills and loss of confidence on the part of workers, who are no longer really part of the effective labour force. On the part of employers, a long spell of unemployment is seen as a signal of unsuitability for employment. Thus the probability of re-employment falls markedly with a long spell of unemployment. This is known as a hysteresis effect, since it implies that a reversal of the forces causing the rise in unemployment will not lead to an equivalent reduction of unemployment (Cross 1988).

A unified labour market?

To what extent is it appropriate, given these divergent micro-economic trends, to talk of a unified labour market for the UK? Fortunately, there is empirical evidence to suggest that over the twentieth century it is possible to work with the assumption of a unified labour market. Salter (1960) shows that for the period 1924–50, productivity movements between industries were strongly associated with movements in relative output prices rather than in earnings. As Salter (1960: 115) puts it,

the finding that inter-industry movements of earnings and output per operative are uncorrelated is not at all surprising. The market for labour is common to all industries and, over the long run, the movement of wages in each industry is primarily determined by the movements of wages in the economy as a whole. This is supported by the relatively small dispersion of earnings movements.

Reddaway (1966) confirms this result for the post-war period.

Explaining unemployment

It is useful to set out a general framework for the analysis of un-employment, to explain both the low unemployment of the 1950s and 1960s and the rising unemployment of the 1970s and 1980s.

The NAIRU

The general framework uses the notion of a NAIRU, or non-accelerating inflation rate of unemployment. This is in turn based on three widely accepted propositions in macro-economics. First, that a fall in un-employment will tend to accelerate wage inflation (Phillips 1958). Second, that there are autonomous 'push' factors such as trade unions which can increase inflation (Hines 1964). Third, that once inflation gets going it tends to continue as expectations adjust (Friedman 1968; Phelps 1967).

Layard (1986: 29–30) provides a good exposition. If unemployment is low, inflation will tend to rise because employers will offer higher wages to

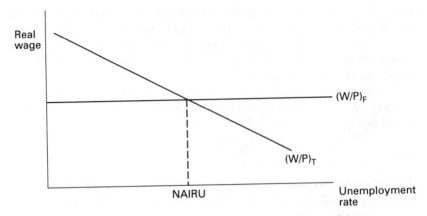

Figure 7.3 The non-accelerating inflation rate of unemployment (NAIRU)

try to attract labour to fill their vacancies. In addition, trade unions will feel in a strong position to press for high wage settlements. On the other hand, if unemployment is high, inflation will tend to fall, as employers will not be trying to attract workers and trade unions will be in a weaker position. Hence there is a critical level of unemployment, at which inflation will be stable, and this is the NAIRU. Low unemployment leads to rising inflation rather than just to a one-off rise in prices, because inflation has a momentum of its own. There is a 'core' inflation rate, so that if there is no upward or downward pressure from the labour market, people expect inflation to continue at this 'core' level. It should be noted that the core rate of inflation in the post-war world has been substantially positive, with governments prepared to settle for stable inflation as the nominal anchor to the economic system. Clearly this has not always been the case and indeed, for the preceding century, core inflation was zero, with governments committed to a stable price level via the gold standard (Gordon 1982; Eichengreen 1985).

The NAIRU can be most easily understood using a diagram from Layard (1986: 35), reproduced here as Figure 7.3. At any time there is a limit to the living standard that workers can have, which Layard calls the feasible real wage $(W/P)_F$. This feasible real wage can be thought of as the inverse of the normal price mark-up (of prices over wages) of firms. Firms have to make profits, so if workers succeed in obtaining an increase in money wages, firms must raise prices. But then there is inflation and the higher money wages negotiated by unions do not translate into higher real wages. The feasible real wage is a horizontal line in Figure 7.3 because the normal price mark-up is assumed not to vary with unemployment. The feasible real wage, then, can be thought of as resulting from the pricing behaviour of firms in imperfectly competitive product markets. If product markets were perfectly competitive, firms would not be able to pass on cost increases by raising prices.

In addition to the feasible real wage, there is a target real wage $(W/P)_T$, which results from the wage-negotiating behaviour of unions in an imperfectly competitive labour market. Thus the target real wage may not be the same as the feasible real wage. However, if the target real wage is greater than the feasible real wage, inflation results. Workers press for higher money wages in an attempt to raise the real wage, but firms respond by increasing prices so that the workers' attempt to raise the real wage is frustrated. A rise in unemployment is then needed to moderate the target real wage and to stop inflation from accelerating. This effect is represented by the downward-sloping target real wage curve, indicating that as unemployment rises, unions reduce their wage aspirations in line with their reduced bargaining power.

The NAIRU is given by the intersection of the feasible and target real wage curves. Where the two curves meet, the target real wage is consistent with the real wage that is feasible, so that there is no pressure for inflation to accelerate. Note that the NAIRU could rise because of a fall in the feasible real wage (caused, for example, by a rise in the price of imported raw materials), or because of a rise in the target real wage (caused, for example, by trade union militancy). Note also that unemployment could rise because of a rise in the NAIRU or because of a rise in unemployment above the NAIRU (caused, for example, by a disinflationary aggregate demand policy).

Imperfect competition in Britain

It should be clear that the model assumes imperfect competition in labour and product markets. Without market power, unions could not press for inflationary wage settlements and firms could not afford to concede them, because it would not be possible to pass on increased costs with higher selling prices. Before using this model, then, it is reasonable to ask what evidence there is for treating British labour and product markets as imperfectly competitive. In fact, the evidence for this assumption is overwhelming.

Studies of the restricted nature of competition in post-war British product markets abound. It shows up not just in terms of high and rising levels of concentration (Hannah 1983; Prais 1976; Hannah and Kay 1977), but also in the widespread use of restrictive agreements, particularly before the Restrictive Practices Act of 1956 and the Resale Price Maintenance Act of 1964 (Yamey 1962b; Elliott and Gribbin 1977). Broadberry and Crafts (1990b) note the strengthening of these restrictive agreements during the Depression of the 1930s, when governments were concerned to avoid the unemployment consequences of the elimination of inefficient producers. Although the post-war period has seen some moves by governments against monopoly and restrictive practices, British anti-trust policy has remained weak by comparison with the United States (Neale 1960; Sawyer 1981: ch. 16). It should be borne in mine, however, that the British economy is open to international competition, which sets limits to the extent of market power that can be enjoyed by domestic producers. During the early post-war period, however, domestic producers were protected by tariffs, which were successively reduced under GATT, the General Agreement on Tariffs and Trade. Britain's accession to the European Economic Community (EEC) in 1973 has seen a further exposure of British industry to competition from abroad (Foreman-Peck 1991; Winters 1987).

The conclusion that the labour market in post-war Britain has been imperfectly competitive is difficult to avoid, with trade union density rising from over 40 per cent at the end of the war to over 50 per cent by the late 1970s (Bain and Price 1980: 38). Even this understates the influence of collective bargaining through unions, since many non-union members receive wages negotiated by unions. The coverage of collective agreements in the late 1970s was over 70 per cent.

It should be noted that once the assumption of the all-pervasiveness of imperfect competition is accepted, it is useful to think in terms of bargaining between firms and unions. Machin and Wadhwani (1989) propose the modelling of wages and effort as the outcome of a Nash bargain between firms and unions. In this approach, changes in the relative bargaining strengths of unions and firms can affect effort as well as wages, and thus lead to changes in the feasible real wage as well as the target real wage. Thus a strengthening of union bargaining power may result in a higher target real wage. However, it may also result in a lower level of effort, lower labour productivity and hence a lower feasible real wage. The net outcome of these two effects would be to raise the NAIRU.

The post-war boom

The trans-war period and the NAIRU

The NAIRU model was originally used to explain the rise in unemployment during the 1970s and early 1980s (Grubb et al. 1983; Layard and Nickell 1985). In the Layard and Nickell paper, the results are presented in terms of explaining the increase in unemployment since the period 1956–66, because the absolute level of the NAIRU is not determined. The values for the NAIRU in subsequent periods are therefore dependent on the assumption that the actual unemployment rate was equal to the NAIRU during the baseline period 1956–66. It should also be noted that there is a non-linearity in the Layard and Nickell post-war model, such that as unemployment falls below the NAIRU the gap between the target and feasible real wage grows very fast and there are strong upward effects on inflation. However, if unemployment rises above the NAIRU, the gap between the feasible and target real wage grows only slowly, so that there is only weak downward pressure on inflation. The model is thus calibrated to explain the rise in unemployment during the 1970s and early 1980s, and the persistence of high unemployment together with persistent inflationary tendencies.

It is interesting, however, to speculate on what the Layard and Nickell model would suggest about the value of the NAIRU for the inter-war period. Could the variables that have been used to explain the high unemployment of the 1970s and 1980s also explain the high unemployment of the 1920s and 1930s? At first sight it would appear doubtful. On the target real wage side, the key variables are the benefit replacement ratio, union power and mismatch. As Metcalf *et al.* (1982) show, the replacement ratio was similar in the inter-war period and early post-war periods, while trade union density was much lower in the 1930s than the 1950s (Bain and Price 1980). In addition, structural change was faster in the post-1945 period, suggesting a greater degree of mismatch and upward wage pressure than in the inter-war period (Matthews *et al.* 1982: ch. 9). Thus all the variables on the target real wage side would suggest a lower NAIRU in the inter-war period. On the feasible real wage side, real import prices and employers' labour taxes are the key variables. There was a deterioration in Britain's terms of trade across the Second World War, although the effect was neither large nor sustained (Feinstein 1972: Table 64; Matthews *et al.* 1982: Table 16.1). To some extent this can be seen as the downside of the competitive gain from exchange rate devaluation (Cairncross and Eichengreen 1983). Employers' labour taxes increased across the war (Feinstein 1972: Tables 3 and 12). Thus on the feasible real wage side we would expect to see a lower NAIRU in the inter-war period. All the variables which Layard and Nickell use to explain a low NAIRU in the 1950s and 1960s compared with the 1970s and 1980s, then, would suggest an even lower NAIRU for the 1920s and 1930s. Yet the inter-war period was characterised by persistently high levels of unemployment.

The problem could be stated the other way round by starting with the estimates of the NAIRU for the 1930s from Dimsdale *et al.* (1989) and projecting forwards into the 1950s. The model is estimated on quarterly data for the period 1924–38, and again the absolute level of the NAIRU is not determined. Rather, the model is used to explain changes in unemployment from a baseline period, much as in the Layard and Nickell (1985) model. But if the model is calibrated with a high NAIRU for the 1930s, forward projection would suggest a high NAIRU for the 1950s, since the explanatory variables are basically the same as those used by Layard and Nickell.

How, then, can the two periods be reconciled? In fact, there are two important differences between the 1930s and the 1950s which can be used within the NAIRU framework to explain the dramatic decline in unemployment across the Second World War. First, a sharp rise in labour productivity growth from 1 per cent per annum during 1924–37 to 2.4 per cent per annum during 1951–73 raised the feasible real wage (Matthews *et al.* 1982: Tables 16.1 and 3.9). Second, the post-war settlement ensured that restraint was exercised by unions on the target real wage side. Hence there was a substantial fall in the NAIRU.

This explanation for the low NAIRU in the post-war period, then, depends on factors which affected both the target real wage and the feasible real wage. On the target real wage side there was a strong dampening effect from the post-war settlement, acting as a kind of implicit incomes policy. On the feasible real wage side, Britain's productivity gap with America opened up the possibility of catch-up growth, thus underpinning the growth of the real wage (Abramovitz 1986; Broadberry and Crafts 1990b). However, Britain's rate of convergence on US productivity levels was much slower than in many OECD countries (Maddison 1987). This persistence of low relative productivity levels in Britain can also be seen as a legacy of the post-war settlement. This means that as well as the positive aspect of wage restraint, there was a negative aspect to the post-war settlement, in terms of the entrenched restrictive practices and low productivity levels. Thus, although during the 1950s and 1960s low unemployment was secured as the target real wage was held back in line with the feasible real wage, Britain's relative productivity position also suffered as the feasible real wage was held back. It should be noted that this negative effect of the post-war settlement on productivity is quite consistent with the fact that productivity growth was higher in the post-war period than during the inter-war period. This is because the opportunities for growth were greater in the post-war period through catching up the USA. The post-war settlement acted only to slow down convergence on American levels of productivity.

The post-war settlement, wages and productivity

The above argument has relied on the notion of a post-war settlement to explain the avoidance of a massive wage inflation given the low rate of unemployment. Hence it is necessary to define precisely what is meant by the post-war settlement, since there is a plethora of definitions available in the literature. The simplest definition would be an implicit income policy, representing a bargain between the government and the Trades Union Congress (TUC), whereby the government agreed to use demand management to maintain a high level of employment in return for wage restraint on the part of unions. This appears to be the view of Jones (1987) and Flanagan et al. (1983).

However, this misses a vital component of the post-war settlement, which helped to entrench low productivity in Britain, thus affecting the feasible real wage as well as the target real wage. The key feature of the post-war settlement was that it involved a consensus between all the major economic interest groups, forged during the exceptional circumstances of the Second World War. The key interest groups came together during the war in a number of tripartite bodies such as the Joint Consultative Committee to settle industrial relations issues and the National Production Advisory Committee to settle production issues (Tomlinson 1990: 154).

Middlemas (1979) argues that unions and employers' organisations thus became 'governing institutions' rather than mere lobbying organisations, exercising restraint over their members in return for participation in the process of government. Yet he also sees them as resisting formal incorporation into the state because of their need to remain representative of their members' interests.

Middlemas (1986) makes the clearest attempt to set out the details of the settlement and how it was perceived by the different interest groups. However, Middlemas never sets out clearly the incentives facing the interest groups, which is essential to explain the persistence of the settlement. What, then, did the various groups get out of the post-war settlement?

For most authors, full employment is at the centre of the 'post-war settlement', even if that term is not used. Other commentators have used other terms such as 'the Keynesian revolution' (Winch 1972), 'the triumph of social democracy' (Gamble 1985), 'tacit cooperation'(Flanagan et al. 1983), or 'the Dream of New Jerusalem' (Barnett 1986).

Governments wanted full employment for political reasons, fearing the electoral consequences of association with the mass unemployment and deflation of the 1930s. The competition between the Labour and Conservative parties for the working-class vote meant that this would be true whichever party was in power. Governments were prepared to use demand management to maintain full employment so long as the situation was not exploited by unions and employers. Hence a form of self-regulation was required.

Unions were prepared to accept the need for wage restraint in return for full employment, although the importance of plant-level bargaining made it difficult for the central unions to deliver (Clegg 1979). The voluntary, consensual nature of the agreement meant that government implicitly agreed to keep out of matters such as restrictive practices, immunities and union activity on the shop floor, where self-regulation was deemed appropriate (Flanagan *et al.* 1983: 379).

For industry, high demand plus wage restraint could still deliver high profits despite restrictive practices in the labour market, so long as the cosy system of cartelisation and restrictive practices in labour markets that had been built up during the 1930s was allowed to continue (Broadberry and Crafts 1990b). Hence the post-war settlement also depended on industry being left to a form of self-regulation through trade associations rather than a vigorous anti-trust policy. There was a striking contrast between the loose, discretionary approach to competition policy in post-war Britain and the tight, non-discretionary policy in the United States (Sawyer 1981: ch. 16; Elliott and Gribbin 1977; Neale 1960).

Hence the post-war settlement came to underwrite low productivity, with the implicit consensus leading to an avoidance of difficult issues that impinged directly on the interests of one of the key institutions. As Middlemas writes of the fudging of key issues in the 1944 White Paper on *Employment Policy*, 'three crucial issues had been laid aside, wrapped in platitudes to enable the White Paper to appear at all' (1986: 94). On the issue of oligopoly power and restrictive practices, he writes 'in the apparently overriding interests of consensus about the full employment package, a vast question had been buried, which would not be resurrected until the early 1960s' (1986: 95).

This avoidance of difficult decisions in the interests of consensus shows up in studies of early post-war British industry, surveyed in Broadberry and Crafts (1989). For example, in the Anglo-American Council on Productivity (AACP) reports on individual industries, union and management attitudes and restrictive practices are usually cited as major contributors to Britain's productivity shortfall. In his overall assessment, based on the AACP reports, Hutton (1953) concludes that British managers and unions had settled for a quiet life in which overmanning and restrictive practices were accepted. Thus he writes, 'The drawbacks or shortcomings in Britain, the brakes on productivity, are not due to the quality of industrial relations between unions. The hindrances seem due more to the restricted content of those relations' (Hutton 1953: 144). Detailed studies such as those by Scott *et al.* (1956), Zweig (1951) and Flanders (1964) provide support for this view.

In terms of Olson's (1965, 1982) analysis, British society became highly sclerotic, with growth slowed down by entrenched interest groups. British trade unions and employers' organisations exhibited narrow scope and low sophistication; that is, they bargained on behalf of small groups and exercised only weak central control over members. As Batstone (1986) notes, countries such as Sweden, with unions and employers' organisations which exhibited broad scope and high sophistication, had superior growth performance in the post-war period. This can be explained by the fact that small bargaining groups can gain by increasing their share of society's resources at the expense of others. They could also make themselves better off by working to increase the size of the national output cake to be distributed, but in that case they might not be able to appropriate all the gain, so that there is a public good problem. For large, encompassing groups, however, it is not possible to gain by redistribution. Hence encompassing unions are seen by Batstone as less likely to press for inflationary wage settlements, and more likely to accept the changes in employment conditions necessary for productivity growth. Calmfors and Driffill (1988) argue that extremes work best; either a highly decentralised bargaining system free from union influence or a highly centralised system in a highly unionised economy. An intermediate case such as Britain, with a high degree of unionisation but decentralised wage bargaining, captures the worst of both worlds.

Thus although the post-war settlement can be seen as restricting the growth of the target real wage and thus promoting full employment, as in the conventional view, there was also a darker, negative side to the settlement, with the entrenchment of restrictive practices and low pro-ductivity, holding back the growth of the feasible real wage.

Pressures undermining the post-war settlement

Before examining the rising unemployment of the 1970s in detail, it is worth noting the forces which undermined the incentives that underpinned the consensus of the post-war settlement. From the point of view of the workers who were being asked to hold back on wage claims so as to sustain a low productivity, low wage economy, it is not difficult to see the possibility of a better deal. When Frank Cousins became General Secretary of the Transport and General Workers' Union (TGWU) in 1956, and began to undermine the consensual policies of the TUC, his starting point was the belief that 'wages in British industry were too low, especially among the majority of workers represented by the TGWU: the semi-skilled and unskilled workers' (Goodman 1979: 116). There may be doubts about the willingness of Cousins to accept the measures necessary for the higher productivity needed to underpin the higher wages (Goodman 1979: 128), but there is little doubt that he was championing a popular cause in opposition to wage restraint. This illustrates a tension that arose between workers' interests as producers and as consumers. As producers, workers wanted to retain restrictive practices and the relaxed pace of work depicted by the AACP reports, but as consumers they were not prepared to pay for this in terms of cost and quality, as evidenced by the growing import penetration (Foreman-Peck 1991). The fragmented structure of British unions, however, meant that small groups of workers could press for higher wages and block the measures necessary to raise productivity, hoping to gain by redistribution from the rest of society (Olson 1982).

From the point of view of firms, paying higher wages without correspondingly higher productivity meant that prices had to be raised, which made British industry uncompetitive under a fixed exchange rate regime. Loss of export markets and import penetration thus increasingly became a problem (Foreman-Peck 1991; Krause 1968). Also, consumer interests led to pressure on product market restrictive practices, with legislation in 1956 and 1964 (Elliott and Gribbin 1977). Firms were thus faced with growing product market competition at home and abroad, which put downward pressure on profitability (Matthews et al. 1982: ch. 6; Hill 1979).

From the government's point of view, the problems were the build-up of inflationary pressure as workers refused to accept wage restraint, and the relative decline of British living standards (and economic power and influence) as productivity grew faster abroad (Caves 1968a; Crafts 1991a). There were thus strong forces at work undermining the post-war settlement during the golden age of the 1950s and 1960s.

The return of mass unemployment

Layard and Nickell's (1985) estimates of the NAIRU are presented in Table 7.3. The model has been calibrated so that the actual unemployment rate was equal to the NAIRU for the period 1956–66. Inflation remained low and stable during this period. As we have seen, the low NAIRU was the result of the post-war settlement, which held the growth of the target real wage back in line with the growth of the feasible real wage. However, this fragile equilibrium was undermined, as it also resulted in the feasible real wage being held back through the entrenchment of restrictive practices and low productivity.

Table 7.3. *Estimates of the NAIRU for males, 1956–83 (percentage points)*

	1956–66	1967–74	1975–9	1980–3
NAIRU	1·96	4·12	7·80	10·72
Actual male unemployment rate	1·96	3·78	6·79	13·79

Source: Layard and Nickell (1985: Table 7).

For the period 1967–74, the NAIRU rose as wage restraint broke down and productivity growth faltered with the ending of the post-war world boom. Since the actual unemployment rate did not rise by as much, however, actual unemployment remained below the NAIRU and inflation accelerated. For the period 1975–9, although actual unemployment continued to rise, the NAIRU rose further, with union militancy, stagnation of productivity growth and adjustment to the oil price shock of 1973–4, so that inflationary pressure remained. This inflationary pressure was initially dampened down by incomes policy, but only temporarily. During 1980–3, the NAIRU rose further, in the face of continued target wage growth and a further jolt to the price of oil. However, with the deflationary policy of the Thatcher government the actual unemployment rate rose above the NAIRU and inflation was reduced.

Table 7.4 gives the reasons for the rise in the male unemployment rate, obtained from the Layard and Nickell study. The benefit replacement ratio, the union wage mark-up, mismatch and incomes policy all represent factors affecting the target real wage, while real import prices and employers' labour taxes affect the feasible real wage. Finally, demand factors affect the extent to which unemployment deviates from the NAIRU.

Of the factors which affected the target real wage, the benefit replacement ratio had a small positive effect on unemployment during the late 1960s and early 1970s, but since that date any effect has been negative, since the replacement ratio has fallen. The notion that the mass unemployment of the 1970s and 1980s can be regarded as voluntary in response to generous unemployment benefits is difficult to sustain. Although some economists claim to have found high estimates of the elasticity of unemployment with respect to benefits from time series data (Maki and Spindler 1975; Minford 1983), the consensus of estimates from cross-sectional data is that the elasticity is low (Narendranathan *et al.* 1985).

It is worth noting at this point that Benjamin and Kochin (1979b) also attempt to attribute the high unemployment of the inter-war period to a

Table 7.4. *Breakdown of the change in the male unemployment rate, 1956–83 (percentage points)*

	1956–66 to 1967–74	1967–74 to 1975–9	1975–9 to 1980–3
Benefit replacement ratio	0·54	−0·09	−0·10
Union wage mark-up	0·84	0·86	0·57
Mismatch	0·14	0·18	0·44
Incomes policy	0·00	−0·31	0·43
Real import prices	−0·36	1·01	−0·67
Employers' labour taxes	0·42	0·67	0·78
Demand factors	0·47	0·82	5·14
Total	2·05	3·14	6·59
Actual change	1·82	3·01	7·00

Source: Layard and Nickell (1985: Table 6).

high replacement ratio. Again, the micro-evidence suggests that the elasticity of unemployment with respect to benefits was low (Eichengreen 1987), and since the replacement ratio was of the same order of magnitude in the inter-war and post-war periods, the benefit system cannot explain the difference between the high inter-war unemployment and the low post-war unemployment.

Trade union power is measured in the Layard and Nickell model by the union wage mark-up (of union over non-union wages). This is seen as a more accurate measure of union power than trade union density, which is often seen as linking wage inflation to trade union power (Hines 1964). Although the proportion of the labour force which was unionised fell during the recession after 1979, the union mark-up continued to rise, and this is seen by Layard and Nickell as a more accurate reflection of labour market realities, with wage inflation remaining a problem despite the high level of unemployment.

The other two factors affecting the target real wage are mismatch and incomes policy. Mismatch or frictional unemployment has risen slightly, which suggests a minor role for structural change. With rapid structural change, the unemployed would be less suited to the available vacancies and hence there would be greater upward pressure on wages as firms tried to fill the vacancies. Incomes policy had an effect of dampening down wage inflation during the period 1975–9, but this was more than offset by catch-up effects during 1980–3.

Turning to the factors affecting the feasible real wage, real import prices had their strongest effect during the 1970s, with the oil price shock of 1973–4 and the explosion of commodity prices (Bruno and Sachs 1983). By the time of the second oil shock in 1979–80, Britain was a net exporter of oil (Bean 1987: 69) and the early 1980s saw a fall in real import prices, which acted to raise the feasible real wage and thus lower the NAIRU. Rising employers' labour taxes exerted downward pressure on the feasible real wage throughout the period, especially from the late 1960s (Layard 1986: 41).

However, the single most important factor behind the surge in unemployment after 1979 was the deflation of demand as a counter-inflation policy. The sharp rise in unemployment during 1979–83 was thus to a large extent the cost of the reduction of inflation. In this approach, the traditional macro-economist's distinction between Keynesian unemployment (due to demand deficiency) and classical unemployment (due to excessive wages) disappears. For although the proximate cause of the rise in unemployment was the result of a deflation of aggregate demand, this deflationary policy must in turn be seen as a response to inflationary pressures arising from the excessive target wages of workers.

Given the relatively short run of annual time series data available, the precise magnitude of these estimates should be treated with some caution and the results seen as illustrative rather than definitive. In particular, one shortcoming of the Layard and Nickell estimates is the absence of a separate term for productivity growth, which plays such an important role in the estimates of Grubb et al. (1983).

A Thatcher miracle?

The NAIRU since 1983

The Layard and Nickell estimates of the NAIRU do not cover the period since 1983. However, using a similar model, Jenkinson (1987) finds a reduction in the NAIRU for the period 1983–7. It seems likely that this reduction in the NAIRU was largely the result of improvements on the feasible real wage side, since wage increases remained relatively high. In addition to a substantial reduction in the price of oil from 1986, the British economy experienced a period of relatively rapid output and productivity growth from the trough of the recession in 1981 to the peak of 1988.

To what extent does this improved productivity performance of the 1980s represent a new sustainable trend of higher growth (a Thatcher miracle) rather than simply a one-off shift to a new higher level of productivity? Whereas there seems to be a clear gain over the disappointing productivity growth of the 1970s, as Muellbauer (1986) notes, this represents at best a return to the growth rates of the 1950s and 1960s, albeit against a background of a much less favourable international economic environment. Hence, as Crafts (1988) notes, Britain no longer languished at the bottom of the world growth league during the 1980s.

Note, however, that as the actual unemployment rate fell sharply during 1987–8, inflation once again picked up, suggesting that actual unemployment was again below the NAIRU. The government responded by tightening monetary policy to reduce inflation. Another way of assessing the extent to which there has been a Thatcher miracle is to examine the trade-off between inflation and unemployment. To what extent has the government been able to attain the twin goals of low inflation and low unemployment? A popular indicator in the United States has been the index of economic misery, which is obtained as the sum of the unemployment rate and the inflation rate (Calmfors and Driffill 1988: 19). Clearly, during the 1980s this index has been lower than during the 1970s. Although unemployment increased during the 1980s, inflation fell sharply, to give a lower value for the misery index. However, compared with the low inflation and low unemployment of the 1950s and 1960s, the 1980s has generated a lot more economic misery. Once again, then, performance seems better during the 1980s than during the 1970s, but not as good as during the 1950s and 1960s. Again, however, it should be noted that world economic conditions during the 1980s were far less favourable than during the 1950s and 1960s.

Explaining the improvements of the 1980s

There may be some doubts about whether the performance of the 1980s compared favourably with the performance of the 1950s and 1960s, but there seems little doubt that it represents an improvement over the 1970s. Inflation was reduced and productivity growth increased, but at a cost of higher unemployment for a sustained period.

One explanation for this might be that the trade union legislation of the 1980s severely weakened unions, which resulted in less inflationary wage claims and also faster productivity growth as unions no longer blocked technical change which threatened workers' jobs (Matthews and Minford 1987). This then led to favourable effects on both the feasible real wage and target real wage sides. The resurgence of inflation during the late 1980s must cast some doubt on this optimistic interpretation of events.

An alternative view, argued forcefully by Wadhwani (1989) and Brown and Wadhwani (1990) stresses the shift in bargaining power from workers to management brought about by the recession and the threat to the existence of firms. Wadhwani (1989) argues that the union legislation of the 1980s, which outlawed mass secondary picketing, reduced trade union immunities, outlawed the closed shop and increased the democratic accountability of union leaders, had little impact. He notes that although productivity growth was faster in unionised firms than in non-unionised firms during 1980–4, there was no difference between union and non-union firms during 1975–9 and 1985–6. If the anti-union legislation was important in explaining the superior performance of unionised firms during 1980–4, Wadhwani argues, the pro-union legislation of the 1970s should have worsened the performance of the unionised firms during 1975–9. However, Wadhwani may be considering too short a time period. We have already seen the importance of restrictive practices noted in the early post-war literature on productivity in Britain. Compared with the massive change to the generally favourable treatment of unions which was embodied in the post-war settlement, the pro-union legislative changes of the 1974–8 period were relatively minor.

Bean and Symons (1989) accept that both legislative changes and the recession had roles to play in the reduction of union power and hence in the improved productivity performance of the 1980s. Their explanation of how reduced union power led to improved productivity performance is also of some interest. They note that the productivity improvement was greatest in firms where multi-unionism was present, which links back to the Olson thesis. Bargaining in isolation, a union can perceive overmanning and other restrictive practices as being in its interests. A reduction in union power in these circumstances can result in a rise in productivity and wages.

Conclusion

Low unemployment of the 1950s and 1960s should therefore be seen as exceptional. During this period low unemployment was reconciled with stable inflation through the exercise of wage restraint. Yet the post-war settlement which underpinned this wage restraint also allowed the entrenchment of overmanning and other restrictive practices, which inevitably slowed the growth of productivity and the feasible real wage. The breakdown of this post-war consensus led to accelerating inflation during the 1970s, with the abandonment of wage restraint. This was followed by a return of mass unemployment during the early 1980s as the government pursued an anti-inflationary monetary policy.

The abandonment of the post-war consensus also freed the government to move against trade union power, which resulted in improved pro-ductivity performance during the 1980s. However, the difficulties of achieving the twin goals of low unemployment and low inflation which continue to beset the British economy suggest that there are still problems with British labour market institutions. The combination of a high degree of unionisation and decentralised wage bargaining continues to deliver a high degree of inflationary pressure, which can only be kept in check by a high level of unemployment.

8 Money and monetary policy in Britain, 1945–1990

Susan Howson

Introduction

In the four and a half decades since 1945 the role of money, and the use of monetary policy, has been peculiarly subject to the whims of intellectual fashion in economic thought, in Britain perhaps even more so than elsewhere. At the outset the most commonly held view among British economists was that 'money does not matter (much)' for maintaining high employment, fostering economic growth or controlling inflation. By the 1980s the opposite view, that money matters a lot especially so far as inflation is concerned, a proposition at the heart of what is usually referred to as 'monetarism', had come to dominate among economists and policy makers. The adoption of a 'monetarist' monetary policy in Britain in the mid-1970s had been hastened by frustration with the results of the monetary policy pursued in the previous two decades. Nonetheless, there have been striking continuities in British monetary policy since 1945: an ambivalence about the role of monetary policy and whether it should be assigned to domestic or external objectives; a preoccupation with the management of the national debt; and an apparent inability to control monetary growth (meaning here the growth of some suitable measure of the money supply). The Bank of England has always been reluctant to try to control the monetary base (essentially the reserve base of the commercial banking system) and has always found it difficult to control bank lending.

Post-war monetary policy can be divided into four phases: (i) the immediate post-war policies of the 1945–51 Labour governments under Prime Minister Clement Attlee, when the 'Keynesian' downgrading of monetary policy was still in the ascendant; (ii) the 1950s Conservative governments' 'revival' of monetary policy which in spite of confused aims and uncertain methods effectively reassigned it to the preservation of external balance; (iii) the attempt at a new approach with 'Competition and Credit Control' in 1971 and subsequent gradual moves towards 'monetary targets' (that is, announced targets for the rate of growth of the money supply somehow defined); (iv) the experience and gradual abandonment of monetary targets under the Medium-Term Financial Strategy in the 1980s.

The major policy changes each reflect, with a lag, changes in Britain's external monetary arrangements: the increasing openness of the UK economy after 1947, in spite of the failure of that year's attempt to restore convertibility of sterling into dollars, and the adjustment to post-war realities in the devaluation of the pound from US$4.03 to $2.80 in 1949; the achievement of general convertibility of previously inconvertible European currencies in 1958 which ushered in the operation of the Bretton Woods system; the mounting difficulties of Bretton Woods which included a second post-war devaluation of the pound (to US$2.40) in 1967 and its floating in 1972; and the abolition in October 1979 of the remnants of the comprehensive exchange controls introduced in 1939. Entry into the exchange rate mechanism of the European Monetary System in 1990 returned Britain to a regime of fixed exchange rates against other European currencies but this regime lasted only until 1992.

The next section of this chapter provides a simplified description of the changing theoretical views that lie behind the conduct of British monetary policy since 1945. The same model is used to illustrate the external factors that impinge upon domestic monetary policy and restrict its operation in many circumstances. The section also briefly discusses the definition of the money supply and the methods of controlling it. The following section outlines the conduct of British monetary policy in the four periods mentioned above, indicating for each both the policies pursued and the intellectual rationale for their pursuit or abandonment. The final section suggests some conclusions, especially in relation to Britain's experience of inflation in the post-war period.

Theory

In a modern capitalist economy the supply of money, used for making payments and in final settlement of debts, consists of currency (notes and coin) in circulation with the public together with bank deposits. (Credit cards provide credit, not money, because they do not finally extinguish debts.) The money supply can therefore be defined in different ways depending on the categories of bank deposits included. The most widely used definition in the UK has been M3 or 'broad money', which includes 'all deposits, whether denominated in sterling or non-sterling currency, held with the UK banking sector by UK residents in both the public and private sectors, together with notes and coin in circulation with the public'. This is to be distinguished from 'narrow money', M1, which comprises currency plus sterling current (chequable) accounts held with the private sector, and an intermediate aggregate, M2, which equals M1 plus private sector sterling deposit accounts with UK banks and discount houses (Bank of England 1970: 320–1). (Discount houses are specialist financial institutions, who borrow at very short term (on call) from UK banks and invest in short-term bills, especially British government Treasury bills.)

The monetary base (M0) is the total of currency in the hands of the non-bank public and the cash reserves of the banking system (partly currency but mainly deposits with the Bank of England). In *principle*, the central bank (Bank of England) controls the supply of reserves to the banks, and if the supply is increased (decreased) then since banks hold reserves equal to only a fraction of their deposits, this will have a multiplier effect on bank lending and hence bank deposits and the money supply. In practice, the Bank of England has always disliked the idea of 'monetary base control' and preferred to influence banks' behaviour by altering short-term interest rates (on, say, Treasury bills) and the rate at which it is prepared to *lend* cash reserves to the discount houses and hence the banking system, a rate traditionally known as 'Bank Rate'. If the Bank raises these rates, the willingness of banks to lend should then be reduced, given the increased cost of acquiring additional reserves to support deposit expansion.

Monetary *policy* includes all central bank attempts to influence the money supply directly (e.g. by controlling the monetary base) or indirectly (i.e. via changing those interest rates which the central bank can easily influence). 'Open-market operations' by the Bank, such as purchases of Treasury bills from the public, will reduce the supply and hence lower the interest rates on Treasury bills, as well as increasing bank reserves. The monetary authorities' intervention in the gilt-edged market – purchases or sales of marketable British government securities as distinct from Treasury bills which are part of the 'floating debt' – whether undertaken for monetary policy reasons or as part of the management of the national debt, will also alter interest rates and the supply of money.

The monetarist–Keynesian debate over the effectiveness of monetary policy can in the first instance be described in terms of the well-known IS–LM model. Indeed the debate was initially, and unrealistically, conducted in this framework. Until the 1960s most (but not all) 'Keynesian' economists tended to believe that domestic monetary policy had little impact on aggregate demand and hence on output and employment. This followed from their view of the 'transmission mechanism' of monetary policy that a change in monetary conditions engineered by a central bank would influence demand through nominal interest rates on bank advances and on financial assets which were alternatives to investment in real assets. This meant that monetary policy primarily influenced firms' investment

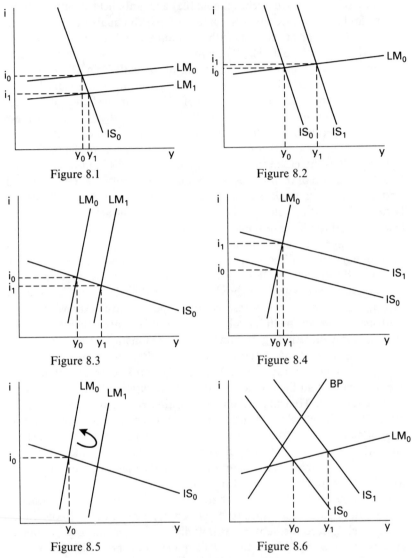

Figure 8.1

Figure 8.2

Figure 8.3

Figure 8.4

Figure 8.5

Figure 8.6

Figures 8.1 to 8.6 For legend see facing page

rather than consumers' expenditure, and investment decisions were also thought to be rather insensitive to changes in interest rates. Thus the demand for money was fairly elastic with respect to the nominal rate of interest, while investment was relatively interest-inelastic, making for a flat LM curve and a steep IS curve.

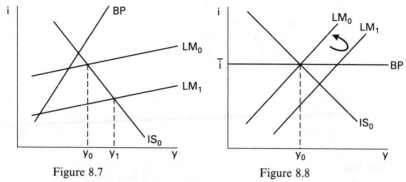

Figure 8.7   Figure 8.8

Figures 8.1 to 8.8 Different formulations of the IS–LM model

An increase in the nominal money supply, shifting the LM curve to the right, produces only a small fall in nominal interest rates and a small rise in income (Figure 8.1). An expansionary *fiscal* policy, on the other hand, which increases aggregate demand either directly by increasing government expenditure or through reduced taxation, has a large impact on income and employment in this framework (Figure 8.2).

A more realistic variant, to be found implicitly at least in the Radcliffe Report (1959), argued that the Bank of England did not control the money supply, which accommodated itself to money demand generated by the level of economic activity and nominal income and the level of interest rates (which were influenced by the Bank's actions). Then the LM curve was essentially horizontal. Again, this made monetary policy relatively ineffective compared with fiscal policy.

In the 1960s the monetarists, led by Milton Friedman of the University of Chicago, challenged the 'Keynesian' view as seriously underestimating the potency of monetary policy, by taking too narrow a view of the transmission mechanism and by neglecting the contribution of monetary expansion to price inflation. Whereas the Keynesians described the demand for nominal money balances as a function of nominal income and a representative interest rate on those *financial* assets regarded as alternatives to money, the monetarists argued that the demand for money was a demand for real balances (M/P), dependent on real income (Y), wealth and the expected rates of return on a wide range of financial and real assets (including housing and consumer durables, for instance). The rates of return would themselves depend *inter alia* on the expected rate of price changes. The proportion of real income held as real money balances was fairly stable in the short run, so that the elasticity of money demand with respect to interest rates could be regarded as low. A change in the real money stock could therefore affect firms and household demands for real assets 'directly' rather than just through changes in interest rates on financial assets. In the IS–LM model the IS curve is then relatively flat and the LM curve relatively steep; monetary policy is a more powerful instrument for influencing aggregate demand than fiscal policy (Figures 8.3 and 8.4).

Moreover, expansionary monetary policy can only increase real income and employment when unemployment is above the 'natural' rate of unemployment determined by demographic and social factors and institutional arrangements in the labour market. If aggregate demand is boosted too much it will raise prices rather than real output; and if the authorities persist in trying to raise output the inflation will not only persist but will come to be anticipated, to be reflected in wage bargains, and to accelerate. (The so-called natural rate of unemployment is thus better known as the non-accelerating inflation rate of unemployment, NAIRU; see chapter 7.) In IS–LM terms, rising prices caused by an increase in the nominal money supply when the natural rate of unemployment prevails and real output cannot be increased other than temporarily, will reduce the real value of the money supply, shifting LM leftwards (Figure 8.5) – unless there is a continuous and accelerating expansion of the nominal money supply, when inflation will also continue at an accelerating rate. (Fiscal policy can also not reduce unemployment other than temporarily above the NAIRU, but if an expansionary fiscal policy is *not* accompanied by monetary expansion then the inflation cannot continue indefinitely.)

This is a crude characterisation of the monetarist–Keynesian debate in the 1960s and early 1970s. It is crude for at least two reasons: (1) as the debate itself implies, the IS–LM model is inadequate for discussing the causes and consequences of inflation; (2) the external constraints on domestic monetary policy have been ignored. The model has been retained in spite of the first defect because it can conveniently be used to illustrate the external constraints.

The balance of payments (B) of a small open economy can be written as

$$B = pX(ep^*/p) - ep^*M(Y, ep^*/p) + K(i, i^*)$$

where p and p^* represent domestic and foreign prices and e the nominal exchange rate (domestic currency, e.g. pounds, per unit of foreign currency, e.g. dollars), so that ep^*/p is the *real* exchange rate; X and M are the volumes of exports and imports of goods and services, so that $pX - ep^*M$ is the current account of the balance of payments; and K stands for net capital flows, whose short-term behaviour is largely determined by interest rates at home and abroad (i, i^*). The combinations of real income and domestic interest rates which produce 'external balance' (B = 0) given the levels of the other variables can be added to the IS–LM diagram; the line will be flatter the freer are international capital movements to respond to changes in relative interest rates.

This expanded IS–LM model, usually known as the Mundell–Fleming model after Mundell (1962 and 1963) and Fleming (1962), implies that the effectiveness of domestic monetary and fiscal policy depends on the exchange rate regime as well as on the degree of international capital mobility. With fixed exchange rates, which the UK enjoyed from 1945 to 1972, and a low degree of capital mobility (which may have prevailed until the later 1950s), the use of monetary policy to increase income would have the disadvantage of producing a larger balance of payments deficit than would have a fiscal policy with the same effect on income (figures 8.6 and 8.7; the vertical distance of the intersection of IS and LM from the external balance line BP measures the increase in domestic interest rates necessary to bring about external balance and hence the size of the deficit).

A balance of payments deficit with fixed exchange rates will oblige the authorities (Treasury and Bank of England) to sell foreign currency in exchange for pounds in order to maintain the value of the pound; hence UK official international reserves (of US dollars and other foreign currencies) will decline. This exchange market intervention will also reduce the money supply unless the Bank takes offsetting action by, for instance, buying Treasury bills from the non-bank private sector. If international capital mobility is high the running down of international reserves necessary to maintain a fixed exchange rate will be large and may be unsustainable, since the reserves are not infinite. The size of the reserve changes may also be too large for the authorities to 'sterilise' their effects on the money supply. In the limit, with 'perfect capital mobility', monetary policy is powerless to influence income (Figure 8.8). If interest rates fall below i, because of an expansionary monetary policy, there will be a massive capital outflow and fall in official international reserves: the money supply will fall back, interest rates will return to i, and income will be unchanged at Y_0.

With flexible exchange rates, which the UK resorted to in 1972 and retained until 1990, an independent monetary policy can be regained. In such a case, a balance of payments deficit does not necessitate either a fall in reserves or the need for sterilisation of the effect of a fall in reserves on the money supply. Furthermore, with high international capital mobility as we have had since the 1960s, monetary policy becomes *more* powerful than fiscal policy in its effects on the domestic economy, regardless of Keynesian–monetarist considerations. A fall in interest rates due to an expansionary monetary policy will both directly increase aggregate demand and depreciate the exchange rate. Unless domestic prices rise immediately, a fall in the real exchange rate (ep*/p) will increase exports of goods and services and reduce imports of goods and services, thus further increasing aggregate demand as well as offsetting the balance of payments deficit caused by the capital outflow. (This statement ignores lags in the response of the current account to exchange rate changes but the principle nonetheless holds.)

The increased effectiveness of monetary policy under floating exchange rates is not an unmixed blessing: expansionary monetary policy can be particularly damaging to the domestic economy because of the increased possibilities of generating inflation if output and employment cannot respond sufficiently to increased demand. By the same token, however, restrictive monetary policy becomes a more powerful anti-inflationary weapon under floating exchange rates when an exchange rate appreciation will reduce aggregate demand and reduce the domestic currency price of imports, which are a major item in the retail price index.

Discussion of inflation strictly goes beyond the confines of the essentially Keynesian Mundell–Fleming model. On the other hand, the original monetarist attack on the Keynesian model ignored the external sector of the economy. The 'monetary theory of the balance of payments', developed in the 1970s, by Harry Johnson (of the University of Chicago and the London School of Economics) among others, rectified this shortcoming. A small open economy in a global financial and trading system has to adapt both to interest rates set in international financial markets and to the world prices of internationally traded goods. Under fixed exchange rates domestic interest rates will have to be kept in line with foreign interest rates (for otherwise capital flows would through their impact on the domestic money supply bring them back in line) and domestic prices will also largely reflect world prices. An unduly expansionary monetary policy will show up not in increased inflation but in a balance of payments deficit until the rate of monetary expansion is cut back (hence the '*monetary* theory of the *balance of payments*'). As the Mundell–Fleming model with perfect capital mobility also implies, there is no scope for an independent monetary policy under fixed exchange rates.

The monetary theory also implies that if a country with a balance of payments deficit under fixed exchange rates devalues its currency to try to eliminate the deficit, any improvement will only be temporary without a reduction in the rate of monetary growth. Older and more 'Keynesian' theories, such as the absorption approach (Alexander 1952; Johnson 1958b), agreed that devaluation, in conditions of high employment such as the late 1940s and the 1960s, would not cure a deficit without a reduction in domestic demand, but they did not imply that the instrument of demand reduction would have to be monetary.

Finally, once inflation is taken into account, it is necessary to distinguish between nominal and real interest rates. The former will tend to be higher, the higher is the (expected) rate of inflation, which should therefore be deducted from observed interest rates to arrive at a measure of the real interest rates which are relevant to borrowers' and lenders' decisions. In the early post-war years, however, when persistent inflation was not generally anticipated, 'cheap money' was taken to mean low nominal interest rates and 'dear money' a Bank Rate of over 3 per cent.

With these theoretical considerations as background, it is possible to turn to the monetary policy practised by the UK monetary authorities (Treasury and Bank of England) since 1945.

Policy

The monetary policies of the 1945–51 Labour governments

The Second World War left Britain with a balance of payments deficit on current account equivalent to over one sixth of her national income (which was just under £10,000 million), a central government budget deficit of about the same size and a national debt more than double national income (Feinstein 1972: Tables 3 and 12; Pember and Boyle 1950: 447). At the same time, with wartime exchange controls in force, the UK economy was *financially* closed, with low international capital mobility. This had allowed the government to maintain cheap money throughout the war, with Bank Rate at 2 per cent, the rate of interest on Treasury bills fixed at 1 per cent and nominal yields on gilt-edged government securities ranging from 1.75 per cent for bonds with five years to maturity to 3 per cent for those with maturities of twenty years or more (see Sayers 1956: chs. 5 and 7). The money supply (M3) had doubled during the war and there had been a large increase in the amount of short-term government debt held by the banks and the non-bank private sector, but direct controls had prevented serious open inflation. In 1945 government officials and economists, including Lord Keynes, James Meade and Lionel Robbins, recommended the retention of cheap money and direct controls for at least a transitional period after the war. Their advice reflected widespread anticipation of a post-war slump like that which followed the First World War, recognition that relying on high nominal interest rates (dear money) to restrain inflation without controls would substantially increase the interest cost of the large post-war national debt, and, to a lesser extent, scepticism as to the influence of interest rates on private sector expenditure (Howson 1987: 438–41).

The first post-war Labour Chancellor of the Exchequer, Hugh Dalton, tried, however, to go further and to *lower* nominal interest rates on

Table 8.1. *Growth rates of monetary aggregates, 1945–90*
(% p.a.) (December to December)

	M0	M1	£M3	M3
1945	9·7	8·6		8·3
1946	5·6	15·3		14·3
1947	−3·8	1·4		3·5
1948	−3·5	2·4		2·2
1949	1·6	−0·5		0·3
1950	1·0	3·7		2·2
1951	4·9	−0·3		−0·3
1952	4·9	−0·7		2·0
1953	4·7	2·6		4·0
1954	6·2	4·4		3·9
1955	3·3	−1·9		−2·9
1956	4·6	0·4		1·4
1957	5·3	−0·3		3·4
1958	2·3	2·4		3·5
1959	4·1	4·9		4·4
1960	3·9	−1·4		0·6
1961	3·6	−0·5		2·1
1962	−0·1	2·3		2·8
1963	4·5	7·0		4·2
1964	7·7	3·2	5·6	5·5
1965	5·2	3·9	7·6	7·6
1966	3·4	−0·1	3·4	3·6
1967	4·0	7·6	10·0	10·7
1968	4·2	4·1	6·8	7·3
1969	3·3	0·3	2·4	3·1
1970	2·1	9·3	9·5	9·5
1971	5·1	15·1	13·8	13·0
1972	15·4	14·2	26·5	27·8
1973	10·4	5·1	26·0	27·6
1974	15·4	10·8	10·2	12·6
1975	11·6	18·6	6·5	7·6
1976	10·9	11·3	9·6	11·2
1977	16·8	21·5	10·0	9·8
1978	12·9	16·4	15·0	14·9
1979	10·6	8·4	9·9	9·6
1980	5·3	4·0	18·1	18·5
1981	1·0	17·7	25·0	27·6
1982	5·8	11·3	8·9	11·0
1983	5·3	11·2	11·1	13·2
1984	6·9	14·1	9·4	11·9
1985	1·9	18·2	13·4	10·7
1986	10·4	22·5	19·0	22·2
1987	4·2	23·0	22·8	20·4
1988	8·5	14·0	20·5	18·9
1989	5·4			
1990	2·5			

Sources: M0: calculated from Capie and Webber (1985: Tables I (1) and III (2));
M1 and M3 1945–62: Capie and Webber (1985: Tables I (2) and I (3)); M1 and M3
1963–90, £M3: *Bank of England Quarterly Bulletins.*

government debt after the war. He lowered the fixed Treasury bill rate to 0.5 per cent in October 1945 and then during 1946 issued two long-term securities which yielded only 2.5 per cent at the time of issue. (His second issue, of 2.5 per cent Treasury Stock 1975 or after, has always been nicknamed 'Daltons'.) His success in this extraordinary endeavour was short-lived. Nominal yields on long-term government securities returned to their wartime 3 per cent during 1947, once the authorities stopped buying in long-term government securities to keep up their market prices. This intervention caused a very rapid expansion in bank deposits (and hence the money supply: Table 8.1), creating expectations of higher nominal interest rates. The 'cheaper money policy' was effectively abandoned early in 1947, well before the 'convertibility crisis' of the summer (Howson 1987: 441–50).

The Labour government had attempted to cope with the balance of payments problem by seeking large-scale financial assistance from the US and Canadian governments. Under the Anglo-American Financial Agreement of December 1945 it was committed to restore convertibility of sterling into US dollars (in principle only for current transactions) by 15 July 1947. The crisis erupted when it tried to fulfil the commitment. The loss of international reserves, which prompted the suspension of convertibility after less than six weeks on 20 August, was caused by an increased UK current account deficit, by a current account deficit in the rest of the sterling area and by capital movements permitted by the exchange controls (Cairncross 1985: ch. 6; see Table 8.2 for reserve figures). The cheaper money policy contributed, however, to the excessive domestic demand which produced the deterioration in the UK current account in 1947 (Howson 1993: ch. 4). (This view differs from the earlier views of, say, Kennedy (1952: 193–5) and Dow (1964: 21–2), that the cheap money policy had little effect because it was short-lived and because investment was subject to controls; the older view reflects the Keynesian view of the transmission mechanism which relies on the interest-elasticity of investment.)

Economists today are clearer about why 'cheaper money' failed than about why it was undertaken. The official records show that the reason was not so much a belief that monetary policy was unimportant as the choice of a particular assignment of policy instruments. Dalton thought that immediate post-war inflation could be kept at bay by controls and was more concerned to prevent unemployment in the anticipated post-war slump. He believed that the current balance of payments problem could be contained by the US Loan and that the existing exchange controls *completely* insulated the domestic monetary system from external influences. His Treasury and Bank of England advisers also feared a severe

Table 8.2. *UK official international reserves, end-years, 1945–90 (US$ equivalent)*

	US$M
1945	2,476
1946	2,696
1947	2,079
1948	1,856
1949	1,688
1950	3,300
1951	2,335
1952	1,846
1953	2,518
1954	2,762
1955	2,120
1956	2,133
1957	2,273
1958	3,069
1959	2,736
1960	3,231
1961	3,318
1962	2,806
1963	2,658
1964	2,315
1965	3,004
1966	3,009
1967	2,695
1968	2,422
1969	2,528
1970	2,827
1971	6,582
1972	5,646
1973	6,476
1974	6,789
1975	5,429
1976	4,129
1977	20,557
1978	15,694
1979	22,538
1980	27,476
1981	23,347
1982	16,997
1983	17,817
1984	15,694
1985	15,543
1986	21,923
1987	44,326
1988	51,685
1989	38,545
1990	38,464

Source: Economic Trends Annual Supplement 1991.

post-war slump and saw the advantages to the budget of low nominal interest rates on government debt (Howson 1987, 1988 and 1989).

Dalton resigned as Chancellor in November 1947 after inadvertently leaking the contents of an autumn budget. By then he had begun a 'disinflationary' budgetary policy which his austere successor, Sir Stafford Cripps, retained for the next three years. Monetary policy was a relatively passive accompaniment (Dow 1964: 48–9, 227–30). While Bank Rate stayed at 2 per cent and the fixed Treasury bill rate at 0.5 per cent, nominal yields on longer-term government bonds crept up to 4 per cent by 1951. The money supply (M3) grew slowly (at about 2 per cent a year instead of the annual rates in excess of 10 per cent which had been experienced in 1946 and during the war: Table 8.1), so that with prices rising slightly faster real money balances were declining. Since rising bank lending tended to offset the effect of government budget surpluses on the money supply, the clearing banks were from time to time ineffectually 'requested' by the Chancellor of the Exchequer via the Governor of the Bank of England to moderate the growth of their advances.

Behind this inactivity lay a prolonged dispute between Ministers, Treasury officials and the Bank of England about the use of monetary policy. The government side wanted in one way or another, but preferably without raising *short-term* interest rates and hence the cost of the floating debt, to control the growth of bank deposits as a contribution to the policy of disinflation. The Bank wanted to restore the traditional weapons of monetary policy, especially the variability of Bank Rate and short-term money market interest rates, and hence its own pre-war position in the UK monetary system (Howson 1991; Fforde 1992: ch. 5). The new Governor of the Bank, C. F. Cobbold, opened his campaign during the balance of payments crisis which preceded the devaluation in September 1949. (On the devaluation see Cairncross 1985: ch. 7, and ch. 2 above.) Although some government officials, especially Robert Hall, the Director of the Economic Section, were prepared to see higher nominal interest rates, Cobbold lost his opportunity – partly because he also wanted large government expenditure cuts as a way of avoiding a devaluation and partly because he could not convince the Treasury that a small rise in the rate of interest on Treasury bills would produce a reduction in monetary growth sufficient to justify the increased interest cost to the budget (Howson 1991; Fforde 1992: 373–7; see also Roberthall 1989). There was no significant change in monetary stance to accompany the 30 per cent devaluation, merely another call for the bankers to restrain their lending.

After Hugh Gaitskell succeeded the ailing Cripps as Chancellor in October 1950, the dispute over monetary control was rekindled, fanned by the inflationary pressures arising out of British rearmament and world-

Table 8.3. *Market holdings of UK national debt, 1945–90, selected dates, by maturity, as percentage of total market holdings,[a] at 31 March*

	1945	1952	1957	1969	1979	1990
Treasury bills[b]	26·1	12·5	12·9	13·4	3·4	5·9
Stocks						
Up to 5 years to final maturity	7·6	15·6	18·1[c]	19·9	26·7	20·3
Over 5 years and up to 15 years	15·5	11·1	19·4[c]	} 42·2 {	15·5	30·3
Over 15 years and undated	33·4	44·8	34·6		36·3	19·7
Non-marketable debt[d]	17·3	16·0	15·0	24·5	18·1	23·8
Total market holdings	100·0	100·0	100·0	100·0	100·0	100·0

[a] Market holdings = total outstanding *minus* official holdings by Bank of England, government departments and the National Debt Commissioners; hence they include holdings of overseas residents, including overseas official holders.
[b] Includes Treasury deposit receipts in 1945.
[c] Includes holdings of exchange equalisation account and Banking Department of Bank of England.
[d] Mainly national savings securities.
Sources: calculated from: 'Exchequer financing and national debt, 1945–51', *Economic Trends* (December 1961), Tables 2b, 3 and 4; Committee on the Working of the Monetary System, *Principal Memoranda of Evidence*, vol. 1, pp. 56, 111, 125; 'Distribution of the national debt: March 1969', *Bank of England Quarterly Bulletin* 10 (March 1970), Table C; 'Distribution of the national debt at end-March 1979', *Bank of England Quarterly Bulletin* 19 (December 1979), Table B; and 'The net debt of the public sector: end-March 1990', *Bank of England Quarterly Bulletin* 30 (November 1990), Table H.

wide commodity price inflation during the Korean War. Gaitskell wished to pursue a more deflationary policy but was thwarted by his own (and his ministerial colleagues') reluctance to increase the cost of the floating debt, while Cobbold would countenance no tightening of monetary stance without some movement in the fixed Treasury bill rate (Howson 1991, 1993; Fforde 1992: 387–94; see also Williams 1983: 227; Roberthall 1989: 134, 143). The Bank also rejected quantitative direct controls on bank assets or liabilities as administratively impossible. The authorities did, however, begin in 1950 to 'fund' the floating debt, that is, to replace it by longer-term securities, a habit that was to persist for three decades (Table 8.3).

In the 1940s the Bank of England exercised no control over the monetary base. It supplied the banks with sufficient reserves for them to take up each week the quantity of floating debt desired by the government while maintaining a constant ratio of reserves to deposits (8 per cent for the London clearing banks from December 1946). If the Bank had not done so the banks could have replenished their reserves anyway, for the fixed Treasury bill rate was maintained by the authorities' willingness to buy in bills from the discount houses at that rate. Bank Rate was ineffective and the banks were always able easily and cheaply to acquire additional reserves to support additional lending. Any serious attempt to limit monetary growth would have to close the 'open back door' to the Bank of England as well as to allow more movement in interest rates.

The revival of monetary policy

The Labour Party was defeated in the October 1951 general election during another acute balance of payments crisis. A new Conservative Chancellor of the Exchequer, R. A. Butler, announced a rise in Bank Rate to 2.5 per cent on 7 November in a package of emergency measures (mainly cuts in imports which were still subject to controls). Although most economists now favoured higher interest rates (Dow 1964: 67–9; Howson 1988: 562–3; Roberthall 1989: 168–221), it is not clear that the new administration knew what to expect from higher short-term rates. (The remarks about official intentions in the next seven paragraphs are based mainly on unpublished papers in the Public Record Office.)

From the Bank's point of view what was important was the introduction of a new rate of 2 per cent at which the discount houses could borrow from the Bank against Treasury bills, the closing of the Bank's 'open back door' and a special funding issue of £1,000 million short-term bonds to replace outstanding Treasury bills (which totalled £5,000 million), which reduced the clearing banks' liquid assets from 39 to 32 per cent of their deposits. The Bank hoped that the banks, which had kept their liquid assets ratio around 30 per cent before the war, would not let the ratio fall significantly below 30 per cent, but for most of the 1950s it was comfortably above that conventional minimum. There was also a further request to the banks on their advances in late November 1951. A new instrument, restrictions on the terms of hire purchase lending, which had been in preparation for some months, was added in February 1952. (For details see Johnson 1952 and Fforde 1992: 398–411.) The Governor of the Bank told the Permanent Secretary of the Treasury, Sir Edward Bridges, that these measures would 'necessarily be experimental'.

The Bank Rate increase had little impact on the exchange rate, and a 'crisis' rise to 4 per cent, with a corresponding rise in the operative lenderof-last-resort rate to 3.5 per cent, was announced in the budget in March 1952. During 1952 the balance of payments turned round dramatically, thanks to an improvement in the terms of trade as import prices fell and to the beginnings of recession at home (Dow 1964: 73–4; Cairncross 1985: 255–6, 266–7). The recession also reduced the private sector's demands for bank loans, but the authorities succumbed to the temptation to attribute the rapid fall in advances to their monetary measures and thus overestimated the impact of changes in short-term money market interest rates (Cairncross 1987: 11–13).

In September 1953 Bank Rate was reduced to 3.5 per cent and the special rate for borrowing against Treasury bills introduced in November 1951 was merged with it, so that Bank Rate became again the effective rate for last-resort lending to the discount market. (For a list of changes in Bank Rate up to its abolition in 1972, see Table 8.4.) When the balance of payments went into deficit again, the authorities hoped to repeat their favourable 1952 experience with monetary policy. A 'package' of measures in February 1955, intended both to curb domestic demand and to support sterling externally, included a 1 per cent Bank Rate rise (following a 0.5 per cent rise in January) and the reimposition of hire purchase restrictions which had been lifted in July 1954. Since Butler went on to introduce an expansionary budget in April 1955, 'To a cold eye it may seem that he was relying on monetary policy to work wonders' (Dow 1964: 79). Further measures had to be taken: in July 1955 a request to the bankers for a 'positive and significant reduction in their advances over the next few months', an autumn budget, another Bank Rate rise in February 1956 and further requests to the bankers (Radcliffe 1959: paras. 415–22; Cairncross 1987: 14–17; Fforde 1992: ch. 10; see also Smith and Mikesell 1957).

The Treasury was by now rather disillusioned with the Bank's claims for traditional monetary policy. One consequence was the appointment in May 1957 of the Radcliffe Committee on the Working of the Monetary System, which reported two years later (see below). Another was the authorities' resort to quantitative direct controls which the Bank had previously rejected. The July 1955 request to the bankers has been seen as the first step (Radcliffe 1959: para. 417), but it was only a little one. The Treasury wished the Chancellor's request to include a figure of 10 per cent for the desired reduction in bank advances, but the Governor of the Bank refused. After his conversations with the bankers' representatives, however, they agreed amongst themselves to aim for a 10 per cent reduction by the end of the year. Bank advances fell by about 8 per cent in the second half of 1955, but rose again by a similar amount in the first half of 1956 (Cairncross 1987: 16–17; Fforde 1992: 637–40). In July 1956 and again in March 1957 (after a reduction in Bank Rate in February!) new requests

Table 8.4. *Bank Rate changes, 1951–72*

Date of change	Amount of change (%)	New rate (%)
8 November 1951	$+\frac{1}{2}$	$2\frac{1}{2}$
12 March 1952	$+1\frac{1}{2}$	4
17 September 1953	$-\frac{1}{2}$	$3\frac{1}{2}$
13 May 1954	$-\frac{1}{2}$	3
27 January 1955	$+\frac{1}{2}$	$3\frac{1}{2}$
24 February 1955	$+1$	$4\frac{1}{2}$
16 February 1956	$+1$	$5\frac{1}{2}$
7 February 1957	$-\frac{1}{2}$	5
19 September 1957	$+2$	7
20 March 1958	-1	6
22 May 1958	$-\frac{1}{2}$	$5\frac{1}{2}$
19 June 1958	$-\frac{1}{2}$	5
14 August 1958	$-\frac{1}{2}$	$4\frac{1}{2}$
20 November 1958	$-\frac{1}{2}$	4
21 January 1960	$+1$	5
23 June 1960	$+1$	6
27 October 1960	$-\frac{1}{2}$	$5\frac{1}{2}$
8 December 1960	$-\frac{1}{2}$	5
26 July 1961	$+2$	7
5 October 1961	$-\frac{1}{2}$	$6\frac{1}{2}$
2 November 1961	$-\frac{1}{2}$	6
8 March 1962	$-\frac{1}{2}$	$5\frac{1}{2}$
22 March 1962	$-\frac{1}{2}$	5
26 April 1962	$-\frac{1}{2}$	$4\frac{1}{2}$
3 January 1963	$-\frac{1}{2}$	4
27 February 1964	$+1$	5
23 November 1964	$+2$	7
3 June 1965	-1	6
14 July 1965	$+1$	7
26 January 1967	$-\frac{1}{2}$	$6\frac{1}{2}$
16 March 1967	$-\frac{1}{2}$	6
4 May 1967	$-\frac{1}{2}$	$5\frac{1}{2}$
19 October 1967	$+\frac{1}{2}$	6
9 November 1967	$+\frac{1}{2}$	$6\frac{1}{2}$
18 November 1967	$+1\frac{1}{2}$	8
21 March 1968	$-\frac{1}{2}$	$7\frac{1}{2}$
19 September 1968	$-\frac{1}{2}$	7
27 February 1969	$+1$	8
5 March 1970	$-\frac{1}{2}$	$7\frac{1}{2}$
15 April 1970	$-\frac{1}{2}$	7
1 April 1971	-1	6
2 September 1971	-1	5
22 June 1972	$+1$	6

were made to the bankers, this time in person, by new Chancellors of the Exchequer (Harold Macmillan and Peter Thorneycroft respectively) but they did not include specific amounts, again because of the Bank's objections.

On 9 April 1957 Thorneycroft announced the 'new Macmillan committee' (Roberthall 1991: 99). (The old Macmillan Committee was the famous Committee on Finance and Industry, of which Keynes was a member and which reported in August 1931.) During its deliberations another sterling crisis blew up: Bank Rate jumped in one step from 5 to 7 per cent (its highest rate for thirty-six years) on 19 September 1957 and the Chancellor asked the banks explicitly to reduce their advances to the 'average level of the last twelve months'. Thorneycroft wanted to go further and call for a 5 per cent cut in advances. He was frustrated by the Governor's refusal to ask this of the banks and annoyed by his officials' apparent acceptance of the resulting limited possibilities of monetary control (Roberthall 1991: 124–8; Fforde 1992: 676–86). In January (1958) he resigned, along with his two junior Treasury Ministers, over his Cabinet colleagues' unwillingness to take stronger deflationary measures, and there was subsequent cautious easing of monetary policy under his successor Heathcoat Amory (Dow 1964: 96–106). Thorneycroft, advised by Lionel Robbins, has been seen as an early convert to 'monetarism'; whether or not this is true, his resignation showed that official opinion was not yet ready for it, as the Radcliffe Report soon demonstrated. (To add to the excitement there were allegations of a 'leak' before the September Bank Rate change and an official inquiry into them.)

The Bank of England claimed in its evidence to the Radcliffe Committee that existing techniques of monetary control were adequate since the banks voluntarily adhered to a cash reserve ratio of 8 per cent and a conventional minimum liquid assets ratio of 30 per cent (Radcliffe Committee 1960b: I, 9–10). However, it considered some 'alternative techniques', one of which it found less objectionable than the others; in light of the previous few years' experience, the Treasury supported this 'special deposits' scheme (Radcliffe Committee 1960b: I, 38–42, 120–1). The Chancellor, encouraged by Macmillan who was now Prime Minister, announced the end of advances requests and the new scheme, under which the Bank could call for special interest-bearing deposits from the clearing banks to reduce their liquidity, on 3 July 1958, without waiting for the Radcliffe Report. The first calls for special deposits were made in April and June 1960 (Dow 1964: 240–2).

Since 1951 monetary policy had been influenced at critical points by the authorities' gradual but hesitant movements towards the convertibility of sterling. Monetary policy in the 1950s was also constrained by their preoccupation with the problems of debt management. In February 1952 the Bank of England and the Overseas Finance Division of the Treasury launched their notorious 'Robot' plan, under which the pound would be made convertible immediately but with a floating exchange rate and blocking of some of the large sterling balances held by Britain's overseas official creditors. Although Robot was effectively shot down by Robert Hall and his allies in Whitehall (Cairncross 1985: ch. 9; MacDougall 1987: ch. 5; Plowden 1989: ch. 14; Roberthall 1989: 202–33; Fforde 1992: ch. 6 (b)), its advocates, especially the Governor of the Bank, continued to urge early convertibility, usually with a floating exchange rate. In the 'collective approach' to convertibility discussed at several Commonwealth conferences from December 1952 and with the American administration in 1953, the major currencies would have become convertible simultaneously with the help of a support fund from the USA. The short-term result was to feed rumours which weakened sterling in the foreign exchange markets and obliged successive Chancellors to disclaim all intentions of letting sterling float (Dow 1964: 80–90, 97–8, 106–8; Fforde 1992: ch. 7). It is not surprising that Bank Rate changes were directed increasingly towards external balance. Sterling became freely convertible – but only for non-residents – in December 1958.

As for debt management, the Governor of the Bank told the Radcliffe Committee that 'it has been the continuous need to raise finance to meet overall Government requirements ... which, coupled with the refinancing of maturing Government loans, has made the monetary situation so difficult' (Radcliffe Committee 1960b: I, 3–4, see also 22–32). The Treasury pointed to 'the perennial possibility of conflict in the aims of monetary policy' created by the need to fund the debt (Radcliffe Committee 1960b: I, 95). There were three related aspects of the debt problem. First, there was the need to sell debt to cover both new borrowing, by nationalised industries and local authorities as well as by central government, and the repayment of maturing debt. Second, there was the funding of floating debt, which was desired mainly for reasons of monetary policy, specifically to keep down the liquidity of the banks (Radcliffe Committee 1960b: I, 105–12). The Bank believed that it could not control the banks' cash reserves (and hence the monetary base) because the banks held so many Treasury bills which could readily be discounted at Bank Rate or allowed to run off as they matured each week (even if they could not obtain cash for Treasury bills quite as easily and cheaply as before November 1951). Hence the authorities' desire after 1951 to keep the banks' liquid assets ratio down to 30 per cent. Both problems provided reasons for wanting *low* nominal interest rates on government debt, which might at times conflict with the needs of monetary policy, but they also meant the authorities wanted to sell a sizeable amount of long-term debt all the time, which might require quite *high* nominal interest rates to persuade the private sector to hold such debt.

The third problem was compounded by the Bank's belief that it could not sell bonds on a falling market, because investors would expect bond prices to fall and give rise to capital losses on bonds – as had happened under the 'cheaper money policy' in 1947. High interest rates would make gilt-edged borrowing expensive but rising interest rates could make it impossible. Hence the Bank concentrated sales of government bonds in the 1950s in periods of declining interest rates and also tended to be 'entirely passive, indeed fatalistic' about long-term interest rates (Radcliffe 1959: paras. 521–2); although the Radcliffe Committee swallowed the Bank/ Treasury line about the importance of funding, it was critical of the Bank's view of the demand for government bonds. The third problem also affected the timing and movement of short-term interest rates: when Bank Rate was raised the Bank often wanted the market to be convinced that this was the 'top' and hence to anticipate falling interest rates; the Bank was also often anxious to lower Bank Rate quickly but in small steps so as to encourage a rising gilts market.

The Radcliffe Report is best known for its statements of the unimportance of the money supply compared to 'the whole liquidity position' – such as 'spending is not limited by the amount of money in existence ... [but] related to the amount of money people think they can get hold of' – and its recommendation that the authorities operate on 'the structure of interest rates' rather than the supply of money, whose control was '[found] to be no more than an important facet of debt management' (1959: paras. 389–97, 514). In the short run the Report provided an intellectual rationale for the authorities to continue their 1950s practice in the 1960s. In the slightly longer run it brought about a permanent improvement in the availability and quality of UK monetary and financial statistics and eventually encouraged UK monetary economists to reconsider their views about the efficacy of monetary policy and to test them empirically.

In both aims and methods, monetary policy in the 1960s was a continuation of 1950s policy (Bank of England 1969; Tew 1978a; Artis 1978). Hire purchase restrictions were reimposed in April 1960 and changed on twelve occasions in the next ten years. The special deposits scheme, supposed to substitute for direct controls on bank lending, was in operation through the 1960s except for about two and a half years between 1962 and 1965, and from July 1961 was always accompanied by requests to at least some banks to limit their advances. (The scheme only applied to the clearing banks; since the deposits of other banks had been growing very rapidly since the restoration of convertibility in 1958 and the rise of the eurodollar market, the authorities invented a 'cash deposits' scheme to apply to them but did not bring it into operation 'because it has continued to be necessary to exercise tighter control through ceilings' (Bank of England 1968 and 1969: 226).) The requests to the banks became explicit quantitative ceilings from May 1965 and applied to commercial bills as well as advances.

The management of the national debt continued to restrict the ambitions of monetary policy. Since 'the chief purpose of debt management ... is to maintain market conditions that will maximise, both now and in the future, the desire of investors at home and abroad to hold British government debt', the Bank operated to stabilise bond prices, buying government securities to slow down price falls and selling them in large quantities when prices were rising (Bank of England 1984a: 75–82; see also Tew 1978a: 229–33; Artis 1978: 274–6). Since this made gilt-edged securities almost as liquid as Treasury bills the maintenance of a minimum liquid assets ratio, even reinforced by special deposits, was not an effective constraint on bank lending: hence the renewed resort to the control of advances.

Bank Rate changes were dictated by the fixed exchange rate, with the pound under severe pressure in 1961 and 1964–9. They were most frequent during the period (1964–7) when the Labour government under Harold Wilson was trying to maintain the pound at US$2.80. As in the 1950s the increases came in 'packages' intended also to deflate domestic demand. Although there was almost no conflict in the 1960s between internal and external balance, the measures were not particularly successful in achieving either. The Labour government eventually decided to devalue the pound to US$2.40 on 18 November 1967 – when Bank Rate went up to 8 per cent for the first time since August 1914. (On the devaluation see Tew 1978b: 310–15, 354–6; Cairncross 1983.)

By the end of the 1960s British monetary economists were coming under the influence of the 'monetarist' ideas associated with Milton Friedman and, nearer to home, Harry Johnson. The Money Study Group was founded in 1969 in order to encourage both discussion of monetary issues and empirical research. (For some of the more notable empirical work, especially on the demand for money, see Walters 1969a and 1969b; Goodhart and Crockett 1970; Laidler and Parkin 1970; Laidler 1971; Price 1972; Artis and Lewis 1976.) The Bank of England began to publish money supply series (for M1 and M3) (Bank of England 1970). In spite of a spirited rearguard action by 'Keynesians' attached to Radcliffean ideas (see, for instance, Kaldor 1970), it was gradually accepted in the 1970s that any successful anti-inflationary policy must include control of the rate of growth of the money supply, which the Bank of England had so far failed to achieve. At the same time, since international capital mobility was now obviously higher than in earlier post-war decades, more economists favoured flexible exchange rates (which Friedman had always advocated) to overcome the external constraints on domestic monetary policy.

A new approach?

The new approach implemented in the early 1970s was 'Competition and Credit Control' (CCC), formally announced in May 1971 (Bank of England 1971a). It turned out to be the most spectacular failure to control monetary growth (see table 8.1).

CCC was intended both to encourage greater competition among UK banks and other financial institutions and to make it easier to control monetary growth by interest rate changes. Quantitative lending ceilings would be abolished; the cash and liquid assets ratios which applied only to the London and Scottish clearing banks would be replaced with a single reserve assets ratio applying to all banks; the clearing banks would abandon long-standing collusive agreements on their deposit and advances rates of interest; and the special deposits schemes would apply to all banks. The new reserve asset ratio was set at 12.5 per cent of sterling deposits or 'eligible liabilities'.

Reserve assets comprised balances with the Bank of England (except special deposits), Treasury bills and government securities with a year or less to maturity, money lent at call to the discount houses, and local authority and commercial bills eligible for rediscount at the Bank, but not till money. 'Eligible liabilities' comprised sterling deposits of an original maturity of two years or under from both UK residents and non-residents (except banks), net interbank deposits, sterling certificates of deposit, net liabilities in sterling to overseas offices or in other currencies, and 60 per cent of net items in transit (Bank of England 1971b).

The London clearing banks also agreed to hold (as part of their reserve assets) non-interest-bearing balances equal on average to 1.5 per cent of their eligible liabilities, to be used for clearing cheques. The clearing banks gave up their interest rate cartel and ceased to tie their lending and deposit rates to Bank Rate in October 1971; a year later the Bank replaced Bank Rate with a Minimum Lending Rate (MLR) which was to move automatically with Treasury bill rate (Bank of England 1984a: 114; Tew 1978a: 238–45). There were also parallel changes in regulations governing the discount houses, who agreed to invest at least half of their borrowed funds in public sector debt as well as to continue to tender for the government's weekly issue of Treasury bills (Bank of England 1971a). (The former regulation turned out to keep down the Treasury bill rate at times

of rising interest rates; it was therefore replaced in July 1973 by the requirement that a discount house's other assets must not exceed twenty times its capital and reserves (Bank of England 1973).) A prerequisite for the variation of interest rates for monetary policy purposes was that the authorities reduce their intervention in the gilt-edged market. This they had already begun to do in 1969 when they ceased to announce the prices at which they would sell government bonds from their own holdings and buy in bonds nearing maturity (Bank of England 1969). In 1971 they reduced their commitment to only buying bonds with a year or less to maturity.

The overall aim of CCC was 'a system under which *the allocation of credit is primarily determined by its cost*' (Bank of England 1984a: 40). Monetary control would operate through the effect of interest rate changes on bank lending. The subsequent 'troublesome and at times unhappy' experience (Goodhart 1975: 91) included a rapid rise in bank lending and hence the growth of the money supply, with M3 running at nearly 30 per cent in 1972 and 1973. M1 grew more slowly, but at double-digit rates, while nominal interest rates also rose to double-digit levels in 1972. After a lag the rate of price inflation also moved into double digits in 1974–5 (Table 8.5). The housing market boomed, and so did the commercial property market, whose collapse caused a banking crisis among secondary banks at the end of 1973 (see Gowland 1978: chs. 3–6, 1982: chs. 6–7; Reid 1982).

Bank lending rose rapidly partly because of the ending of the ceilings and the interest rate cartel – an effect which was anticipated although its size was not known or estimated – and partly because of the growth of 'liability management', which the authorities did not foresee. With greater competition the banks could react to strong loan demand by bidding for funds in the 'wholesale' money markets. They were not constrained by the reserve asset ratio, which was anyway subject to several loopholes (Goodhart 1975: 98–106; Gowland 1982: 96–100; Spencer 1986: 37–44). Hence the 'new approach' failed to control monetary growth because it continued the old practice of trying to control bank lending without controlling bank reserves.

The authorities did not stand idly by, but their reactions were slow – delayed first by fear of unemployment and then by the floating of the exchange rate. In 1972–3 macro-economic policy was designed to stimulate demand, with Anthony Barber, Chancellor of the Exchequer in Edward Heath's Conservative government, pursuing a highly expansionary budgetary policy. When the pound came under pressure the government decided to let it float from 22 June 1972 in order to remove the external constraint on domestic economic policy. When capital outflows reduced

Table 8.5. *Rate of change of retail price index, annual, 1945–89*
(% p.a.)

1945	1·8
1946	4·4
1947	5·5
1948	7·6
1949	2·6
1950	2·9
1951	9·9
1952	8·7
1953	3·3
1954	1·7
1955	4·5
1956	4·9
1957	3·9
1958	3·0
1959	0·5
1960	1·5
1961	3·0
1962	4·4
1963	2·1
1964	3·4
1965	4·7
1966	3·8
1967	2·5
1968	4·8
1969	5·1
1970	6·0
1971	9·7
1972	7·5
1973	9·1
1974	15·9
1975	24·0
1976	16·6
1977	15·9
1978	8·3
1979	13·4
1980	18·2
1981	11·9
1982	8·6
1983	4·5
1984	5·0
1985	6·0
1986	3·3
1987	3·9
1988	4·9
1989	7·8

Sources: calculated from Feinstein (1972: Table 65), and *Economic Trends Annual Supplement* 1989: Table 25.

the banks' deposits and reserves the Bank lent them reserves (by temporarily buying government securities from them) after Bank Rate had been raised to 6 per cent on 22 June. In August the Bank resorted to requesting the banks to cut down their lending for property and stock exchange speculation – with little effect. In November and December it called for special deposits and the newly introduced substitute for Bank Rate rose with Treasury bill rates to reach 9 per cent on 22 December. This had little immediate impact on the growth of M3, which was being increased by 'round tripping': high-money market interest rates made it profitable for bank borrowers to use overdrafts to invest in certificates of deposit (CDs) and other money-market instruments (Price 1978a: 205–7; Tew 1978a: 249–54; Gowland 1982: 104–11; Spencer 1986: 39–42).

It is not clear why there was no further restrictive action in the first half of 1973, when interest rates were allowed to *fall*. (MLR was 7.5 per cent by June; it had been 7.25 per cent when it was introduced the previous October.) It may have been that the rapid growth of M3 was regarded as 'artificial', inflated as it was by round tripping (Goodhart 1975: 104). In July, however, when the floating pound depreciated sharply (see Table 8.6), the authorities at last reacted vigorously. (As Gowland (1982: 111–12) remarks, a 'cynic with a long memory would have commented that the UK authorities had always responded ... with higher interest rates when there was a foreign exchange crisis'.) They made further calls for special deposits in July and again in November, and pushed up MLR, in July to 9 per cent by reducing the supply of reserve assets and in November to 13 per cent by administrative action. The first increase in money-market rates provoked a new bout of round tripping, to which the Bank reacted with a new device quite contrary to the spirit of 'competition and credit control': Supplementary Special Deposits (SSDs) or the 'corset' (Bank of England 1974). The banks now had to make non-interest-bearing deposits with the Bank whenever their interest-bearing eligible liabilities (IBELs) grew at more than a specified rate, initially 8 per cent over the next six months. The required SSDs increased with the amount by which the specified rate was exceeded. Direct quantitative controls on bank activities had returned, but this time on liabilities and with (increasing) penalties for non-compliance. Hire purchase controls were also reimposed in December 1973.

The SSD scheme was used three times: December 1973 – February 1975, November 1976 – August 1977, and June 1978 – June 1980. Until the end of 1979 it did not involve the banks in making large payments to the Bank (Bank of England 1984a: 117–27). Its major and predictable weakness, especially when used for such long periods, was disintermediation, the shifting of borrowing from instruments which were included in banks'

Table 8.6. *Nominal exchange rates, end-years, 1972–90 (foreign currency per £)*

	US$/£	DM/£
1972	2·3481	7·5150
1973	2·3235	6·2788
1974	2·3495	5·6537
1975	2·0283	5·2987
1976	1·7020	4·1016
1977	1·9185	4·0135
1978	2·0410	3·7150
1979	2·2250	3·8400
1980	2·3920	4·6925
1981	1·9110	4·2897
1982	1·6175	3·8505
1983	1·4520	3·9515
1984	1·1580	3·6536
1985	1·4455	3·5299
1986	1·4837	2·8524
1987	1·8870	2·9607
1988	1·8080	3·2047
1989	1·6125	2·7275
1990	1·9295	2·8875

Source: Bank of England Quarterly Bulletins.

IBELs to those which were not included such as commercial bills. In the short run it helped to reduce monetary growth, especially in 1974 when the demand for bank lending was lowered by recession and the aftermath of the secondary banking crisis (Gowland 1982: 145–8; Spencer 1986: 44–5, 98–103). It was, however, an adjunct to other methods of monetary and credit control, which continued to include the old standbys of requests to the banks to restrict their lending to certain types of borrowers and hire purchase controls (Gowland 1982: 198–9).

The second 'new approach' of the 1970s, *monetary targets*, had been waiting in the wings for some time. It could not seriously be adopted until the government had given up the commitment to a fixed exchange rate, since in an open economy, becoming increasingly smaller within an increasingly financially integrated world economy, there was by then little scope for an independent monetary policy. It also assumes that there exists a stable money demand function, that is that the estimated demand for some (controllable) monetary aggregate is related to income and interest rates in a sufficiently predictable way to be used to set monetary policy instruments.

Table 8.7. *Monetary targets, 1976–86*

Period	Announced	Variable(s)	Target (%)	Actual (%)
1976–7	July 1976	M3	12	10·0
1977–8	March 1977	£M3	9–13	16·0
1978–9	April 1978	£M3	8–12	11·0
1979–80	June 1979	£M3	7–11	10·0
1980–1	March 1980	£M3	7–11	18·5
1981–2	March 1981	£M3	6–10	13·0
1982–3	March 1982	£M3	8–12	11·5
		M1	8–12	11·0
		PSL2	8–12	9·0
1983–4	March 1983	£M3	7–11	11·0
		M1	7–11	11·0
		PSL2	7–11	12·3
1984–5	March 1984	£M3	6–10	12·0
		M0	4–8	5·5
1985–6	March 1985	£M3	5–9	15·0
		M0	3–7	3·5
1986–7	March 1986	£M3	11–15	20·0
		M0	2–6	2·0

Source: Dow and Saville (1990: Table 7.1).

From 1973 the Bank adopted an unpublished target rate of growth for M3. It chose this aggregate over M1 because of two 'somewhat fortuitous factors': the behaviour of M3 could be arithmetically related to, and hence analysed in terms of, its 'credit counterparts' (the public sector borrowing requirement (PSBR), government debt sales to the non-bank private sector, bank lending to the private sector and net external flows) and the current statistical series for M1 was less reliable than that for M3 (Bank of England 1984a: 3 and 45). By this time the Bank's estimated demand for money functions for M3 were beginning to show signs of instability (Bank of England 1984a: 172–87) but the Bank retained its preference for a broad aggregate through the 1970s. One reason was the credit counterparts analysis, the other was the acceleration of inflation in 1974–5: 'following closely on the heels of the monetary expansion in 1972–73, [this] led to even greater emphasis being placed on the need for a financial anchor in the form of a monetary target applied in order to constrain and control the rate of inflation'. In 1976, following another sterling crisis when the pound fell to a record low against the US dollar, the Chancellor of the Exchequer announced a target for M3 of 12 per cent for the 1976–7 financial year (Bank of England 1984a: 45–7; see also Table 8.7).

A general election in February 1974 produced a minority Labour government which obtained a majority in another election in October. It was therefore a Labour Chancellor, Denis Healey, who announced the conversion to a more 'monetarist' policy, or at least the acceptance that control of the rate of growth of the money supply is a necessary condition for control of the rate of inflation (Gowland 1982: 153–6). The 1974–9 Labour government's monetary (and fiscal) policies were a continual struggle against inflation and unemployment and, in the early years, a deficit on the current account of the balance of payments and depreciation of sterling. Monetary growth at first helpfully declined following the December 1973 measures, but inflation, in the wake of the first oil price shock, accelerated through 1974 and 1975 to reach an annual rate of over 25 per cent in the second half of 1975. The pound fell during the first half of 1975 and remained weak, prompting increases in interest rates (MLR reached 12 per cent in October); it fell even more in the first half of 1976 despite large-scale exchange-market intervention (Bank of England 1976). In spite of additional support from other central banks, public expenditure cuts, the adoption of an M3 target, calls for special deposits and SSDs, and sharp rises in interest rates, including a 2 per cent jump in MLR to 15 per cent in October, the government had to apply to borrow from the International Monetary Fund in December. As with earlier IMF borrowings, the strings attached to the loan included a target for domestic credit expansion (DCE, roughly equivalent to the growth of M3 less the balance of payments deficit), but the Labour government nonetheless stuck to its money supply target in the following two years. At the beginning of 1977 the target was set in terms of £M3 (that is, excluding residents' foreign currency deposits) and as a range (9–13 per cent for the financial year 1977–8) rather than a single number (Gowland 1982: 154; Bank of England 1977).

The Labour government was generally successful in keeping £M3 within the announced target ranges, except in 1977–8 (see Table 8.7). In the summer and early autumn of 1977 the authorities intervened in the foreign exchange market to prevent a rapid *appreciation* of sterling; in early 1978 they underestimated the actual rate of monetary growth (Gowland 1982: 171–4; Bank of England 1984a: 68). In the spring of 1978 they raised MLR and abandoned its 'automatic' link with the Treasury bill rate (which had already been overridden on several occasions), and reintroduced the SSD scheme. But although monetary growth was brought under control, and the target range reduced to 8–12 per cent for 1978–9, inflation continued to be a problem, especially in the winter of 1978–9 after the second oil price shock.

The Bank's activities in the gilt-edged market in the later 1970s also reflected the 'new approach'. In the early years of CCC it had not sold much gilt-edged to the market. Once it was concerned to control monetary growth it had to sell government bonds more aggressively. (If nothing else the credit counterparts analysis of M3 demonstrates that an increase in debt sales to the private sector will *ceteris paribus* reduce monetary growth and, more usefully in practice, will offset rising bank lending.) It began to manipulate MLR as it had Bank Rate more tentatively in the 1950s so as to encourage gilt-edged sales, pushing it up sharply to foster expectations of future falls in interest rates and only gradually lowering it while selling large quantities of gilt-edged securities. This 'Duke of York' strategy was based on the Bank's belief that the gilt-edged market was dominated by asset-holders with short holding periods and extrapolative expectations. According to Gowland (1982: 149) it was used successfully eight times between January 1974 and August 1980 in spite of the apparently irrational behaviour which it assumes on the part of gilt-edged investors. Empirical studies of the demand for gilts (Goodhart 1969; Norton 1969; Spencer 1981 and 1986: ch. 8) seem surprisingly to support the Bank's view. In the 1970s and 1980s the authorities also tried to facilitate long-term government borrowing by varying the types of securities issued and the methods of issuing them, such experiments including index-linked stocks and auctioning new issues (Bank of England 1984a: 88–104, 1987c, 1988a).

The 1980s

The 1980s witnessed the 'high tide of monetarism' in Britain and several other countries which had tried monetary targeting in the 1970s (Foot 1981; Goodhart 1989: part I). It also saw a rerun in modern dress of the earlier debates about methods of monetary control within the Bank and Treasury and more publicly. Although there were changes in regulations, including the abolition of those introduced under CCC, the Bank remained opposed to monetary base control. Debt management continued to be important, even after the achievement of a budget surplus in the later 1980s. Financial innovation caused problems with monetary targeting, which became less focussed on a single aggregate. By the end of the decade monetary policy was concerned with the exchange rate again.

The general election of May 1979 returned a Conservative government under a Prime Minister (Margaret Thatcher) determined not to repeat the monetary mistakes of 1972–3. Her first Chancellor, Geoffrey Howe, reaffirmed the commitment to achieve a monetary target defined in terms of £M3 and reduced to 7–11 per cent for 1979–80, but he made its achievement more immediately difficult by raising value added tax (VAT) from 8 to 15 per cent in June 1979 and abolishing exchange control in October. With inflation accelerating towards a peak of almost 22 per cent in May 1980, MLR was raised from 14 to 17 per cent on 15 November, partly to set off a 'Duke of York' manoeuvre and encourage gilts sales (Gowland 1982: 190–2; see also Bank of England 1980: 20–2). The Chancellor also announced in November that the authorities were reviewing their monetary control methods and would be issuing a Green Paper, which was published the following March. The debate on monetary base control, which was already underway continued for about a year (Bank of England 1984a: 129–49; below).

The March 1980 budget announced a *Medium-Term Financial Strategy* (MTFS), invented by Nigel Lawson, then Financial Secretary to the Treasury, and intended to commit the government both to reduce the (target and actual) rate of monetary growth steadily year by year and to subordinate fiscal policy as well as interest rates to this anti-inflationary aim. The SSD scheme was abolished as from June 1980, an inevitable consequence of the abolition of exchange control which had increased the opportunities (and the practice) of avoiding direct credit controls by disintermediation. The 'bill leak' (bank bills held outside the banking system) is estimated to have reached £2,700 million in the second quarter of 1980; it fell dramatically after the ending of the corset (by £1,000 million in the first month), while the money supply soared well out of its target range in the second half of 1980 (Bank of England 1984a: 65–73, 117–27). The qualitative guidance on lending priorities in force since August 1972 effectively lapsed, although it was not *formally* withdrawn until 1987 (Bank of England 1987a: 30).

Meanwhile the combination of record high interest rates and North Sea oil had dramatically raised the nominal and real foreign exchange value of sterling and Britain had entered a particularly severe recession. Industrial production fell by 10 per cent in 1980 and unemployment, already over 1 million, rose to over 2 million. (For a sample of the vigorous debate over the relative contributions of contractionary monetary policy and North Sea oil to the appreciation of sterling see Eltis and Sinclair 1981.) In this context it was politically difficult for the authorities to raise interest rates in order to keep monetary growth on target, and short-term interest rates were in fact reduced to 16 per cent in July and 14 per cent in November 1980 (Goodhart 1989: 303–4). In spite of the overshooting of the target for £M3 (which was growing at an annual rate of nearly 25 per cent in the autumn of 1980: see Table 8.1), Howe announced in his March 1981 budget a new target of 6–10 per cent for February 1981 – April 1982, while reducing MLR further to 12 per cent (Bank of England 1981: 3–4). A year later, when £M3 had grown by about 14.5 per cent in 1981–2, the target range was raised again to 8–12 per cent and this time encompassed *three* aggregates, M1, £M3 and a new, even broader one, PSL2. Goodhart

(1989: 306) remarks: 'Outside commentators complained that this would give the authorities a greater chance to hit at least one target; insiders worried that the markets would concentrate on whichever indicator/target was currently doing worst.'

In 1983 and 1984 the government continued to set targets which in line with the MTFS were lowered each year in the budget, but the range of aggregates considered useful as targets or as indicators of the stance of monetary policy widened further. In 1983 the targets for 1983–4 were 7–11 per cent for M1, £M3 and PSL2. In 1984 the £M3 target was duly lowered to 6–10 per cent for £M3, but a new target (4–8 per cent) was set for M0, and 'attention will also be paid to other monetary indicators ... in interpreting monetary conditions', including M2, PSL2 and the exchange rate. This reflected the increasingly divergent behaviour of the different monetary series (see Table 8.1) and the chronic difficulty of controlling bank lending.

In the 1950s the Bank had rejected monetary base control (MBC) because it wanted a stable Treasury bill rate (Radcliffe 1959: para. 376). In 1980 it rejected MBC for a similar reason, as did other central banks, namely that strict control would 'continually threaten frequent and potentially massive movements in interest rates' – a fear to some extent borne out by the US Federal Reserve's experience of operating a modified form of MBC in 1979–82 (Bank of England 1984a: 129–36; Goodhart 1989: 322–6). The Bank and other central banks generally preferred to try and control the rate of growth of the money supply by means of setting and maintaining very short-run (week-to-week) targets for short-term interest rates which were decided upon in accordance with the currently favoured estimated demand for money function.

The authorities did, however, make changes in their practice of monetary policy in 1980–1 which brought that practice closer to the economists' model of central bank control of the money supply. In November 1980 the Chancellor announced that, as the March 1980 Green Paper on *Monetary Control* had proposed, the reserve assets ratio would be eliminated and replaced with a low cash requirement, similar to the 1.5 per cent of eligible liabilities required of the clearing banks since 1971, on all banks and other deposit-taking institutions above a minimum size. The Bank was also to change its money-market intervention so as to rely more on open-market operations in bills than on discount window lending and to use them to keep short-term interest rates within a narrow unpublished band consistent with the current desired rate of monetary growth. It would probably cease to announce an MLR (Bank of England 1984a: 148–9). Accordingly, the 12.5 per cent reserve assets ratio was reduced to 10 per cent in January 1981 and abolished in August, when non-interest-bearing cash deposits at the

Bank of England equal to 0.5 per cent of eligible liabilities were required of all 'eligible banks'. The Bank also abandoned MLR in August but retained the right to call for special deposits (Bank of England 1984a: 152–64).

There have been further developments in the Bank of England's intervention techniques in both the short-term money market and the gilt-edged market in response to structural and regulatory changes in the UK financial system. The most striking of these changes was the 'Big Bang' of 27 October 1986, which eliminated the distinction between brokers and jobbers in the stock market and their fixed commissions for stock transactions; the most noteworthy result for monetary policy is that the Bank now deals directly with a wider group of financial institutions than it used to (see Bank of England 1987b, 1988b, 1989a and 1989b).

Since 1945 UK bank lending has always proved difficult to control by interest rates. In the 1980s it became even more so in a period of widespread financial innovation and deregulation (which both increased the supply of loans and made estimated demand for money functions unreliable for policy purposes: Goodhart 1984 and Bank of England 1986). The problem was aggravated in the early years of the MTFS by the recession which maintained the demand for bank lending (and the PSBR). The Bank resorted, not for the first time, to 'overfunding', that is, selling more gilt-edged debt than was needed to finance the PSBR (Bank of England 1984a: 165, 1984b). This kept £M3 within its target range at the cost of producing other problems, both technical and economic. While previous overfunding had allowed the authorities to redeem short-debt government debt mainly held by the banks, this time the Bank had to buy private sector commercial bills from the banks since their holdings of Treasury bills and other short-term public sector debt were already low. The resulting 'bill mountain' was inconvenient (since a large volume of maturing bills had constantly to be replaced) and also reduced interest rates on commercial bills relative to other short-term assets. It also meant that the resulting reduced growth of bank deposits was largely artificial, raising doubts as to whether this was consistent with the objectives of controlling monetary growth. 'More fundamentally ... was a technique that allowed bank credit expansion to continue roaring ahead, but restrained the growth of bank deposits, achieving any proper purpose, or was it just another "cosmetic" device?' (Goodhart 1989: 327–8).

During 1985 the doubts prevailed over the determination to maintain a £M3 target. With weakening sterling the Bank not only intervened to raise short-term money-market interest rates but also reintroduced MLR (at 12 per cent) on 14 January. In the budget in March the government retained targets for M0 and £M3, but in October the Chancellor (now Lawson) suspended the £M3 target for 1985–6 and announced that he would now aim at fully funding the PSBR rather than overfunding. Over the year the authorities drew less attention to £M3 and more to M0 which was 'probably least affected' by financial innovation (Bank of England 1985a: 362–3, 1985b: 518–20; see also 1987d). Although a £M3 target was reinstated in the March 1986 budget (11–15 per cent for 1986–7 compared with 2–6 per cent for M0), no formal target for it was set in 1987. The preferred monetary target was apparently M0.

Since 1989, when as a result of the structural changes in the UK banking system the Bank of England stopped publishing estimates for some monetary aggregates, including M1 and M3, the Bank has (in common with other central banks such as the Bank of Canada whose experiment with monetary targets in the late 1970s and early 1980s was also undermined by financial innovation and deregulation) been investigating the properties of new aggregates (Bank of England 1990a, 1990c). However, an exchange rate target was becoming more important, with interest rate moves in 1987–9 closely related to the behaviour of the pound against the deutschmark (Goodhart 1989: 309–11). In 1990 Prime Minister Thatcher's notorious reluctance to allow the exchange rate to be tied to other European currencies was overcome. Britain joined the exchange rate mechanism of the European Monetary System on 8 October 1990 and committed itself to maintaining sterling within a ±6 per cent band around a central rate of £1 = DM2.95 (Bank of England 1990b). This regime was also short-lived. Britain made an undignified exit from the ERM on 16 September 1992 and the future course of monetary policy is uncertain.

Conclusion

The problems of the authorities in controlling interest rates, bank lending and the money supply have been stressed in the previous section. By way of conclusion it is useful to look at their achievements (or lack of them) in relation to Britain's inflation experience since 1945 and the behaviour of the exchange rate (see Tables 8.1, 8.5 and 8.6).

The most striking thing about UK monetary growth since 1945–90 is its rapid acceleration after the floating of the pound in 1972. Almost equally striking is the similar behaviour (with a lag) of the rate of inflation up until the early 1980s; in the mid-1980s the relation between the rate of price change and the growth of the *broader* monetary aggregates was seriously disturbed by the structural changes in the financial system.

As the simple Mundell–Fleming model shows, in a small open economy with internationally mobile capital the rate of domestic monetary growth will under a fixed exchange rate tend to reflect the (world) rate of inflation rather than the other way round. As capital mobility increased in the 1950s and 1960s it became increasingly difficult for the UK monetary authorities to control the UK money supply, although it took time for them to recognise this. Once it was recognised, the opportunity to pursue a sensible independent monetary policy given by a floating exchange rate was squandered – under the Thatcher administration as well as its predecessors – by the authorities' lack of determination to keep monetary growth under control. However Keynesian one's preferred approach to economic problems may be, it is difficult to avoid the conclusion implied by monetary theory that if monetary expansion proceeds significantly faster than the growth of real output the rate of price inflation will accelerate a year or two later. A floating exchange rate both permits a rate of monetary growth different from that in other countries and increases the resulting inflation as the pound depreciates.

Many British economists and officials have argued since 1945 that it is virtually impossible to control the domestic money supply even with a floating exchange rate, and that the authorities should give up the attempt to do so and should direct monetary policy towards external balance. The recent attempt to return to a fixed exchange rate regime may imply that their line of argument is dominant again. But it is not the only conclusion that can be drawn from Britain's fairly disastrous experience with trying to control the rate of monetary growth since 1972. That experience does not in itself imply that monetary control is a waste of time. The UK experience in the early 1970s and again in the early 1980s suggests that the growth rates of the monetary aggregates provide a useful *indicator* of the current stance of monetary policy – and a warning if it is expansionary of inflation in the not very distant future.

9 British economic policy since 1945

Jim Tomlinson

Introduction

By most accounts the British economy has suffered from serious deficiencies in its output of goods and services since 1945. But there has been no
such deficiency in the output of economic policy, or commentaries upon
policy. British governments since the war have been activist governments,
and their efforts have in turn produced a mountain of assessment ranging
from the crass and politically tendentious to the highly abstract and
theoretical. The task of this chapter is to give an account and (highly
tentative) assessment of British economic policy since the war. Because of
the scale of the material published on the period this poses major problems
of organisation – how is this myriad of activity best to be understood? The
solution used here is to deploy the notions of policy objectives, instruments
used in the pursuit of these objectives and the constraints faced in that
pursuit.

It is possible to present the relationship between these aspects of policy
in a formal and technocratic manner. Famously this was the approach of
Tinbergen (1952: 4) when he outlined policy procedure as:

(i) the fixation of a collective preference indicator;
(ii) the deduction, from this indicator, of the targets of economic policy
generally;
(iii) the choice of 'adequate' instruments, qualitative and quantitative;
(iv) the determination of the quantitative values of the instrument
variables, as far as such instruments are chosen.

Whatever the usefulness of this kind of approach as an heuristic device,
in practice economic policy making rarely if ever follows such a
straightforward deductive chain. Rather, as Tinbergen (1952: 45) himself
stressed, 'economic policy, like any real activity, has to reckon with many
aspects originating from very different realms of life, and hence certainly
not only economic view-points: institutional, juridical, technical in the
widest sense of the word, and psychological'.

British economic policy making has also to be seen in the context of the international economy. British policy objectives have usually given a high priority to international aspects, such as a stable exchange rate regime. Equally, the instruments used have been strongly affected by the international economy, such as the rejection of explicit and general protectionism. Finally, the constraints on policy have been to a significant extent those flowing from trying to run the economy in a particular international context, either of trends like the freer movement of capital, or episodic like the OPEC crisis of the early and late 1970s. Hence before focussing in on the domestic policy issues, a broad account is given of the international framework in which policy was formed.

The international framework

Britain was a junior partner with the US in the reconstruction of the institutions of the world economy at the end of the Second World War. The central thrust of US policy was to build a non-discriminatory trade system, coupled with an exchange rate regime which at least discouraged competitive currency depreciations. This programme was seen by the US as the way to prevent the recurrence of the economic and political breakdown of the 1930s, and also to make the world safe for American capitalism. Such a programme was highly problematic for Britain, with her legacy of imperial preference and combination of commitment to full employment and overvalued currency. Nevertheless, out of a combination of arm-twisting by the US, great power pretensions relating to the role of the pound and charismatic advocacy by Keynes, Britain committed itself to such a policy regime (Gardner 1969; Pressnell 1986).

Britain's adherence to the Bretton Woods agreement of 1944 committed her in broad terms to a regime of stable (but not unchangeable) exchange rates, and to the abolition of exchange controls. But in practice the transition to such arrangements was slow and painful, even with the eventual support of Marshall Aid from 1948. Exchange controls were lifted in 1947, a condition placed on the US loan to Britain in 1945, but such was the run on the pound that followed that after six weeks controls were reimposed, not to be lifted until the late 1950s. (Minor forms of exchange control continued until 1979.) Despite such controls the pound was devalued in 1949, but then remained unchanged until 1967.

The attempt to establish a parallel body to the International Monetary Fund (IMF) created at Bretton Woods was unsuccessful. The International Trade Organisation (ITO), designed to supervise multilateralism in trade, foundered. In the immediate conditions of the post-war world a general commitment to multilateral trade was contrary to Britain's concerns with employment and a continued commitment to imperial trade, and the contrary US view that such concerns should not derogate from a full 'open-door' policy. The ITO Charter was therefore never ratified (Diebold 1952). Nevertheless the non-discriminatory design was embodied in the General Agreement on Tariffs and Trade (GATT), which from 1947 onwards, in a series of 'rounds' moved much of the world towards free trade, especially in manufactured goods (Van der Wee 1986: 349–51, 382–6). But as with currencies, so with trade, the movement towards the US ideal was halting in most European countries, including Britain. For example, vestiges of imperial preference, by which British goods had privileged access to markets in the empire and vice versa, survived into Britain's entry into the EEC (1973) in the form of 'transitional arrangements' for privileged access of primary products such as New Zealand butter into the UK market.

Down to 1971/2 the international financial regime within which Britain conducted its policy is usually seen as that laid down at Bretton Woods. This needs to be qualified in a number of ways. As already noted, the full movement to that regime cannot be dated before 1954, when *de facto* free convertibility of the pound into US dollars was established. Second, the actual fixity of exchange rates under Bretton Woods was greater than its designers anticipated, in particular because political prestige became attached to a particular exchange rate in an economically irrational manner. Finally, an unintended consequence of Bretton Woods was to encourage the expansion of international capital flows, so that eventually by the 1970s the openness of the economies of western Europe to such capital flows (measured as the ratio of capital flows: GDP) was to rival that of the period immediately before 1914 (Grassman 1980). This was to have highly significant consequences for the capacity of national governments to manage their economies.

After Bretton Woods

Despite these qualifications, the designation of the years up to 1971/2 as the Bretton Woods era makes sense in distinguishing it from the sharply different years that followed, characterised by floating exchange rates and more generally by a much less stable economic environment. The new regime after 1971/2 was initiated by the declining capacity of the US to act as the dominant power in the international economy. The comparative economic performance of the US in the 1950s and 1960s was poor, and most other advanced capitalist countries caught up a considerable part of the gap between themselves and the US. The Bretton Woods arrangements made it difficult for the US to devalue its currency as its situation demanded, and the 1971 raising of the gold value of the dollar heralded the break up of the system. However, that system was already under great pressure from the acceleration of inflation rates in the late 1960s, the destabilising effects of which for exchange rates were transmitted and magnified by the increasing scale of capital flows.

The regime of floating rates was forced on the world but did not lack intellectual support. It could be seen not only as another case of allowing the market to determine a price, but more particularly as a way of resolving the apparent conflict between domestic and external policy objectives, between stability of the pound and domestic growth (Brittan 1969; see below). The hopes entertained at the end of Bretton Woods about the effects of floating rates have not generally been realised. Nominal exchange rates have proved more unstable than expected, and real exchange rates have fluctuated widely, with significant effects on output and employment (Dornbusch 1976; Dunn 1983). The result has been that from the 1980s the leading financial powers have sought to restabilise exchange rates, through a variety of largely *ad hoc* agreements.

Multilateralism in currencies has been accompanied by a parallel trend to multilateralism in trade. This has always been qualified by an almost complete lack of application to agriculture, a very qualified application to many services and periodic 'regression' in the case of manufactured goods. In the 1970s, for example, significant expansions of trade restrictions were made, largely by European countries against Japanese producers. Other measures, such as the Multi-Fibre Agreement, have also acted to reduce penetration of European markets by textile products from poor countries. But whatever the effects of such trade-diverting policies, they have not been the main determinant of the shift in world trade patterns, which has increasingly seen trade concentrated on the swapping of manufactured goods between advanced capitalist countries. This pattern is apparent in the changing geographical pattern of Britain's links (Table 9.1).

Increasingly Britain's economic fortunes have been linked with the EC, and less with the Sterling Area or Commonwealth with which the Area was largely coterminous. The shift away from this Area is obviously linked to Britain's accession to the EC in 1973, but was already apparent before that date. Trading links with western Europe had been growing, especially from the late 1960s. On the other hand, the links with the Common-wealth/Sterling Area suffered from the erosion of imperial preference, but much more from the rapidity of growth of European markets.

By the beginning of the 1990s Britain was doing half its trade with western Europe and was moving closer to a monetary union within the European Monetary System. This movement summarises Britain's path over much of the post-war period – an (eventual) giving up of pretensions

Table 9.1. *Geographical composition of British trade, 1955–85 (percentage share)*

	1955		1967		1972		1985	
	Imports	Exports	Imports	Exports	Imports	Exports	Imports	Exports
Sterling Area	39·4	27·4	47·0	30·4	23·3	24·4	—	—
USA	10·7	12·6	7·0	12·2	10·6	12·5	11·7	14·7
Western Europe	25·7	36·4	28·1	38·0	43·9	42·9	63·1	58·3
EEC	(12·6)	(19·6)	(14·0)	(19·2)	(24·5)	(22·9)	(46·0)	(46·3)
Soviet Union and eastern Europe	2·7	3·9	1·2	3·3	3·5	2·8	2·2	2·0
Japan	0·6	0·6	1·5	1·8	2·8	1·6	4·9	1·3

Source: Prest and Coppock (1984).

to being a world economic power, and a recognition that for good or ill closer collaboration with western Europe was a logical consequence of pursuing economic policy goals in an increasingly interdependent world economy.

Policy objectives: employment

By the end of the Second World War full employment had become established as the central economic policy objective in Britain. The 1944 White Paper on *Employment Policy* committed British governments to pursue a 'high and stable' level of employment, and whilst the means to be used to this end were ambiguous, the commitment itself was both unmistakable and revolutionary. In the 1940s such a commitment was regarded as politically inescapable – its continuation thereafter reflected the same political calculation in a context where the costs of the policy seemed small.

In comparative perspective the strength of this commitment to full employment seems to mark Britain out. Certainly in other major European countries there was not the same emphasis. For example, in France the central objective of pol'cy in the 1940s and 1950s was industrial modernisation, based on the sense of a basic failure of the economy which had led to the military defeat of 1940. Things were different on the other side of the Channel, where in Monnet's words, 'Britain had not been conquered or invaded; she felt no need to exorcise history' (cited Bullock 1983: 778).

This emphasis on full employment stemmed in large part from the experience of the 1930s, coupled with a shift in the balance of power towards labour in the war period. The unemployment of the 1930s had combined demand deficient and structural elements. In the wartime discussions over post-war policy these two elements had been debated, and the result was a policy position which tried to emphasise both the need for adequate demand and labour market and other policies to correct structural imbalances (Tomlinson 1987: ch. 3; Booth 1989: ch. 7). This latter was strongly pursued by what was called distribution of industry (later, regional) policy. This set the stage for an important part of British policy throughout the next five decades (Parsons 1986). Evidence on the effects of this policy is sketchy and controversial, but one major examination found them 'encouragingly large' (Moore and Rhodes 1973: 99; but see ch. 7).

The significance attached to aggregate demand followed from the Keynesian emphasis on this aspect of employment determination, and the embodiment of such an approach in the management of the economy from 1941 onwards. From the war period emerged a 'simple Keynesianism' (Booth 1986) which emphasised the short-run determination of employment by demand, regulated primarily by fiscal policy. This established one pole of the 'stop–go' pattern of the 1950s and 1960s, which flowed from short-run policy adjustment to try and deal with the two alternating problems of rising unemployment and runs on the pound; the latter aspect is returned to below.

Unemployment retained this central place in policy objectives until the 1970s, though the level of unemployment started to drift up from the late 1960s (ch. 7). The erosion of the commitment to this goal in part followed simply from the fact that it was no longer more or less costless to achieve, as it had been in the 1950s and 1960s. As inflation also started to move upwards from the late 1960s the old trade-off between a little more inflation and a little less unemployment broke down. The attractiveness of full employment to policy makers declined as the perceived opportunity costs of achieving it rose.

In the 1972–4 period the Conservative government under Heath changed tack and pursued expansionary macro-economic policies to increase growth and reduce unemployment. The succeeding Labour government initially did the same, even in the face of the deflationary effects of the OPEC price rise of 1973/4. But by 1975/6 the rise in inflation and fall in the value of the pound led to a reversal of priorities, often seen as epochal. In his budget speech of April 1975 Chancellor of the Exchequer Healey, responding to urgings to expand demand to reduce unemployment, rejected this advice because 'I cannot afford to increase demand further

Table 9.2. *Inflation rates since 1945 (annual percentage increase in retail price index)*

1945–50	4·3
1950–67	3·8
1968–73	7·5
1974–80	15·9
1980–7	6·9
1988–90	7·4

Sources: Woodward (1991: 189); *Economic Trends* 1991.

Table 9.3. *UK balance of payments current account/GDP, 1946–90 (annual averages over five-year periods)*

1946–50	1·2
1951–5	−0·1
1956–60	0·7
1961–5	−0·1
1966–70	0·3
1971–5	−1·5
1976–80	0·2
1981–5	1·4
1986–90	−2·1

Source: Economic Trends Annual Supplement.

today when 5p. in every pound we spent at home has been provided by our creditors abroad and inflation is running at its current rate' (House of Commons, 15 April 1975, col. 282).

Despite this disavowal of traditional employment policy, the policies pursued by Labour (1974–9) were equivocal. Whilst the employment objective was downgraded in 1975/6, it had something of a revival in 1978 when the inflation and balance of payments problem receded. Labour's retreat on employment policy seems grudging and driven by perceived constraints, rather than based on a whole-hearted disavowal of the post-war consensus on the importance of full employment.

The Conservatives under Mrs Thatcher after 1979 explicitly eschewed any commitment to short-run policies to contain unemployment. The policies pursued by them did not aim deliberately to create mass unemployment (they believed such mass unemployment to be politically fatal) but the issue was now seen in a new light. The key point from a policy point of view was not a disavowal of the desirability of full employment, but a denial that government could directly do much to bring it about. In

1985 the Thatcher government published a new White Paper on *Employment: The Challenge to the Nation*, in which it is emphasised that the government can 'only set the framework for the nation's effort'. The route to restoration of full employment is a reduction in inflation coupled to radical changes in the labour market and the supply side of the economy. The 1944 White Paper had touched on many of the same points as that of 1985, but the key difference is that all the supply-side aspects had been seen as the corollaries of the maintenance of aggregate demand. By 1985 it is this keystone which is missing, and with it the central role of government in determining the level of employment (Tomlinson 1987: ch. 9).

Policy objectives: inflation

As a broad generalisation we may say that the commitment to full employment weakened as the perceived dangers of inflation loomed larger for policy makers. Inflation is a curious economic policy objective in the sense that unlike unemployment, where the economic loss incurred and social damage occasioned seems obvious, the costs of inflation are relatively obscure. By comparison with politicians, economists of quite different persuasions have tended to play down its harmful effects. These effects mainly arise from the lack of full adaptation of the tax and financial systems to inflation, and the extreme unlikelihood that inflation will be fully anticipated (Fender 1990: ch. 3; also Wadhwani 1987). So in this area of policy in particular it is important to see the political as much as the economic origin of government concern, a concern which surfaced long before the Second World War.

That war and its consequences of full employment led to a new emphasis on containing inflation, and indeed the new apparatus of Keynesian demand management was built up essentially with that purpose in mind. From the beginnings of full employment policy in the war years it was recognised that such a policy would enhance the bargaining power of labour and threaten higher inflation (Jones 1987: ch. 3). This perception did not lead to any clear policy conclusions, and indeed the whole history of policy on inflation is one of episodic scares and hurried policy initiatives, unsustained once the immediate scare is passed.

The main responses to inflation in Britain have been either direct attempts to regulate wages by incomes policies, or attempts to contain it by reducing demand. These instruments of policy are discussed more fully below, but it is important to note that for the period up to the early 1970s much of the concern with inflation flowed from its impact on international competitiveness, given a fixed exchange rate under the Bretton Woods system. Thus attempts to control aggregate demand to contain inflation were usually triggered not by the level of an inflation index but by a run on the pound which threatened to drive it from the fixed level. (For a quantitative analysis of policy makers' responses to different indices in this period, see Pissarides 1972.) Similarly, incomes policies in the pre-1972 period tended to be introduced at times of balance of payments crises and to be discontinued as the immediate danger passed (Blackaby 1979c; Jones 1987: chs. 5–7).

In the 1970s, with the demise of fixed exchange rates, the perception of inflation problems altered somewhat. In principle, under a floating exchange rate regime, international competitiveness should be taken care of by movements in that rate. Whilst governments have rarely been willing to allow the exchange rate to float freely to allow such (alleged) adjustment, certainly in the 1970s the old focus on the strength of the pound as a trigger for anti-inflationary policy declined somewhat. But this change broadly coincided with a (world-wide) upsurge in inflation, which reached its post-war peak in Britain in 1975 at a level of 25 per cent. By the time it reached this level, what can only be called a moral panic was unleashed in Britain (e.g. Jay 1976). Inflation, it was suggested, threatened not just economic danger but the basis of civilisation as we know it – although, as always in these discussions, evidence for such assertions was rather thin on the ground.

One major reason why governments worry about inflation, despite the limited evidence of its harm (at the kinds of levels experienced in the UK), is because of its effects on financial opinion. Financiers rarely lose confidence in government because of mass unemployment, but inflation is a different matter. Thus in 1975/6 the government had little choice but to change its policies to reduce inflation, given the pressures from financial markets, manifest both in the problems of financing the government's budget deficit and the run on the pound (Tomlinson 1990: ch. 10).

From 1979 inflation attained an unchallenged position as public enemy number one for the government. Central to this seemed to be the idea that inflation threatened social order, summed up by Sir Geoffrey Howe the Chancellor of the Exchequer: 'Nothing, in the long-run, could contribute more to the disintegration of society and the destruction of any sense of national unity than continuing inflation' (House of Commons, 26 March 1980).

This seems a much exaggerated view of the effects of inflation in Britain, though it is true that under certain circumstances inflation can bring about significant unintended income redistribution which is likely to be a cause of discontent. One perhaps curious feature of this focus on inflation as a policy objective is that it may well be (unlike unemployment) an area where government claims too much responsibility. According to standard

monetarist views inflation is the one thing which governments unambigu-
ously can control. This seems to locate responsibility fairly and squarely
with government for the inflation level, though inflation trends in Britain
would seem to follow, albeit in exaggerated fashion, those elsewhere,
suggesting that individual national governments may be less than all
powerful in attaining this objective (Brown 1985).

Policy objectives: growth

Whilst policy concern with unemployment was largely a product of the
inter-war and war periods, and that with inflation a perennial of modern
government, a concern with growth is largely a product of the 1950s. Of
course governments had long since been concerned with the wealth of
nations, but only from the 1950s did economic growth join the objectives
which government explicitly committed themselves to achieve and design
policies to secure. This was an international phenomenon, linked in part to
the idea of competition with the communist bloc for political support, by
showing which system could deliver the fastest growth in living standards
(Arndt 1978).

More particularly, once full use of resources had been established it was
plain that only capacity growth could lessen the political strains of
competing claims on resources (Radcliffe 1959: para. 59). The political
incentive to increase growth was increased by the publication for the first
time in the 1950s of comparative growth figures, sponsored by the UN and
OECD (Hutchison 1968: 125–6).

In 1954 the Conservative Chancellor of the Exchequer, R. A. Butler,
spoke of the desirability of doubling the standard of living in twenty-five
years. But at this stage such pronouncements were 'rather a happy
aspiration than a serious statement of purpose or a promise' (Harris 1972:
239). But from 1960 growth moved from aspiration to policy – or at least
to a sense of urgency on the issue and the creation of the National
Economic Development Council. This in turn drew much of its inspiration
from the rhetoric of planning, and the perceived success of indicative
planning in France. The idea of a new body to 'plan' the economy also
drew on the widespread distrust of the Treasury and the belief that its
stop–go approach had damaged the economy's growth prospects. (A view
strongly expressed, for example, in Michael Shanks' book of 1961 whose
title aptly summarised the mood of the times: *The Stagnant Society: A
Warning*.)

The same basic approach lay behind the Labour government's creation
of the Department of Economic Affairs in 1964 and the publication of the
National Plan in 1965. As with the Conservatives, 'planning' was more a

statement of firmness of purpose than a well-thought-out mechanism of policy (Leruez 1975; Hare 1985). The commitment to growth and planning soon fell victim to a reassertion of the priority to defend the pound by deflationary measures, culminating in the 'July measures' of 1966 which effectively marked the end of the planning for growth movement.

Much of this linkage of planning to growth relied on the belief that the key to Britain's low growth lay in too low an investment level. Hence much of the planning effort was aimed at raising that level, a view which could find warrant in traditional growth theory literature (e.g. Solow 1956) but was increasingly challenged by more empirical studies of the growth process (e.g. Denison 1967). The latter suggested that growth rates depended much more on the quality of investment and of labour than on the quantity of these inputs. Such concerns, with research and development and education and training, grew in the 1960s but there was still a common belief that a high level of investment could somehow solve Britain's growth problem, rather than, more plausibly, such an increase being the *result* of policies of a more micro-economic character.

In a two-party system the political imperative to try to increase growth was compelling, and in the early 1970s growth was once again centre-stage, especially from 1972 when the Conservatives launched the 'Barber boom', named after the incumbent Chancellor of the Exchequer. However, planning was no longer coupled with growth, rather the emphasis was on demand-driven expansion plus a willingness to try to ease the balance of payments constraint on such a 'dash for growth' by allowing the pound's value to fall. Thus Britain's floating of the pound in 1972, whilst influenced by the concurrent break-up of Bretton Woods, was also a perceived resolution of long-standing domestic policy dilemmas. Output did indeed expand very rapidly during this period, but inflation rose quickly as the commodity price rise culminated in OPEC I at the end of 1973; eventually this led to one more reversal of policy towards a deflationary stance.

The 1970s were a period of slow growth in Britain as elsewhere in the advanced capitalist world (Beckerman 1982). Policy priority was on unemployment and then inflation. But by the early 1980s growth was again central to the policy agenda, as the economy recovered sharply from the slump of 1979–81. For the Conservatives under Mrs Thatcher the evidence of the link from popular living standards to electoral fortunes compelled a policy of expansion, largely monetarily fuelled, which like the expansion of 1972–4 eventually fell foul of balance of payments and inflation problems and to a recession brought about by tight-money policies at the beginning of the 1990s.

Policy objectives: the balance of payments

The fourth policy objective which must be discussed is the balance of payments. Analytically this is difficult to handle for two reasons. First, a good case can be made that the balance of payments should be treated as a constraint on achieving other policy objectives, rather than an objective in its own right. Plainly there is an absolute constraint in the sense of a country running out of foreign exchange and being unable to borrow. But this is a situation which is rarely reached, and policy usually responds to balance of payments considerations long before such a stage is reached, as other policy objectives are compromised. However, in post-war Britain the balance of payments in some guise or other has usually been treated as a policy objective, and that approach will be followed here.

The second problem is that whilst British government worries about the balance of payments have been almost continuous since 1945, those worries have been both changing and underspecified. Broadly speaking, up to the float of 1972 the key concern was to defend the value of the pound ($4.03 to 1949, $2.80 1949–67, $2.40 1967–72), which in turn led to a desire to strengthen the reserve position, especially to try and improve the asset:liability ratio. A key part of the problem of the pound in this period was the scale of outstanding sterling debts ('sterling balances') originally largely accumulated during the Second World War, but added to periodically thereafter. These balances reflected the old status of the pound as the dominant world currency, a status which the British authorities were reluctant to relinquish, so that the value of the pound became entangled with all sorts of grand issues about Britain's place in the World, rather than being seen as just a question of economic policy (Strange 1971).

After 1972 the balance of payments was still a matter of concern, although the value of the pound lost most of its symbolic role. Rather the focus was now more directly on the current account balance, and the consequences of this on the need to borrow. This approach reached its apogee (or nadir?) in the summer of 1976 when the government was forced to borrow from the IMF, and this particular piper called some unpalatable tunes. In the late 1980s a similar scenario unfolded, except that this time the price to be paid for borrowing was not subordination to the dictates of the IMF, but the payment of usurious interest rates to keep foreign bank deposit holders in sterling.

At the same time, despite the floating of the pound, governments have been generally unwilling to see the pound depreciate 'too much' because of fears for the inflationary effects of this, coupled with a declining faith in the capacity of exchange rate depreciation to deliver a balance of payments improvement (see below, instruments of policy). The combination of these attitudes has led on occasions to the view that a strong pound is positively desirable, as a way of forcing exporters to contain their costs, especially their wage costs. This view was strongly urged in the period of sterling appreciation 1979–81, and at the time of the pound's occasional periods of strength in the late 1980s and beginning of the 1990s.

Concerns relating to the balance of payments have not only been subject to bewildering shifts, they have at almost all times been underspecified. For example in the 1950s the key concern of the authorities – the stimulus to 'stop' in the stop–go cycle – was a run on the reserves (e.g. Scott 1962). This problem led the authorities to talk of a current account surplus of £300–50 million as desirable in the 1950s, rising to £450 million by the end of the decade (*Economic Survey* 1953: paras. 101–3; Radcliffe 1959: paras. 62, 734). But such explicit targets were unusual (as well as being pious hopes) and for most of the period the aims of the authorities in this area were inexact and unclear.

However inexact the goals of the authorities, it is clear that a concern with the strength of the pound, and the belief that this strength was crucial to Britain's financial role, dominated policy making for twenty-five years after the war. Up to the late 1960s this policy position found its rationale partly in the continued importance of the pound as an international currency. Many countries did continue to hold part of their reserves in sterling, and sterling was a widely used vehicle currency (Strange 1971). However, the effects of this on the domestic economy were unclear. The reserve role of the pound led to a destabilising debt overhang which exacerbated the instability of the pound, and possibly magnified the deflationary response to pressure on sterling. Whether this mattered very much for economic performance is debatable, given the supply-side weakness of the economy (Crafts 1988). Nevertheless, it is an important part of the basis of policy making in Britain that from the early 1960s the defence of the pound was seen as an obstacle to more rapid economic growth, and much of the 1960s can reasonably be seen as a battle between those two priorities. The devaluation of 1967 resolved that dispute, and in doing so unintentionally revealed that the financial role of London did not depend on a 'strong' pound, and thus allowed these two issues to be treated separately (Strange 1971, ch. 7). The float of 1972 may be seen as the final nail in the coffin of sterling as a world currency, a pretension which had by then lost any economic rationale (Van der Wee 1986: 491).

Instruments of policy: fiscal policy

The choice and deployment of policy instruments is far from a matter of choosing technical means to politically determined ends. Instruments

Table 9.4. *Fiscal policy, 1972–9*

	(a) Nominal PSBR (£b)	(b) As % GDP		(c) Cyclically adjusted % GDP
1972/3	2·5	3·7	1972	1·3
1973/4	4·5	6·0	1973	−1·0
1974/5	7·9	8·9	1974	1·4
1975/6	10·6	9·6	1975	1·1
1976/7	8·5	6·6	1976	−0·7
1977/8	5·6	3·8	1977	1·5
1978/9	9·2	5·4	1978	0·9

Sources: (a) and (b): *Economic Progress Report* 160, September 1983; (c): Begg (1987: 37).

themselves always carry political connotations which means that part of the choice of instruments depends on politics. The left in Britain has, for example, usually been unenthusiastic about the use of monetary policy, the right similarly about incomes policy. Conversely some instruments – notably fiscal policy – have appeared attractive because their use seems to lack direct political consequences. This account of the use of policy instruments in Britain since 1945 will pay considerable attention to these political aspects.

Fiscal policy has dominated in post-war Britain at least until the 1980s (chs. 2 and 3). This primacy accorded to fiscal policy was not an inevitable consequence of Keynes or Keynesianism, Keynes himself being famously catholic in his advocacy of policy instruments (Booth 1989). But budgetary policy emerged pre-eminent in part at least because it appeared to fulfil Keynes' 'liberal collectivist' dream of allowing regulation of the level of economic activity whilst minimising the state's role in the decisions of individual economic agents (Cutler *et al.* 1987: ch. 1; Hall 1986a: 70–1). Certainly this was a key aspect of support for budgetary Keynesianism in the early post-war years, when the main battle-lines were between the Keynesians and the planners.

Fiscal policy was also plausible because of the growth of public expenditure, especially on welfare, which gave fiscal policy much greater leverage over the economy. Public expenditure (exhaustive expenditures and transfers) in Britain grew from around 25 per cent before 1939 to almost 40 per cent by the late 1940s, and rose very gradually over the next decades, with a sharp rise in the mid-1970s, followed by a fall back to the previous level (Heald 1983: 22–8).

Stop–go in the 1950s and 1960s was largely a matter of fiscal policy, operated predominantly through the alteration of tax rates. Public expenditure was found to be an inappropriate instrument of short-run demand management, given the necessarily long-run decisions involved in that expenditure. Thus the main focus of macro-economic policy in practice was consumption expenditure, the largest component of aggregate expenditure and that most directly affected by tax changes (Dow 1964: ch. 7). Whether this system of policy should be called Keynesian is unclear. As Clarke (1989: 15) notes, 'It is ironical that Keynes, who had spent long tracts of his active life campaigning for the direct control of public investment, should have been commemorated after his death by the appropriation of his name for a system relying on the indirect regulation of private consumption.'

How successful was this 'hydraulic Keynesianism' in its own terms? Dow in 1964 (210–13) argued that tax variations did indeed have significant impact on the economy, but suggested that these interventions were poorly timed and may have exacerbated rather than damped-down fluctuations. Whilst remaining controversial, this conclusion has been broadly supported by Hansen (1969: ch. 8) and later by Price (1978a: 209–12), who extends the point to cover policy into the mid-1970s. This consequence has flowed not just from technical problems of fiscal policy, e.g. errors in forecasting, but also from the highly political desire to manage the economy to achieve electoral success. The Conservatives were notably successful in using this method to increase their voting support in 1955 and 1959, though the method just failed in 1964 (Mosley 1984).

The fiscally dominated policy cycle of stop–go came under increasing challenge as it was perceived to inhibit a faster expansion of output. Despite this challenge, fiscal policy continued to reign supreme as a policy instrument in the 1960s and 1970s. The end of the 1960s saw a savage fiscal deflation by post-war standards, leading to the first negative public sector borrowing requirement (PSBR) since the 1930s (Heald 1983). In 1974/5 fiscal policy was called upon to play the opposite role, to expand aggregate demand in the face of the deflation triggered off by OPEC.

The episode of the 1970s revealed the weakness of fiscal policy in such deflationary circumstances. For most of the post-war period the budgetary position, calculated in Keynesian fashion, had been usually mildly deflationary, the current budget being in surplus, with government financing for investment leading usually to a small borrowing requirement (Matthews 1968; rather different figures are given in Ward and Neild 1978: ch. 4). Nothing more expansionary had been required. Up to the mid-1970s fiscal policy had not had to face a serious depression, rather 'government never had to handle a situation in which full employment was in serious jeopardy ... The techniques of demand management were shot through with Keynesian views; but demand management itself operated on buoyant market forces and even then only within narrow limits' (Cairncross 1981: 374).

In late 1974 the new Labour government hoped to avoid a deflationary response to the oil price rise. There seemed to be an international consensus that if every country deflated to offset the balance of payments consequences of this rise there would be a world-wide slump. However, this expansionary policy stance was quickly reversed in most countries, especially because of the inflation which accompanied the oil price increase and the balance of payments deterioration. Expectations of the future flow of North Sea oil as well as political opposition to deflation may have added to the British government's initial stand on this issue. But it was a stand that nevertheless had to be reversed by late 1974. In Keynesian terms fiscal policy remained broadly neutral on average through the rest of the 1970s (Table 9.4). In this kind of analysis the nominal budget position is adjusted to eliminate the effects of fluctuations in output. The aim is to isolate the effect of policy from exogenous changes in fiscal stance. Thus the cyclically adjusted fiscal deficit is calculated for a constant level of employment.

Increasingly, however, such Keynesian-style calculations of the 'real' impact of budgetary policy were displaced by a concern with the nominal PSBR, which rose to unprecedented heights in the mid-1970s – from £2 billion in 1972 to a peak of £10.5 billion in 1975. This purely financial assessment of the government's policies, coupled to the sharp rise of public expenditure which underlay the fiscal deficit, brought a 'fiscal crisis' in 1975/6. This led to a sharp reversal of policy – public expenditure was cut by 2.4 per cent in 1976/7 and 6.9 per cent the following years – the biggest cuts of the post-war period (Pliatzky 1984: 218). Financing the PSBR was difficult in the face of City resistance to gilt sales and the level of borrowing fell.

The incoming Conservative government's rhetoric in 1979 repudiated the whole of post-war demand management and most especially fiscal policy as a regulator of output and employment (Fforde 1983). The Medium-Term Financial Strategy (MTFS) subordinated fiscal policy to monetary, and fiscal policy became assessed by the size of the PSBR. In Keynesian terms this strategy involved fiscal policy imparting a significant deflationary bias to the economy, as the downturn in the economy generated a fiscal deficit which policy tried to reduce. The cyclically adjusted surplus rose from 0.9 per cent of GDP in 1979 to 5.6 per cent by 1982 (Begg 1987: 37). But the government's aim of reducing the PSBR as a share of GDP was achieved, albeit more slowly than hoped in 1980/1.

As always, fiscal balance reflects to a substantial extent the cyclical status of the economy. The fiscal improvement of the mid-1980s followed the sharp recovery of the economy from the slump of 1979–81, rather than any success for the government's aim of reducing public expenditure. Indeed, public expenditure continued to rise in real terms throughout the Conservative's period in office, and the fall in the PSBR of the mid-1980s reflected a combination of higher tax rates (other than income tax) and fast increasing output and employment. In addition, despite their eschewal of demand management, the Conservatives found it difficult to give up the use of fiscal policy to help their electoral prospects, and the 1987 election was preceded by a budget which boosted an already fast-expanding economy. By 1991 fiscal policy was designed to allow the automatic stabilisers to create deficits in recessions and surpluses in booms, but to balance over the cycle as a whole (Budd 1991).

Policy instruments: monetary policy

Monetary policy for most of the post-war period has been clearly secondary to fiscal policy, as chapter 8 points out. Without going into detail on this, it is worth stressing that this emphasis cannot be seen as simply a technical choice of policy instruments. By 1945 the left had developed a great mistrust of monetary means of regulating the economy, and the (largely notional) nationalisation of the Bank of England in 1944 did little to shift this view. Coupled to this historical distrust was the fact that the use of monetary instruments has tended to be linked to priority being given to defeating inflation, rather than reducing unemployment, again contrary to the left's usual priorities. So, much more than in the case of fiscal policy, the use of monetary instruments has been partisan in character, though through most of the 1950s and 1960s both major parties subordinated monetary to fiscal policy. In the 1970s Labour came to employ monetary instruments, including control of the money supply, but this seems to have been the consequence of *force majeure* (i.e. the perceived need to appease financial opinion) rather than a real change of heart about the preferred policy instruments.

Policy instruments: incomes policy

The political connotations of policy instruments is nowhere more apparent than in the case of incomes policy. Here the political divide has been less stable than over monetary policy, often running through political parties as much as between them. Indeed in the 1960s and early 1970s the divide seemed to be between the same parties depending on whether they were in or out of office (Stewart 1977).

Britain's first and possibly most successful incomes policy came under the Labour government in 1948 (ch. 2). This initial experience of incomes policy in many ways set a pattern that was to be followed more than once in the following years. First, whilst the TUC was unenthusiastic about the whole idea, it went along with the policy to support 'its' Labour government. Second, the policy was basically about controlling wages, but the TUC was able to bargain for parallel concessions by employers, e.g. dividend restraint. Third, the policy, whilst showing some initial success, broke down eventually, largely because of repudiation of the policy by rank and file trade unionists. Finally, the policy was always conceived as an interruption to normality, a normality defined by free collective bargaining, rather than as an attempt seriously to restructure the collective bargaining system (Jones 1987: ch. 10; Fishbein 1984).

Attempts at incomes policy were made by Conservative governments in 1961 and again in 1972, but against trade union opposition little was achieved; the second episode led to the 1974 coal-mining strike and the defeat of the Heath government. Unsurprisingly the Conservative leadership then repudiated the whole idea.

Labour tried incomes policy on a voluntary basis in 1964 and on a statutory basis in 1966 (ch. 3). The attempt was renewed after 1974 under the name of the Social Contract. Within this the unions were promised changes in the law on industrial relations and a say in macro-economic and other policies in return for (unclear) restraint on wage claims. The policy failed disastrously in the early part of Labour's period in office in 1974/5, but as before when the going got tough the TUC got going, and for the period 1975 to 1978 the policy helped to reduce inflation from around 25 per cent to around 8 per cent without any rise in unemployment (Layard 1986: 127–9). This view is highly controversial, but the experience of the 1980s seems to suggest that the only alternative instrument for reducing inflation in Britain is massive deflation of demand.

Such success as was achieved in the 1970s was not based on any fundamental reappraisal of the wage bargaining system, but on a reaction to the inflationary crisis of 1975, as well as stemming from some claim by Labour on the political loyalty of trade union members. The underlying commitment of most of the British left to free collective bargaining was not challenged, and as in the late 1940s the TUC found it increasingly hard to hold the line against growing trade union hostility to the policy; it eventually had to repudiate it. This commitment to free collective bargaining was underpinned by a highly fragmented trade union and bargaining system, in which the focus of union activity was the local bargain, rather than nation-wide issues (Donovan Report 1968).

The weakness of the incomes policy instrument in Britain, in comparison to countries like Sweden and Austria, was grounded in the weakness of

'corporatist' structures. For successful incomes policies the need seems to be for both strong employer and union 'peak associations' which are able to 'deliver' on bargains struck with government. In turn such capacity to deliver requires a degree of political consensus or political sophistication which has been simply unavailable in Britain (Katzenstein 1985). The absence of effective incomes policies in Britain provides perhaps the most tantalising might-have-been in the whole history of post-war economic policy.

From 1979 the whole idea of incomes policy was decisively rejected by the Conservatives. The grounds for this were both economic and political. Economically, opposition to incomes policies was grounded on the belief that such policies obscured the monetary origins of inflation. Equally, incomes policies were believed to impose an economic cost both by disrupting the working of the labour market, and because they led to undesirable concessions to trade union views on economic policy. But, above all, hostility to incomes policy was grounded on the belief that it was politically unacceptable for government to bargain over its policy with producer groups, especially the trade unions. Hence the concept of parliamentary sovereignty played a decisive role in the political opposition to 'corporatist' arrangements such as incomes policy (Brittan and Lilley 1977). Of course, such notions of parliamentary sovereignty contain a very substantial element of illusion, as producer groups necessarily have great power in all economies, but the doctrine served to give a constitutional gloss to a rejection of the political claims of trade unions in particular.

Policy and the exchange rate

As is evident from the discussion of policy objectives, the sterling nominal exchange rate has usually been seen as an objective of policy rather than an instrument in post-war Britain. Changes in the value of the currency, when deliberately engineered as in 1949 and 1967, were basically reluctant reactions to external pressures rather than part of a strategy to use the exchange rate positively to improve competitiveness (Cairncross and Eichengreen 1983). The logic of the floating of the pound in 1972 was to free the economy from a constraint, but again not deliberately to manipulate the rate. Such a manipulation was undertaken in 1976, when the Treasury encouraged a fall in the pound to try to restore competitiveness in the wake of the 1975 inflation (Pliatzky 1984: 143). But the fall in the pound quickly went much further than the authorities desired (ch. 3).

This episode illustrated the extent to which policy makers lack the power to control the exchange rate, an incapacity increased as the scale and volatility of international capital flows has increased. Thus, under floating rates, the British authorities have persistently intervened in the foreign exchange market, directly or indirectly, but their impact was marginal. The great appreciation of the pound from 1977 to 1981 was largely outside governmental control (though affected by government policy, especially the financial conservatism after 1979). This real appreciation was a key reason for the slump of 1979–81, but there was little the Conservative government could do about it (except reverse their whole policy position), and they settled for making a virtue of necessity by celebrating its anti-inflationary effects.

Similarly, the Conservative government was able to do little to stem the resumption of the pound's long-term depreciation after 1981, such that by the end of the decade its nominal effective rate was down to 75 (1975 = 100), though the real rate had fallen much less, from 112 in 1981 to 107 in 1990. This is not to say that national governments are powerless in relation to the exchange rate, but their capacity to go against market sentiment is limited simply by the scale of capital flows in world financial markets, against which an individual government's reserves are a pittance. Interest rates are also used to affect currency values, but of course the costs of such policies for the economy may be high. Thus there is a simple logic in Britain's membership of the exchange rate mechanism of the European Monetary System, which may be seen as trying to regain a policy capacity at international level which has been largely lost at a national level.

A central assumption of post-war British policy has been that price competitiveness is the key to success in international trade. But from the mid-1970s there were growing doubts about this, as more and more evidence was adduced to support the view that, certainly for many sophisticated manufactured goods, competition was much more in quality, design, reliability and other 'non-price' aspects (e.g. Stout 1977). This suggested that the scope for maintaining competitiveness by continuous depreciation was, at the least, more limited than many had believed (e.g. Kaldor 1971).

British policy on the balance of payments has been largely indirect, based on manipulation of domestic demand. Industrial policies (see below) might be seen as attempting to raise industrial competitiveness over the long run, but in the short run there has not usually been a separate instrument aimed at the balance of payments. Protectionist measures such as the import surcharge of 1964–6, or the voluntary export restraints of the 1970s and 1980s, have been marginal deviations from the dominance of free trade, at least since the 1950s. Protectionism of a general character was powerfully advocated by the Cambridge Economic Policy Group in the 1970s, but even in those crisis years the commitment of the major interest groups to free trade remained largely untouched. In Tinbergen's frame-

work, the policy objective of improving the balance of payments has lacked its own policy instrument – though as Kaldor (1971 : 4) noted this had 'far more deep-seated causes than the failure by Ministers or officials to make a proper study of the writings of Professor Tinbergen'.

Industrial policies

No post-war British government has restricted its policy instruments to the macro-economic devices enumerated so far. All have had industrial policies, though that omnibus term covers a multitude of virtues and sins.

Apart from its well-known policies of nationalisation, the Labour government of 1945 pursued a range of policies to try to raise the efficiency of the private sector of British industry (Tiratsoo and Tomlinson 1993; Tomlinson 1993). This policy focus was largely driven by short-term macro-economic policy concerns, especially over the balance of payments, though the initiatives pursued would have had long-term effects if successful – for example the encouragement of rationalisation of industry and the standardisation of production.

The real stimuli to sustained intervention in the industrial sector came from two main sources. On the one hand there were policies primarily aimed at reducing unemployment. This led to regional policy on a considerable scale – beginning in the 1940s, waning in the 1950s and then substantially expanding again in the 1960s and into the 1970s. Expenditure in this area fell sharply in the 1980s, but the principle of regional policy still holds some sway in British policy making (Parsons 1986; Thompson 1990). Unemployment fears have also led to a bewildering variety of industrial subsidies to declining industries – from the subsidies for cotton reorganisation in the late 1940s onwards. Between 1960 and 1974, for example, shipbuilding received £153 million in subsidies, textiles £32 million (Mottershead 1978: 478). Such interventions expanded in the 1970s as the economy moved into crisis, and led to a new round of nationalisations such as those of British Leyland and shipbuilding. Again the 1980s saw a retreat from support for such 'lame ducks' but the Conservatives were not entirely immune from political pressures to sustain enterprises whose closure would threaten significant unemployment.

The other policy objective which spurred industrial intervention was that of growth. As noted above, one of the symbols of this concern was the creation of the NEDC in 1961, followed by that of the DEA in 1964. Also under Labour after 1964 a Ministry of Technology was created to emphasise the commitment to submitting British industry to the 'white heat' of technological change.

Whilst the political compulsion to be seen to be doing something is apparent, the analytic basis for government's role in industry was often unclear. For example, in 1965 the Monopolies and Mergers Act was introduced to police merger activity as well as to replace the almost worthless Monopolies Act of 1948. At almost the same time the government established the Industrial Reorganisation Corporation to encourage mergers, in order to gain perceived economies of scale.

Both policies to support declining industries and those to encourage expanding industries tended to be *ad hoc* and a-strategic. A very large proportion of total government effort went into military areas, or those where commercial benefits were poor, such as nuclear power. R & D expenditure in particular was dominated by such areas, and this may have crowded out other R & D effort, especially by soaking up scarce technical manpower (Smith 1989).

In the long boom period there was not much difference between the policies of the two parties in government. The Heath government of 1970 came to power eschewing lame-duck rescues and generally aiming to retreat from industrial intervention, but changed tack radically in 1972 with an Industry Act which allowed a range of industrial rescues, most famously of Rolls Royce and Upper Clyde Shipbuilders. The Labour government of 1974 also promised a new departure and attacked 'lame-duckery', not in the name of laissez-faire, but in the name of intervention aimed at modernisation and creating national champions to compete in international markets. The chosen instrument of this policy was to be the National Enterprise Board (NEB). The aim was to create a state holding company to take over companies in key sectors of the economy. Coupled with this was the idea of planning agreements – contracts made by governments with firms, whereby firms would promise to deliver, for example, investment projects in return for government aid or permission to raise prices.

This was probably the most coherent industrial policy produced by the left in the post-war period. But whatever the economic logic of the ideas, politically the NEB posture was unsustainable. On the one hand, in the crisis of the mid-1970s the Labour government found it impossible to focus attention on 'picking winners', and the NEB's portfolio became dominated by rescued companies like Rolls Royce and British Leyland. On the other hand, the positive role envisaged for the NEB was deemed by the Labour leadership to be too radical for business and marginal opinion, and the exercise was largely aborted following the sacking of Tony Benn as Industry Minister in 1975. The NEB did register some successes; it 'turned round' Ferranti from bankruptcy to viability and created the successful silicon chip company INMOS. But this was small beer in comparison with the hopes of its founders (Grant 1982: chs. 3, 5; Sawyer 1991).

In theory the Conservatives after 1979 determinedly rejected such dirigisme. In practice the picture was more complex. Whilst the scale of industrial subsidies fell (especially in the nationalised industries) they still gave money, particularly to small and high-tech firms and paradoxically in a more discriminatory fashion than their predecessors, in the name of 'targeting'. A similar evolution occurred in regional policy (Thompson 1990). So industrial policy survived, albeit radically reshaped, into the 1990s. Given the combination of high and concentrated unemployment, and the continuing competitive failings of British industry it is doubtful if any government would pursue the degree of disengagement suggested by neo-liberal rhetoric.

Constraints: international integration

Before the First World War the British economy was highly integrated with the world economy through goods and capital markets, but this was not a constraint on national economic management, as such management was not on the agenda. From 1945 the economy began from a much lower level of integration than that attained by 1913, but this level increased rapidly especially from the 1960s and increasingly constrained the capacity of individual national governments to achieve their economic policy objectives.

Integration poses problems for all national governments, but plainly bears hardest on less internationally competitive economies, both because of the impact of competitive failure on the current account, but also because, other things being equal, such failure discourages capital inflows. Domestic institutional arrangements can, however, also 'push out' international constraints. In Sweden in the early 1980s, for example, the corporatist wage-bargaining arrangements allowed the government to deliver a real depreciation of the kroner, an achievement almost impossible in Britain.

Britain then was constrained by growing economic integration in part because of the domestic problems of the competitive failures of its manufacturing industry and the incapacity to deliver consensual policies. But even in more successful countries, the scale of capital flows and the level of trade dependency, plus the increasing role of multinational enterprises, hemmed in national policy makers. Stewart (1983) has pointed out how capital flows have tended to act asymmetrically to reinforce national policies of deflation but undermine policies of demand expansion. Examples of this in operation would be France in 1980/1 and Britain in 1975/6.

Recognition of such constraints has led to proposals for 'dis-integration' as in the protectionist proposals of the 1970s, but these were decisively rejected. Another response has been to emphasise the possibility of regaining powers at a supra-national level lost at the national level – most evident in the bipartisan enthusiasm for European monetary integration which emerged in the late 1980s. Above all, a perception of the limits of national macro-economic policies has led to a striking and again bipartisan shift to emphasising policies for the supply side of the economy. By the end of the 1980s an increased emphasis was being placed on national economic competitiveness, somewhat displacing the previous stress on national economic management.

Internal constraints

Internally, policy has been constrained by the mechanisms of policy formation and the ideas at work in that formation, as well as by the wider cultural and political context in which policy is made. In discussions of policy formation, two recurrent themes have been the dominance of the Treasury and the role of the City of London.

Though with a reluctance and ambiguity that stretched into the 1950s, the post-war Treasury was eventually converted to a version of Keynesianism (Rollings 1988). This was 'hydraulic Keynesianism', which manifested itself in 'stop–go' and took for granted the defence of the pound. By the end of the 1950s this policy and the Treasury were subject to serious attack as a major obstacle to faster economic growth, and attempts were made to create institutions, notably the DEA, to assert the needs of industry.

This argument assumed that stop–go was significantly damaging for British industry, by harming investment intentions. However the cyclical fluctuations in the British economy in the stop–go period were no worse than in comparable economies with much better growth records (Whiting 1976), which rather undercuts the commonly postulated link between 'stop–go' and the failings of British industry. Secondly, the Treasury's support for maintaining the value of the pound in the years up to 1967 was not by any means a position that it alone pressured the government to adopt. Rather, the major basis for resisting devaluation from 1964 to 1967 seems to have been a combination of belief that other policies could render such a devaluation unnecessary and that Labour, following 1949, should not become the party of devaluation. In addition, $2.80 was 'clung to partly as a matter of preserving the "status of sterling" as an international transactions currency, and also as a reserve currency which would stiffen the wilting bonds of Commonwealth policy' (Strange 1971: 337; Cairncross and Eichengreen 1983: ch. 5).

The picture sometimes drawn of the Treasury as the major obstacle to reform of British economic policy (e.g. Ham 1981) seems to be overdrawn. The Treasury has usually represented a position widely held in Britain, rather than standing out against a widespread consensus.

The role of the City of London is equally ambiguous. The City undoubtedly operated as a pressure group for a strong pound in the period up to the end of the 1960s, and this pressure was powerfully reinforced by the role of the Bank of England as purveyor of City opinion in the inner counsels of policy making. Again, however, this position was little challenged by Labour governments, despite criticisms from writers on the left such as Shonfield (1959), Hirsch (1965) and Strange (1988). Most strikingly, the Attlee government, despite its leaders' assertion that 'the City of London in a socialist economy is like the Pope in Moscow' (Durbin 1985: 74), encouraged the idea of re-creating London as a major financial centre and the pound as a top currency, and thus restoring the power of the City of London.

Whilst the specific role of the City as a pressure group for a strong pound fell away from the late 1960s, the general constraining impact of financial markets has been enhanced since that time. As already noted, the scale and volatility of capital movements has inhibited expansionary policies in Britain and elsewhere in the last two decades, because of the effects of such policies on financial confidence and thereby on the exchange rate and the rate of inflation. In addition, financial confidence has directly constrained the capacity of governments to pursue desired fiscal policies by constraining their ability to borrow (as well as enhancing its cost) as in the British 'gilt strike' of 1976 (Keegan and Pennant-Rea 1979: 131–7). The difficulty of discussing financial confidence is that it is impossible to locate a single decision-making body which determines the state of that confidence. The most one can say is that the maintenance of financial confidence seems to have been based on semi-permanent notions of sound money and 'prudent' fiscal policy. What has changed has been the increased capacity of such confidence to constrain policy, via the increase in capital flows and fiscal deficits.

Ideas and policy

Constraints are not just external brick walls against which policy makers can only beat their heads. Constraints also flow from the ideas which inform policy – policy is necessarily to a degree a process of putting ideas into practice.

Much of the post-war history of British economic policy has been written in terms of the waxing and waning of certain economic theories –

especially the theories of Keynesianism, monetarism and the New Classical economics. Unless one adopts the view that theories are just masks to hide true intentions (as in the view, mocked by Marx, that all priest are atheists who are also liars), theoretical ideas must be seen as having some impact on policy. Discussion of post-war Britain has probably exaggerated the impact of such economic ideas on policy formation. If one takes Keynes' ideas, it is clear that the policies which emerged in the late 1940s and 1950s, most obviously the general idea of managing demand, owe something to him, but the form of implementation of those policies cannot be reduced to an expression of Keynesianism (Dow 1964: ch. 7; Hall 1986a: ch. 10). Equally, the policies pursued after 1979 owed rather little to Friedman's theories beyond a general emphasis on containing inflation by monetary means.

It is surely unsurprising that by and large the exigencies of policy making escape the formulations of economic theorists. The focus on the alleged impact of economic theories on economic policy has probably acted to oversimplify our understanding of the policy-making process, certainly in some of the writing on economics. But to be sceptical of that impact is not to counterpoise some equally dubious notion of the impact of 'interests' on policy, as is commonly done (Institute of Economic Affairs 1990). The problem with this approach is not that vested interests do not affect policy, but that the policies which those interests advocate cannot be reduced to a consequence of their position in the social structure, but are themselves constructed with theories or 'ideas'. For example, the pursuit of a strong pound by the City of London in the 1950s and 1960s rested on a particular view of where the City's interest lay, a view which can be challenged. If, for example, a weaker pound in the 1950s and 1960s had allowed a more competitive British industry to develop, this might have advantaged the City in the long run. Thus an adequate account of policy making must explain both how ideas became incorporated into institutions of that policy making, and how and why different interests perceive their interests in particular ways.

Politics and policy

Such an account must also take on board the wider political context in which economic policy is pursued. A substantial part of the discussion so far in this chapter has been on macro-economic policy, with much less said on industrial or micro-economic aspects. This balance reflects the historiography of the period but also a real and highly significant feature of British policy in this period. To a significant extent, in comparison with other major advanced capitalist countries, Britain has lacked a coherent pattern of micro-economic or industrial intervention. Industrial policy has not lacked attention nor expenditure of effort and money, but it has lacked continuity and much of a strategic vision.

Ultimately this pattern must be explained to a significant extent by the nature of the post-war political settlement in Britain (Marquand 1989; Cutler *et al*. 1987). That settlement embodied (eventually) a kind of 'lowest common denominator' of Keynesian macro-economic management. This liberal Keynesianism emerged triumphant from the policy battles of the 1940s, defeating the planners, though with more of a struggle than is commonly recognised (Rollings 1992). Its appeal to the dominant elements in both political parties and in the bureaucracy was that it promised economic stability and full employment, whilst maintaining a 'hands-off' approach to the private sector. 'Hands-off' did not mean literally quite that, but it meant no attempt to subject the private sector or a significant section of it to overarching plans of any kind.

Of course Britain had a very large nationalised sector (ch. 6), but the particular form of that nationalisation, the Morrisonian corporation, meant that it was not a ready instrument of government economic policy, and therefore not a mechanism for commanding the economy from its heights. Hence nationalisation, for the period up to the 1980s at least, was largely uncontroversial but also rather unimportant for the management of the economy, for all the *ad hoc* interventions to which nationalised firms were subject.

The rise of economic growth as a policy concern from the 1950s challenged this post-war settlement, and brought forth calls for a more interventionist stance. Whilst these could not be entirely resisted, they largely led to a rhetoric of planning coupled with an actuality of extended *ad hoc* interventions. The same point can be made about attempts at incomes policy, which came and went with successive economic crises. Hence in essentials the post-war settlement survived at least until the traumas of the 1970s.

Perversely enough, these half-hearted attempts at an extended role for the state, plus the crisis of the mid-1970s, led eventually to a neo-liberal reaction and a diagnosis which proposed a route to industrial modernisation which no other advanced capitalist country has successfully pursued. By the end of the 1980s it was apparent that this strategy had failed to stem the tide of relative impoverishment which has seen Britain fall from the highest per capita income in Europe in 1945 to the lowest in north-west Europe by 1990.

Conclusion

Would-be revolutionaries necessarily decry the achievements of previous regimes. Much of the policy discussion of the post-1979 years presented economic policy since 1945 as a story of failure, a view neatly summarised by Barnett's (1985: ch. 1) view that post-war Britain had set off down the wrong road to 'New Jerusalem' rather than to 'industrial modernisation'.

Such a negative view of post-war policy obviously gained credence from the combination of high inflation, high unemployment and low growth of the 1970s, together with the continuing vulnerability of the British economy to balance of payments worries. However, whether these problems should lead to a wholesale condemnation of British policy over the post-war period is doubtful.

In terms of the standard indices of economic performance the post-war period presents a mixed picture. For most of the period, and for all the years up to the end of the 1970s, unemployment was low both in historical and comparative perspective (ch. 7). Whether this success was wholly due to policy is doubtful. Any idea that low unemployment simply reflected governmental commitment to Keynesian demand management seems unacceptable (Matthews 1968). But in less direct ways policy contributed to this outcome. The commitment to a liberal trade regime certainly helped Britain in the 1950s and 1960s, though its effects were more ambiguous later. The degree of political commitment to the full employment goal may have encouraged an expansionary outlook amongst investors, and more specifically ruled out whole-hearted deflationary responses to balance of payments problems.

Of course it can be and is argued that this success on unemployment caused excessively high inflation rates. But in fact up to the late 1960s Britain's inflation rate was no higher than those of other OECD countries, so in fact the comparatively poor performance on that indicator of the 1970s and 1980s post-dates Britain's exceptional unemployment success.

Even on growth, the evaluation depends on the perspective adopted. From an historical view post-war growth was at a level never previously sustained for an extended period. It is the introduction of a new perspective, of international comparison, which throws British performance into the shadows.

The balance of payments is an area of recurrent failure by almost any standard. It would be hard indeed to argue that policy has not been highly constrained through much of this period by different aspects of the payments position, and these problems seem to have been worsening if we judge by the current account deficits occurring at anything approaching full employment of resources.

Have the failings of performance been caused by policy errors? Some of the issues raised by such a question seem to be relatively straightforward to settle. Britain has not had particularly high levels of public expenditure, taxation, public borrowing or public ownership in comparison with other OECD countries (Brittan 1978) so it would seem difficult to blame policy in these areas for British failings.

'Stop–go', often identified in the 1960s as a culprit for Britain's poor growth, seems implausible as a significant contributor given the evidence on the relative fluctuations in output in OECD countries. Such a conclusion would also seem to suggest that the undoubted obsession of governments of the 1950s and 1960s with the value of the pound could not have been crucial to Britain's balance of payments problems, though uncompetitiveness may have been worsened by the failure to devalue in the early 1960s. The experience of the years after the float of 1972 does not suggest that the pound's value was quite so central to the balance of payments problems as writers in the period of fixed exchange rates commonly suggested.

Policy is subject to failures of omission as well as commission. Could policy have done significantly more to improve performance?

One failure has plainly been in the area of incomes policies. The significance of this failure is not that it meant an inability to secure a lower trend level of real wage costs in Britain, which many commentators on left and right have seen as the aim of incomes policy. It is doubtful if such costs have been crucial to Britain's economic failings (Williams *et al.* 1989). Rather the absence of successful incomes policies has reduced the effectiveness of other policy instruments, especially changes in the exchange rate, and led to an excessive reliance on others, such as deflation, as, for example, in the period after 1979.

But ultimately it is difficult to escape the conclusion that the major error of omission in policy has been in the area of industrial policy, broadly defined. It seems clear that the constraint on performance from the failings of the supply side of the British economy outweighs any macro-economic policy errors. Such a statement implies neither that such failings have been constant over the post-war period, nor that policy could readily have corrected them. Nevertheless, and especially if we look at Britain in a comparative perspective, what seems striking is the extent to which policy has been dominated by macro-economic considerations and the absence not of interest in industry, but lack of both an intellectual and political basis for a strategy directed towards industrial modernisation.

10   The welfare state

Paul Johnson

Introduction

In the four decades since 1948 government social expenditure in the UK has risen from less than a third to over half of total government expenditure, and from one tenth to over one fifth of GNP (Barr 1987: 170). This enormous expansion of the cash transfers and publicly provided services that constitute the British 'welfare state' has been variously credited with creating a more just society and a more stable economy and blamed for eroding incentives and retarding economic growth. Supporters of the welfare state emphasise the equity achievements while detractors stress the efficiency losses of this massive system of resource redistribution. In 1956 the socialist thinker and Labour MP Antony Crosland argued that there was a 'direct and intimate' relationship

between social expenditure and social equality. The former can promote the latter in two ways: first, by removing the greater handicap which poorer families suffer as compared with richer, during sickness, old age and the period of heaviest family responsibility, and secondly by creating standards of public health, education and housing which are comparable in scope and quality with the best available for private purchase. (Crosland 1956: 519)

Crosland's views gained widespread support during the 1950s and 1960s when there was a broadly based political consensus about the desirability of public social expenditure, but by the beginning of the 1980s a new anti-welfare orthodoxy had emerged. According to Milton and Rose Friedman (1980: 158): 'The waste is distressing, but it is the least of the evils of the paternalistic programs that have grown to such massive size. Their major evil is their effect on the fabric of society. They weaken the family, reduce the incentive to work, reduce the accumulation of capital, and limit our freedom.'

Simplistic and doctrinaire assertions such as these about the role of the welfare state in the post-war economy take little account of the complexity of structure, function and outcome of the diverse range of transfers that together make up the British welfare state.

284

This chapter examines the extent to which the welfare state justifies the extravagant claims made for and against it. The emphasis is on the economic impact of the welfare state, and in particular the effect which government social expenditure has had on economic equity and economic efficiency. An assessment is also made of the success or failure of the welfare state in achieving the many (sometimes conflicting) goals that have been set for it by successive politicians and administrators. But before assessing the outcomes, it is necessary to know something of the origins, structure and development of the welfare state since 1945.

Origins

The British welfare state is not simply a creation of the Second World War, nor has it remained in a fixed form since the 1940s, but the war was an important watershed in the development of the welfare functions of government in Britain (ch. 1 above). Support of the destitute poor had been a legitimate function of local government since the Elizabethan Poor Law of 1601, and in the late nineteenth and early twentieth centuries state provision was extended to the fields of elementary education, pensions, health and unemployment insurance, asylums and sanatoriums (Thane 1982; Digby 1989). On the eve of the First World War Britain had a public welfare system with many of the characteristics found in the post-1945 welfare state: provision of both cash benefits and direct services, administration by both central and local government, finance from a mixture of direct and indirect taxes, and an explicit element of re-distribution from richer to poorer elements of society. But the differences between the pre-1914 and post-1945 welfare states were as great as the similarities. The most obvious difference was that of scope.

Before the First World War most social expenditure in Britain was based on the concept of a *residual* welfare state, a system of physical and financial safety nets which prevented absolute destitution and relieved chronic ill-health where it could be shown, on the basis of a means test, that the recipient was without alternative resources. The limited scope of this early twentieth-century welfare state is reflected by its cost – public social expenditure in 1920 accounted for just over one quarter of total public expenditure, and less than 6 per cent of GNP.

By 1948 the welfare state was very different in size and character. It accounted for over 10 per cent of GNP, and was more centralised and much more comprehensive in terms of the proportion of the population and the type of social contingencies covered. It had changed from being a *residual* to an *institutional* welfare system, integral to the structures of modern industrial society (Wilensky and Lebeaux 1958: 138–47). Some of these changes were a direct response to the unprecedented requirements that the waging of 'total war' placed on British society. Hospitals were reorganised to cope with the anticipated civilian and military casualties of war (Titmuss 1950: 55), and means-tested 'public assistance' payments (the Old Poor Law relief renamed) evolved into non-means-tested benefits payable to many thousands of households suffering financially from the effects of bombing, military conscription and wartime inflation. But wartime welfare developments were not simply reactive, a government response to exogenous circumstances. British politicians and civil servants themselves generated, from the early years of the war, an ambitious and wide-ranging set of proposals for an extension of government involvement in many areas of social provision.

A multitude of advisory committees was established from 1940 to develop plans for post-war reconstruction and social reform, although they worked with little coordination or agreement over values and goals (Harris 1986: 238). Whilst education planning (culminating in the 1944 Education Act) followed administrative lines established in the 1930s and health proposals were conditioned by the practical achievements of running the wartime Emergency Medical Service, employment and social security proposals had more distinct ideological roots. The White Paper on *Employment Policy* (UK 1944) was an explicitly Keynesian document which committed post-war governments to 'the maintenance of a high and stable level of employment' through a conscious policy of economic management. And the report of a committee chaired by Sir William Beveridge on *Social Insurance and Allied Services* (UK 1942), which advocated a comprehensive system of social insurance 'against interruption and destruction of earning power and for special expenditure arising at birth marriage and death', was a direct descendant of 'New Liberal' ideology which aimed at preventing destitution without undermining market structures and incentives (Harris 1977).

This 'Beveridge Report', as it came to be known, promised freedom from want for all citizens from the cradle to the grave in exchange for weekly insurance contributions (paid jointly by worker and employer) from all those in employment. Beveridge assumed that positive economic management after the war would prevent long-term unemployment and that medical services would be available through a comprehensive health care system; his insurance scheme was designed primarily to relieve the financial costs of temporary unemployment and sickness, long-term disability and old age. The Report attracted enormous publicity and public support, partly because its ambiguity, breadth of vision and overall optimism meant that almost everyone could find something in it with which they agreed (Harris 1986). It was, however, little more than one man's blueprint for the consolidation and extension of existing and overlapping schemes of social protection, and was accepted only grudgingly as a policy document by the wartime government, with no move made towards implementation. It came, nevertheless, to take a central position in the plans for a post-war welfare state designed to destroy what Beveridge called the five giant evils of 'Want, Disease, Ignorance, Squalor and Idleness' (UK 1942: 6).

In the general election, fought at the end of the war in July 1945, the Labour Party readily adopted the major proposals of the Beveridge Report, together with commitments to better housing, greater educational opportunity and full employment, a strategy which undoubtedly contributed to Labour's electoral victory (Addison 1975). With this Labour government came a flurry of legislation which established the foundations of the post-war welfare state: in 1945 the Family Allowance Act, in 1946 the National Insurance and National Health Service Acts, in 1948 the National Assistance and Children's Acts and in 1949 the Housing Act. Although there is disagreement among historians about the extent to which the specific institutions of the post-war welfare state reflected the novelty of wartime thought and action or the continuity of inter-war developments (Titmuss 1955; Harris 1981), there can be little doubt that the impetus to legislative action came from a desire, shared by many Conservative as well as Labour politicians, to build a better and more equal Britain after the sacrifices of five years of total war. The idea of a residual welfare state that would merely respond to economic and social problems was replaced by a comprehensive welfare ideology in which public social expenditure could be used to change and improve society. How much this comprehensive welfare state would cost, how it would be funded or what impact it would have on macro-economic performance or micro-economic incentives was never fully considered.

Structure and finance

The structure of the welfare state that had emerged by 1948, and which has remained fundamentally the same since that date, is shown in Figure 10.1. There were two broad types of benefit, directly provided services and cash transfers. The cash transfers were themselves of two types, some being provided through the contributory system of National Insurance closely modelled on Beveridge's plan, and others being paid on a non-contributory basis from general tax revenue. National insurance benefits were to be paid to individuals (and their dependants) who had made a sufficient number of actuarially calculated contributions to the National Insurance Fund, in the event that they succumbed to any of the contingencies most likely to lead

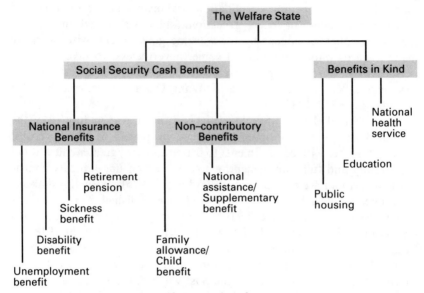

Figure 10.1 Main welfare state benefits

to poverty – particularly sickness, unemployment, disability and old age. Membership of the national insurance scheme was compulsory, and the contributions and benefits were flat-rate with benefits set at a subsistence level to encourage additional private saving for emergencies. The National Insurance Fund was to be managed as an independent account, ultimately to be self-financing and entirely separate from all other government revenues. By contrast, non-contributory national assistance benefits were intended to be a means-tested safety net for the few groups (for instance vagrants) who did not have an adequate contribution record to qualify for, or whose needs were not sufficiently met by, national insurance benefits. National Assistance was financed from general tax revenues and was intended to be a modern (and more humane) continuation of the residual welfare function performed in the nineteenth century by the Poor Law. In addition, families were to be assisted quite independently from central government revenues with the payment of weekly benefits (family allowances) to all parents with two or more dependent children, together with the granting to fathers of additional tax allowances related to family size.

The comprehensive nature of the post-war welfare state needs to be stressed. Partly in reaction to the stigma associated with the Victorian Poor Law and the resentment towards the means test imposed on the unemployed during the inter-war years, it was insisted that national insurance benefits were a *right*, paid in equal amounts to everyone in exchange for their equal insurance contributions. Furthermore, the centrally funded National Health Service made medical attention available to everyone free of charge, with access determined only by medical assessment of relative need, and all school-age children were entitled (and required) to receive an education provided entirely without charge in state schools. Almost every household in the country was in regular, and in many cases daily, receipt of services and/or cash benefits from the all-embracing welfare state. But even as Clement Attlee, the Labour Prime Minister, was claiming in 1950 that 'the foundations of the Welfare State have been well and truly laid' (Pelling 1984: 117–18), there were appearing substantial cracks in these foundations relating to the cost and adequacy of welfare state benefits.

Beveridge had always held the vision of social insurance to be more important than the details of finance, and it was not until his 1942 report was in draft form that a detailed attempt was made to cost its proposals (Barnett 1986: 46–7). This exercise revealed a fundamental problem – if National Insurance was to operate on true actuarial principles, pensions could be paid only after a full contribution period of around forty-five years, and the first national insurance pensioners would not receive their pensions until the 1990s. Such a long delay was incompatible with the social and political goals of the social insurance scheme, and a compromise was proposed by the Government Actuary, whereby old age pensions would be paid at a reduced rate for the first twenty years of the scheme, with the inevitable income shortfall being made up by direct subventions from central government revenue (UK 1942). But in order to assist pensioners on fixed incomes who were struggling to cope with the after-effects of wartime inflation, the Labour government began in 1946 to pay the full state pension to all retired people over pension age (sixty for women, sixty-five for men). The Government Actuary expressed his concern at the size of future pension liabilities that were not being covered by adequate contributions, although the lower than anticipated expenditure on unemployment benefit in the immediate post-war period allowed the national insurance scheme to preserve a temporary financial balance. This fortuitous financial equilibrium could not continue, if only because the number of pensioners in the population was projected to rise by 4 million over a thirty-year period from a baseline figure of 5.6 million in 1941. The decision taken in 1946 to pay full pensions to all people above the qualifying age had the inevitable consequence of creating large and growing deficits for the National Insurance Fund (Dilnot *et al.* 1984).

Only by substantially raising contributions without offering any improved benefits for two or three decades could the long-run financial solvency of the national insurance scheme be re-established, but political expediency demanded the reverse, an increase in benefits, which were falling behind earnings as real incomes rose in the 1950s. The way out of this problem was to abandon the idea of building up a fund which would cover future pension liabilities, and instead to use current contributions to pay current benefits. By 1958 National Insurance had changed from being a 'funded' to a 'pay-as-you-go' system, with the insurance 'fund' aiming merely to balance income and expenditure over each year. Future pension liabilities were to be financed out of future economic growth – or to be worried about by future generations. As Dilnot *et al.* (1984: 13) note, 'the device of meeting yesterday's claims from today's premiums has been familiar to fraudulent and foolish financiers for millennia', and it was now to become the financial model for what was somewhat ironically called 'social security'. This shift from a 'funded' to a 'pay-as-you-go' basis for contributory benefits created great potential for expansion of the national insurance system, potential which, as is shown in the next section, was fully realised by politicians and administrators.

Concern about the overall cost of the scheme was matched by a concern, from the very beginning, about the adequacy of benefits. Beveridge explicitly stated that the national insurance benefit should 'provide by itself the income necessary for subsistence in all normal cases', and though he intended that this subsistence level should be austere, it was supposed to be sufficient to ensure that members of the national insurance scheme need have no resort to means-tested National Assistance. But there is an obvious contradiction between the goal of flat-rate cash benefits for all beneficiaries and the goal of providing a subsistence income for families whose size, needs and resources may vary enormously. The size of this contradiction can be seen in Figure 10.2, which shows that since 1950 around 25 per cent of national insurance benefit recipients (and substantially more of those in receipt of unemployment benefit) have had incomes so low that they have also qualified for means-tested National Assistance (from 1966 called 'supplementary benefit'). Beveridge believed that means-tested poverty relief would wither away as the entire population was incorporated in the national insurance scheme but insurance benefits have always been set at too low a level to achieve this goal; Digby (1989: 68–9) has noted that the proportion of the British population receiving means-tested benefits has risen from just over 4 per cent in 1948 to 12 per cent by 1981. This has involved not only costly, cumbersome and overlapping administration, but, as will be shown below, has also reduced the incentives for some benefit recipients to work and save.

The disincentive effect of overlapping benefit systems has been exacerbated by changes to the structure of the income tax and national insurance

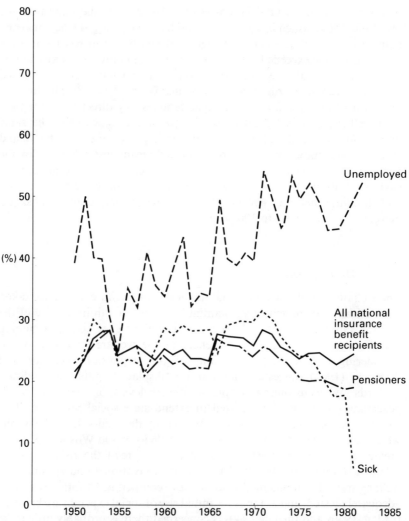

Figure 10.2 Percentage of all benefit recipients dependent (in whole or part) on National Assistance/supplementary benefit, 1950–81
Source: Dilnot *et al.* (1984: 22).

contribution systems. The abandonment of the concept that premiums should be actuarially related to benefits allowed governments first to increase the level of contribution in order to pay for current benefits, then in 1961 to introduce graduated contributions, in 1975 to relate contributions to earnings, and in the 1980s to increase contributions in order to gain additional general revenue rather than to balance the nominal

National Insurance Fund (Dilnot *et al.* 1984: 29). At the same time the threshold above which income tax is paid has fallen; in 1949–50 a married man with two children under the age of eleven began to pay income tax when his income exceeded 120 per cent of average manual earnings, but by 1980–1 an identical household began to pay tax when its income exceeded only 50 per cent of average manual earnings (Wicks 1987: 28). This has had the effect of making more low-income families pay direct taxes for their own welfare, and has created the bizarre situation whereby the same households are regarded as sufficiently rich to be taxed by the Inland Revenue, and sufficiently poor to be granted means-tested benefits by the Department of Social Security. Poor households frequently find that a slight increase in their income will simultaneously raise their tax liability and eliminate their entitlement to benefit, thereby effectively imposing a marginal tax rate close to 100 per cent.

Development

These changes in the structure and finance of the welfare state have taken place within the context of substantial long-run growth in the size of the welfare state budget and in the scope of its activities, so before examining the efficiency and equity consequences of the welfare state it is worth considering alternative explanations of this expansion. Peacock and Wiseman (1961) suggested that warfare 'displaced' public expenditure upwards by accustoming people to higher levels of taxation, which peacetime governments then used to extend state social provision. This supply-side hypothesis has been countered by demand-side explanations which stress a heightened sense of altruism (Wilson and Wilson 1982) or a greater desire on the part of individuals to spread the risks of social calamity (Goodin and Dryzek 1987) as the motivational underpinnings of welfare state development. None of these competing hypotheses can be adequately tested, and as far as the initial rise of social expenditure between the late 1930s and the late 1940s is concerned there is probably little to be gained from pursuing a wholly economic explanation of welfare developments in this period of exceptional administrative, social and political change.

The expansion of public social expenditure since the establishment of the welfare state structure is, however, worth examining closely. It is not immediately obvious why social expenditure should have doubled as a proportion of GDP in the three decades since 1950, since sustained economic growth over this period has raised most incomes well above the subsistence thresholds set in 1948. A preliminary view of the process of

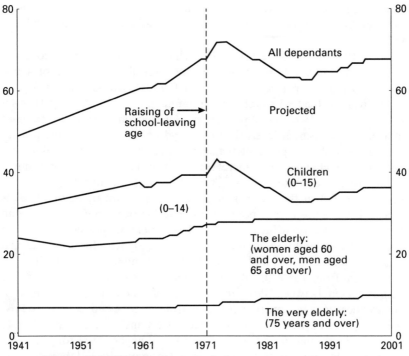

Figure 10.3 UK dependant population as a percentage of population
of working age, 1941–2001
Source: Glennerster (1985: 240).

expenditure growth can be gained by separating this growth into its
constituent parts. Social expenditure can grow first because of demographic change which increases the number of people in certain defined
benefit categories; second because of changes in coverage which alter the
boundaries of benefit categories; third because of changes in the value of
benefits. Governments have little control over the first of these factors, but
coverage and benefit levels are directly determined by political decisions.

As Figure 10.3 shows, demographic change imposed a consistent upward
pressure on welfare state spending until at least the mid-1970s as the
proportion both of children and of the elderly in the British population
rose. This pressure has continued through the 1980s with an increase in the
population aged over seventy-five, since as well as receiving pensions this
group is a major beneficiary of health service expenditure. The diagram
also shows what can happen when coverage is extended. In 1947 the school
leaving age was set at fifteen, but in 1972 this was raised to sixteen,
immediately involving the government in additional welfare state ex-

penditure both in the provision of additional schooling and in the granting of benefit payments (such as child benefit) for which all school-age children were eligible.

Table 10.1 shows the relative role of changes in demography, coverage and real benefit levels in influencing the overall growth rate of social expenditure in the periods 1960–75 and 1975–81. In the first period real expenditure on the four specified programmes grew at an annual rate of 4.9 per cent, most of which (3.2 per cent p.a.) was a consequence of increases in average real benefit levels. In the second period, however, the growth rate fell to only 1.8 per cent p.a., half of which was accounted for by demographic changes, with increases in real benefit levels playing only a minor role. The continued rise over 1975–81 in the number of elderly people and fall in the number of children (as shown in Figure 10.3) is reflected in the positive demographic impact on pension expenditure and negative impact on education. The large increase in the size of the unemployed population in the late 1970s accounted for a substantial 'demographic' boost to real expenditure on unemployment benefit.

It is clear from Table 10.1 that the rapid growth of welfare expenditures that occurred between 1960 and 1975 came about largely because of positive decisions by governments, both Conservative and Labour, to raise the real level of welfare benefits. Such decisions were not peculiar to Britain; the annual growth rate of real social expenditure for the seven major OECD countries (Canada, France, Germany, Italy, Japan, the UK and the USA) was 8 per cent over the period 1960–75, of which 4.6 per cent p.a. was accounted for by real benefit increases. In fact, of these seven countries the UK had both the lowest overall growth rate of social expenditure and the lowest rate of growth of real benefits (OECD 1985b).

Several alternative scenarios can be developed to account for this growth of social expenditure; they depend on different assumptions about the net direction of transfers between those who pay the extra taxes and those who receive the enhanced benefits. If taxes are paid primarily by the rich majority and benefits received mainly by the poor minority, then an apparent increase in humanitarian sentiment among the rich may induce them to support governments which use the tax/benefit system to improve the lot of the poor. Such behaviour is often attributed to non-economic 'altruism', though it can equally be explained by interdependent personal utility functions; for example the utility of the rich may be raised by transferring sufficient resources to the poor to remove the need of the latter to go begging. A second possibility is that taxes are paid and benefits received by most people in society, with little by way of redistribution between different economic or social categories. In this case a substantial increase in social expenditures could occur if voters perceived the state to

Table 10.1. *Decomposition of the growth rate of social expenditure in the UK, 1960–75 and 1975–81*

	Education	Health	Pensions	Unemployment	Total of four programmes	Total social expenditure
Expenditure share in 1960 as % GDP	3·7	3·4	4·1	0·2	11·4	13·9
1960–75 real expenditure growth, % per annum:	5·0	3·4	5·9	10·3	4·9	5·0
of which						
Demography	0·6	0·4	1·6	6·5	1·0	
Coverage	1·1	0·0	0·9	−0·8	0·7	
Benefits	3·2	3·0	3·3	4·4	3·2	
Expenditure share in 1975 as % GDP	6·8	5·0	6·3	0·7	18·8	22·5
1975–81 real expenditure growth, % per annum:	−2·0	2·0	4·5	14·2	1·8	2·5
of which						
Demography	−0·4	0·0	1·0	19·1	0·9	
Coverage	−0·5	0·0	0·8	5·3	0·3	
Benefits	−1·1	2·0	2·6	−8·9	0·7	
Expenditure share in 1981 as % GDP	5·8	5·4	7·4	1·4	20·0	23·7

Source: OECD (1985b: 39).

be a more efficient provider of welfare or insurance services than the private market. A third possibility is that taxes are paid by the rich minority and benefits received by a relatively poor majority who consistently vote for more redistributive transfers – a case of the tyranny of the majority, or of democracy in action, depending on one's outlook.

These three potential explanations for the growth of public social expenditure rest on two common assumptions: that majority electoral preference determines policy and that benefits have to be paid from taxes. Neither assumption necessarily holds for Britain after 1945. Electoral preferences are mediated by government bureaucracies which exercise enormous power over the formulation and execution of public policy. Bureaucracies may strive for objectives such as the maximisation of size and spending power which differ sharply from those preferred by the electorate (Niskanen 1971; Heclo and Wildavsky 1974). Furthermore the post-war acceptance of Keynesian deficit financing together with the adoption of pay-as-you-go social security financing opened up the possibility of current benefits being funded not from current taxes but from loans, which ultimately have to be repaid from future taxes. Politicians had a new opportunity to offer electoral bribes today for which someone else would have to pick up the tab tomorrow. According to Buchanan and Wagner (1977) it was the electorally attractive spending opportunities which opened up for politicians, together with the self-aggrandising designs of bureaucrats, which fuelled the rapid growth of public expenditure. To determine which of these alternatives provides the most convincing explanation of the growth of the welfare state requires empirical investigation of a range of questions. Who paid the taxes? Who received the benefits? Did public welfare provision develop only in those areas where market forces failed adequately to meet demand? Was public provision efficient? Was welfare state growth responsive to electoral pressure? It is to these questions about the performance and economic impact of the post-war welfare state, at both the macro- and micro-level, that the discussion now turns.

Aggregate economic impact of the welfare state

Assessing the aggregate impact of the welfare state on the British economy, whether in terms of efficiency and growth or equity and distribution, is fraught with technical and empirical difficulties (Atkinson and Stiglitz 1980: ch. 9). The distributional effect of increasing a particular benefit or the incentive effect of cutting a particular tax can be readily assessed if all other conditions of production, consumption and distribution remain the same, but in practice these other conditions also change. To determine the overall effect on efficiency and equity of even a simple change in the tax and benefit system requires a general equilibrium analysis, and so far little has been achieved in this area by economists because of both computational difficulties and the lack of sufficiently detailed data. These problems of analysis and evidence have not, of course, prevented people from making far-reaching claims about the equity gains and efficiency losses of the welfare state, as can be seen above in the quotations from Crosland and Friedman. Such claims inevitably rest on a partial analysis of imperfect data, and sometimes on no analysis at all.

Efficiency effects

The criticisms of welfare expansion fall into two separate but related strands: that the tax and benefit system reduces the incentive for individuals to work and save, and that the supply of services by government is necessarily wasteful because government agents are not subject to the competitive pressures of the market. Both strands lead towards the conclusion that a reduction in the role of government and the level of taxes will increase the efficiency of the economy. This was a minority view in the 1950s and 1960s, although attempts were made within the Conservative Party to develop an alternative approach to social policy critical of the drift towards universal provision and re-emphasising the virtue of the insurance principle and the means test (Macleod and Powell 1952). The election of a Conservative government in 1951 led to the establishment of a whole series of policy reviews which were designed to curtail the creeping universalism and rising cost of health and welfare provision. By the late 1950s, however, electoral and administrative discontent with welfare budgets that were static or declining as a proportion of GNP, and social investigations which revealed extensive old age and child poverty, spurred governments to expand welfare state expenditure and provision (Glennerster 1990).

In the 1960s Labour and Conservative administrations were equally lavish towards the welfare state, but the economic stagnation and high inflation ushered in by the first oil price shock of 1973–4 forced a reassessment of the economic consequences of a growing public sector. Glennerster (1980: 15) has noted that while in the 1960s the social services were viewed as the handmaidens of a growing economy, by the mid-1970s they were labelled a 'burden'. Far from helping the government to manage the economy out of short-run difficulties in good Keynesian fashion, the social services were now seen to be hindering economic management because of the political and practical difficulties of cutting their budgets. Cuts were reluctantly imposed by the 1974–9 Labour government, particularly on the housing and education budgets (see Figure 10.4). The

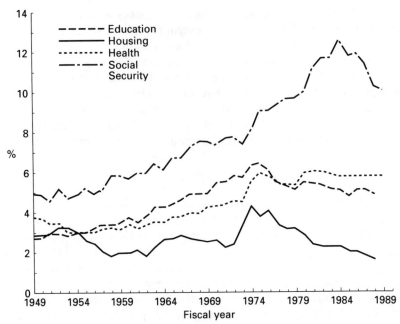

Figure 10.4 Social expenditure in the UK as a percentage of GDP,
1949–89
Source: Hills (1990).

result was that the growth rate of social expenditure fell abruptly, though
it remained just above the growth rate of GDP over the period 1975–81.
What was a reluctant retrenchment for Labour was a positive policy goal
for the Conservative Party under Margaret Thatcher. The first policy
statement on public spending issued by the Conservative government in
1979 was forthright: 'Public expenditure is at the heart of Britain's present
economic difficulties' (UK 1979), and much effort and even more rhetoric
in the following decade was devoted to 'rolling back the frontiers of the
state', including, of course, the welfare state.

This policy was based as much on faith as on fact. It was argued, for
instance, that the high taxes needed to pay for the welfare state reduce
work incentives, and thereby retard economic growth. It is certainly true
that an increase in the marginal tax rate will lower the opportunity cost of
leisure, so encouraging people to work less and play more (the substitution
effect). But it also lowers people's income, and so may induce them to work
harder in order to maintain their standard of living (the income effect).
Which effect will dominate is entirely an empirical question, and the
limited evidence for the UK is wholly inconclusive (Le Grand 1982: 148).

In the case of most cash benefits there is no ambiguity – an increase in benefits reduces work incentives, but how important the effect is for the economy as a whole is again an empirical question. Although much has been made of the possibility of some people being better off 'on the dole' rather than in work, the numbers so affected (as is shown below) are small and the aggregate effect is probably minimal.

There may be more evidence to support the other strand of criticism – that the direct provision of services by the government involves gross inefficiency because of the absence of price signals and competitive market pressures (Minford 1991: ch. 7). This argument can apply only to services provided directly by the state (primarily health, education and housing), since cash transfers enable recipients to buy goods and services in the free market. As Figure 10.4 shows, cash transfers (usually given the generic name 'social security') have dominated social expenditure growth from the early 1970s to the mid-1980s, a consequence of rising unemployment rates. Public expenditure on directly supplied welfare services has actually declined as a proportion of GDP since the peak year of 1975 when it reached 14 per cent (Berthoud 1985: 7), and so any associated efficiency losses are likely to have declined in tandem. The magnitude of such losses is very difficult to estimate. Bacon and Eltis (1976) believed that it was considerable both because public services were themselves inefficient and because they were too large, soaking up unproductive labour which the free market, if left to its own devices, would allocate to the more productive private sector. While this may have been true of non-welfare public services such as energy supply and transport, which could equally well be provided privately, there are good reasons, discussed in the next section, for believing that the health and education sectors may have been too small rather than too large.

The enormous practical difficulty of identifying and measuring the overall disincentive effects and inefficiencies of the welfare state has often led critics to adopt a more *ad hoc* approach based on the association between the late 1960s and the late 1970s of a rise in social expenditures and a corresponding decline in growth rates and increase in unemployment and inflation rates. The idea that rising social expenditure was a *source* of the economic problems moved from the extremist wings to centre-stage of economic analysis; the OECD gave its official sanction to this view with the publication in 1981 of a report on *The Welfare State in Crisis*.

This was a profoundly unhistorical document; although rapid growth of social expenditure was associated with poor economic performance in Britain and other OECD countries from the late 1960s, a longer-term analysis would have shown that the even faster rates of social expenditure growth from the 1950s to the mid-1960s were associated with the strongest and most sustained economic boom ever experienced by the developed economies (Johnson 1986). Somewhat embarrassed by its own lack of historical understanding, the OECD conducted an investigation into the longer-run development of social expenditures which 'failed to reveal an inverse relationship between public sector size and economic performance as reflected in GDP growth rates, unemployment levels and inflation rates, or between public sector growth and inflation rates' (OECD 1985b: 15). Between 1960 and 1981 the country with the highest growth rate of social expenditure, Japan, also had the highest annual growth rate of GDP, while the UK had the lowest growth rates of both GDP and social expenditure. Germany, the other star economic performer, had the highest share of social expenditure as a proportion of GDP of all the major OECD countries in both 1960 and 1981. At the level of casual empiricism allowed by this aggregate data, there appears to be little support for the hypothesis that public expenditure, and social expenditure in particular, was at the heart of Britain's economic difficulties. This does not mean that social expenditure has no macro-economic impact, but rather that its impact appears to be slight relative to the many other factors that determine the long-run performance of the economy.

Distributional effects

Supporters of the welfare state argue, however, that the distributional impact of social expenditure has been great, that it has scored a major success in increasing the equality of British society since 1945. The concept of equality is ambiguous and requires two separate issues to be considered – equality of what (for instance, income, wealth, consumption, life expectancy) and equality between whom (rich and poor, young and old, men and women, black and white, and so on). In practice most of the claims about the distributional successes of the post-war welfare state relate to the income of rich and poor either in terms of a more equal distribution of income or in terms of an absolute reduction of poverty. It should be noted that these policy goals are quite distinct; a redistribution of income from very rich to moderately rich will make the overall distribution of income more equal, but will do nothing to alleviate the poverty of the poorest.

It is clear that Beveridge had in mind the prevention of poverty rather than the redistribution of income as the primary goal of social insurance when he put forward his proposals in 1942. Benefits were to be limited to a subsistence level and the flat-rate basis of contribution meant that redistribution would occur only to the extent that the incidence of the insurance contingencies (sickness, unemployment, disability and old age) varied between income groups.

It seemed in the immediate post-war period that the welfare state had indeed succeeded in preventing poverty. Seebohm Rowntree published a third poverty survey of York in 1951 which showed only 3 per cent of the population living in poverty, compared with 31 per cent in his inter-war study and 30 per cent in his original investigation in 1899 (Rowntree and Lavers 1951). But this was a false dawn. In the mid-1960s social researchers discovered widespread poverty in many families with dependent children and among pensioner households, two groups who were specifically supported by the welfare state through the payment of family allowances and old age pensions (Abel-Smith and Townsend 1965). Subsequent studies (Townsend 1979; Fiegehen *et al.* 1977) found that poverty continued to be a major social problem throughout the 1960s and 1970s, despite the rapid growth of social expenditure, and a survey of evidence in 1987 concluded 'that the burden of poverty has increased grotesquely over the last eight years' (Piachaud 1987: 26). The number of people receiving means-tested benefits because of poverty doubled from 1 to 2 million between 1948 and 1966, and doubled again to reach over 4 million in the deep recession of the early 1980s, with many more living on incomes only marginally above this poverty threshold. Digby (1989: 68, 107) summarises the pessimistic view by concluding that, in 1983, 16.3 million people in the UK lived in households on or just above the poverty line (defined as incomes of no more than 140 per cent of the supplementary benefit level) – almost one in three of the population. Yet a prominent Conservative politician, Sir Keith Joseph, confidently claimed in 1979 that 'by any absolute standard there is very little poverty in Britain today' (Joseph and Sumption 1979: 27).

Joseph viewed poverty as an absolute condition: a lack of the food, clothing and shelter necessary for survival. Since there are very few people starving on the streets there is, by this definition, very little absolute poverty in Britain. But the Royal Commission on the Distribution of Income and Wealth (1978: 3) noted that the poverty line 'is now generally accepted as a standard which changes with the general standard of living in society'; in other words, poverty is usually regarded as a relative concept, so that in a wealthy society people can be considered poor long before they are destitute. A shift from an absolute (subsistence) definition to a relative definition of poverty during a period of increasing average living standards involves 'moving the goal posts' in a way that is likely to increase the numbers falling into the poverty net.

This is what has happened since the Second World War; Atkinson (1989: 49–50) shows that poverty standards have risen significantly in real terms over the last fifty years, though because of the way different types of household are treated by the social security system, the increase for pensioners has been greater than that for families with children, which has been greater than the minimal gain for single persons. The shift of the official poverty line away from Beveridge's subsistence concept to a relative concept came in 1959 with an announcement that national assistance recipients would be given a share in increasing national prosperity (Atkinson 1991). Through the 1960s both national insurance and means-tested cash benefits were increased roughly in line with average earnings, although there was a pronounced jump in the value of pensions relative to earnings in the mid-1970s which was maintained for almost a decade. For unemployment and supplementary benefits, increases in the 1970s broadly maintained their relation to net earnings, but the relative values of both pensions and other cash benefits have declined from the early 1980s as the Conservative government has explicitly returned to the practice of increasing benefits in line with prices rather than earnings (Barr and Coulter 1990: 304–7).

If the official poverty line today were drawn at the income level equivalent to Beveridge's subsistence income, adjusted only for price inflation over the intervening five decades, then the number of households found to be living in poverty would be very small. But these households would be much more deprived today, according to advocates of relative poverty concepts, than would their equivalents in 1948, because to participate fully in the community's style of living today requires more resources than it did in 1948 (Townsend 1979: 249). Access to a car, a telephone or a television are requirements for general participation in normal social and economic life in a way in which they clearly were not in the immediate post-war years. Once a relative definition of poverty is accepted as the appropriate one, however, enormous scope emerges for argument over the setting of the relativities and over the true extent of need, since the number of people living in poverty will come to be determined by administrative definitions of subsistence income. If we simply take the size of the population in receipt of or eligible for means-tested state benefits as a measure of the extent of poverty, then there was unequivocally more poverty in Britain in 1990 than in 1948, despite the overall rise in average income in the intervening period and the great growth of social expenditure.

This conclusion at first sight seems to confirm the argument that the welfare state has done very little except consume enormous resources in a vastly inefficient bureaucratic merry-go-round. Yet critical assessments of the administrative costs of the entire cash benefit system have shown them to be only 4.6 per cent of total payments in 1971/2 and 4.2 per cent in 1981/2 (Dilnot et al. 1984: 44). To see more clearly what has happened to welfare state resources it is necessary to shift focus from the incomes of the

Table 10.2. *Distribution of personal income, 1949 to 1976–7 (%)*

Income group	1949	1959	1967	1976–7
Before income tax				
Top 1 per cent	11·2	8·4	7·4	5·6
2–10 per cent	22·0	21·0	20·6	20·4
11–20 per cent	14·1	15·1	15·2	16·1
21–30 per cent	11·2	12·6	12·6	13·3
31–40 per cent	9·6	10·7	11·1	11·1
41–50 per cent	8·2	9·1	9·1	9·2
51–100 per cent	23·7	23·1	24·1	24·5
Gini coefficient	41·1	39·8	38·2	36·6
After income tax				
Top 1 per cent	6·4	5·3	4·9	3·5
2–10 per cent	20·7	19·9	19·4	18·9
11–20 per cent	14·5	15·7	15·2	15·9
21–30 per cent	11·9	12·9	13·0	13·4
31–40 per cent	10·5	11·2	11·0	11·3
41–50 per cent	9·5	9·9	9·7	9·4
51–100 per cent	26·5	25·0	26·8	27·6
Gini coefficient	35·5	36·0	33·5	31·5

Source: Royal Commission on the Distribution of Income and Wealth 1977, Report 5.

poor to the distribution of taxes and benefits across the whole of the population. Supporters of the welfare state claim it has played a major role in promoting equality by redistributing from rich to poor. This is an unexceptional claim; because taxes are progressive the rich pay more and because many benefits are means tested, the poor receive more. The important issue, however, is whether the proportionate redistribution away from the rich and to the poor has increased as social expenditures have grown since 1948.

Table 10.2 presents data on the distribution of personal incomes in the UK before and after income tax for selected years from 1949 to 1976–7. Two features are immediately apparent: first, the share of before-tax income received by the top 1 per cent of earners fell dramatically between 1949 and 1976–7, and second, the income tax system consistently worked to reduce the share of after-tax income received by the top 1 per cent. These two features are captured by changes in the Gini coefficient, a summary measure of distributional equality. A coefficient of 0 indicates absolute equality (the top 1 per cent and bottom 1 per cent and all percentiles in between each receive 1 per cent of total income), while a coefficient of 100 indicates complete inequality (the top 1 per cent receive all the income, the rest getting nothing). The decline of the Gini coefficient of both before- and after-tax income between 1949 and 1976–7 shows that the distribution became more equal over time, and the fact that for each year the after-tax Gini coefficient was always below the before-tax figure shows that the income tax system was consistently redistributive. But nearly all this equalisation occurred within the top half of the distribution, with transfers over time going from the top 10 per cent (and especially the top 1 per cent) of income units to those in the next 40 per cent. The before-tax income share of the poorest half of the distribution fell slightly between 1949 and 1976–7; the after-tax income share showed a barely perceptible rise.

An assessment of the affect of income tax alone on the income distribution cannot capture the full effect of the welfare state, which also involves indirect taxes and non-cash benefits. Table 10.3 presents the Gini coefficients at five different stages of the tax/benefit system for the period 1975–87, and Figure 10.5 shows the effect of each of these stages for households in different quintiles of the income distribution in 1987. All five groups of households in Figure 10.5 experienced an increase in income from cash benefits (moving from *original* income to *gross* income), a consequence of non-means-tested benefits being paid to all households regardless of their original income. Poorer households, however, also receive means-tested benefits, so it is the lowest quintile that experiences the largest proportionate and absolute increase in moving from original to gross income.

The Gini coefficient for gross income was therefore below that for original income since the distribution of gross income was more equal. All five household groups then experience a decline in income, because they move from *gross* income to *disposable* income, as they all pay some direct tax, though since the richest pay most the Gini coefficient continues its fall from gross to disposable income definitions. Household income continues to fall as indirect taxes are imposed (a move from *disposable* income to *post-tax* income), but indirect taxes, being flat-rate, tend to have a higher incidence for poorer households (they reduce the income of the lowest quintile by around one quarter, of the highest quintile by less than one fifth). They therefore make the distribution of income less equal, so the Gini coefficient is higher for post-tax than for disposable income. All households then benefit by roughly the same absolute amount through the receipt of services in kind, and as the proportionate value is greater for low-income families, the Gini coefficient for *final* income is below that for *post-tax* income.

All five income quintiles make direct and indirect tax contributions to the welfare state and enjoy benefits in cash and kind, and these tax and

Table 10.3. *Gini coefficients for the distribution of income at each stage of the tax-benefit system, 1975–87*

Gini coefficients (%)	1975	1979	1983	1987
Original income	43	45	49	52
Gross income	35	35	36	40
Disposable income	32	33	33	36
Post-tax income	33	35	36	40
Final income	31	32	33	36

Source: Economic Trends 1990: no. 439, 118.

benefit effects together make the distribution of final income considerably more equal than the distribution of original income. But there is little sign that the *expansion* of the welfare state over time has promoted *greater* equality. The gross income and disposable income definitions in Table 10.3 are roughly equivalent to the before-tax and after-tax definitions in Table 10.2, and comparing the Gini coefficients for the whole post-war period suggests that the final income distribution in the UK in 1987 was almost exactly the same as in 1949. There has been some slight move towards equality up to 1975 and away from it since then. Table 10.3 shows that the drift towards greater inequality since the mid-1970s was due to changes in original income rather than to changes in the structure of taxes and benefits, the main cause being the substantial increase in unemployment since the late 1970s (Nolan 1987: 150–1).

Neither the poverty nor the income distribution evidence provides much support for Crosland's assertion that social expenditure and social equality are intimately linked. The enormous growth of social expenditure since the Second World War does not appear to have reduced relative poverty or promoted greater income equality. Nor do the aggregate and comparative data on growth rates of social expenditure and GDP provide clear support for the argument that expansion of the welfare state in Britain has sapped incentives and retarded economic growth. Yet individual elements of the welfare state could have had strong and possibly conflicting distributional or incentive consequences for sub-groups of the population which have either cancelled each other out or have been too small to be observed in aggregate data. In order to identify such effects it is necessary to look at each part of the welfare state in turn.

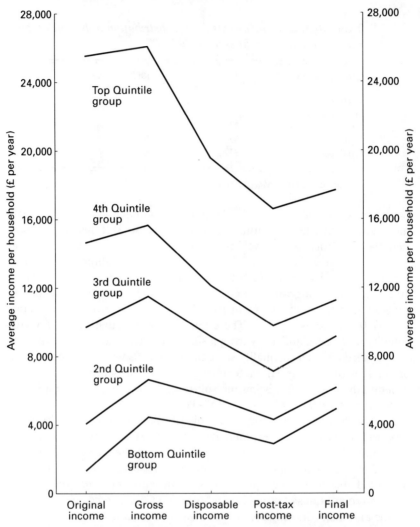

Figure 10.5 The effects of taxes and benefits on quintile groups of households, 1987

Original income   = employment and investment income before government intervention
Gross income   = original income plus cash benefits
Disposable income = gross income minus direct taxes
Post-tax income   = disposable income minus indirect taxes
Final income   = post-tax income plus benefits in kind (e.g. health, education)

Source: Economic Trends 1990: no. 439, 88.

Micro-economic impact of the welfare state

In 1942 Beveridge identified five giant evils – disease, ignorance, squalor, idleness and want – which it was the purpose of social insurance to destroy. These five evils have been matched by welfare state expenditure in the areas of health, education, housing, employment and income support

Disease and health

The National Health Service (NHS) came into operation in July 1948 to provide comprehensive health care and treatment which would be free at point of use and financed from general tax revenue. According to Aneurin Bevan, the Minister of Health in the post-war Labour government, 'a free health service is pure socialism and as such it is opposed to the hedonism of capitalist society' (Bevan 1952: 81). The clear intention was to provide equality of access to health care and to promote equality of health. Although direct charges have been introduced for some minor parts of the health service (prescription charges, for instance, were introduced in 1951, abolished in 1965, reimposed in 1968) medical consultation and treatment remains free, so equality of access has been achieved. But consumer demand has not been satisfied; queues for treatment, particularly for 'non-urgent' surgery, have been a constant reminder of health service 'failure'. Although the share of GDP spent on health care has risen by around 50 per cent since 1951 (Figure 10.4), it has consistently grown at a slower rate than total social expenditure (Table 10.1). In the 1980s there was a *perceived* decline in the resources available to the NHS, although in practice real spending on health grew at 2.8 per cent per annum between 1979 and 1987 compared with 1.6 per cent per annum for real GDP (Hills 1987: 89). But demographic pressure from the rising number of very elderly patients, medical pressure from the development of new and expensive treatments and rising expectations of treatment and service from the public together have meant that increased health service expenditure has not kept pace with demand.

This excess demand is to some extent a function of free access – under the NHS anyone can make their implicit demand for health care effective simply by visiting a doctor for an initial consultation and if necessary by being put on a waiting list for further treatment. Under a free market system the implicit demand can be made effective only by those who can afford to buy access to medical services; the implicit demand of the rest goes unnoticed and untreated. The two different systems of rationing – by queue or by price – involve different costs borne by different groups, and judgements about their relative merit are more likely to be determined by moral and political than by economic arguments. Public opinion polls in the 1970s and 1980s have consistently found very strong support throughout the British population for the principle of a free NHS funded by general tax revenue (Taylor-Gooby 1985). And two detailed official enquiries into the operation of the NHS, the Guillebaud Committee in 1956 and the Royal Commission on the National Health Service in 1979, concluded that in the main the service provided value for money (Klein 1983).

This generally positive judgement of NHS performance has been tempered by enduring criticisms about the structure of the system. In order to secure the grudging support of the doctors' trade organisation, the British Medical Association, and the hitherto independent voluntary hospitals, the 1946 National Health Service Act enshrined a tripartite administrative division between the family practitioner, hospital and local authority health services, which allowed each a large degree of financial and managerial autonomy (Webster 1988). This framework also encouraged an inefficient use of resources, particularly in the hospital sector where many high-cost beds were filled with long-term or convalescent patients who required less intensive care and who could benefit from a less institutional environment. A unification of the administrative structure in 1974, together with the closure of many small hospitals, certainly improved efficiency – between 1959 and 1989 the number of beds fell from 455,000 to 283,000, while the average length of stay in hospital fell from forty-five days in 1951 to fourteen days in 1988 (Scrivens 1991: 34). Meanwhile, however, staff numbers have more than doubled to reach almost 1 million, making the NHS the largest single employer in Europe.

Despite this rise in the number of medical and support staff and the long-run increase in real resources, in comparison with health care systems in other countries the NHS appears consistently to have been kept short of funds by successive governments, both Labour and Conservative. Total expenditure on health as a proportion of national income in Britain has been below the OECD average since 1960, and the gap has widened over time. In 1982 the UK spent 5.9 per cent of GNP on health; by contrast the US spent 10.6 per cent, Germany 8.2 per cent, France 9.3 per cent, Spain 6.3 per cent (OECD 1985a: 12). Since these large differences in average per capita health spending do not appear to be related to national differences in life expectancy, the low spending and resource constraints on health care in Britain can be interpreted as much as a sign of macro-efficiency as of allocative failure.

In one respect, however, the NHS may have failed in its original intention to bring about equality of health in Britain. Although life expectancy has continued to rise in the post-war period, *class* differentials in mortality rates appear to have widened since the establishment of the NHS rather than narrowed (Black 1980). On the other hand, dispersion around the mean individual age of death has narrowed since the mid-1970s, indicating greater equality of life expectancy between *individuals* (Le Grand *et al.* 1990: 128–9). It is still the case, however, that rates of both mortality and morbidity (sickness) for unskilled manual workers are considerably above the population average and, for professional workers, below the average. This probably has little to do with the NHS; inequalities in health are a function of many factors including low income, and as we have already seen, income inequality has not narrowed over time.

Ignorance and education

State funding and direct provision of education in Britain dates from 1870, and the 1944 Education Act can best be seen as an incremental development of a well-established system. Public expenditure on education as a share of GNP in Britain since the 1950s has been close to the average for the seven major OECD countries, but strong arguments have been made that the educational system has failed to achieve both efficiency and equality.

Since there is no convincing way of measuring the quality of output of the educational system, assessment of efficiency is very much a matter of judgement. There is considerable evidence to suggest that young adults in Britain are not as well trained as their counterparts in other developed countries (Prais 1988), but this may be a consequence of employers failing to train their workers rather than schools failing to educate their pupils. There is no doubt, though, that in the tertiary education of twenty- to twenty-four-year-olds, Britain has increasingly lagged behind her competitors. Between 1960 and 1980 the proportion of this age group enrolled in tertiary education in Britain rose from 9 to 20 per cent, in Japan from 9 to 30 per cent, in Germany from 6 to 28 per cent, in the US from 32 to 57 per cent (Heller *et al.* 1986: 69). This low enrolment has not led to low expenditure, because the cost per student has been high. In 1980 expenditure per tertiary student in Britain equalled 62 per cent of average per capita income, compared with 30 per cent in the US and 37 per cent in Japan, though the German figure was 61 per cent. By this measure, therefore, higher education in the UK is less efficient than in most other developed countries. Whether a higher quality of product justifies the higher unit cost is difficult to discern. It has been claimed that 'from an economic point of view Britain's educational provision during the postwar period has been little short of disastrous. Both in quantity and quality there has been a shortfall compared with other countries' (Aldcroft 1990: 239). But until the contribution of education to economic growth can be more accurately identified and measured, such sentiments will remain a matter of speculation.

The failure of educational spending to achieve educational equality in the post-war period is more a matter of fact. Among the pre-welfare state cohort of boys reaching age twenty between 1933 and 1942, 1 per cent of working-class boys and 7 per cent of middle-class boys entered university. For the cohort reaching age twenty between 1963 and 1972 these figures had risen to 3 per cent and 26 per cent respectively; both the proportionate and the absolute increase was greater for middle-class children (Halsey *et al.* 1980: 188). Such class inequalities in access to higher education are not unique to Britain, but the small size of this sector in Britain makes the access particularly restrictive for lower-class children. Access to post-school education is rationed by competitive examinations at age eighteen and working-class children have a much lower chance even of sitting the exams because of their low rate of continuation in school beyond the minimum school leaving age.

This inequality was to some extent a structural consequence of the post-war secondary education system, in which pupils were tested at age eleven, with the 'bright' children going to grammar schools, the 'non-academic' majority going to secondary modern schools. Dissatisfaction with the rigidity and divisiveness of this system, together with a commitment to extending equality of opportunity, led the Labour government in 1965 to attempt to replace grammar and secondary modern schools with non-selective 'comprehensive' schools. By 1986 almost all state school pupils in Scotland and Wales and 85 per cent of those in England were in comprehensive schools. The reforms of the 1960s do appear to have had some impact on educational performance and equality, with average ability pupils benefiting most from the introduction of comprehensive schooling (Glennerster and Low 1990: 55–75). It is still true, however, that at all stages of the education system the cost of continued education is greater for people from working-class families (Le Grand 1982: 63); low income again seems to be a determining factor.

Squalor and housing

At the end of the Second World War there was an acute housing shortage in Britain, the result of wartime destruction and an absence of new building since 1939. In July 1945 both major political parties promised the electorate better housing conditions; the Labour government put promises into practice by launching a major public sector house-building programme which was continued by the Conservatives after their 1951 election victory. Because of the acute post-war shortage of construction materials, private building was severely restricted and public residential construction was seen as a way of allocating scarce resources to maximise social returns. After 1954 licensing restrictions on private construction were removed, but public expenditure on the building and maintenance of the publicly owned housing stock ('council houses') continued at around 2 per cent of GNP, rising somewhat from 1964 on the election of a Labour government committed to improving public housing, and rising again for the same reason in 1974 (Figure 10.4). The constraints on public expenditure imposed by macro-economic problems from 1975, and the policy preference of the Conservative government since 1979 to reduce the size of the public housing sector has produced an almost continuous decline in housing expenditure since 1975.

The size and the quality of the housing stock have both increased in the post-war period. The housing shortage of the early 1950s had been transformed into a surplus by 1976, the number of households lacking basic amenities had plummeted (for instance, 38 per cent lacked a fixed bath or shower in 1951, 12 per cent by 1971, only 2 per cent by 1986), and the biggest improvements were experienced by poorer working-class families (Wicks 1987: 118–19). Much of this was a direct consequence of subsidised public housing which enabled poorer families to move out of low-quality private rented accommodation. Between 1951 and 1981 council housing increased from 17 per cent to 31 per cent of the total housing stock of England and Wales while private rented housing declined from 52 per cent to 12 per cent. The decline of the private rented sector was not simply a consequence of declining demand; supply fell sharply as rent controls, in existence since 1915 but more effective after the 1965 Rent Act, made private rental uneconomic. Many landlords sold their properties; the rest had little incentive to improve the quality of accommodation since they could not recoup the capital expenditure by charging higher rents. The third part of the housing stock, owner-occupied property, rose from 31 per cent to 57 per cent of the total in the thirty years from 1951, and had further increased to 65 per cent by 1988, partly as a result of the Thatcher governments' policy of selling council houses to their tenants (Central Statistical Office 1990). Property ownership has also been encouraged throughout the post-war period by granting tax relief on mortgage interest payments and by exempting housing from capital gains tax. In 1986–7 the cost of this tax relief to the Exchequer was £7.3 billion, almost twice the UK public housing budget.

If the 'fiscal welfare' of tax relief is included in an assessment of housing policy, then it seems clear that the post-war policy has increased inequality since owner-occupiers receive a greater subsidy than do tenants, and rich owner-occupiers have received the largest subsidy because the tax relief is worth most to those paying higher rates of income tax. Le Grand (1982) has estimated that in 1977 the housing subsidy received by households in his top income group was almost double that received by the lowest income group. Housing policy has also unquestionably reduced the efficiency of the housing market. The quality and quantity of private rented accommodation has been driven down by rent controls, the price of owner-occupied property has been artificially inflated by tax subsidies and the very localised system by which council housing is allocated restricts labour mobility.

Idleness and employment

The wide-ranging nature of employment policy in the post-war period is analysed in detail in chapter 7 so the discussion here is confined to the equity and efficiency consequences of the national insurance unemployment benefit. Since 1948 this benefit has been paid as an insurance entitlement for up to twelve months to unemployed workers with an appropriate contribution record. When drawing up his report in 1942, Beveridge assumed a future unemployment rate of 8.5 per cent which proved to be unduly pessimistic, but he also assumed that this unemployment would be almost entirely of short duration, which turned out to be unduly optimistic. A significant (and since the 1970s a growing) proportion of the unemployed has had to rely on National Assistance/supplementary benefit either because they have had an inadequate contribution record or because they have been unemployed for over a year. In 1975–6, one third of the unemployed did not qualify for unemployment benefit and received means-tested supplementary benefit alone. By 1983–4 the enormous rise of unemployment in general and long-term unemployment in particular meant that over half the unemployed did not qualify for unemployment benefit and had to rely solely on means-tested supplementary benefit. Over this nine-year period total expenditure on supplementary benefits for the unemployed rose three times as fast as expenditure on unemployment benefits (Creedy and Disney 1985: 104). The rapid growth of social security expenditure from the early 1970s to 1984 shown in Figure 10.4 was, therefore, largely a function of rising unemployment which greatly increased expenditure on both national insurance and means-tested benefits for the unemployed. The improvement in employment opportunities in the latter part of the 1980s led to a significant reduction in social security benefit expenditure.

There is little doubt that these cash transfers promote equality between rich and poor, but it is frequently claimed that they significantly reduce work incentives by paying people to remain idle. This belief lay behind the thirty-eight or more important changes made between 1979 and 1988 to benefits for the unemployed, changes which have resulted in a substantial reduction in national insurance benefits for people out of work (Atkinson 1989: ch. 8). The potential financial attraction of unemployment has been reduced; in 1968 one in three workers suffering a thirteen-week period of unemployment received benefit payments equal to or greater than 90 per cent of their previous employment income, but by 1978 this number had fallen to one in five, and by 1983 it was only one in thirty-five (Dilnot *et al.* 1984: 59). How much effect these reductions in the value of benefits relative to earnings have had on the numbers of unemployed or the duration of unemployment is unknown. After surveying the econometric studies, Atkinson (1987) has concluded that the lack of robustness in the results means that the conclusions drawn are largely dependent on the prior beliefs of the investigators.

Want and income support

Support for the unemployed is just one element of the extensive system of social security cash benefits that has dominated welfare state expenditure since the Second World War. Cash benefits themselves have been dominated by old age pensions which have consistently accounted for around half of all social security expenditure since 1948 (Johnson and Falkingham 1988: 141). Income support for families has also been a major item, with child benefit accounting for around 20 per cent of social security expenditure (Barr and Coulter 1990: 288). Although old age pensions are a national insurance benefit, whereas child benefit is paid for out of general tax revenue, neither of them are means tested. Because they are paid to all households containing people in the relevant age group their total cost is high, but because of their universal and automatic coverage their role in relieving poverty is considerable. Many of the means-tested elements of the income support system such as supplementary benefits, rent and rate rebates have had low take-up rates, possibly because of ignorance of entitlements, stigma associated with having to ask for public assistance, complicated claims procedures which deter applicants, or because of a 'poverty trap' created by the interaction of means tests and tax liabilities (Barr and Coulter 1990: 296–302; Deacon and Bradshaw 1983).

The criticism that because of low take-up rates means-tested benefits do not adequately relieve poverty is valid, but universal benefits may also perform poorly because of their institutional rigidity. Eligibility for the most important universal benefits – pensions and child benefit – is determined predominantly by age. If age is a strong correlate of need, then age-determined universal benefits will be an effective way of relieving poverty. This was certainly the case with the retirement pension after the Second World War, since almost all elderly people were poor. But poverty has become more diversified over time, with social categories not recognised in the Beveridge scheme being particularly subject to poverty. In the 1970s and 1980s single parents and juveniles and young adults living away from the parental home have constituted important groups of the 'new poor'. The social security benefits to which they are entitled are generally low, and although this is partly the result of a deliberate design to create strong incentives for these social groups to participate in the labour market, it is also a consequence of the rigidity of Beveridge's social categories, which assumed that mothers would reside with breadwinning fathers (and would gain their social security entitlements as unpaid houseworkers) and that older children would live with their parents until economically independent (Williams 1989).

Single parent families, a social category which in the period 1971–87 has increased from 8 per cent to 14 per cent of all families with dependent children (Central Statistical Office 1991: 38), seem to be particularly disadvantaged by social security rules. They frequently face 'multiple deprivation', experiencing low income, few employment opportunities, high food, clothing and housing costs, and often poor housing conditions, and so will receive a variety of benefits in cash and kind relating to these various circumstances. However, the *ad hoc* way in which many of these benefits have been amended or added to over time has resulted in them having different qualifying income limits. When poor families, in receipt of multiple benefits, increase their employment income they quickly lose benefits and become liable to income tax, so that they face marginal tax rates over 70 per cent. In addition, single parents who re-enter the labour market have to buy child care out of their taxed income, with the result that their disposable income can be significantly lower if they engage in paid employment. Dilnot *et al.* (1984: 56) have shown that in 1983 the net income of a family with two children remained virtually constant at £110 per week when its employment income rose from £50 to £120 per week. Such a family was caught in a poverty trap created by the social security and tax system from which it could not escape by its own efforts without an improbable leap to a much higher income bracket.

Benefit changes in the 1980s have reduced the severity of the poverty trap for some low-income households, but little has been done to assist the growing number of poor single women with dependent children. In fact the proportion of single parents living in poverty rose from 47 per cent in 1979 to 64 per cent in 1985 (Barr and Coulter 1990: 309). There is considerable disagreement about the macro-economic significance of the work disincentives which are created by poverty traps and social security entitlements, but the best guess is that it is relatively slight. Only 3.5 per cent to 4.5 per cent of tax units are affected by the poverty trap (Atkinson 1989: 184), and any work disincentive will have diminished over the decade since 1977 as the standard rate of supplementary benefit has fallen from over 17 per cent to under 14 per cent of average adult male earnings (Barr and Coulter 1990: 307).

Although much attention has been devoted to investigating the potential efficiency costs of the income support system, its greater failing has been in the field of the alleviation of poverty. The inability of means-tested benefits to reach between a quarter and a half of those eligible has resulted in the *least* redistributive cash benefits, universal old age pension and child benefit, being among the most effective ways of alleviating poverty. Despite a great deal of discussion since the mid-1960s about how better to target income support, the lack of coordination between the income tax and social security systems, and the complex patchwork of universal and means-tested benefits has prevented an effective and consistent targeting of benefits to the most needy.

Efficiency, equity and the economy

At the micro-economic level the theoretical costs of the welfare state in adversely affecting economic efficiency can be clearly specified, but they can seldom be adequately measured. The efficiency impact of state intervention in the housing market seems to be unequivocally negative, though the cost in terms of macro-economic performance is quite unknown. Public provision of education and health care may have involved a misallocation of resources which has kept these sectors smaller than would have been the case under a free market. However, since the economic returns to education and health spending do not appear to be closely related to the level of aggregate spending, budget restrictions may have *promoted* macro-economic efficiency rather than retarded it. Empirical uncertainty about the efficiency impact of income support did not deter the Thatcher governments from a vigorous pursuit of greater work incentives for the poor. Since 1979 a multitude of restrictions to benefit entitlements and reductions in their value relative to average earnings, together with substantial income tax cuts for high earners, have been part of a deliberate design to restore the 'work ethic' (Walker and Walker 1987). This design is based more on vision and faith than on estimation and fact; economic evidence that the welfare state has retarded macro-economic performance since the Second World War is unconvincing.

The micro-economic analysis does, however, give some insight into the apparent paradox of why the enormous expansion of the welfare state since the 1940s has neither eradicated poverty nor further redistributed final income. First, many of the transfers effected through the welfare state involve only a limited degree of inter-class transfers. The majority of social security expenditure goes in universal cash benefits which can redistribute only to the extent that they are paid for disproportionately by the rich. Furthermore, many welfare benefits in kind, though apparently available to all, have in practice been 'captured' by the middle classes who make disproportionate use of them. Le Grand and Winter (1987) have estimated that only in the areas of council housing and rent allowances do welfare services favour the poor. And much of the redistribution that does take place occurs across generations but within the same families: from working age adults to their children (education, child benefit) and their parents (old age pensions, health care). It is obviously wrong, therefore, to see the growth of welfare spending since 1945 as a straightforward 'loss' to the economy, since it seems reasonable to presume that, in the absence of public provision, many households would have provided health care, education and income support for the young and the old through private agencies, and possibly in a less efficient manner.

Second, and more importantly, the underlying state of the economy and the nature and extent of social need were profoundly different in 1990 compared with 1948. The proportion of the population over pension age was under 13 per cent in 1948 but over 18 per cent in 1990, the unemployment rate was only 1.3 per cent when the post-war welfare state was inaugurated, but reached 12.4 per cent in the deep recession of 1983, the number of people receiving means-tested benefits because of their poverty rose from around 1 million in 1948 to almost 7 million by 1985. This enormous change in the economic and social structure of Britain since the Second World War, and particularly since the economic stagnation of the mid-1970s, is why the explicit commitment by Mrs Thatcher to roll back the frontiers of the state had only muted effect. Total taxes and social security contributions in 1987 represented 44 per cent of GNP, virtually the same level as in 1982 (45 per cent) and in 1970 (43 per cent) (*Economic Trends* 1978, 1990). The fact, therefore, that the distribution of final income in the late 1980s (as measured by the Gini coefficient) appears to be very similar to the distribution in the late 1940s is an indicator of the *success* of the welfare state in moderating the social and economic effects of much greater inequality in employment opportunities and earnings.

This success of the welfare state in relieving poverty and promoting equity is not unqualified, as the unsatisfactory treatment of single parent families demonstrates, but it is sufficient to attract broad public support for welfare state services and transfers, and for the concomitant level of taxation. As the inequities of the labour market have increased in the

1980s, so popular support for the public finance of welfare (as recorded in the British Social Attitudes Survey) has risen (Le Grand 1990: 355). This may reflect a little more altruism on the part of rich tax payers or a little more envy on the part of poor beneficiaries, but with only 3 per cent of respondents wishing to reduce taxes and benefits in 1987 it seems that the great majority of people in Britain regard the state as a worthwhile and efficient mechanism for providing social insurance and welfare services.

11   British economic decline since 1945

Barry Supple

On what principle is it that, when we see nothing but improvement behind
us, we are to expect nothing but deterioration before us?

(Macaulay 1829: 122)

Introduction

For almost exactly 100 years, the decline of the British economy has
provided fertile subject matter for journalists, politicians, social commentators and academic researchers. But it is only in the last thirty years or so
that the idea that Britain is in decline, possibly even heading for national
ruin, has dominated economic and political debate.

What is meant by 'decline' and how it is explained, are questions with
considerable historical resonance. On the one hand, the sense of potential
deterioration has, paradoxically, marched in step with Britain's industrial
evolution since the late eighteenth century. On the other, Britain's
experience and the responses to it are not unique: other nations – Venice in
the sixteenth century, Spain and Holland in the seventeenth century, the
United States since the 1960s – have experienced some sort of decline.

This chapter is, however, concerned less with comparative history than
with the general issues raised by Britain's economic performance since
1945, and more specifically with the fear and presumed symptoms of
national economic decline that have come to the surface in the last
generation.

One reason why this is an interesting as well as important topic is its
contradictory character: anxiety about decline has coincided with a period
of unprecedented growth. Indeed, in spite of Britain's unenviable reputation, national premonitions have been blatantly disproportionate to the
bare statistics of (relative or absolute) economic achievement.

Such contrasts raise intriguing questions about the meanings of
'decline'. In what senses has Britain suffered a serious or historically
significant deterioration? Why do people worry about relative accomplish-
ments? How are poverty and deprivation defined? How has the performance of the economy, in all its diversity, been perceived and explained?

318

Obviously, it will be necessary to cover again some of the ground discussed by earlier chapters in this volume which survey economic performance more broadly, or examine specific aspects of that performance or at the principal areas of policy. In contrast to these chapters, however, this one will examine rather disparate issues from a single perspective: the character of Britain's presumed decline and the anxieties which it has generated.

The meanings of decline

The most straightforward quantitative meaning of national economic decline is also the least commonly experienced: a sustained fall in the total or per capita output of goods and services. With the exception of very brief periods, that has not happened in Britain for 200 years or more.

More subtly and more realistically, decline can refer to a *retardation* in growth rates (output continues to grow, but at a slower rate than earlier). And that is, of course, a more familiar experience.

But the most common sense in which decline is discussed is in *relative* terms: the rate of growth, which may in fact be high by historical standards, is overtaken by that of other leading countries.

These statistical meanings have the advantage of being unambiguous – especially when the outcome of relative decline can be measured by an international comparison of growth rates or levels of income. But aggregate statistics of absolute and relative growth do not provide particularly sensitive indications of national economic progress or decline. For one thing, the adequacy of economic performance is partly a matter of realising what is imagined to be the national potential – even if this is neither a fixed level nor an objective concept. Thus an economy may be experiencing slower growth than others not because its institutions, techniques and attitudes are less efficient or buoyant, but because the countries that are growing faster have more and cheaper resources, or are 'catching-up' (closing a technological gap), or recovering from disruption caused by abnormal events (e.g. war), or making use of hitherto idle or low-productivity resources (e.g. a pool of underemployed agricultural labour – as was the case with France and Germany in the post-war years). In effect, then, assessments of apparent economic decline need to take some account of performance relative to what an economy 'should' be capable of achieving.

Of course, the preoccupations with success or failure transcend a country's position in a league table of production. The concept of 'decline' also raises broader questions of means and ends and national self-confidence. Thus a deterioration in performance may occur relative not merely to the past or to the achievement of other countries, but also to the aspirations of a society and its citizens. A country may be underperforming even if its rate of growth has not changed or is increasing, if critical aspects of its economy (prices or the balance of payments, for example) appear out of control or if it fails to provide resources sufficient to meet some more or less realistic set of national goals (generous allowances for one-parent families, more finance for schools and the National Health Service, better housing and more washing machines, a more effective navy and air force to sustain Britain's influence in the Falklands or the Middle East). And since such goals may well vary over time, as perceptions and aspirations change or as the example of other societies is observed, the sense of 'decline' will fluctuate independently of purely objective measures of productivity and output. Certainly, that appears to have happened in Britain's case over the last two centuries.

Finally, it is important to bear in mind that 'decline' may be perceived in terms not simply of macro-economic performance, but of inadequate achievement in areas where the economy was once dominant or outstanding, or of disconcerting patterns of structural change. The great staple industries – coal, iron and steel, cotton, shipbuilding – may collapse; manufacturing competitiveness may deteriorate; the industrial sector may shrink; technological leads (the jet engine, electronics, computers, machine tools) may be lost. Decline may therefore be perceived not merely as the aggregate outcome of economic activity, but in terms of the way in which an economy operates (or fails to operate). This is the case even though the actual *workings* of an economy are more properly to be considered as symptoms and causes of economic performance: if the rate of growth of output and income were satisfactory, there would no doubt be less reason to complain about such matters as the rise and decline of particular industries or sectors of the economy.

Measuring Britain's economic performance

When Britain's economic performance since 1945 is compared solely with what went before, the picture is one of progress rather than decay. As Table 11.1 shows, over the last two centuries national income (gross domestic product) has grown at about 2 per cent per annum. But within this long-run average, growth accelerated (albeit mildly) – from just under 2 per cent in 1873–1913, to just over 2 per cent in the years 1924–37 (i.e. in peacetime years, less affected by the two world wars), and to almost 3 per cent in the period 1951–73. Similarly, the rate of growth of GDP per capita

Table 11.1. *Annual growth rate, British GDP, 1856–1973 (%)*

	GDP	GDP per capita
1856–1973	2·0	1·2
1856–73	2·4	1·2
1873–1913	2·0	0·9
1913–24	−0·1	0·3
1924–37	2·2	1·8
1937–51	1·8	1·0
1951–73	2·8	2·4

Source: Matthews *et al.* (1982: 22).

Table 11.2. *Annual growth rate, GDP, 1870–1984 (%)*

	Change between periods					
	I 1870/1913	II 1913–50	III 1950–73	IV 1973–84	II/III	III/IV
France	1·7	1·1	5·1	2·2	+4·0	−2·9
Germany	2·8	1·3	5·9	1·7	+4·6	−4·2
Japan	2·5	2·2	9·4	3·8	+7·2	−5·6
Netherlands	2·1	2·4	4·7	1·6	+2·3	−3·1
UK	1·9	1·3	3·0	1·1	+1·7	−1·9
Average	2·2	1·7	5·6	2·1	+4·0	−3·5
USA	4·2	2·8	3·7	2·3	+0·9	−1·4

Source: Maddison (1987: 650).

Table 11.3. *Annual growth rate, per capita GDP, 1960–87 (%)*

	1960–8	1968–73	1973–9	1979–87	1981–7	1960–87
UK	2·4	2·9	1·5	1·7	2·9	2·1
USA	3·1	1·8	1·4	1·2	1·6	1·9
Japan	9·3	6·8	2·5	3·1	3·0	5·5
Germany	3·2	4·0	2·5	1·6	1·9	2·7
France	4·2	5·0	2·6	0·9	1·1	3·0
Italy	5·0	3·9	2·1	1·5	1·3	3·1

Source: Meen (1988: xxiii).

rose from about 1 per cent in the late nineteenth century, to 1.8 per cent during the 'normal' inter-war years, and to just over 2 per cent in the decades after 1951. In spite of some retardation during the mid-1970s (when the absolute level of output continued to rise, but the rate of growth of per capita GDP fell back to just below the inter-war average), the recovery which characterised most of the 1980s meant that taken as a whole the post-war performance of the British economy continued to be an improvement on that of the nineteenth and early twentieth centuries: per capita GDP grew at 2.4 per cent annually in 1951–73 (Table 11.1) and at 2.1 per cent in 1960–87 (Meen 1988: xxiii) – although it should be noted that the annual rate of growth of GDP decelerated, from 2.4 per cent to 1.9 per cent, between 1969/79 and 1979/88 (Coutts and Godley 1989: 138).

The rate of growth of efficiency also increased after the Second World War, although the acceleration was not maintained. For example, the annual growth rate of UK total factor productivity (i.e. allowing for changes in the quantity and quality of labour and capital) has been estimated as 0.38 per cent in 1913–50, 1.53 per cent in 1950–73 and 0.64 per cent in 1973–84.

Indeed, as Table 11.1 shows, not only has British national income continued to grow over the last 200 years (with the exception of the period of economic dislocation around the First World War), but total and average incomes actually grew faster after the Second World War (i.e. precisely when complaints about decline have been at their most anguished) than during any other period since the industrial revolution.

On the other hand, this picture of long-run acceleration is put in a very different light when the British growth rate is compared with that of most other industrial countries. Indeed, during the post-war decades the British economy certainly did decline in relative terms: the rates of growth of its total and per capita GDP were persistently lower than those of its rivals (Tables 11.2 and 11.3); and its rate of productivity growth, although comparing favourably with that of the USA, was resoundingly exceeded by that of France, West Germany and Japan: in 1950–73 each of these three enjoyed an annual growth rate of total factor productivity of more than twice that of Britain (Crafts 1988: 5).

The inevitable result of these developments was a substantial fall in Britain's relative level of output per head (Table 11.4) and its standing as a world economic power. And although Britain's growth rate reached record heights during the three decades after 1950, this was also the period when the biggest gap opened up between its rate of expansion and that of other industrial countries.

As with all statistics of growth in national income and productivity, especially when they are used to compare different economies, these data

Table 11.4. *Levels of GDP, 1950–84 ($1984)*

	Per head of population				Per hour worked			
	1950	1960	1973	1984	1950	1960	1973	1984
France	4,147	5,933	10,514	12,643	4·54	6·95	14·31	20·78
Germany	3,600	6,985	10,899	13,267	3·67	7·13	13·94	19·28
Japan	1,486	3,136	8,987	12,235	1·51	2·70	8·39	11·85
Netherlands	4,884	6,703	10,581	11,710	6·17	8·62	16·77	20·72
UK	5,000	7,093	9,902	11,068	6·41	8·04	13·19	17·17
USA	8,261	9,608	13,741	15,829	10·93	13·98	19·16	21·31

Source: Maddison (1987: 683).

Table 11.5. *GDP per hour worked, 1870–1984 (UK = 100 in each year)*

	USA	France	Germany	Japan
1870	90	49	53	17
1913	105	50	58	19
1938	143	84	78	36
1950	171	71	57	24
1960	174	86	89	34
1973	145	108	106	64
1979	140	117	120	71
1984	124	121	112	69

Source: Crafts (1988: 3).

Table 11.6. *Rate of growth of productivity (real values added per employee) in manufacturing, 1960–85 (%)*

	1960–8	1968–73	1973–9	1979–85	1960–85
USA	3·2	3·8	0·9	3·5	2·8
Japan	9·0	10·4	5·0	6·3	7·7
Germany	4·7	4·5	3·1	2·4	3·7
France	6·8	5·8	3·9	n.a.	5·0
UK	3·4	3·8	0·6	3·7	2·9
Italy	7·2	5·6	2·9	3·0	4·8

Source: Meen (1988: xxvi).

Table 11.7. *Rate of growth of real output per person employed, 1873–1987 (% per annum)*

	UK	USA	Germany	Japan
1873–99	1·2	1·9	1·5	1·1
1899–1913	0·5	1·3	1·5	1·8
1924–37	1·0	1·4	3·0	2·7
1951–64	2·3	2·5	5·1	7·6
1964–73	2·6	1·6	4·4	8·4
1973–9	1·2	−0·2	2·9	2·9
1979–87	2·1	0·6	1·5	2·9

Source: Crafts (1988: 2).

need some care in interpretation. Nevertheless, a number of points about Britain's economic performance seem beyond dispute:

1. The post-war rate of growth, and the associated increase in living standards, were impressive, at least when judged by the standards of Britain's own economic history.

2. The growth rates of other economies (notably Japan, but also the leading countries of western Europe) was even more impressive, or at least greater – in some cases spectacularly so (Tables 11.2, 11.3, 11.6 and 11.7). However, the growth record of the United States economy was much more like the British than the Japanese or western Europe model. This situation may have reflected fundamental contrasts between different sorts of economies. But it may also have reflected the fact that Britain and the United States had already achieved a measure of economic maturity (McCloskey 1990: 40–55), so that other countries grew more rapidly in part because they were catching-up with the pioneers.

3. The inevitable outcome of these differential growth rates was a long-run decline in Britain's relative economic standing measured in terms of GDP per capita (Table 11.4). Average living standards, although rising throughout the period, were ultimately matched or overtaken by those of most of western Europe.

4. These aggregate statistics conceal striking sectoral changes – notably the relatively slow rate of expansion of manufacturing and manufacturing productivity in Britain (Tables 11.6 and 11.8), the eventual result of which was a dramatic fall in its share of world manufacturing output. That share was almost halved, although there is some disagreement about the absolute amounts: one (official) source estimates that the proportion fell from a fairly impressive 14 per cent in 1964 to barely 8 per cent in the early 1980s; another, however, suggests a fall from less than 7 per cent in 1964 to 4 per

Table 11.8. *Ratios of output per employee in manufacturing, 1951–87*

	1951	1964	1979	1987
USA:UK	2·73	3·04	2·99	2·80
West Germany:UK	0·77	1·10	1·39	1·13

Source: Crafts (1988: 2).

cent in 1980 (House of Lords 1985: 12; Bairoch 1982: 304). At the same time its share of global trade in manufactured products, which had been 30 per cent or more before the First World War, and regained that level during the immediate post-war export drive, fell from some 25 per cent in 1950 to 14 per cent in 1964, 9 per cent in 1973 and less than 8 per cent in the early 1980s (Matthews *et al.* 1982: 435; House of Lords 1985: 23). In the early 1980s Britain, to the consternation of many, became a net importer of manufactures. The fact that this could be in part 'explained' by the buoyancy of North Sea oil production and exports (the resulting strong pound made it more difficult to export other goods, and encouraged abundant imports) was relatively little compensation to those who found it difficult or painful to transfer their resources or skills into more remunerative uses. More generally, it was a cause for great anxiety for those who assumed that Britain's future prosperity depended on its role as a manufacturing nation – even though it is not obvious that a successful economy in the late twentieth century needs to do quite what a successful early nineteenth-century economy did.

5. Britain's relative decline after the early 1950s did not proceed at a steady pace. During the 1970s, as world economic growth slowed abruptly, Britain's growth rate did not fall as fast as some of its competitors, and during the 1980s its performance (in terms of per capita output and productivity) managed, albeit briefly, to rival or outpace those of many other industrial economies. The narrowing, and in many instances the reversal, of the productivity gap was proximately at least as much attributable to the deteriorating performance of others as to a trans-formation of Britain's efficiency. But the fact remains that, just as the British economy had not been able to take as much advantage as its rivals of the prolonged post-war boom up to the early 1970s, it seemed to be somewhat less constrained by the subsequent retardation in global growth (Table 11.2).

6. The mid-1980s appeared to be a period of outstanding improvement in British manufacturing productivity, leading some observers to talk of a

decisive British 'economic miracle'. Soon, however, more cautious assessments prevailed: the spurt in manufacturing productivity was not accompanied by an improvement in the rate of growth of output or GDP per head (Coutts and Godley 1989: 37); and in any case a sharp reduction in the pace of GDP growth occurred at the end of the decade, once again throwing into high relief the problems of manufacturing competitiveness and import penetration, together with those of an imbalance of trade. By 1990–2 the economy was in the grip of a severe recession and GDP fell.

7. On the other hand, the retardation of productivity growth in such economies as Germany and Japan during the 1970s and even more the 1980s resulted in a degree of convergence which suggests that important changes were taking place (Tables 11.3, 11.5–8) – even if the relevant changes were located in other economies than Britain's. There was certainly some evidence that as industrial economies matured their levels of productivity converged (Feinstein 1988).

The perception of economic decline

The central meaning of economic decline is undoubtedly derived from relative efficiency, competitiveness and international standing – from the sense of a loss of status as a world power and a leading industrial nation. But even the *economic* measure of performance cannot be approached solely in terms of rates of change in output and productivity. It must also be assessed in terms of an economy's presumed competitive outcomes, the structure and balance of its economic activity, the degree of stability and security afforded by economic processes, and the satisfaction of needs. These are in part matters of subjective perception; but they are nonetheless of great significance.

It so happens that economic pessimism has, however intermittently, accompanied much of Britain's economic progress over the last 200 years: Malthus' apprehensions about overpopulation at the end of the eighteenth century, the anxiety expressed by classical economists concerning the inevitability of stagnation, fears concerning the exhaustion of cheap coal supplies in the 1860s, intermittent gloom about the loss of Britain's industrial competitiveness from the late nineteenth century – all bore witness to the insecurity that could accompany economic success.

But the perception of decline that has increasingly characterised Britain since the 1940s has been both more general and more insistently fearful. Even so, these fears took time to appear: in spite of the austerity of the immediate post-war years, the first decade or so after the war was characterised by a sense of genuine accomplishment as output, trade and private affluence all increased. Dissatisfaction with the performance of the economy only arose tentatively in the course of the 1950s but more decisively in the 1960s.

That it did so then was no doubt partly due to the growing awareness (facilitated by the rising production of official statistics by international agencies) that other economies were now overtaking Britain. From the early 1960s, the sense of a threat to Britain's industrial standing was aggravated by abundant information concerning the superior growth performance of other countries. The anguish was sharpened by the obvious erosion of Britain's place as a world power, and both the economic and the political anxieties encouraged the swirling gloomy premonitions about the country's long-run prosperity.

Among the pessimists, there were increasing doubts about the future viability of much manufacturing. The industrial base of Britain's former economic supremacy appeared frail and uncompetitive, seemingly inadequate to the tasks of maintaining a vigorous and sustained national prosperity into an indefinite future. The perception of decline was therefore initially based on what seemed an unsatisfactory manufacturing performance and a serious structural imbalance – although, in the nature of such mild bouts of near panic, it was soon reinforced by more general fears about economic stability and viability, and by the frustration of collective and private aspirations.

Structural change and deindustrialisation

In recent decades, the most potent indicator of decline has been taken to be a dislocation in the balance of economic activity. Of course, if output, income and productivity are growing at rates judged to be both significant and satisfactory, the actual composition of output or the distribution of jobs and skills are the less important. On the other hand, it is possible that differential expansion or contraction in some activities and skills may have long-run consequences not reflected in current statistics of aggregate output. A major example of this sort of anxiety was the argument – much canvassed in the 1970s (Bacon and Eltis 1976) – that a shift of capital or labour into 'non-market' activities (in particular into the public sector) may place too great a burden on the market sectors and on a diminishing proportion of the workforce actually engaged in 'productive' activities. Here, in spite of the element of social choice (and therefore presumably satisfaction) involved in the growth of public services, economic utility is identified with output that is marketed commercially – and decline with the growth of government.

More cogently, however, the greater anxiety has been reserved for those

Table 11.9. *Annual average growth rate of sectoral labour
productivity (value added per person employed), 1950–73 (%)*

	Agriculture	Industry	Services
UK	4·6	2·9	2·0
France	5·9	5·2	3·0
Germany	6·3	5·6	2·8
Japan	7·3	9·5	4·0
Netherlands	6·0	5·6	1·8
USA	5·4	2·2	1·4

Source: Maddison (1987: 684).

structural changes which result in the reduced importance of employment
and/or output in the manufacturing sector – whether in absolute terms
(which is rare) or relatively, as compared with the service sector (which is
very common) (see also ch. 5).

Those who measure decline in terms of a fall in the relative size of the
manufacturing sector do so because they see industry as the primary source
of productivity gains, wealth and growth for the economy as a whole. On
this argument, the diversion of labour and capital into other sectors of the
economy will ultimately retard national efficiency and expansion, and
impair the country's international trading position.

During the last twenty years or so this process has been labelled
'deindustrialisation' by those who distrust its consequences. And it has
given rise to the fear that the long-term basis of Britain's prosperity would
be eroded by a reduction in the importance (usually the relative
importance) of industry, and the associated destruction of jobs, undermining of national efficiency, and the diminution of export potential. How
far have the presumed symptoms of such a process of deindustrialisation
been exemplified in recent British history?

Certainly, employment and output in manufacturing industry have
borne the brunt of economic fluctuations and adjustments. And, while
Britain's manufacturing productivity has grown much more slowly than
among her competitors (Tables 11.6 and 11.9), the proportion of the
employed labour force engaged in manufacturing, mining, construction
and public utilities fell from about 45 per cent in the early 1950s to about
38 per cent in 1981 (Rowthorn and Wells 1987: 10) while the proportion in
manufacturing alone, which had been about 35 per cent in the early 1960s,
was 26 per cent in 1981 and fell to 20 per cent and less by the end of the
1980s.

In fact, most of this decline came after the 1960s, and most dramatically in the early 1980s, when resources were squeezed out of manufacturing as the result of a severe slump, which was itself related to increasing exchange and interest rates. Sterling's 'strength' was in part the result of high rates of interest, but also (in the absence of countervailing government policies) of the growing production of North Sea oil. Both oil revenues and interest rates increased the attraction of sterling and enhanced export earnings so that manufactured imports became cheaper to British consumers, British manufactures became more expensive to foreign purchasers, and the incentive to export capital funds exceeded those to export manufactured goods. High interest rates also hindered manufacturing investment and profitability, thus further devastating the manufacturing sector.

As a result of this combination – reflected commercially in bankruptcies, streamlining and rationalisation – between 1978 and 1983 the country's manufacturing capacity fell by virtually 25 per cent (House of Lords 1985: 46) and employment in major companies shrank: between 1977 and 1983 British Steel shed 61 per cent of its labour force, British Leyland 53 per cent, British Shipbuilders 28 per cent, and a large number of major British firms (e.g. Courtaulds, Tube Investments, Dunlop, Talbot) each lost in excess of 50 per cent of its workforce.

Not surprisingly, such developments helped British industry to attain almost unprecedented rates of increase in labour productivity through the 1980s (about 4 per cent annually), although the 1979 level of total manufacturing output was not regained until late in the decade. Given (often unexamined) assumptions about the primacy of industrial activity, the sharp retardation of manufacturing growth and the fall in industrial employment confirmed those who identified decline with deindustrialis- ation, and deindustrialisation with a relatively large non-manufacturing sector. On the other hand, it remains to be seen whether the problems of manufacturing industry during the 1980s will prove to be handicaps for the future development of the economy, or will embody a rapid and therefore painful adjustment to a new balance of economic activity in a maturing society. This, however, is not to deny that the fall in manufacturing employment went far beyond what might have been provoked simply by changes in the balance of exports and imports. It seems likely that a degree of chronic industrial uncompetitiveness was also to blame. In any event, between 1966 and 1984 employment in industry (including mining, construction and public utilities) fell with gathering speed – from an all-time peak of 11.5 million to 7 million. In manufacturing the labour force plunged from 8.7 to 5.4 million (Martin and Rowthorn 1986: 2).

Nor were such aggregate changes the sole cause of alarm. The widespread anxiety about the health of industry was related to economic structures within manufacturing as well as between the manufacturing and service sectors as a whole. Within post-war British manufacturing, it has been increasingly argued, prosperity *may* be (temporarily) sustained by the growth of some industries, but the economy would ultimately suffer unless some way was found of fostering *sophisticated* industries, those using skilled labour and advanced techniques, those with high value added, and those likely to enjoy the most buoyant increases in international demand.

The decline, first of Britain's staple industries, and (even more important) then of industries of the second or third industrial revolutions – motor vehicles, machine tools, electrical engineering, electronic equipment, cameras, household durables – are offered as cogent arguments in favour of the view that the long-run basis of prosperity has, indeed, been eroded. And this is not simply a matter of trade competition and market shares, but of the deleterious effects of low-level activities on the national pool of human skills and capital, on research and development and training, and therefore on the potential for continued and diversified growth in the evolving manufacturing sector in the future.

By the same token, pessimists about structural deterioration point to the growth of services as an enfeebling rather than a strengthening factor as far as future rapid economic growth is concerned. First, not all services offer equal prospects of growth and income generation. Much of the expansion in service employment in recent years, for example, has been in relatively low value-added and unskilled occupations (retail distribution, catering and fast food services, cleaning, security, tourism), where the potential for cumulative expansion of productivity and national income is limited. Second, it is argued, it is misleading to imagine that 'services' and 'manufacturing' are distinct from and unrelated to each other. High value-added services, of the sort which can be traded internationally and provide the basis for cumulative expansion, need a sophisticated and vigorous manufacturing base. Thus, it is asserted, healthy service industries in such fields as information technology, computer software, advanced engineering design and consultancy, insurance, banking and the like cannot thrive and provide foreign exchange earnings on a competitive basis unless firmly rooted in the practices that make use of and generate them (Cohen and Zysman 1987).

In effect, runs the conclusion, the growth of British service-sector employment is not sufficient compensation for the reduced significance of British industry. As was argued in a pessimistic report from a House of Lords Committee in the mid-1980s, British economic decline is exemplified by virtue of the fact that 'manufacturing is vital to the prosperity of the country and that services, important as they are, are no substitute for manufacturing because they are too heavily dependent upon it and only 20 per cent are tradable overseas ... The Committee believe that expansion of

the manufacturing base is the principal means of achieving growth'
(House of Lords 1985: 41–3).

Paying our way and maintaining stability

Although the concern about industrial productivity and 'deindustrialisation' has been central to the debate about decline, it is far from the only
consideration. Another important manifestation of the putative weakness
of the economy has been identified with the problem of the nation 'paying
its way' – that is the tendency towards an unfavourable and unstable
balance of payments and a consequent weakness of sterling.

In practice, however, payments balances and exchange rates are
uncertain measures of economic processes. In the first case, the former can
be determined by (as well as determine) exchange rates. Secondly, the
demand and supply of currency which influence both payments balances
and exchange rates reflect not merely productive efficiency but also
patterns of savings and consumption, credit policies, wage bargaining and
costs, speculative capital movements and (most importantly in the case of
post-war Britain) the need to raise money overseas to fulfil political and
military ambitions and obligations. Hence, although the strengths and
weaknesses of the British economy were in part reflected in the course of its
payments balance and sterling's exchange rate – so was much besides.

But whatever their ultimate significance, balance of payments crises,
particularly in the 1960s and 1970s, were one element in a general sense of
economic insecurity which focussed on incipient inflation, lagging productivity and similar frictions and imperfections in the workings of the
economy. The feeling grew that the nation's economic destiny might be
beyond control – or, at least, that official policies were seriously mis-
directed (Gwyn 1980: 2–3). And the apparent inability of the economy to
expand without generating inflation and trade imbalances and threatening
financial instability was undoubtedly a persuasive symptom of weakness –
in productive potential as well as in structure (Coutts and Godley 1989:
150–1).

Indeed, in the 1970s the failure to control inflation, by undermining cost
competitiveness and severely constraining the power of governments to
initiate expansion, was the central emblem of the political economy of
Britain's relatively poor performance. And by the end of that decade,
although pessimism was not universal (Nossiter 1978), the augmentation
of economic difficulties by political tensions, bitter industrial disputes, and
the apparent threat of 'ungovernability', led to what appeared to many as
a chronic 'crisis of confidence', and with it an almost unreasoned fear of
some terminal disaster lying in wait for the economy (Hutber 1978;

Kramnick 1979). Yet this apocalyptic interpretation of Britain's problems was, almost literally, irrational: no good reason has ever been offered for assuming that relatively slow growth will give way to absolute decline.

Relative deprivation

The presumed symptoms of decline are not, of course, confined to Britain's international status or the small size of its industrial sector or the course of its exports, imports and prices. There is also the vital question of how far the economy succeeds in supplying the perceived material needs of its population. Here the problem is that there is no adequate objective definition of 'need'. Rather, perceptions of affluence or poverty, material privilege or deprivation are the product of comparison, experience and expectation. A sense of poverty or decline – for individuals, classes or nations – can therefore be generated by subjective comparisons with others, or with past experience, or even with newly forged expectations.

The concept of economic decline in perspective

The case in favour of the view that Britain has undergone a severe economic decline is obviously strong – and sufficiently strong to have persuaded large numbers of well-informed people over many years. On the other hand, the fact that the belief has endured for so long with no sign of any immediate collapse should provide some food for thought. More significantly, the precise meaning of 'decline' and the evidence that would demonstrate its existence are not always specified as clearly as they need to be.

A second-class power

Take, in the first instance, the most obvious fact: the reduction in Britain's share of world production and trade, and its consequent decline as an international power. Given the size and resources of other countries, together with the diffusion of industrialisation among nations more comparable to Britain itself, it was inconceivable that the country could continue to occupy a very significant or autonomous position in international affairs. Britain simply lacked the distinctive wealth necessary to maintain anything like its 'historical' role, first as a major policeman in imperial and quasi-imperial affairs, and then as a premier 'player' on the world scene.

Indeed, Britain's transformation from imperial superpower to geopolitical innocuousness turned out to be a relatively slow process, although it was dramatised by the extraordinary circumstances of Britain's role in the Second World War, followed by the rapidity of post-war recovery and decolonisation elsewhere in the world. Even so, and ignoring the one or two superpowers still remaining, there are important respects in which Britain still retains a relatively powerful role on the world stage.

On the other hand, there can be little doubt that a major transformation has taken place over the last 100 years. Signs of this transformation became obvious with the disintegration of the empire (and particularly with Indian independence) in the years immediately following the Second World War; it was confirmed by the ignominious attempt to subdue Egypt in 1956; and in effect acknowledged with extensive troop withdrawals and the announcement of an end to the East of Suez policy in January 1968. And although Britain shares with almost every other country an inability to take independent international initiatives, that fact establishes a sharp distinction between her position in the late nineteenth and the late twentieth centuries.

Disturbed as some observers have been at which they see as 'the bleak and even terrifying reality of Britain's fallen place in the world' (Barnett 1978: 34), given Britain's size and her resources, such a diminution of power could hardly have been avoided (though it might have been briefly retarded). A country with such a small proportion of the world's population cannot indefinitely deal on equal terms with developed nations bigger by anything between 50 and 400 per cent. More than this, it is not at all clear that this aspect of decline has been of principal concern to the majority of the population. While such a trend in public opinion may itself have reflected a philosophical resignation in the face of the inevitable, the fact is that the intensity and implications of perceptions of decline will always vary between social groups. The greatest sensitivity to Britain's diminishing international role has been felt by those who principally determined economic and political policy and were more directly involved in formulating explanations of Britain's economic performance. The bulk of the population have other perceptions of national welfare.

Given that a significant relative decline was inevitable, it follows that some adjustment in attitudes to Britain's position in the world was equally unavoidable, even if painful and humiliating to some. What was clear was that the erosion first of Britain's dominance, and then of its standing as one of the world's handful of powerful economies, meant that it could not afford the psychological luxury of political and economic independence. Of course, given the character of political economy in the modern world, the same could be said even about such an economic superpower as the United States from the 1960s. But compared with America, Britain lacked even a degree of quasi-autonomy. Willy-nilly, it was integrated into the world economy in a dependent rather than an autonomous way.

The resulting quest for a framework of cooperation, for allegiances and networks which might generate mutual support and strength, dominated much of British international political and economic policy after the war. Britain's membership of the European Community is an acknowledgement, but not yet a resolution, of its new difficulties on the world economic stage. Clearly, Britain has declined from the position of supremacy that it enjoyed when it counted as a big economy. But just as the industrialisation of other countries made it inevitable that it should become a relatively less big economy, so it was inevitable that it should assume a quite different role in the world. Other countries (but not many) were bound to become more important.

Structural change and manufacturing productivity

Turning away from economic superpowers and power politics, how far are the changes within Britain's economic structure – and in particular the relative shrinkage of manufacturing industry – to be identified with distinctive economic decline?

Here, the first point to be emphasised is that trends in British manufacturing since the Second World War have been the outcome of *various* developments, and that not all of them have implied relative inefficiency.

In particular, some decline in manufacturing industry's share of employment and output in a mature economy is to be expected – and welcomed. For it reflects economic progress in the form of relatively rapid productivity growth in many manufacturing sectors and the continued enhancement of living standards. High productivity means that manufacturing industry's demand for labour expands relatively slowly, or not at all, while the relative cost of fabricated goods and (therefore) their prominence in the national accounts fall. Further, private affluence and 'maturing' consumption patterns bring disproportionate increases in the demand for leisure, health, educational, and public and personal services, and these tend to be labour intensive. The inevitable result is that industry's shares of employment, consumption and current output fall, while those of the service sectors rise. To a large extent, such structural changes are symptoms of maturity rather than decline.

And at this general level, many of the fears about structural change have been misplaced. Output, consumption and wealth are embodied no less in services than in manufactures; and the view that tangible goods are more important than intangible services because (in the words of the Committee

Table 11.10. *Economic structure, 1913–84 (% of total employment)*

		1913	1950	1960	1973	1984
UK	Agriculture	11·0	5·1	4·6	2·9	2·6
	Industry	44·8	46·5	46·7	41·8	32·4
	Services	44·2	48·4	48·7	55·3	65·0
France	Agriculture	37·4	28·5	21·9	11·0	7·6
	Industry	33·8	34·8	36·3	38·4	32·0
	Services	28·8	36·7	41·8	50·6	60·4
Germany	Agriculture	34·6	22·2	13·8	7·2	5·5
	Industry	37·8	43·0	48·2	46·6	40·5
	Services	27·6	34·8	38·0	46·2	54·0
Japan	Agriculture	64·3	48·3	30·2	13·4	8·9
	Industry	13·9	22·6	28·5	37·2	34·8
	Services	21·8	29·1	41·3	49·4	56·3
Netherlands	Agriculture	26·5	13·9	9·5	5·7	4·9
	Industry	33·8	40·2	39·2	35·7	26·4
	Services	39·7	45·9	51·3	58·6	68·7
USA	Agriculture	32·3	13·0	8·2	4·1	3·3
	Industry	29·3	33·3	34·3	32·5	28·0
	Services	38·4	53·7	57·5	63·4	68·7

Source: Maddison (1987: 684).

of the House of Lords, quoted earlier) only 20 per cent of the latter are tradable overseas, runs the mercantilist risk of assuming that only foreign trade creates wealth.

The international universality of the divergence between the growth of labour productivity in the industry and service sectors is well exemplified in Table 11.9 – although the universal decline in the proportion of the labour force engaged in industry proceeded unevenly as between different economies. Those which matured later or (as with Germany) had their growth gravely disrupted by war, experienced the reduction later, whereas the relative decline in Britain's industrial labour force was (with that of the Netherlands) earliest and most dramatic.

It is, therefore, possible that Britain's experience of structural change has been a function of its economic maturity – and that structural change has in part been feared primarily because it involves abandoning the concentration of jobs and output in manufacturing that was assumed to have generated the prosperity and trading success of the nineteenth century.

Certainly, Britain's experience of general structural change measured in terms of industrial *employment* did not diverge very much from other (and faster-growing) economies: by 1984, notwithstanding British complaints

Table 11.11. *Value added in manufacturing as a share (%) of total GDP, 1960 and 1983*

	1960	1983
West Germany	40·3	31·8
Japan	33·9	30·5
UK	32·1	21·0
France	29·1	25·3
USA	28·6	21·1
Italy	28·6	27·1

Source: House of Lords (1985: 12).

about indigenous deindustrialisation, many industrial societies had an even lower proportion of their workforce in industry (Table 11.10). And even after the extreme slump of 1979–81 Britain still had a higher proportion of its labour force engaged in manufacturing alone than did the USA, Japan, France, Sweden or Belgium (Martin and Rowthorn 1986: 7). Whatever the other signs of pressures on British industry, Britain still had a relatively high rather than a distinctively low proportion of its workers in manufactures.

But this is by no means the whole story. Compared with other developed economies, the decline in manufacturing's share of output in Britain was more precipitous and reached much lower levels (Table 11.11). And one reason why British manufacturing employed a somewhat higher proportion of the nation's labour force was its relatively inferior productivity.

It is, therefore, hard to deny that the experience of manufacturing industry (which has borne the brunt of economic fluctuations for a generation after 1960) has been painful and occasionally worrying. And, given the precipitousness of the decline in the size and commercial competitiveness of much British industry in recent years, a healthy maturity is unlikely to have been the sole reason for structural change in the economy – even if the deleterious consequences of that change have been exaggerated.

Economic stability

Many observers interpreted national decline or decadence as an inability to conduct an orderly and reasonably stable national economic life, to guard a society against the apprehension of insecurity and lack of control, or to meet such proximate objectives of economic and social policy as a healthy balance of payments, price stability, high and stable employment levels

Table 11.12. *Annual average current account balances, 1960–87*
(*$USb*)

	1960–8	1969–73	1974–9	1980–7
USA	3·66	2·83	−1·12	−71·74
Japan	0·10	3·30	2·84	34·10
Germany	0·60	1·78	4·26	10·86
France	n.a.	−0·15	2·50	−3·16
UK	−0·38	0·76	−2·12	1·37
Italy	1·08	0·97	0·46	−3·84

Source: Meen (1988: xxv).

and a steady growth in income. Insofar as this is the case, then the post-war record does, indeed, suggest failure, for it seems to be one of instability and fluctuation – in prices, employment, exchange rates, balance of payments, interest rates, etc. Even so, when applied to the British experience, this meaning of decline is amongst the least persuasive.

First, although Britain's record with respect to inflation, payments deficits and unemployment is far from impressive, other developed countries, with higher growth rates, have not been immune to economic fluctuations and instability.

Second, although in some respects (particularly with regard to the record on inflation) the British performance may, indeed, have been among the worst of all industrial societies, these deficiencies are in the last resort not the essence of 'decline'. Rather, they are the focus of attention because of the concern about relatively slow growth. It is reasonable to assume that, had the rates of growth of British productivity and output been closer to those of western Europe, there would have been far fewer anxieties about the value of sterling, the level of prices and the availability of work.

More than this, it is far from clear that some of the supposed instances of insecurity reflected as bad a record as is sometimes assumed. Take, for example, the balance of payments. Here, although the persistence of deficits and the resulting pressures and crises were influential and disruptive enough, most trouble was generated on the official account. As a 'problem', the balance of payments embodied less the competitive weakness of British enterprises than the negative effects of Britain's continued attempts to play a role as a world and imperial power. Thus, between 1958 and 1969 the cumulative balance on private account was a credit of £5,800 million, whereas the balance on official account was a debit of £7,810 million (Manser 1971: 25), and an even more dramatic contrast (between a private credit of £11,169 million and an official debit of £22,747 million) was apparent in 1970–81. Moreover, the frequent *sterling* crises resulted as much from volatile movements of capital in anticipation of changes in the strength of the currency, as from immediate weakness in the balance of payments.

Obviously, it is not possible to claim that either public or private activity is the more 'important' determinant of a favourable or unfavourable balance of payments. Nevertheless, public outlays are much more obviously matters of choice, and throughout most of the post-war period, in the absence of a defence establishment, foreign loans and overseas aid, the balance of payments would in all likelihood have been consistently favourable and the pressure on sterling (and the presumed need for violent 'stop–go' policies) much less (Manser 1971). Only in recent years has the private or marketed sector of trade and capital flows raised serious problems for policy and domestic activity.

Nor can 'decline' be defined as a failure to provide continuity of employment (although chronic unemployment may well be a *consequence* of relatively poor economic performance). Here, although the inter-war record was clearly poor, the first thirty years or so of post-war history exemplified an unprecedented degree of full employment, security and provision against the costs of unemployment. Indeed, there are better grounds for arguing that productivity and structural change in Britain during the thirty or more years after 1945 were restrained by *high* levels of employment, which retarded mobility and adaptability of the labour force. Security and stability could be considered alternatives to adaptation and change.

In this respect, of course, the record since the mid-1970s provides an important contrast – in the form of a serious increase in unemployment, and a trend away from generosity in social service policies. Increased unemployment may in part be the consequence of structural imperfections (the slow pace at which resources flow from declining to expanding sectors). However, in recent years the problem of unemployment has been keenly experienced in other countries with a superior growth record – while, in any case, as with other economic problems (rapid inflation, severe trade imbalances, uneven and retarded structural change, inadequate social expenditures), chronic unemployment is neither the quintessence nor the explanation of decline. Rather, it is, if anything, a symptom of deeper aspects of economic performance, which must be explained in more fundamental ways.

Falling behind, catching-up and convergence

Attempts to explain the rate of growth of British productivity and output have tended to concentrate on long-run considerations and on enduring aspects of British society, culture and economic arrangements. But there is also a sense in which it is possible to explain *too much*. For although the change in Britain's relative position has often been painfully abrupt, it is by no means obvious either that such international adjustments were avoidable or (more important) that the apparent divergence of growth rates would endure. In other words, the persistence of Britain's 'decline' can easily be exaggerated.

The point has already been made that relative growth rates might be determined by the levels of maturity as well as by the intrinsic characteristics of the economies concerned. From one viewpoint, there is some evidence that stable economies ultimately tend towards lower growth rates (Olson 1982). And by the same token the rapid, even dramatic, growth rates of late-comers to industrialisation or of advanced societies after they have been disrupted by war (Germany, Japan, France from the 1950s) may be a function of the institutional flexibility of a particular stage of development combined with the possibility of closing technical and organisational gaps that were opened up by immaturity and/or conflicts.

The convergence of rates of productivity growth in the 1970s and 1980s (Tables 11.3, 11.5–8) may, therefore, reflect not a transitory phenomenon, but a 'dramatic drawing together of the level of productivity in the leading industrialized countries' (Feinstein 1988: 6). And it is possible that this convergence will prove a more enduring feature of comparative economic performance than the spectacular and distinctive rates of growth of output and productivity achieved by late-comer or follower countries in the initial stages of their growth, or during recovery from such misfortunes as the Second World War (Feinstein 1988; Abramovitz 1986; Baumol 1986; McCloskey 1990: 40–55).

This is not to say that Britain will necessarily be able to recapture the ground lost during the initial post-war decades: the vigour with which now-leading industrial societies expanded after 1945 gave them a momentum which could have established a once-for-all superiority. As a result the gap in growth rates might well be closed while that in the levels of output and productivity might remain. But certainly, it would be curious if, in a world increasingly characterised by ease of communication, mobility of capital and enterprise, flexibility of technology transfer and the internationalisation of knowledge, advanced economies could permanently sustain major differences of economic attainment measured in terms of rates of expansion.

The relativity of relative deprivation

As has been seen, the fears and intuitions that have shaped the post-war debate about economic decline have not been confined to a concern about the level or structure of GDP. With a growing intensity, they have themselves been shaped by subtler definitions of decline: other countries were growing faster; Britain was losing world power as well as ease of control over its economic relationships; public and private, social as well as economic, aspirations were being frustrated; and pressing social problems (homelessness, extreme if still relative poverty, deteriorating social capital, lawlessness, poor public transport), for the alleviation of which increased resources were a necessary if not a sufficient condition, were eroding the conventional argument that Britain's superior quality of life was a compensation for its low growth rate.

The issue of this sort of perception of decline is by no means straightforward. Admittedly, some of the proximate causes of dissatisfaction – a low growth rate, an unfavourable balance of payments, inflation, unemployment, strife over wage determination – were apparent for all to see. And in the eyes of the critics, inept government policy and the clash of social classes excited equal amounts of blame. Nevertheless, the various possible reasons for dissatisfaction with this state of affairs were not always clear, while there were other presumed symptoms which were even more doubtful.

Within Britain, for example, one of the presumed indications of a poor economic performance has been the apparent inability to provide resources for an adequate supply of public goods and services – economic infrastructure, health and education services, welfare income, collective capital of various sorts. But the adequacy or otherwise of such provision is itself a subjective and historically determined matter.

The point is that Britain's public expenditure on social purposes (although not outstandingly high compared to other countries: Tables 11.13–15) has grown fairly substantially – to the point at which it has been argued that welfare expenditure has been excessive rather than meagre in relation to the country's economic situation.

But in this matter the fact of growth or the use of objective criteria of 'adequacy' may be singularly irrelevant. What is considered to be a desirable or realistic level of public services (or of material security or employment or income equality) is *socially* determined. As in the private sphere, affluence or deprivation in the collective provision of goods and services are relative matters: observation, experience, changing aspirations and (perhaps above all) comparison all play their part. The levels which are deemed appropriate in one age or by comparison with some potential or

Table 11.13. *Social expenditure as a percentage of GDP, 1960–80*

	UK	USA	OECD (Europe)
1960	13·9	10·9	16·9
1970	18·6	15·7	20·5
1980	22·1	20·7	28·3

Source: Sked (1987: 74).

Table 11.14. *Government expenditure as a percentage of GDP, selected OECD countries, 1964–81*

	Final consumption		Social security		Total expenditure	
	1964/5	1980/1	1964/5	1980/1	1964/5	1980/1
Sweden	17·2	29·1	9·3	19·3	35·6	63·7
Netherlands	14·8	18·0	13·3	28·0	38·3	60·6
Belgium	12·7	18·6	11·8	22·0	31·6	53·9
Germany	15·0	20·4	12·9	17·9	36·4	48·8
Italy	14·7	17·3	12·1	17·1	33·1	48·4
France	13·2	15·5	16·5	24·4	38·2	47·7
Britain	16·7	21·9	7·9	13·3	35·2	46·5

Source: Cameron (1985: 17).

Table 11.15. *Social expenditure as a percentage of GDP in the UK, 1960 and 1981*

	1960	1981
Education	3·7	5·8
Health	3·4	5·4
Pensions	4·1	7·4
Unemployment benefit	0·2	1·4
Total of above	11·4	20·0
Total social expenditure	13·9	23·7

Source: Gillion and Hemming (1985: 27).

actual foreign level may be judged scandalously low at another period or on the basis of new knowledge and comparisons.

In the case of modern Britain, expectations, the definition of what makes for a tolerable and civilised existence, the sense of deprivation among the relatively poor, the awareness of the desirability of high standards of health and education, the social acceptability of minimum housing standards – have all been transformed in ways which, *in spite of the vast increase in provision*, have served to increase the gaps between 'need' (as newly perceived) and resources (as newly made available).

In effect, and paradoxically, economic and social progress almost inevitably increases dissatisfaction by making the definition of need more demanding, constantly raising the 'poverty line' as average incomes grow, and transforming the public judgement of what are acceptable standards of social existence.

Similar, or even more powerful, sorts of arguments can be made about private needs and aspirations as indicators of decline. Once again, as with public expenditures, but perhaps even more strikingly, the actual post-war achievement of the British economy (the growth in average personal income and consumption) has been considerable. But, once again, the socially determined 'needs' and appetites of the population have diverged from the enhanced output of goods and services. In this respect, of course, dissatisfaction is primarily generated by the comparison of living standards and life styles – between social groups within Britain, between Britain and other countries and between actual levels of consumption and widely publicised and advertised levels of potential consumption.

This is not to deny that there have been instances of groups which have become absolutely poorer. But such immiseration has been rare. More common in recent years has been the coincidence of almost universal material improvement and a worsening distribution of income. In effect, real or perceived comparabilities have changed; poverty has come to mean relative rather than absolute deprivation; and economic growth inevitably brings frustration as 'need' outpaces means and the unavoidable limit on the availability of 'positional goods' become clear (Hirsch 1976). Little wonder, then, that an intermittent perception of national economic decline in the sense of the chronic persistence or even extension of 'poverty', has endured even while the British people have, on average, experienced improvements in living standards faster than at any other time in their history.

In practice, economic growth itself tends to augment the appetite for consumption, and if that appetite is determined by observation of even faster-growing societies, or more rapidly enriched groups, then any improvement will appear *increasingly* inadequate – and as the gap between the actual and the presumed possible increases, so social dissatisfaction and disappointment will be intensified. Nor is that gap solely a matter of autonomous personal perception: the development of modern mass communication, the perfection of the art of advertising and the 'globalisation' of consumption have all served to aggravate the tensions between actual and apparently potential levels of consumption and security.

Images of decline: interpretations of the British experience

The argument in this chapter has been that the perceptions of Britain's economic decline, at least in the form and to the extent generally asserted, have been mistaken or distorted. On the other hand, to assert that the British economy has grown at an apparently 'satisfactory' rate, or that faster growth might have brought social and psychological disadvantages, is not to dispute the view that growth *could* well have been more rapid – or that the frustrations of slower growth have their own drawbacks. And it has to be acknowledged that even if relative decline has been inevitable, in the sense that other major powers were bound to overtake Britain's growth rate, it is certainly possible that the economy's relegation need not have been so rapid. Why, then, has Britain's rate of economic growth not been faster?

The menu from which possible answers to this leading question may be chosen is rich, varied and occasionally indigestible. Familiar and much-canvassed items are: a shortage or diversion of investment; lack or disruption of demand; inflexible labour attitudes and poor industrial relations; imperfect training and skills; unimaginative and ineffective managerial outlook and business organisation; a conservative and anti-enterprise national culture; rigid and antagonistic class structures and mature and inflexible institutions.

Some of these arguments have already been touched on. For example, imperfections in the provision of capital figure prominently in many explanations of Britain's lower growth rates. Yet there is, in fact, relatively little hard evidence that British industry has suffered unduly from a shortage of investment funds, while the internationalisation of capital markets makes the possibility of such a shortage hard to imagine. Indeed, the post-war record (investment as a proportion of output) is a clear improvement on pre-war experience. Further, although British investment ratios have still been distinctly less than those of continental countries or Japan, capital accumulation only accounted for a relatively small part of the shortfall in the growth rate of British productivity. Differences were much more attributable to rates of growth in total factor productivity (i.e. increases in output after allowing for changes in the quantity and quality of labour and capital) (Crafts 1988: 4, 20). More to the point, therefore, was the efficiency with which capital was used. Here, the crucial fact is that Britain has had a low, and sometimes a very low, level of output per unit of investment (for much of the post-war period it was almost half the amount enjoyed by West Germany). Correspondingly, the returns to investment, the level of demand for capital and the rate at which the capital stock has grown have all been relatively low. In the 1960s and 1970s, for example, the growth in the productivity of German capital was between 70 and 90 per cent higher than that of British (Crafts 1988: 20–1; Cairncross 1981: 380).

As in so much analysis of economic processes, the causal sequence may, therefore, be the opposite of that generally assumed: Britain's relatively low rate of investment and capital accumulation may be the outcome rather than the cause of its relatively low rate of output growth (Cairncross 1981: 379).

These arguments are very important both in themselves and for the light they throw on other, less direct, explanations of Britain's relatively depressed rate of economic growth. For insofar as inadequacies in economic performance cannot be attributed to deficiencies in savings and investment ratios, a popular and significant range of other hypotheses are commensurately weakened. Thus, the possible effect of official policy in destabilising or restricting demand (and thereby inhibiting investment and the expansion of capacity) becomes the less significant – simply because there is little evidence for the primacy of an investment famine in any explanation of Britain's slow growth. Nor is it clear that the country's competitors benefited from a more stable environment for growth-inducing capital accumulation. Such arguments (Dow 1964; Pollard 1982) assume that (a) the British climate for business activity was exceptionally uncertain, (b) there existed a potential for productivity growth which went unrealised largely because of the absence of a continuous demand stimulus and (c) there was a critical role for the investment of more funds than were actually invested.

In fact, each of these assumptions is questionable: first, economic fluctuations and balance of payments fluctuations were not obviously more volatile than those in much faster-growing economies (Crafts 1988: 12); second, the stimulus of demand, far from engendering sustainable growth, often exposed structural weaknesses which threatened economic stability through inflation; third, as we have already seen, it was less the amount of investment than the efficiency with which capital was used that proved a consistent handicap for industrial productivity in Britain.

It certainly seems that the slow growth of British productivity relative to that of other countries cannot easily be attributed to restrictions on the level or growth of demand. Indeed, just as the stimulus to investment was impaired by the effectiveness with which new investment was used, so any explanation of Britain's economic performance must focus on the supply side of economic activity and the *determinants* of productivity: the potential for human and organisational and technical change; the flexibility of economic arrangements and outlooks; the vigour and success of research and development effort; the responsiveness and efficiency of enterprise and management; the quality and skills of labour; the posture of trade unions; and social attitudes towards business activity generally (see also ch. 5).

Such 'supply-side' arguments were, of course, influential in the policy of the Thatcher administration of 1979–90, albeit not always consistently formulated or successfully pursued. In effect, the social and institutional structures, and the accompanying attitudes, that explain the vigour with which an economy operates and adapts are deeply rooted and resistant to sudden (or externally imposed) change. It therefore proved easier to lower income tax rates, or introduce private ownership to formerly nationalised industries, or reduce the power of trade unions, than to transform entrepreneurial policies towards research and development, or enhance the level of the labour force's skills, or overcome engrained attitudes to class or industrial and geographical mobility.

This is not to deny that structural and psychological changes have taken place, and continually do. But in the last resort, a nation is what it is and has become, socially, culturally, politically – and economically.

Much of the post-war concern with Britain's supposed decline either assumes that drastic, even volatile, reversals are always feasible, or pessimistically concludes that the unavoidably slow pace of historical evolution has condemned Britain to economic decay and ruinous impoverishment.

Neither of these views is well founded. 'Decline' has certainly occurred: over the last 100 years Britain has lost its former pre-eminent position in the world's economy and polity; since the Second World War it has grown at a slower pace than most other industrial nations; and in recent decades it has had to share its role as a second-rank power with an increasing number of other countries. But much of this change was inevitable in the sense that it was a logical consequence of the resources, aptitudes, institutions and attitudes that were inherent and fostered in Britain since at least the eighteenth century. More significantly, the experience of 'decline', although uncomfortable for a nation formerly accustomed to supremacy, has been only ambiguously painful. Living standards have risen, affluence has been diffused, wealth has accumulated. Frustration and a consciousness of deprivation have, of course, continued – and, perhaps unavoidably, increased. But these are subjective matters, determined by constantly changing aspirations and appetites, in both the collective and the private spheres. And it has been perceptions of this sort, more than any quantitative retrogression or ebbing of national prosperity, that have given point to the idea of decline. Adam Smith's advice to an anxious correspondent remains as valid in the late twentieth as in the late eighteenth century: 'Be assured my young friend, that there is a deal of *ruin* in a nation' (Sinclair 1831: 390–1).

Chronology

Wade E. Shilts

The University of Iowa

1940s

ECONOMIC AND SOCIAL CONDITIONS

Inflation (1945–50): 4·3 per cent per annum.

1945	Britain's current account deficit reaches one sixth of national income.
1947	Convertibility crisis.
1949	Pound devalued by 30 per cent against dollar.

TECHNOLOGY AND IDEAS

1947   Use of streptomycin to treat tuberculosis.

POLITICS, LAW AND PUBLIC POLICY

1942	Beveridge Report calls for 'cradle to grave' social services.
1944	Education Act creates general programme of secondary education. White Paper on *Employment Policy* commits government to a full-employment policy.
1945–51	Labour government under Attlee.
1945	Distribution of Industry Act places emphasis on regional economic development. Anglo-American Financial Agreement whereby UK commits to convertibility by 1947.
1946	Nationalisation of coal, Bank of England.
1947	Nationalisation of transport, electrical power.
1948	National Health Service begins operation. Republic of Ireland Act.
1949	Nationalisation of iron and steel.

INTERNATIONAL EVENTS

1941	American government passes Lend-Lease Act.
1944	Bretton Woods Agreement.
1945	End of Second World War. Formation of United Nations. Yalta and Potsdam meetings. Founding of Fourth Republic in France.
1947	General Agreement on Tariffs and Trade. Independence of India and Pakistan. Truman doctrine.

347

1947–54	War between French and Vietnamese.
1948–9	Berlin Blockade.
1948–50	Marshall Plan aid to United Kingdom.
1948–9	Israeli war of independence.
1949	Formation of North Atlantic Treaty Organisation (NATO). Formation of Council of Mutual Assistance (COMECON) between Soviet Union and States of eastern Europe.

1950s

ECONOMIC AND SOCIAL CONDITIONS

Output growth rate (constant factor cost, 1951–73): 2·8 per cent per annum.
Inflation (1950–67): 3·8 per cent per annum.

1950	Public expenditure exceeds 39 per cent of GDP.
1954	*De facto* free convertibility of pound into dollar.

POLITICS, LAW AND PUBLIC POLICY

1950	Rearmament begins.
1951–64	Conservative governments (Churchill, Eden, Macmillan, Douglas-Home).
1953–5	Steel privatised.
1954	Withdrawal of troops from Egypt.
1956	Suez Crisis.
1959	Report of the Radcliffe Committee on the Working of the Monetary System.

INTERNATIONAL EVENTS

1950s–60s	Civil rights movement in the United States.
1950–3	Korean War.
1951	Formation of European Coal and Steel Community. Establishment of European Payments Union.
1955	Formation of Warsaw Pact.
1957	Treaty of Rome establishes European Economic Community. Soviet Union launches *Sputnik*.
1958	General convertibility of European currencies. Creation of Fifth Republic in France.
1959	Formation of European Free Trade Area.

1960s

ECONOMIC AND SOCIAL CONDITIONS

Population of Great Britain (1961): 51·3 million. Life expectancy at birth (1960):
    68·2 years (men); 74·1 years (women).
Inflation (1968–73): 7·5 per cent per annum.

| 1966 | Seamen's strike. |
| 1967 | Devaluation of pound from $2·80 to $2·40. |

POLITICS, LAW AND PUBLIC POLICY

1961	First use of 'tax regulator' whereby Chancellor of Exchequer could change indirect taxation between budgets.
1965	Monopolies and Mergers Act. Establishment of National Board for Prices and Income.
1967	Renationalisation of steel.
1968	Donovan Report calls for reform of industrial relations. End of 'east of Suez' policy.

INTERNATIONAL EVENTS

1961	Erection of Berlin Wall.
1962	Cuban Missile Crisis.
1962–5	Second Vatican Council of the Roman Catholic Church.
1963	France vetoes United Kingdom membership in the EEC. Test-ban treaty limits nuclear testing.
1965	Tonkin Gulf Resolution and escalation of Vietnam War.
1968	The 'Year of Protest'. Invasion of Czechoslovakia by Soviet troops.
1969	First landing on the moon.

1970s

ECONOMIC AND SOCIAL CONDITIONS

Inflation (1974–80): 15·9 per cent per annum.
1970	Public expenditure exceeds 47 per cent of GDP.
1972	First national coal strike since 1926. Britain floats pound.
1972–3	Wages and prices frozen.
1974	Coal strike. Majority of voting shares in British Leyland held by government (until 1988).
Late 1970s	North Sea oil comes on stream.
1979–82	Major recession.

POLITICS, LAW AND PUBLIC POLICY

1972	Britain suspends Northern Irish Parliament, begins direct governance.
1973	Britain becomes part of European Community.
1974	Election of Labour government in 'Who governs Britain?' election.
1975	Establishment of state-owned National Enterprise Board.
1979	Election of Conservative government under Margaret Thatcher. Privatisation of British Petroleum. Recognition of Zimbabwean independence.

1970	United States and China re-establish relations.
1972	Break-up of Bretton Woods Agreement.
1972	Strategic Arms Limitation Treaty.
1972–4	Watergate crisis in United States.
1973–4	International oil crisis.
1979	Soviet Union invades Afghanistan.

1980–92

ECONOMIC AND SOCIAL CONDITIONS

Population of Great Britain (1981): 54·3 million.
Inflation: 1980–7 6·9 per cent per annum; 1988–90 7·4 per cent per annum.

1980	Public expenditure exceeds 50 per cent of GDP.
1980–3	Recession.
1983–9	Recovery.
Early 1980s	Britain becomes net importer of manufactures.
1984–5	Miners' strike.
1990	Public expenditure down to 37 per cent of GDP.
	SSHYpolitics, law and public policy
1981	Founding of Social Democratic Party.
1986	Channel Tunnel treaty signed with France.
1988	Reprivatisation of steel.
1990	Privatisation of electricity.
1990	Britain joins European Monetary System.

INTERNATIONAL EVENTS

1982	Falklands War.
1986	Chernobyl nuclear disaster.
1989	Berlin Wall falls. Revolutions throughout eastern Europe.
1990	Reunification of Germany.
1990–1	Mobilisation and war in Persian Gulf.

NOTE ON SOURCES

Economic and demographic statistics found under 'Economic and social conditions' above were taken from the following sources:

Income/output. Rate of growth, 1856–1973: Feinstein (1972: 11, 19), as updated in Matthews et al. (1982: 28).
Population. 1801–1981: Mitchell (1988: 9).
Prices. 1945–90: ch. 9.
Public expenditure. 1950–90: ch. 9.

Bibliography

Place of publication is London unless otherwise stated. All references to the *Economic History Review* are to the Second Series, unless otherwise stated.

Abel-Smith, B., and Townsend, P. 1965. *The Poor and the Poorest.*

Abramovitz, M. 1986. Catching up, forging ahead and falling behind. *Journal of Economic History* 46: 385–406.

1989. *Thinking about Growth.* Cambridge.

Ackrill, M. 1988. British managers and the British economy, 1870s to the 1980s. *Oxford Review of Economic Policy* 4: 59–73.

Addison, P. 1975. *The Road to 1945.*

Albu, A. 1980. British attitudes to engineering education: a historical perspective. In Pavitt 1980.

Aldcroft, D. H. 1984. *Full Employment: The Elusive Goal.* Brighton.

1990. Education and Britain's growth failure, 1950–1980. In Tortella 1990.

Alexander, S. S. 1952. The effects of devaluation on a trade balance. *IMF Staff Papers* 2: 263–78.

Alford, B. W. E. 1988. *British Economic Performance 1945–1975.*

Allen, G. C. 1951. The concentration of production policy. In Chester 1951.

Allen, R. G. D. 1946. Mutual aid between the U. S. and the British empire, 1941–1945. *Journal of the Royal Statistical Society* 109: 243–71.

Armstrong, H. W. 1991. Regional problems and policies. In Crafts and Woodward 1991.

Armstrong, H. W., and Taylor, J. 1987. *Regional Policy: The Way Forward.*

Arndt, H. W. 1978. *The Rise and Fall of Economic Growth.* Melbourne.

Artis, M. J. 1978. Monetary policy. In Blackaby 1978.

Artis, M. J., and Cobham, D. 1991. *The Labour Government 1974–79.* Oxford.

eds. 1991. *Labour's Economic Policies 1974–79.* Manchester.

Artis, M. J., and Lewis, M. K. 1976. The demand for money in the United Kingdom 1963–1973. *Manchester School of Economic and Social Studies* 44: 147–81.

Artus, J. R. 1975. The 1967 devaluation of the pound. *IMF Staff Papers*, November.

Ashworth, W. 1986. *The History of the British Coal Industry, vol. V: The Nationalised Industry, 1946–1982.* Oxford.

Atkinson, A. B. 1987. Income maintenance and social insurance. In Auerbach and Feldstein 1987.

1989. *Poverty and Social Security.*

351

1991. A national minimum? A history of ambiguity in the determination of benefit scales in Britain. In Wilson and Wilson 1991.

Atkinson, A. B., and Stiglitz, J. E. 1980. *Lectures on Public Economics*. New York.

Atkinson, F. J., Brooks, S. J., and Hall, S. G. F. 1983. The economic effects of North Sea oil. *National Institute Economic Review*, May.

Auerbach, A. J., and Feldstein, M. S., eds. 1987. *Handbook of Public Economics* vol. II. Amsterdam.

Averch, H., and Johnson, L. 1962. Behavior of the firm under regulatory constraint. *American Economic Review* 52: 1052–69.

Aylen, J. 1988. Privatisation of the British Steel Corporation. *Fiscal Studies* 9,3: 1–25.

Bacon, R., and Eltis, W. A. 1976. *Britain's Economic Problem: Too Few Producers*.

Bain, G. S., and Price, R. 1980. *Profiles of Union Growth: A Comparative Statistical Portrait of Eight Countries*. Oxford.

Baines, D. 1981. The labour supply and the labour market, 1860–1914. In Floud and McCloskey 1981.

Bairoch, P. 1982. International industrialization levels from 1759 to 1980. *Journal of European Economic History* 11: 269–310.

Ball, R. J., and Burns, T. 1976. The inflationary mechanism in the U. K. economy. *American Economic Review* 66: 467–84.

Bank of England. 1968. Control of bank lending: the cash deposits scheme. *Bank of England Quarterly Bulletin* 8: 166–70.

1969. *The Operation of Monetary Policy since the Radcliffe Report*.

1970. The stock of money. *Bank of England Quarterly Bulletin* 10: 320–6.

1971a. Competition and credit control: the discount market. *Bank of England Quarterly Bulletin* 11: 314–15.

1971b. Reserve ratios: further definitions. *Bank of England Quarterly Bulletin* 11: 482–9.

1973. Competition and credit control: modified arrangements for the discount market. *Bank of England Quarterly Bulletin* 13: 306–7.

1974. Credit control: a supplementary scheme. *Bank of England Quarterly Bulletin* 14: 37–9.

1976. The balance of payments and the exchange rate developments in the first half of 1976. *Bank of England Quarterly Bulletin* 16: 308–13.

1977. DCE and the money supply – a statistical note. *Bank of England Quarterly Bulletin* 17: 39–42.

1980. Financial review. *Bank of England Quarterly Bulletin* 20: 19–32.

1981. Economic commentary. *Bank of England Quarterly Bulletin* 21: 3–18.

1984a. *The Development and Operation of Monetary Policy 1960–1983*. Oxford.

1984b. Funding the public sector borrowing requirement: 1952–83. *Bank of England Quarterly Bulletin* 24: 482–92.

1985a. Operation of monetary policy. *Bank of England Quarterly Bulletin* 25: 361–70.

1985b. Operation of monetary policy. *Bank of England Quarterly Bulletin* 25: 517–25.

1986. Financial change and broad money. *Bank of England Quarterly Bulletin* 26: 499–507.

1987a. Operation of monetary policy. *Bank of England Quarterly Bulletin* 27: 26–38.

1987b. Changes in the Stock Exchange and regulation of the City. *Bank of England Quarterly Bulletin* 27: 54–65.

1987c. The gilt-edged market: auctions. *Bank of England Quarterly Bulletin* 27: 203.

1987d. The instruments of monetary policy. *Bank of England Quarterly Bulletin* 27: 365–70.

1988a. The experimental series of gilt-edged auctions. *Bank of England Quarterly Bulletin* 28: 194–7.

1988b. Bank of England operations in the sterling money market. *Bank of England Quarterly Bulletin* 28: 390–409.

1989a. The gilt-edged market since Big Bang. *Bank of England Quarterly Bulletin* 29: 49–58.

1989b. Bank of England operations in the sterling money market. *Bank of England Quarterly Bulletin* 29: 92–103.

1990a. The determination of the monetary aggregates. *Bank of England Quarterly Bulletin* 30: 380–3.

1990b. The exchange rate mechanism of the European Monetary System. *Bank of England Quarterly Bulletin* 30: 479–81.

1990c. Monetary aggregates in a changing environment: a statistical discussion paper. *Bank of England Discussion Papers* 47: 1–44.

Barker, T. C., and Robbins, M. 1974. *A History of London Transport, vol. II: The Twentieth Century to 1970.*

Barlow Report. 1940. *Royal Commission on the Distribution of the Industrial Population.*

Barnett, C. 1978. Obsolescence and Dr Arnold. In Hutber 1978.

1985. Long-term industrial performance in the U. K.: the role of education and research 1850–1939. In Morris 1985.

1986. *The Audit of War: The Illusion and Reality of Britain as a Great Nation.*

Barr, N. 1987. *The Economics of the Welfare State.*

Barr, N., and Coulter, F. 1990. Social security: solution or problem? In Hills 1990.

Batstone, E. 1986. Labour and productivity. *Oxford Review of Economic Policy* 2: 32–43.

Baumol, W. J. 1986. Productivity growth, convergence and welfare: what the long-run data show. *American Economic Review* 76: 1072–85.

Bean, C. 1987. The impact of North Sea oil. In Layard and Dornbusch 1987.

Bean, C., and Symons, J. 1989. Ten years of Mrs. T. *Centre for Economic Policy Research Discussion Paper* no. 316.

Beck, G. 1951. A survey of British employment and unemployment. *Oxford University Institute of Statistics* 19: 27–45.

Beckerman, W., ed. 1972. *The Labour Government's Economic Record 1964–70.*

1982. *Economic Slowdown in the Western World.* Cambridge.

Beesley, M. E., Gist, P., and Glaister, S. 1983. Cost-benefit analysis in London's transport policies. *Progress in Planning* 19: 171–269.

Begg, D. 1987. Fiscal policy. In Layard and Dornbusch 1987.

Benjamin, D. K., and Kochin, L. A. 1979a. Searching for an explanation of unemployment in interwar Britain. *Journal of Political Economy* 87: 441–78.

1979b. What went right with juvenile unemployment policy between the wars: a comment. *Economic History Review* 32: 523–8.

Berthoud, R. 1985. *Challenges to Social Policy*. Aldershot.

Bevan, A. 1952. *In Place of Fear*.

Beveridge, W. H. 1942. *Social Insurance and Allied Services*. Cmd 6404.

1944. *Full Employment in a Free Society*.

Bishop, M., and Kay, J. 1988. *Does Privatisation Work? Lessons from the UK*.

Black, D. 1980. *Inequalities in Health: Report of a Research Working Group*.

Blackaby, F. T., ed. 1978. *British Economic Policy 1960–74*. Cambridge.

ed. 1979a. *British Economic Policy 1960–74: Demand Management*. Cambridge.

ed. 1979b. *Deindustrialisation*.

1979c. General appraisal. In Blackaby 1979a.

Boltho, A., ed. 1982. *The European Economy: Growth and Crisis*. Oxford.

Bolton Committee. 1971. *Report of the Committee on Small Firms*. Cmnd 4811.

Booth, A. 1983. The 'Keynesian Revolution' in economic policy making. *Economic History Review* 36: 103–23.

1985. Economists and points rationing in the Second World War. *Journal of European Economic History* 14: 297–317.

1986. Simple Keynesianism and Whitehall 1936–47. *Economy and Society* 15: 1–22.

1989. *British Economic Policy 1931–49: Was There a Keynesian Revolution?* Hemel Hempstead.

Booth, A., and Coats, A. W. 1980. Some wartime observations on the role of the economist in government. *Oxford Economic Papers* 32: 177–99.

Bowden, S., and Turner, P. 1990. *Productivity and Long-Term Growth Potential in the U. K. Economy 1924–1968*. University of Leeds, mimeo.

Brech, M. J. 1985. Nationalised industries. In Morris 1985.

Briggs, A. 1979. *The History of Broadcasting in the U. K, vol. IV: Sound and Vision*. Oxford.

Brittan, S. 1969. *Steering the Economy*. Harmondsworth.

1970. *The Price of Economic Freedom: A Guide to Flexible Rates*.

1978. How British is the British disease? *Journal of Law and Economics* 21: 245–68.

Brittan, S., and Lilley, P. 1977. *The Delusions of Incomes Policy*.

Britton, A. J. 1991. *Macroeconomic Policy in Britain 1974–87*. Cambridge.

Broadberry, S. N. 1986. *The British Economy between the Wars: A Macroeconomic Survey*. Oxford.

1988. The impact of the world wars on the long run performance of the British economy. *Oxford Review of Economic Policy* 4: 25–37.

Broadberry, S. N., and Crafts, N. F. R. 1989. *Supply Side Problems and the Potential for Growth in Interwar Britain*. Warwick University, mimeo.

1990a. Explaining Anglo-American productivity differences in the mid-twentieth century. *Oxford Bulletin of Economics and Statistics* 52: 375–402.

1990b. The impact of the depression of the 1930s on productive potential in the United Kingdom. *European Economic Review* 34: 599–607.

Brown, A. J. 1955. *The Great Inflation 1939–51*. Oxford.

1972. *The Framework of Regional Economics in the United Kingdom*. Cambridge.

1985. *World Inflation since 1950: An International Comparative Study*. Oxford.

Brown, H. Phelps. 1983. *The Origins of Trade Union Power*. Oxford.

Brown, M., and Baldwin, S., eds. 1980. *Year Book of Social Policy in Britain 1979*.

Brown, W. 1991. Industrial relations. In Artis and Cobham 1991.

Brown, W., and Wadhwani, S. 1990. The economic effects of industrial relations legislation since 1979. *National Institute Economic Review* 131: 57–70.

Bruno, M., and Sachs, J. D. 1983. Input price shocks and the slowdown in economic growth: the case of UK manufacturing. In Greenhalgh *et al.* 1983.

1985. *Economics of Worldwide Stagflation*. Oxford.

Buchanan, J. M., and Wagner, R. E. 1977. *Democracy in Deficit: The Political Legacy of Lord Keynes*. New York.

Budd, A. 1991. The 1991 budget in its historical context. *Fiscal Studies* 12: 18.

Bullock, A. 1967. *The Life and Times of Ernest Bevin*, vol. II: *Minister of Labour, 1940–1945*.

1983. *Ernest Bevin, Foreign Secretary*. Oxford.

Burk, K., and Cairncross, A. 1992. *Good-Bye Great Britain: The 1976 IMF Crisis*.

Burn, D., ed. 1958. *The Structure of British Industry: A Symposium*. Cambridge.

Cairncross, A., ed. 1971. *Britain's Economic Prospects Reconsidered*.

1979. What is de-industrialisation? In Blackaby 1979a.

1981. The post-war years, 1945–77. In Floud and McCloskey 1981.

1983. The 1967 devaluation of sterling. In Cairncross and Eichengreen 1983.

1985. *Years of Recovery: British Economic Policy 1945–51*.

1987. Prelude to Radcliffe. *Rivista di Storia Economiche* December: 1–20.

1989. The United Kingdom. In Pechman 1989.

1992. *The British Economy since 1945*. Oxford.

Cairncross, A., and Eichengreen, B., eds. 1983. *Sterling in Decline*. Oxford.

Cairncross, A., and Watts, N. 1989. *The Economic Section 1939–61: A Study in Economic Advising*.

Cairncross, F., and Cairncross, A. 1992. *The Legacy of the Golden Age. The 1960s and their Economic Consequences*.

Callaghan, J. 1987. *Time and Chance*.

Calmfors, L., and Driffill, J. 1988. Centralisation of wage bargaining. *Economic Policy* 6: 13–61.

Cameron, D. R. 1985. Public expenditure and economic performance in international perspective. In Klein and O'Higgins 1985.

Capie, F., and Webber, A. 1985. *A Monetary History of the United Kingdom 1870–1982*, vol. I: *Data, Sources, Methods*.

Caves, R. E. ed., 1968a. *Britain's Economic Prospects*. Washington D. C.

1968b. Market organisation, performance and public policy. In Caves 1968a.

1980. Productivity differences among industries. In Caves and Krause 1980.

Caves, R., and Krause, L., eds. 1980. *Britain's Economic Performance*. Washington D. C.

Central Statistical Office. 1951. *Statistical Digest of the War*.

1990. *Social Trends*.

1991. *Social Trends*.

Chancellor of the Exchequer and the Secretary of State for Industry. 1975. *An Approach to Industrial Strategy*. Cmnd 6315.

Chandler, A. D. 1990. *Scale and Scope: The Dynamics of Industrial Competition*. Cambridge, Mass.

Channon, D. 1973. *The Strategy and Structure of British Enterprise.*
    1976. Corporate evolution in the service industries. In Hannah 1976a.
    1978. *The Service Industries.*
Chester, D. N., ed. 1951. *Lessons of the British War economy.* Cambridge.
    1975. *The Nationalization of British Industry.*
Chick, M., ed. 1990. *Governments, Industries and Markets: Aspects of Government–Industry Relations in the U. K., Japan, West Germany, and the United States since 1945.* Aldershot and Brookfield, Vt.
Churchill, W. S. 1949. *The Second World War, vol. II: Their Finest Hour.* 1985 edn.
Clare Group. 1982. Problems of industrial recovery. *Midland Bank Review* Spring: 9–16.
Clark, C. 1961. *Growthmanship.*
Clarke, P. 1989. The decline of post-war consensus: commentary two. In Gorst *et al.* 1989.
Clarke, R. W. B. 1982. *Anglo-American Collaboration in War and Peace.* Ed. A. Cairncross. Oxford.
Clayton, G., Gilbert, J. C., and Sedgwick, R., eds. 1971. *Monetary Theory and Monetary Policy in the 1970s.*
Clegg, H. A. 1979. *The Changing System of Industrial Relations in Great Britain.* Oxford.
Cohen, C. D. 1971. *British Economic Policy 1960–69.*
Cohen, S. S., and Zysman, J. 1987. *Manufacturing Matters: The Myth of the Post-Industrial Society.* New York.
Combined Committee on Non-Food Consumption. 1945. *The Impact of the War on Civilian Consumption in the United Kingdom, the United States and Canada.*
Coopey, R. 1992. The white heat? Labour's industrial policies in the 1960s. In vol. VI of *Labour: The Party of Industrial Organisation?* Business History Unit Conference, London School of Economics and Political Science.
Council on Prices, Productivity and Incomes. 1958–61. *Reports 1–4.*
Coutts, K., and Godley, W. 1989. The British economy under Mrs Thatcher. *Political Quarterly* 60: 137–51.
Crafts, N. F. R. 1987. Long term unemployment in Britain in the 1930s. *Economic History Review* 40: 418–32.
    1988. British economic growth before and after 1979: a review of the evidence. *Centre for Economic Policy Research Discussion Paper* no. 292.
    1991a. Economic growth. In Crafts and Woodward 1991.
    1991b. Reversing relative economic decline?: the 1980s in historical perspective. *Oxford Review of Economic Policy* 7: 81–98.
Crafts, N. F. R., and Woodward, N., eds. 1991. *The British Economy since 1945.* Oxford.
Creedy, J., and Disney, R. 1985. *Social Insurance in Transition.* Oxford.
Croome, D. R., and Johnson, H. G., eds. 1969. *Money in Britain 1959–1969.*
Crosland, C. A. R. 1956. *The Future of Socialism.*
Cross, R. 1982. *Economic Theory and Policy in the UK.* Oxford.
    ed. 1988. *Unemployment, Hysteresis and the Natural Rate Hypothesis.* Oxford.
Cutler, A., Williams, K., and Williams, J. 1987. *Keynes, Beveridge and Beyond.*
Davies, G. 1989. A decade of Britain's supply-side revolution. *Evidence to Treasury and Civil Service Committee,* 17 April 1989.

Davies, S., and Caves, R. E. 1987. *Britain's Productivity Gap*. Cambridge.

Deacon, A., and Bradshaw, J. 1983. *Reserved for the Poor: The Means-Test in British Social Policy*. Oxford.

Dell, E. 1991. *A Hard Pounding: Politics and Economic Crisis 1974–76*. Oxford.

Denison, E. F. 1967. *Why Growth Rates Differ*. Washington D. C.

    1980. *Accounting for Slower Economic Growth: The United States in the 1970s*. Washington.

Department of Economic Affairs. 1965. *The National Plan*. Cmnd 2764.

Department of Employment, *Employment Gazette*. 1975, 1990.

Department of Employment and Productivity 1971. *British Labour Statistics: Historical Abstract, 1886–1968*.

Devons, E. 1950. *Planning in Practice*. Cambridge.

    1961a. Economic planning in war and peace. In Devons 1961b.

    ed. 1961b. *Essays in Economics*.

    1970a. *Papers on Planning and Economic Management*. Ed. A. Cairncross. Manchester.

    1970b. Planning by economic survey. In Devons ed. 1970a.

Diebold, W. 1952. The end of the I. T. O. *Princeton Essays in International Finance* 16, Princeton N. J.

Digby, A. 1989. *British Welfare Policy: Workhouse to Workfare*.

Dilnot, A. W., Kay, J. A., and Morris, C. N. 1984. *The Reform of Social Security*. Oxford.

Dimsdale, N. H., Nickell, S. J., and Horsewood, J. 1989. Real wages and unemployment in Britain during the 1930s. *Economic Journal* 99: 271–92.

Donoghue, B. 1987. *Prime Minister. The Conduct of Policy under Harold Wilson and James Callaghan*.

Donovan Report. 1968. *Report of Royal Commission on Trade Unions and Employers' Associations 1965–68*. Cmnd 3623.

Dornbusch, R. 1976. Expectations and exchange rate dynamics. *Journal of Political Economy* 84: 1161–76.

Dow, J. C. R. 1964. *The Management of the British Economy, 1945–1960*. Cambridge.

    1990. *How Can Real Wages Ever Get Excessive?*

Dow, J. C. R., and Saville, I. D. 1990. *A Critique of Monetary Policy*. 2nd edn. Oxford.

Dunn, R. M. 1983. The many disappointments of flexible exchange rates. *Princeton University Essays in International Finance* 154, Princeton, N. J.

Durbin, E. F. M. 1949. *Problems of Economic Planning*.

    1985. *New Jerusalems: The Labour Party and the Economics of Democratic Socialism*.

Eatwell, J., and Robinson, J. 1973. *An Introduction to Modern Economics*. Maidenhead.

Eatwell, J., Milgate, M., and Newman, P., eds. 1987. *The New Palgrave: A Dictionary of Economics*.

Economic Implications of Full Employment. 1956. Cmd 9725.

Economic Survey. Annual from 1947 to 1962.

Economic Trends.

Economic Trends Annual Supplement.

Economist. 1990a. 13 October 1990: 117.

1990b. 15 December, 1990: 106.

Eichengreen, B., ed. 1985. *The Gold Standard in Theory and Practice.*

1987. Unemployment in interwar Britain: dole or doldrums? *Oxford Economic Papers* 39: 597–623.

1990. Hegemonic stability theories of the international monetary system. *Centre for Economic Policy Research Discussion Paper* no. 193.

Eichengreen, B., and Hatton, T. J., eds. 1988. *Interwar Unemployment in International Perspective.*

Elbaum, B., and Lazonick, W., eds. 1986. *The Decline of the British Economy.* Oxford.

Elliott, D., and Gribbin, J. D. 1977. The abolition of cartels and structural change in the United Kingdom. In Jacquemin and de Jong 1977.

Elliot, I. 1976. Total factor productivity. In Panic 1976.

Eltis, W. A., and Sinclair, P. J. N., eds. 1981. *The Money Supply and the Exchange Rate.* Oxford.

Employment Policy. 1944. Cmd 6527.

Englander, A. S., and Mittlestaat, A. 1988. Total factor productivity: macroeconomic and structural aspects of the slowdown. *OECD Economic Studies* 10: 17–56.

Ergas, H. 1984. *Economic Evaluation of the Impact of Telecommunications Investment in the Communities.* Berlin.

Feinstein, C. H. 1972. *National Income, Expenditure and Output of the United Kingdom 1855–1965.* Cambridge.

ed. 1983. *The Managed Economy.* Oxford.

1988. Economic growth since 1870: Britain's performance in international perspective. *Oxford Review of Economic Policy* 4: 1–13.

Feinstein, C. H., and Matthews, R. C. O. 1990. The growth of output and productivity in the UK: the 1980s as a phase of the postwar period. *National Institute Economic Review* 133: 78–90.

Fellner, W. 1961. *The Problem of Rising Prices.* Paris.

Fender, J. 1990. *Inflation: A Contemporary Perspective.*

Fforde, J. S. 1983. Setting monetary objectives. *Bank of England Quarterly Bulletin* 23: 200–8.

1992. *The Bank of England and Public Policy 1941–1958.* Cambridge.

Fiegehen, G. C., Lansley, P. S., and Smith, A. D. 1977. *Poverty and Progress in Britain, 1953–73.* Cambridge.

Fishbein, W. H. 1984. *Wage Restraint by Consensus: Britain's Search for an Incomes Policy Agreement, 1965–79.*

Flanagan, R. J., Soskice, D. W., and Ullman, L. 1983. *Unionism, Economic Stability and Incomes Policies: European Experience.* Washington, D. C.

Flanders, A. 1964. *The Fawley Productivity Agreements.*

Fleming, J. M. 1962. Domestic financial policies under fixed and under floating exchange rates. *IMF Staff Papers* 9: 369–79.

Flemming, J. 1976. *Inflation.* Oxford.

Floud, R. and McCloskey, D., eds. 1981. *The Economic History of Britain since 1700.* 1st edn. Cambridge.

Foot, M. D. K. W. 1981. Monetary targets: their nature and record in the major economies. In Griffiths and Wood 1981.

Foreman-Peck, J. 1989. Competition, cooperation and nationalisation in the nineteenth century telegraph system. *Business History* 31: 81–101.

1991. Trade and the balance of payments. In Crafts and Woodward 1991.

Foreman-Peck, J., and Manning, D. 1988. How well is BT performing? An international comparison of telecommunications total factor productivity. *Fiscal Studies* 9: 54–67.

Foreman-Peck, J., and Waterson, M. 1985. The comparative efficiency of public and private enterprises in Britain: electricity generation between the wars. *Economic Journal* 85, supplement: 84–106.

Forsyth, P. J., and Kay, J. A. 1980. The economic implications of North Sea oil revenues. *Fiscal Studies* 1: 9–17.

Forsyth, P. J., Hill, R. D., and Trengove, C. D. 1986. Measuring airline efficiency. *Fiscal Studies* 7: 61–81.

Freeman, C. 1979. Technical innovation and British trade performance. In Blackaby 1979a.

1987. *Technology Policy and Economic Performance: Lessons from Japan.*

Friedman, M. 1968. The role of monetary policy. *American Economic Review* 58: 1–17.

1975. *Unemployment versus Inflation.*

Friedman, M., and Friedman, R. 1980. *Free to Choose.*

Furner, M., and Supple, B., eds. 1990. *The State and Economic Knowledge: The American and British Experiences.* Cambridge.

Gamble, A. 1985. *Britain in Decline: Economic Policy, Political Strategy and the British State.* 2nd edn.

1990. Britain's decline: some theoretical issues. In Mann 1990.

Gardner, N. 1987. *Decade of Discontent.*

Gardner, R. N. 1969. *Sterling–Dollar Diplomacy.* New York.

1980. *Sterling–Dollar Diplomacy in Current Perspective.* Oxford.

Garside, W. R. 1977. Juvenile unemployment and public policy between the wars. *Economic History Review* 30: 322–45.

1990. *British Unemployment 1991–1939: A Study in Public Policy.* Cambridge.

Gerschenkron A., 1962. *Economic Backwardness in Historical Perspective.* Cambridge, Mass.

Gilbert, M. 1980. *Quest for Monetary Order.* New York and Chichester.

Gillion, C., and Hemming, R. 1985. Social expenditure in the United Kingdom in a comparative context. In Klein and O'Higgins 1985.

Glennerster, H. 1980. Public spending and the social services: the end of an era? In Brown and Baldwin 1980.

1985. *Paying for Welfare.* Oxford.

1990. Social policy since the Second World War. In Hills 1990.

Glennerster, H., and Low, W. 1990. Education and the welfare state: does it add up? In Hills 1990.

Goldthorpe, J. H., and Hirsch, F. 1978. *The Political Economy of Inflation.*

Goodhart, C. A. E. 1969. The gilt-edged market. In Johnson 1972.

1975. Problems of monetary management: the UK experience. In Goodhart 1984.

1982. Structural changes in the banking system and the determination of the stock of money. In Goodhart 1984.

ed. 1984. *Monetary Theory and Practice: The U. K. Experience.*

1989. The conduct of monetary policy. *Economic Journal* 99: 293–346.

Goodhart, C. A. E., and Crockett, A. D. 1970. The importance of money. *Bank of England Quarterly Bulletin* 10: 159–98. Reprinted in Johnson 1972.

Goodin, R. E., and Dryzek, J. 1987. Risk-sharing and social justice: the motivational foundations of the post-war welfare state. In Goodin and Le Grand 1987.

Goodin, R. E., and Le Grand, J., eds. 1987. *Not Only the Poor.*

Goodman, G. 1979. *Cousins: The Awkward Warrior.*

Gordon, R. J. 1982. Why US wage and employment behaviour differs from that in Britain and Japan. *Economic Journal* 92: 13–44.

Gorst, T., Johman, L., and Lucas, W. S., eds. 1989. *Post-War Britain 1945–64: Themes and Perspectives.*

Gourvish, T. R. 1986. *British Railways 1948–73: A Business History.* Cambridge.

Gourvish, T. R., and O'Day, A., eds. 1991. *Britain since 1945.*

Gowing, M. M. 1972. The organisation of manpower in Britain during the Second World War. *Journal of Contemporary History* 7: 147–67.

Gowland, D. 1978. *Monetary Policy and Credit Control: The UK Experience.*

1982. *Controlling the Money Supply.*

Graham, A. 1972. Industrial policy. In Beckerman 1972.

Graham, A., with Seldon, A., eds. 1990. *Government and Economies in the Post-War World: Economic Policies and Comparative Performance 1945–85.*

Grant, W. 1982. *The Political Economy of Industrial Policy.*

1990. Government–industry relations in the British chemical industry. In Chick 1990.

1991. Government and manufacturing industry since 1900. In Jones and Kirby 1991.

Grassman, S. 1980. Long-term trends in openness of national economies. *Oxford Economic Papers* 32: 123–34.

Greenhalgh, C. A., Layard, P. R. G., and Oswald, A. J., eds. 1983. *The Causes of Unemployment.* Oxford.

Griffiths, B. 1973. The development of restrictive practices in the UK monetary system. *The Manchester School of Economic and Social Studies* 41: 3–18.

Griffiths, B., and Wood, G. E., eds. 1981. *Monetary Targets.*

Grubb, D., Jackman, R. and Layard, R. 1983. Causes of the current stagflation. In Greenhalgh *et al.* 1983.

Gwyn, W. B. 1980. Jeremiahs and pragmatists: perceptions of British decline. In Gwyn and Rose 1980.

Gwyn, W. B., and Rose, R., eds. 1980. *Britain: Progress and Decline.*

Hall, M. 1962. The consumer, capital and labour markets. In Worswick and Ady 1962.

Hall, P. A. 1986a. *Governing the Economy: The Politics of State Intervention in Britain and France.* Cambridge.

1986b. The state and economic decline. In Elbaum and Lazonick 1986.

Hall, R., *see* Roberthall, Lord.

Halsey, A. H., Heath, A. F., and Ridge, J. M. 1980. *Origins and Destinations.* Oxford.

Ham, A. 1981. *Treasury Rules.*

Hammond, R. J. 1951. *Food, vol. I: The Growth of Policy.*

Hannah, L. 1974. Managerial innovation and the rise of the large-scale company in interwar Britain. *Economic History Review* 27: 252–70.

ed. 1976a. *Management Strategy and Business Development.*

1976b. *The Rise of the Corporate Economy.*

1976c. Strategy and structure in the manufacturing sector. In Hannah 1976b.

1979. *Electricity before Nationalisation: A Study of the Development of the Electricity Supply Industry in Britain to 1948.*

1982. *Engineers, Managers and Politicians: The First Fifteen Years of Nationalised Electricity Supply in Britain.*

1983. *The Rise of the Corporate Economy.* 2nd edn.

1986. *Inventing Retirement: The Development of Occupational Pensions in Britain.* Cambridge.

1989. Cultural and social roots of British economic decline and renaissance: businessmen's alibi or Thatcher triumph. *Centre for Business Strategy, London Business School, Working Paper 6.*

1990. Economic ideas and government policy on industrial organization in Britain since 1945. In Furner and Supple 1990.

Hannah, L., and Kay, J. 1977. *Concentration in Modern Industry: Theory, Measurement and the UK Experience.*

Hansen, B. 1969. *Fiscal Policy in Seven Countries 1955–1965.* Paris.

Hare, P. G. 1985. *Planning the British Economy.*

Hare, P. G., and Kirby, M. W., eds. 1984. *An Introduction to British Economic Policy.*

Hargreaves, E. L., and Gowing, M. M. 1952. *Civil industry and trade.*

Harris, J. 1977. *William Beveridge: A Biography.* Oxford.

1981. Some aspects of social policy in Britain during the Second World War. In Mommsen 1981.

1986. Political ideas and the debate on state welfare, 1940–1945. In Smith 1986.

Harris, N. 1972. *Competition and the Corporate Society.*

Harrison, M. 1988. Resource mobilization for World War II: the U. S. A., the U. K., U. S. S. R. and Germany, 1938–1945. *Economic History Review* 41: 171–92.

1990. The volume of Soviet munitions output, 1937–1945: a reevaluation. *Journal of Economic History* 50: 569–90.

Hart, P., ed. 1986. *Unemployment and Labour Market Policies.* Aldershot.

Heald, D. 1980. The economic and financial control of UK nationalised industries. *Economic Journal* 90: 243–65.

1983. *Public Expenditure, Its Defence and Reform.* Oxford.

Healey, D. 1989. *The Time of My Life.*

Heath, J. B. 1961. Restrictive practices and after. *The Manchester School of Economic and Social Studies* 29: 173–202.

Heclo, H., and Wildavsky, A. 1974. *The Private Government of Public Money.*

Heller, P. S., Hemming, R., and Kohnert, P. W. 1986. Ageing and social expenditure in the major industrial countries, 1980–2025. *IMF Occasional Paper* 47.

Henderson, H. D. 1947. *The Use and Abuse of Economic Planning.* Cambridge.

Henderson, P. D. 1962. Government and industry. In Worswick and Ady 1962.

Hill, T. P. 1979. *Profits and Rates of Return.* Paris.

Hills, J. 1987. What happened to spending on the welfare state? In Walker and Walker eds. 1987.

    1989. Counting the family silver: the public sector's balance sheet 1957 to 1987. *Fiscal Studies* 10: 66–85.

    ed. 1990. *The State of Welfare: The Welfare State in Britain since 1974.* Oxford.

Hines, A. G. 1964. Wage inflation in the United Kingdom, 1893–1961. *Review of Economic Studies* 31: 221–52.

Hirsch, F. 1965. *The Pound Sterling: A Polemic.*

    1976. *Social Limits to Growth.* Cambridge, Mass.

HM Treasury. 1961. *Economic and Financial Objectives of the Nationalised Industries.* Cmnd 1337.

    1967. *Nationalised Industries: A Review of Economic and Financial Objectives.* Cmnd 3437.

    1978. *The Nationalised Industries.* Cmnd 7131.

HMSO 1941. *Analysis of the Sources of War Finance and Estimate of the National Income and Expenditure in 1938 and 1940.* Cmd 621.

Hogan, M. J. 1987. *The Marshall Plan.* Cambridge.

Holmans, A. Demand management in the United Kingdom 1952–58. (MS).

House of Commons. 1968. Select Committee on Nationalised Industries *Ministerial Control of the Nationalised Industries.*

House of Lords. 1985. *Report from the Select Committee on Overseas Trade.*

Howson, S. 1987. The origins of cheaper money, 1945–7. *Economic History Review* 40: 433–52.

    1988. 'Socialist' monetary policy: monetary thought in the Labour Party in the 1940s. *History of Political Economy* 20: 543–64.

    1989. Cheap money versus cheaper money: a reply to Professor Wood. *Economic History Review* 42: 401–5.

    1991. The problem of monetary control in Britain, 1948–51. *Journal of European Economic History* 20: 59–92.

    1993. *British Monetary Policy 1945–51.* Oxford.

Hutber, P., ed. 1978. *What's Wrong with Britain?*

Hutchison, T. W. 1968. *Economics and Economic Policy in Britain 1946–66.*

Hutton, G. 1953. *We Too Can Prosper.*

Ince, G. 1946. The mobilization of manpower in Great Britain for the Second World War. *Manchester School of Economic and Social Studies* 14: 17–52.

Incomes Policy: The Next Step. 1962. Cmnd 1626.

Institute of Economic Affairs. 1990. *Ideas and Policy.*

Jacquemin, A., and de Jong, H. W., eds. 1977. *Welfare Aspects of Industrial Markets.* Amsterdam.

Jay, D. 1980. *Change and Fortune.*

Jay, P. 1976. *Employment, Inflation and Politics.*

Jenkinson, T. 1987. The natural rate of unemployment: does it exist? *Oxford Review of Economic Policy* 33: 20–6.

Johnes, G., and Taylor, J. 1989. Labour. In Artis and Cobham 1991.

Johnman, L., and Tiratsoo, N., eds. Forthcoming. *The Attlee Years.*

Johnson, C. 1982. *MITI and the Japanese Miracle: The Growth of Industrial Policy, 1925–1975.* Stanford, Calif.

Johnson, H. G. 1952. The new monetary policy and the problem of credit control. *Oxford Bulletin of Economics and Statistics* 14: 117–31.

    ed. 1958a. *International Trade and Economic Growth.*

    1958b. Towards a general theory of the balance of payments. In Johnson 1958a.

    ed. 1972. *Readings in British Monetary Economics.* Oxford.

Johnson, P. 1986. Some historical dimensions of the welfare state 'crisis'. *Journal of Social Policy* 15: 443–65.

    ed. 1988. *The Structure of British Industry.* 2nd edn.

Johnson, P., and Falkingham, J. 1988. Intergenerational transfers and public expenditure on the elderly in modern Britain. *Ageing and Society* 8: 129–46.

Jones, G. 1990. The British government and foreign multinationals before 1970. In Chick 1990.

Jones, G., and Kirby, M. W., eds. 1991. *Competitiveness and the State: Government and Business in Twentieth Century Britain.* Manchester.

Jones, R. B. 1987. *Wages and Employment Policy 1936–1985.*

Joseph, Sir K., and Sumption, J. 1979. *Equality.*

Kaldor, N. (Lord). 1966. *Causes of the Slow Rate of Growth of the United Kingdom.* Cambridge.

    1970. The new monetarism. *Lloyds Bank Review* 97: 1–18.

    1971. Conflicts in national policy objectives. *Economic Journal* 81: 1–16.

    1982. *The Scourge of Monetarism.* Oxford.

Kaplan, J., and Schleiminger, G. 1989. *The European Payments Union: Financial Diplomacy in the 1950s.* Oxford.

Katzenstein, P. 1985. *Small States in World Markets.* Ithaca, N.Y.

Kay, J., and King, M. 1986. *The British Tax System.* 4th edn. Oxford.

Kay, J., and Thompson, D. 1987. Policy for industry. In Layard and Dornbusch 1987.

Keegan, W. 1984. *Mrs Thatcher's Economic Experiment.*

    1989. *Mr Lawson's Gamble.*

Keegan, W., and Pennant-Rea, R. 1979. *Who Runs the Economy?*

Kenen, P. 1960. *British Monetary Policy and the Balance of Payments 1951–59.* Cambridge, Mass.

Kennedy, C. M. 1952. Monetary policy. In Worswick and Ady 1952.

Keynes, J. M. 1927. J. M. Keynes on banking service. *Journal of the Institute of Bankers* 48: 494–7.

    1936. *The General Theory of Employment, Interest and Money.* 1973 edn. Basingstoke.

    1940. *How to Pay for the War: A Radical Plan for the Chancellor of the Exchequer.*

Kindleberger, C. P. 1967. *Europe's Postwar Growth: The Role of Labour Supply* Oxford.

    1987. *Marshall Plan Days.* Boston.

Kirby, M. W. 1984a. De-industrialisation in Britain: an Appraisal. In Hare and Kirby 1984.

1984b. Industrial policy in Britain. In Hare and Kirby 1984.

1991. Supply side management. In Crafts and Woodward 1991.

Klein, B. H. 1959. *Germany's Economic Preparations for War*. Cambridge, Mass.

Klein, R. 1983. *The Politics of the National Health Service*.

Klein, R., and O'Higgins, eds. 1985. *The Future of Welfare*. Oxford.

Knight, K. G. 1987. *Unemployment: An Economic Analysis*.

Kohan, C. M. 1952. *Works and Buildings*.

Kramer, D. C. 1989. *State Capital and Private Enterprise: The Case of the UK National Enterprise Board*.

Kramnick, I., ed. 1979. *Is Britain Dying? Perspectives on the Current Crisis*. Ithaca, N. Y.

Krause, L. B. 1968. British trade performance. In Caves 1968a.

Krause, L. B., and Salant, W. S. 1973. *European Monetary Unification*. Washington D. C.

1977. *World-Wide Inflation*. Washington D. C.

Kuznets, S. 1945. *National Product in Wartime*. New York.

Laidler, D. 1971. The influence of money on economic activity – a survey of some current problems. In Clayton *et al.* 1971.

1981. Monetarism: an interpretation and an assessment. *Economic Journal* 91: 1–28.

Laidler, D., and Parkin, J. M. 1970. The demand for money in the United Kingdom 1956–1967: preliminary estimates. *Manchester School of Economic and Social Studies* 38: 187–208. Reprinted in Johnson 1972.

Landymore, P. J. A. 1985. Education and industry since the war. In Morris 1985.

Law, C. M. 1981. *British Regional Development since World War I*.

Layard, R. 1986. *How to Beat Unemployment*. Oxford.

Layard, R., and Dornbusch, R., eds., 1987. *The Performance of the British Economy*. Washington D.C.

Layard, R., and Nickell, S. J. 1985. The causes of British unemployment. *National Institute Economic Review* 111: 62–85.

1987. The labour market. In Layard and Dornbusch 1987.

Lazonick, W. 1983. Industrial organisation and technological change: the decline of the British cotton industry. *Business History Review* 57: 195–236.

1986. The cotton industry. In Elbaum and Lazonick 1986.

Leadbeater, C. 1990. The road to privatisation: political debate too simplistic. *Financial Times*, 8 August 1990: 9.

Le Grand, J. 1982. *The Strategy of Equality*.

1990. The state of welfare. In Hills 1990.

Le Grand, J., and Winter, D. 1987. The middle-class use of the British social services. In Goodin and Le Grand 1987.

Le Grand, J., Winter, D., and Wooley, F. 1990. The National Health Service: safe in whose hands? In Hills 1990.

Leibenstein, H. 1966. Allocative efficiency vs 'X' efficiency. *American Economic Review* 56: 392–415.

1976. *Beyond Economic Man*. Cambridge, Mass.

Leruez, J. 1975. *Economic Planning and Politics in Britain*. Oxford.

Lewchuk, W. 1986. The motor industry. In Elbaum and Lazonick 1986.

Lindbeck, A. 1983. The recent slowdown of productivity growth. *Economic Journal* 93: 13–34.

London and Cambridge Economic Service. *Key Statistics.*

Lorenz, E., and Wilkinson, F. 1986. The shipbuilding industry 1880–1965. In Elbaum and Lazonick 1986.

Macaulay, Lord. 1829. *Southey's Colloquies,* review of Robert Southey, Sir Thomas More: or, Colloquies on the Progress and Prospect of Society. Reprinted in Lord Macaulay *Critical and Historical Essays Contributed to the Edinburgh Review.* Edinburgh 1894.

McCloskey, D. N. 1990. *If You're So Smart.*

MacDougall, D. 1987. *Don and Mandarin.*

Machin, S., and Wadhwani, S. 1989. The effects of unions on organisational change, investment and employment: evidence from WIRS. *Centre for Labour Economics, London School of Economics, Discussion Paper 355.*

Macleod, I., and Powell, E. 1952. *The Social Services: Needs and Means.*

Maddison, A. 1964. *Economic Growth in the West.* New York.

1982. *Phases of Capitalist Development.* Oxford.

1984. Origins and impact of the welfare state, 1883–1983. *Banca Nazionale del Lavoro Quarterly Review* 148: 55–87.

1987. Growth and slowdown in advanced capitalist economies: techniques of quantitative assessment. *Journal of Economic Literature* 25: 649–98.

1989. *The World Economy in the Twentieth Century.* Paris.

1991. *Dynamic Forces in Capitalist Development: A Long-Run Comparative View.* Oxford.

Major, R. L. 1979. *Britain's Trade and Exchange Rate Policy.*

Maki, D., and Spindler, Z. 1975. The effect of unemployment compensation on the rate of unemployment in Great Britain. *Oxford Economic Papers* 27: 440–54.

Mann, M., ed. 1990. *The Rise and Decline of the Nation State.* Oxford.

Manser, W. A. P. 1971. *Britain in Balance.*

Marglin, S., and Schor, J., eds. 1990. *The Golden Age of Capitalism: Reinterpreting the Postwar Experience.* Oxford.

Marquand, D. 1989. *The Unprincipled Society.*

Mars, J. 1952. British social income estimates, 1938–1950. *Manchester School of Economic and Social Studies* 20: 25–56.

Martin, R., and Rowthorn, R. W. 1986. *The Geography of De-Industrialisation.* Basingstoke.

Matthews, K., and Minford, A. P. L. 1987. Mrs Thatcher's economic policies, 1979–1987. *Economic Policy* 5: 57–102.

Matthews, R. C. O. 1968. Why has Britain had full employment since the war? *Economic Journal* 82: 195–204.

ed. 1982. *Slower Growth in the Western World.*

Matthews, R. C. O., Feinstein, C. H., and Odling-Smee, J. C. 1982. *British Economic Growth, 1856–1973.* Oxford.

Maynard, G. 1988. *The Economy under Mrs Thatcher.*

Meade, J. E. 1948. *Planning and the Price Mechanism.*

1990. *Collected Papers, vol. IV: The Cabinet Office Diary 1944–46.* Ed. S. Howson and D. Moggridge.

Meade, J. E., and Stone, R. 1941. The construction of tables of national income, expenditure, savings and investment. *Economic Journal* 51: 216–33.

Meadows, P. 1978. Planning. In Blackaby 1978.

Meen, G. 1988. International comparisons of the UK's long-run economic performance. *Oxford Review of Economic Policy* 4: xxii–xli.

Mercer, H. 1991. The Monopolies and Restrictive Practices Commission 1949–56: a study of regulatory failure. In Jones and Kirby 1991.

Mercer, H., Rollings, N., and Tomlinson, J., eds. 1992, *Labour Governments and Private Industry: The Experience of 1945–1951*. Edinburgh.

Metcalf, D., and Richardson, R. 1984. Labour. In Prest and Coppock 1984.

Metcalf, D., Nickell, S. J., and Floros, N. 1982. Still searching for an explanation of unemployment in interwar Britain. *Journal of Political Economy* 90: 386–99.

Middlemas, K. 1979. *Politics in Industrial Society*.
   1986. *Power, Competition and the State*, vol. I: *Britain in Search of Balance, 1940–1961*.

Middleton, P. 1989. Economic policy formulation in the post-war period. *National Institute Economic Review* February: 46–51.

Milanovic, B. 1989. *Liberalization and Entrepreneurship*. New York.

Mills, G., and Rockoff, H. 1987. Compliance with price controls in the United States and the United Kingdom during World War II. *Journal of Economic History* 47: 197–213.

Millward, R. 1988. The U. K. services sector, productivity change and the recession in long term perspective. *The Service Industries Journal* 8: 263–76.
   1990. Productivity in the UK services sector: historical trends 1856–1985 and comparisons with the USA 1950–85. *Oxford Bulletin of Economics and Statistics* 52: 423–36.

Millward, R., and Ward, R. 1987. The costs of public and private gas enterprise in late nineteenth century Britain. *Oxford Economic Papers* 39: 719–37.

Milward, A. S. 1977. *War, Economy and Society*. 1987 edn. Harmondsworth.
   1984a. *The Economic Effects of the Two World Wars on Britain*. 2nd edn. Basingstoke.
   1984b. *The Reconstruction of Western Europe 1945–51*.

Minford, A. P. L. 1983. *Unemployment: Cause and Cure*. Oxford.
   1991. *The Supply Side Revolution in Britain*.

Ministry of Labour and National Service. 1947. *Ministry of Labour and National Service Report for the Years 1939–45*. Cmd 7255.

Mishan, E. J. 1967. *The Costs of Economic Growth*.

Mitchell, B. R. 1975. *European Historical Statistics, 1750–1970*.
   1982. *International Historical Statistics: Africa and Asia*.
   1983. *International Historical Statistics: The Americas and Australasia*.
   1988. *British Historical Statistics*. Cambridge.

Molyneux, R., and Thompson, D. 1987. Nationalised industry performance: still third-rate? *Fiscal Studies* 8: 48–82.

Mommsen, W. J., ed. 1981. *The Emergence of the Welfare State in Britain and Germany, 1850–1950*.

Moore, B., and Rhodes, J. 1973. Evaluating the effects of British regional economic policy. *Economic Journal* 83: 87–110.

Morgan, K. O. 1984. *Labour in Power 1945–51.* Oxford.

Morris, D. J., ed. 1985. *The Economic System in the U. K.* Oxford.

Morris, D. J., and Stout, D. K. 1985. Industrial policy. In Morris 1985.

Mosley, P. 1984. *The Making of Economic Policy.* Brighton.

Mottershead, P. 1978. Industrial policy. In Blackaby 1978.

Muellbauer, J. 1986. Productivity and competitiveness in British manufacturing. *Oxford Review of Economic Policy* 23: 1–25.

Mundell, R. A. 1962. The appropriate use of monetary and fiscal policy for internal and external stability. *IMF Staff Papers* 9: 70–7.

1963. Capital mobility and stabilization policy under fixed and flexible exchange rates. *Canadian Journal of Economics and Political Science* 29: 475–85.

Narendranathan, W., Nickell, S. J., and Stern, J. 1985. Unemployment benefits revisited. *Economic Journal* 95: 307–29.

Nash, E. F. 1951. Wartime controls of food and agricultural prices. In Chester 1951.

Neale, A. D. 1960. *The Anti-Trust Laws of the United States of America.* Cambridge.

Niskanen, W. 1971. *Bureaucracy and Representative Government.* Chicago.

Nolan, B. 1987. *Income Distribution and the Macro-Economy.* Cambridge.

Norton, W. E. 1969. Debt management and monetary policy in the United Kingdom. *Economic Journal* 79: 475–94. Reprinted in Johnson 1972.

Nossiter, B. D. 1978. *Britain: A Future that Works.*

OECD 1981. *The Welfare State in Crisis.* Paris.

1985a. *Measuring Health Care.* Paris.

1985b. *Social Expenditure 1960–1990.* Paris.

Ofer, G. 1987. Soviet economic growth: 1928–1985. *Journal of Economic Literature* 25: 1767–833.

Olson, M. 1965. *The Logic of Collective Action.* Cambridge, Mass.

1982. *The Rise and Fall of Nations: Economic Growth, Stagflation and Social Rigidities.* New Haven, Conn.

Overy, R. J. 1980. *The Air War 1939–1945.*

1988. Mobilization for total war in Germany 1939–1941. *English Historical Review* 103: 613–39.

Paige, D., and Bombach, G. 1959. *A Comparison of National Output and Productivity of the UK and the US.* Paris.

Paish, F. W. 1962. *Studies in an Inflationary Economy. The United Kingdom 1948 to 1961.*

1970. *How the Economy Works.*

Panic, M., ed. 1976. *The United Kingdom and West German Manufacturing Industry, 1945–72.*

Papps, I. 1975. *Government and Enterprise: An Analysis of the Economics of Governmental Regulation or Control of Industry.*

Parker, H. M. D. 1957. *Manpower: A Study of Wartime Policy and Administration.*

Parker, W. N. 1971. From new to old to new in economic history. *Journal of Economic History* 31: 3–14.

Parkin, M., and Sumner, M. T. 1978. *Inflation in the United Kingdom.* Manchester.

Parsons, D. W. 1986. *The Political Economy of British Regional Policy.* Beckenham.

Pathirane, L., and Blades, D. W. 1982. Defining and measuring the public sector:

some international comparisons. *Review of Income and Wealth*, 28th Ser., 3: 261–89.

Pavitt, K., ed. 1980. *Technical Innovation and British Economic Performance*.

Pavitt, K., and Soete, L. 1980. Innovative activities and export shares: some comparisons between industries and countries. In Pavitt 1980.

Peacock, A. T., and Wiseman, J. 1961. *The Growth of Public Expenditure in the United Kingdom*. Princeton.

Pechman, J. A., ed. 1989. *The Role of the Economist in Government*. Hemel Hempstead.

Peck, M. J. 1968. Science and technology. In Caves 1968a.

Peden, G. C. 1983. Sir Richard Hopkins and the 'Keynesian Revolution' in employment policy, 1929–45. *Economic History Review* 36: 281–96.

1985. *British Economic and Social Policy*. Oxford.

1987. *Keynes, the Treasury and British Economic Policy*.

Pelling, H. 1984. *The Labour Governments, 1945–51*.

Pember and Boyle. 1950. *British Government Securities in the Twentieth Century*.

Phelps, E. 1967. Phillips curves, expectations of inflation and optimal unemployment over time. *Economica* 34: 254–81.

Phillips, A. W. 1958. The relation between unemployment and the rate of change of money wage rates in the UK, 1861–1957. *Economica* 25: 283–99.

Piachaud, D. 1987. The growth of poverty. In Walker and Walker 1987.

Pissarides, C. 1972. A model of British macroeconomic policy, 1955–69. *Manchester School of Economic and Social Studies* 40: 245–59.

Pliatzky, L. 1984. *Getting and Spending: Public Expenditure, Employment and Inflation*. 2nd edn. Oxford.

1989. *The Treasury under Mrs Thatcher*.

Plowden, E. 1989. *An Industrialist in the Treasury: The Post-War Years*.

Plowden Report. 1961. *Control of Public Expenditure*. Cmnd 1432.

Pollard, S. 1982. *The Wasting of the British Economy: British Economic Policy, 1945 to the Present*.

1983. *The Development of the British Economy 1914–80*.

Posner, M. 1987. Nationalisation. In Eatwell, Milgate and Newman 1987.

Postan, M. M. 1952. *British War Production*.

Prais, S. J. 1976. *The Evolution of Giant Firms in Britain*. Cambridge.

1988. Qualified manpower in engineering. *National Institute Economic Review* 127: 76–83.

Pressnell, L. S. 1986. *External Economic Policy since the War, vol. I: The Post-War Financial Settlement*.

Prest, A. R., and Coppock, D. J., eds. 1984. *The UK Economy: A Manual of Applied Economics*. 10th edn.

Price, L. D. D. 1972. The demand for money in the United Kingdom: a further investigation. *Bank of England Quarterly Bulletin* 12: 43–56.

Price, R. W. R. 1978a. Budgetary policy. In Blackaby 1978.

1978b. Public expenditure. In Blackaby 1978.

Pryke, R. 1971. *Public Enterprise in Practice: The British Experience of Nationalisation over Two Decades*.

1981. *The Nationalised Industries: Policies and Performance since 1968*. Oxford.

1982. The comparative performance of public and private enterprise. *Fiscal Studies* 3: 68–81.

Radcliffe. 1959. *Committee on the Working of the Monetary System: Report* Cmnd 827.

Radcliffe Committee. 1960a. *Minutes of Evidence*.

1960b. *Principal Memoranda of Evidence*, vols. I–III.

Ranki, G. 1988. Economy and the Second World War: a few comparative issues. *Journal of European Economic History* 17: 303–47.

Reddaway, W. B. 1951. Rationing. In Chester 1951.

1966. Addendum: the postwar scene. In Salter 1966.

Rees, G. L. 1963. *Britain and the Post-War European Payments System*. Cardiff.

Reid, M. 1982. *The Secondary Banking Crisis 1973–75*.

Rhys, D. G. 1988. Motor vehicles. In Johnson 1988.

Richardson, R. 1991. Trade unions and industrial relations. In Crafts and Woodward 1991.

Robbins, L. C. 1947. *The Economic Problem in Peace and War*.

Roberthall, Lord. 1989 and 1991. *The Robert Hall Diaries*, vol. I: *1947–53*, vol. II: *1954–61*. Ed. A. Cairncross.

Robertson, A. J. 1987. *The Bleak Midwinter 1947*. Manchester.

Robinson, E. A. G. 1951. The overall allocation of resources. In Chester 1951.

1967. *Economic Planning in the United Kingdom: Some Lessons*. Cambridge.

Rogow, A. A., and Shore, P. 1955. *The Labour Government and British Industry*. Oxford.

Rollings, N. 1985. The 'Keynesian Revolution' and economic policy making: a comment. *Economic History Review* 38: 95–100.

1988. British budgetary policy, 1945–54: a Keynesian Revolution? *Economic History Review* 41: 283–98.

1992. 'The Reichstag method of governing'? The Attlee governments and permanent economic controls. In Mercer, Rollings and Tomlinson 1992.

Rostas, L. 1948. *Comparative Productivity in British and American Industry*. Cambridge.

Rowntree, B. S., and Lavers, G. R. 1951. *Poverty and the Welfare State*.

Rowthorn, R. E., and Wells, J. R. 1987. *De-Industrialization and Foreign Trade*. Cambridge.

Royal Commission on the Distribution of Income and Wealth. 1978. *Lower Incomes* Report no. 6, Cmnd 7175.

1979. *Lower Incomes* Report no. 7, Cmnd 6999.

Rubinstein, W. D. 1988. Social class, social attitudes and British business life. *Oxford Review of Economic Policy* 4: 51–8.

Rupp, L. J. 1978. *Mobilizing Women for War*. Princeton, NJ.

Salant, W. S. 1980. The collected writings of John Maynard Keynes: activities 1940–43 and 1944–46: a review article. *Journal of Economic Literature* 18: 1056–62.

Salter, W. E. G. 1960. *Productivity and Technical Change*. Cambridge.

ed. 1966 *Productivity and Technical Change*. 2nd edn. Cambridge.

Sanderson, M. 1988. Technical education and economic decline: 1890–1980s. *Oxford Review of Economic Policy* 4: 38–50.

1990. Social equity and industrial need: a dilemma of English education since 1945. In Gourvish and O'Day 1991.

Sargent, J. R. 1979. U. K. performance in services. In Blackaby 1979a.

Saunders, C. T. 1946. Manpower distribution, 1939–45. *Manchester School of Economic and Social Studies* 14: 1–39.

Sawyer, M. 1991. Industrial policy. In Artis and Cobham 1991.

1992. *Labour's Industrial Policies in the 1970s: Debates and Disagreements, vol. VI of Labour: The Party of Industrial Modernisation?* Business History Unit Conference, London School of Economics and Political Science, April.

Sawyer, M. C. 1981. *The Economics of Industries and Firms.* 2nd edn.

Sayers, R. S. 1952. *Modern Banking.* Corrected 3rd edn. Oxford.

1956. *Financial Policy, 1939–1945.*

1983. 1941 – the first Keynesian budget. In Feinstein 1983.

Scott, M. 1962. The balance of payments crises. In Worswick and Ady 1962.

Scott, W. H., Halsey, A. H., Banks, J. A., and Lupton, T. 1956. *Technical Change and Industrial Relations.* Liverpool.

Scrivens, E. 1991. Disease. *Social Policy and Administration* 25: 27–38.

Seldon, A. 1981. *Churchill's Indian Summer: The Conservative Government 1951–55.*

Shanks, M. 1961. *The Stagnant Society: A Warning.* Harmondsworth.

Shaw, C. 1983. The large manufacturing employers of 1907. *Business History* 25: 42–60.

Shonfield, A. 1959. *British Economic Policy since the War.* Harmondsworth.

Silberston, A. 1958. The motor industry. In Burn 1958.

Sinclair, Sir J. 1831. *Correspondence of Sir John Sinclair: Volume I.* Edinburgh.

Singh, A. 1977. U. K. industry and the world economy: a case of de-industrialisation. *Cambridge Journal of Economics* 1: 113–36. Reprinted in Feinstein 1983.

Singleton, J. 1986. Lancashire's last stand: declining employment in the British cotton industry. *Economic History Review* 39: 92–103.

1990. Showing the white flag: the Lancashire cotton industry, 1945–65. *Business History* 32: 129–49.

1991. *Lancashire on the Scrap-Heap: The Cotton Industry 1950–1970.* Oxford.

Sked, A. 1987. *Britain's Decline: Problems and Perspectives.* Oxford.

Smith, A. D., Hitchens, D. M. W., and Davies, S. W. 1982. *International Industrial Productivity: A Comparison of Britain, America and Germany.* Cambridge.

Smith, D. C. 1980. Trade union growth and industrial disputes. In Caves and Krause 1980.

Smith, H. L., ed. 1986. *War and Social Change.* Manchester.

Smith, K. 1989. *The British Economic Crisis.* Harmondsworth.

Smith, W. L., and Mikesell, R. F. 1957. The effectiveness of monetary policy: recent British experience. *Journal of Political Economy* 65: 18–39.

Smithies, E. 1984. *The Black Economy in England since 1914. Social Trends.* Dublin.

Solomon, R. 1982. *The International Monetary System 1945–81: An Insider's View.* New York.

Solow, R. M. 1956. A contribution to the theory of economic growth. *Quarterly Journal of Economics* 70: 65–94.

Spencer, P. D. 1981. A model of the demand for British government stocks by non-bank residents 1967–77. *Economic Journal* 91: 938–60.

1986. *Financial Innovation, Efficiency and Disequilibrium: Problems of Monetary Management in the United Kingdom 1971–1981*. Oxford.

Stelser, I. 1988. Britain's newest import: America's regulatory experience. *Oxford Review of Economic Policy* 4: 68–79.

Stewart, M. 1967. *Keynes and After*. Harmondsworth.

1977. *The Jekyll and Hyde Years: Politics and Economic Policy since 1964*.

1983. *Controlling the Economic Future*. Brighton.

Stone, R. 1951. The use and development of national income and expenditure estimates. In Chester 1951.

Stout, D. 1977. *International Price Competitiveness, Non-Price Factors and International Trade*.

Strange, S. 1971. *Sterling and British Policy*. Oxford.

1988. *The Casino Economy*. Oxford.

Summerfield, P. 1984. *Women Workers in the Second World War*.

Supple, B. 1987. *The History of the British Coal Industry*, vol. IV: *1913–1946: The Political Economy of Decline*. Oxford.

Swords-Isherwood, N. 1980. British management compared. In Pavitt 1980.

Taylor-Gooby, P. 1985. *Public Opinion, Ideology, and the Welfare State*.

Tew, J. H. B. 1965. *International Monetary Co-Operation 1945–65*. (8th edn).

1978a. Monetary policy. In Blackaby 1978.

1978b. Policies aimed at improving the balance of payments. In Blackaby 1978.

Thane, P. 1982. *The Foundations of the Welfare State*.

Thirlwall, A. P. 1981. De-industrialisation in the U. K. *Lloyds Bank Review* April: 22–37.

1982. *Balance of Payments Theory and the U. K. Experience*.

Thomas, M. 1988. Labour market structure and the nature of unemployment in interwar Britain. In Eichengreen and Hatton 1988.

Thompson, G. 1990. *The Political Economy of the New Right*. Cambridge.

Tinbergen, J. 1952. *On the Theory of Economic Policy*. Amsterdam.

Tiratsoo, N., ed. 1992. *The Attlee Years*.

Tiratsoo, N., and Tomlinson, J. 1993. *Industrial Efficiency and State Intervention: Labour 1939–51*.

Titmuss, R. M. 1950. *Problems of Social Policy*.

1955. *Essays on 'The Welfare State'*.

Tolliday, S. 1991. Ford and Fordism in post-war Britain: British management and the control of labour 1937–1987. In Tolliday and Zeitlin 1991.

Tolliday, S. and Zeitlin, J., eds. 1991. *The Power to Manage? Employers and Industrial Relations in Comparative Historical Perspective*.

Tomlinson, J. 1987. *Employment Policy: The Crucial Years 1939–1955*. Oxford.

1990. *Public Policy and the Economy since 1900*. Oxford.

1991. A missed opportunity? Labour and the productivity problem 1945–51. In Jones and Kirby 1991.

1993. Mr Attlee's supply-side socialism. *Economic History Review* 47: 1–23.

Tortella, G., ed. 1990. *Education and Economic Development since the Industrial Revolution*. Barcelona.

Townsend, P. 1979. *Poverty in the United Kingdom*.

Treasury and Bank of England. 1980. *Monetary Control*. Cmnd 7858.

Triffin R. 1957. *Europe and the Money Muddle*. New Haven, Conn.

UK 1942. *Social Insurance and Allied Services*.

    1944. *Employment Policy*.

    1979. *The Government's Expenditure Plans, 1980–81*.

Ulman, L. 1968. Collective bargaining and industrial efficiency. In Caves 1968a.

US Bureau of the Census. 1960. *Historical Statistics of the United States, Colonial Times to 1970*. Washington D. C.

Van der Wee, H. 1986. *Prosperity and Upheaval: The World Economy 1945–1980*. Harmondsworth.

Vatter, H. G. 1985. *The U.S. Economy in World War II*. New York.

Vickers, J., and Yarrow, G. 1988. *Privatisation: An Economic Analysis*. Cambridge, Mass.

Wadhwani, S. 1987. Effects of inflation on real wages and employment. *Economica* 54: 21–40.

    1989. The effect of unions on productivity growth, investment and employment: a report on some recent work. *Centre for Labour Economics, London School of Economics, Discussion Paper* 356.

Walker, A., and Walker, C., eds. 1987. *The Growing Divide: A Social Audit, 1979–1987*.

Waller, P. J. 1983. *Town, City and Nation*. Oxford.

Walshe, J. G. 1991. Industrial organisation and competition policy. In Crafts and Woodward 1991.

Walters, A. A. 1969a. Money in boom and slump. *Hobart Paper* 44.

    1969b. The Radcliffe Report – ten years after: a survey of empirical evidence. In Croome and Johnson 1969.

    1986. *Britain's Economic Renaissance*. Oxford and New York.

Ward, T. S., and Neild, R. R. 1978. *The Measurement and Reform of Budgetary Policy*.

Wardley, P. 1991. The anatomy of big business: aspects of corporate development in the twentieth century. *Business History* 33: 268–96.

Wass, D. 1978. *The Changing Problems of Economic Management*. Lecture to the Johnian Society, Cambridge.

Webster, C. 1988. *The Health Services since the War*.

Whitehead, C. 1988. *Reshaping the Nationalised Industries*. Oxford.

Whiteman, J. C. 1985. North Sea oil. In Morris 1985.

Whiting, A. 1976. An international comparison of the instability of economic growth. *Three Banks Review* 109: 26–46.

Wicks, M. 1987. *A Future for All: Do We Need a Welfare State?* Harmondsworth.

Wiener, M. J. 1985. *English Culture and the Decline of the Industrial Spirit 1850–1980*. Harmondsworth.

Wilensky, H. L., and Lebeaux, C. N. 1958. *Industrial Society and Social Welfare*. New York.

Wilks, S. 1990. Institutional insularity: government and the British motor industry since 1945. In Chick 1990.

Williams, F. 1989. *Social Policy: A Critical Introduction*.

Williams, K., Williams, J., and Haslam, C. 1989. Do labour costs really matter? *Work, Employment and Society* 3: 281–305.

Williams, P. M., ed. 1983. *The Diary of Hugh Gaitskell 1945–1956*.
Wilson Committee. 1980. *Report of the Committee to Review The Functioning of Financial Institutions*. Cmnd 7937.
Wilson, T. 1966. Instability and the rate of growth. *Lloyds Bank Review* July.
Wilson, T., and Wilson, D. 1982. *The Political Economy of the Welfare State*.
eds. 1991. *The State and Social Welfare*.
Winch, D. 1972. *Economics and Policy*.
Winters, L. A. 1987. Britain in Europe: a survey of quantitative trade studies. *Journal of Common Market Studies* 25: 315–36.
Woodward, N. W. C. 1991. Inflation. In Crafts and Woodward 1991.
Worswick, G. D. N. 1991. *Unemployment: A Problem of Policy*. Cambridge.
Worswick, G. D. N., and Ady, P., eds. 1952. *The British Economy 1945–50*. Oxford.
eds. 1962. *The British Economy in the 1950s*. Oxford.
Wright, J. F. 1979. *Britain in the Age of Economic Management*. Oxford.
Wrigley, C. 1991. Trade unions, government and the economy. In Gourvish and O'Day 1991.
Yamey, B. S., ed. 1962a. *Resale Price Maintenance*.
1962b. United Kingdom. In Yamey 1962a.
Zweig, F. 1951. *Productivity and Trade Unions*. Oxford.

List of British Isles cities, towns, villages, parishes, counties, regions and other geographic landmarks cited

Note: in 1974 county boundaries in Britain were redrawn; many were consolidated and renamed. Post-1974 county names and descriptions have been given *only* in those instances where they were cited in the text; otherwise all county references are to the pre-1974 counties and boundaries. Not all counties are included.

MAJOR DIVISIONS AND COUNTRIES

England
  The southern portion (excluding Wales) of Great Britain; roughly 50,875 square miles; London is its capital.
Great Britain
  England, Wales and Scotland.
Ireland (Eire)
  Western island of the British Isles; by a new constitution effective 29 December 1937, Ireland declared itself a 'sovereign, independent, democratic state'; full independence from the British Commonwealth was achieved with the Republic of Ireland Act in 1948; 27,137 square miles; Dublin is the capital.
Northern Ireland
  A self-governing state established in 1920 with the Government of Ireland Acts; made up of the former counties of Antrim, Armagh, Down, Londonderry, Tyrone and Ulster; area of 5,238 square miles; a focal point of social, economic and political unrest between Protestants and Catholics; Belfast is the seat of government.
Scotland
  The northern part of Great Britain; 29,796 square miles in area; the border with England extends from roughly the Solway Firth to the Cheviot Hills to the river Tweed; composed of the Southern Uplands, the Central Lowlands (frequently referred to in combination as 'the Lowlands'), the Northern and Western Highlands ('the Highlands'), the Hebrides or Western Isles and the Orkney and Shetland Isles; Edinburgh is Scotland's capital.
United Kingdom of Great Britain *and Ireland*
  Political union established 1 January 1801; comprised of England and Wales, Scotland and Ireland; superseded by the United Kingdom of Great Britain *and Northern Ireland* on 6 December 1921; the Irish Free State recognised as a free member of the British Commonwealth (until 1937 when Ireland declared its independence).
Wales (Cymru)
  Principality in the SW of Great Britain; area of some 8,000 square miles;

commonly divided according to 'North Wales' and 'South Wales'; the Welsh capital is Cardiff.

CITIES, TOWNS AND VILLAGES

Aberdeen
  Seaport city and county town of Aberdeenshire, Scotland; $130\frac{1}{2}$ miles N of Edinburgh and 524 miles N of London.
Ayr
  Seaport and county town of Ayrshire, Scotland, on river Ayr; $41\frac{1}{2}$ miles SW of Glasgow and $87\frac{1}{2}$ miles WSW of Edinburgh.
Balcarres (House)
  In E Fifeshire, Scotland; $\frac{3}{4}$ miles NW of Colinsburgh.
Banbury
  Town in Oxfordshire; 22 miles N of Oxford.
Barnsley
  Town in Yorkshire (West Riding); 16 miles N of Sheffield, on river Dearne.
Bedford
  County town of Bedfordshire, straddles river Ouse; $49\frac{3}{4}$ miles NW of London.
Belfast
  Principal town of county Ulster in Northern Ireland; 113 miles N of Dublin, across the Irish Sea from Glasgow (135 miles) and from Liverpool (156 miles); site of Queens University.
Billingham
  Urban district in SE Durham; $2\frac{1}{2}$ miles NE of Stockton-on-Tees.
Birmingham
  City in Warwickshire; 113 miles NW of London; located roughly in the centre of England on the edge of a major coal and iron district; metal manufactures were central to Birmingham's industrial development.
Blackpool
  Town in N Lancashire; $16\frac{1}{2}$ miles NW of Preston and 227 miles NW of London by rail.
Blackwell Hall
  Seat in S Durham, on river Tees; $1\frac{1}{2}$ miles SW of Darlington.
Bradford
  City in Yorkshire (West Riding); 9 miles W of Leeds, 35 miles SW of York and 192 miles from London by rail; England's primary seat for woollens and worsteds manufacture; nicknamed 'Worstedopolis'.
Bristol
  Seaport city in Gloucestershire (and Somerset); port 26 miles from Cardiff, Wales, and 71 miles from Swansea, Wales; $117\frac{1}{2}$ miles W of London.
Cambridge
  County seat of Cambridgeshire; 57 miles NE of London by rail; most notably the site of Cambridge University and its related colleges.
Cardiff
  Seaport and county town of Glamorgan, Wales; 152 miles W of London; voluminous exports of coal and iron from nearby Taff and Rhymney Valleys made through the port; industries also included iron foundries, tinplate manufactures and iron shipbuilding.
Carnarvon
  County town of Carnarvonshire, Wales; 246 miles NW of London by rail.

Carron
> Village in Stirlingshire, Scotland; near river Carron; ironworks established there in 1760.

Coventry
> City of Warwickshire; 19 miles SE of Birmingham and 94 miles NW of London by rail; manufactures included cycles, motors, ribbons, silk, watches, woollens, carpets, cotton, metalwork and iron founding.

Crook
> Village in S Durham.

Derby (där′bē)
> County town of Derbyshire; 42½ miles NE of Birmingham, 60 miles SE of Manchester and 129 miles NW of London by rail.

Dublin
> Metropolis of Eire (Ireland); port 60 miles from Holyhead, Carnarvonshire, Wales, 196 miles from Glasgow.

Dudley (and Ward)
> Town in Worcestershire; 8 miles NW of Birmingham; 121½ miles NW of London.

Dundee
> Seaport city on the Tay in Angus, Scotland; 59½ miles N of Edinburgh, 84 miles NE of Glasgow, and 452¾ miles NW of London by rail; principal manufactures included jute and linen, shipbuilding, engineering, foundries and brewing.

Dundonald
> Village in Ayrshire, Scotland.

Dunkinfield
> Municipal borough in Cheshire.

Edinburgh
> Capital of Scotland and county town of Midlothian, on the Firth of Forth; 392½ miles N of London; seaport section known as 'Leith'; principal industries included printing, bookbinding, machine-making, rubber and brewing.

Edgbaston
> Parliamentary division of Birmingham.

Etruria
> Village near Stoke-upon-Trent, N Staffordshire; site of Josiah Wedgwood's earthenware manufactures.

Gainsborough
> Town in Lincolnshire; 15 miles NW of Lincoln and 145 miles NW of London; a sub-port of Grimsby.

Gateshead
> Town in N Durham on river Tyne, opposite Newcastle; industrial composition mimicked that of Newcastle.

Glasgow
> City on the river Clyde in Lanarkshire, Scotland; 47½ miles W of Edinburgh and 401½ miles NW of Euston Station in London by rail; principal industries were textiles, printing, iron manufacture, engineering; regarded as the seat of the Scottish iron trade.

Gleneagles
> Place in Perthshire, Scotland; site of grand hotel with golf course and tennis grounds.

Hereford
> County town of Herefordshire on river Wye; 144 miles NW of London by rail.

Hull
> City at the confluence of the river Hull and the estuary the Humber; $55\frac{1}{2}$ miles SE of Leeds and $173\frac{1}{2}$ miles N from London; one of England's largest ports; also known as 'Kingston-upon-Hull'.

Huntingdon
> County town of Huntingdonshire on river Ouse; 59 miles N of London.

Inverness
> County town of Inverness-shire, Scotland, at NE end of Caledonian Canal; 192 miles from Edinburgh, 585 miles from London; principal industries included railway repair, shipbuilding, iron founding and woollen cloth.

Keighley (kēth'lē)
> Town in Yorkshire (West Riding); 9 miles NW of Bradford; connected to Hull by the Leeds & Liverpool Canal.

Leeds
> City on river Aire in Yorkshire (West Riding); 25 miles SW of York, 43 miles NE of Manchester and 186 miles NW of London by rail; site of most major industrial undertakings.

Leicester (les'ter)
> Capital city of Leicestershire on river Soar; 99 miles by rail NNW of London; principal centre for a large agricultural market, including wool-producing districts.

Lincoln
> County town of Lincolnshire; 120 miles NW of London.

Liverpool
> Seaport city in Lancashire on the river Mersey; 31 miles W of Manchester by rail, 201 miles NW of London; chief port for Britain's transatlantic trade.

London
> Capital city of England; seat of government for Great Britain; on the Thames; principal financial and commercial centre for Britain; the financial centre is sometimes simply referred to as 'the City'.

Macclesfield
> Town in Cheshire; $17\frac{1}{2}$ miles S of Manchester, 166 miles NW of London by rail; adjacent to the Macclesfield Canal.

Manchester
> City in Lancashire, separated from Salford by river Irwell; connected to the sea $35\frac{1}{2}$ miles away by the Manchester Ship Canal; 183 miles NW of London.

Marston
> Village in Cheshire on river Trent and on Mersey Canal.

Meriden
> Village in Warwickshire; $5\frac{1}{2}$ miles NW of Coventry.

Monmouth
> County town of Monmouthshire, England; 19 miles S of Hereford.

Newbury
> Town in Berkshire on river Kennet; 17 miles SW of Reading, 53 miles WSW of London by rail.

Newcastle-upon-Tyne
> City in Northumberland on river Tyne; $268\frac{1}{2}$ miles N of London; being the port

nearest one of the largest coalfields in England, immense quantities of coal were exported from there; played a central role in the coal trade.

Northampton
Capital of Northamptonshire on river Nene; 65¾ miles NW of London; principal seat of boot and shoe manufactures; also host to the Pytchley Hunt in March and November.

Nottingham
Capital of Nottinghamshire; 123½ miles by rail NW of London's St Pancras Station; important industries were lace making and cotton hosiery manufacture.

Oldham
Town in SE Lancashire on river Medlock; 6 miles NE of Manchester.

Oxford
County town of Oxfordshire between rivers Cherwell and Thames; 63 miles from London by rail; principally an educational centre, site of Oxford University.

Prescott
Town in SW Lancashire; 7½ miles E of Liverpool; site of Liverpool Corporation's water supply reservoirs.

Preston
Port and manufacturing town in Lancashire; on the Lancaster Canal near the head of river Ribble's estuary; 28 miles NE of Liverpool and 31 miles NW of Manchester.

Salford
City in Lancashire, W of Manchester; 'it forms practically a part of Manchester'.

Sheffield
City in Yorkshire; 42½ miles SE of Manchester, 158½ miles NW of London; long recognised for its cutlery industry, but had almost every other manufacturing industry, too.

Southampton
Seaport in Hampshire; 79 miles SW of London; one of Britain's major port centres, particularly for passengers.

Southend-on-Sea
Town in Essex on the Thames; 42 miles E of London by rail.

Stirling
County town of Stirlingshire, Scotland on river Forth; 20½ miles NE of Glasgow and 36½ miles NW of Edinburgh by rail.

Turnberry
Place on Ayrshire coast on Turnberry Bay; 56 miles SW of Glasgow by rail.

Warrington
Town in Lancashire; 16 miles WSW of Manchester.

Warwick
County town of Warwickshire on river Avon; 108 miles NW of London.

York
County town of Yorkshire; 188 miles NW of London.

COUNTIES

Ayrshire
Maritime co. in SW of Scotland; mineral deposits included coal, iron, limestone and sandstone – all extensively worked; had manufactures of woollens, cotton, iron and earthenware; also dairying.

Bedfordshire
    Inland co. N of London; primarily agricultural, with some manufactures related to agricultural implements; some mineral extraction.
Berkshire (Bark'shir)
    Inland co. W of London; agriculture included dairying and crop cultivation; manufactures of agricultural implements and malt making; Reading had a large biscuit enterprise.
Berwickshire
    Maritime co. in SE of Scotand; mineral deposits of limestone, coal and copper; coastal location supported an important fishing industry; agriculture limited to a fertile area called 'the Merse'.
Borders
    (Post-1974) co. in SE of Scotand; encompasses the former counties of Berwickshire, Roxburghshire, Selkirkshire, Peebles-shire and parts of Midlothian.
Buckinghamshire
    Inland co. adjacent NW to London; agriculture centred around grazing in the south and cultivation of wheat, beans, etc., to the north.
Cambridgeshire
    Inland co. N of London; large fens and marshlands drained for agriculture.
Cheshire
    Maritime co. S of Lancashire; serviced by the Manchester Ship Canal; mineral deposits of salt, coal and ironstone; railway rolling-stock manufacture was an important industry.
Cornwall
    Maritime co. at the extreme SW of England; tin and copper mining and manufacture were dominant industries.
Derbyshire
    Inland co. in N central England; pasture and crop lands as well as endowments of coal, iron ore, lead, limestone and marble; manufactures included paper making, silk, lace, cotton, brewing and iron founding.
Devon
    Maritime co. in SW of England; like Cornwall, tin and copper mines and manufactures, as well as lead, iron and various clays; industries were coarse woollens, linens, lace, paper, and gloves and shoes.
Durham
    Maritime co. in N of England; some of England's most important coalfields located here; many various industries, including chemicals, glass, shipbuilding, paper, woollens & worsteds, large ironworks and machine making.
Essex
    Maritime co. adjacent NE to London; primarily agricultural with few industries not related to local supply of agricultural implements.
Glamorgan
    Maritime co. in S of Wales; commercially the most important Welsh county due to its endowment of coal and iron ore and its convenient seaboard location; home to some of the world's largest ironworks of the time.
Gloucestershire
    Co. in W of England; two large coalfields in the west; industries included silk, woollens and cotton, gloves, glass and dairying.
Hampshire
    Maritime co. in S of England; also called 'Hants'; rolling countryside supported

sheep and pigs; main industry located at the ports – shipbuilding and shipping services.

Hertfordshire

Inland co. N of London; economy dominated by agriculture: animal husbandry, grains, hay, fruit and vegetable gardens for urban markets; very few manufactures.

Humberside

(Post-1974) co. on the NE English coast; composed the former counties of East Riding, Yorkshire, parts of West Riding, Yorkshire and the Lindsey division of Lincolnshire; 'Humberside North' is that part of the co. N of the Humber, previously East Riding.

Huntingdonshire

Inland co. in E of England; primarily agricutural with market gardens and dairying; manufactures essentially limited to the local supply of implements.

Kent

Maritime co. in SE of England; largely agricultural, producing more hops than the rest of the country; manufactures centred around paper, gunpowder and pottery; late exploitation of a coal measure on the eastern coast.

Lancashire

Maritime co. in the NW of England on the Irish Sea; major industrial area: coal and iron, shipbuilding and immense cotton and textile manufactures.

Limerick

County in Munster province, Ireland; rolling plain considered quite productive; chief manufactures were woollens, paper and milled grains; also town on river Shannon, W Ireland.

Lincolnshire

Maritime co. in E of England; divided into divisions of Holland, Kesteven and Lindsey; primarily agricultural with a few heavy industries of shipbuilding and machine making.

Midlothian

Co. in SE of Scotland on Firth of Forth; formerly Edinburghshire; mineral deposits of coal, shale, ironstone and limestone; principal industries were brewing, paper manufacture and brick and tile making.

Monmouthshire

Maritime co. in W of England, adjacent to border with Wales; some agricultural production (wheat, rye, barley and oats); best known for its large industries centred around iron and coal; occasionally included as part of the 'South Wales' region.

Norfolk

Maritime co. in the E of England; principal industries were fishing and agriculture: livestock – including cart horses and poultry.

Northamptonshire

Inland co.; hilly district with large deposits of iron; dominant industry centred around iron, but also had boot and shoe industries; colloquially 'Northants'.

Northumberland

Most northerly co. in England; coalfields and lead deposits dominated economy; major industrial area with ironworks, shipbuilding and chemicals manufacture.

Nottinghamshire

N central co. in England; several coal mines, but primarily agricultural; hosiery, cycles, woollens and cotton, and iron foundries among the industries.

Oxfordshire
Central inland co.; primarily engaged in agriculture.
Ross and Cromarty
Co. in extreme NW of Scotland; encompassed some mainland areas and islands of the Outer Hebrides and Lewis (except Harris); lowlands cultivated and industry limited to the distillation of whiskey.
Shropshire
Inland co. in W central England; famous for its breed of sheep; cattle and dairying; deposits of coal and ironstone – only heavy industries related to iron.
Staffordshire
Co. in NW central England; two major coalfields; heavy industry drawn to nearby coal; 'the Black Country' well known for all branches of iron and related industries.
Strathclyde
(Post-1974) co. in W Scotland; formerly counties of Argyllshire, Ayrshire, Lanarkshire, Dunbartonshire and parts of Stirlingshire.
Suffolk
Maritime co. in E England; produced agricultural crops of wheat, barley, peas and beans, butter, sheep and cart-horses; manufactures limited to agricultural implements.
Surrey
Inland co. adjacent S to London; some industries: pharmaceuticals, tobacco, calicoes and woollen goods.
Sussex
Maritime co. in SE England; administratively divided into East and West Sussex; coastal lowlands cultivated with grains and hay; primary sheep pastures; manufactures included woollens, paper, gunpowder and brick and tile making.
Sutherland
Maritime co. in extreme N of Scotland; economy dominated by fishing and sheep-grazing.
Western Isles
(Post-1974) co. in far NW Scotland; formerly parts of Ross and Cromarty and Inverness-shire.
Wiltshire
Inland co. W of London; woollens, carpets, cutlery and steel goods, and iron-founding traditional industries; a unique industry was training dogs for truffle-hunting.
Yorkshire
Large co. on NE coast; major deposits of limestone and coal; divided into three Ridings: North, East and West.
> North Riding, in N of co.; endowments of limestone, lead, and ironstone; industries related to iron smelting.
> East Riding, in SE of co.; primarily agriculture-related industry; included major seaport of Hull.
> West Riding, in W and SW of co.; centre of Yorkshire's industry; encompassed the major Yorkshire coalfield in an area 45 miles × 20 miles; industrial centres in West Riding included Barnsley, Bradford, Dewsbury, Halifax, Huddersfield, Leeds and Sheffield.

REGIONS

arable zone
  Counties of Yorkshire (East Riding), Lincolnshire, Nottinghamshire, Rutland, Huntingdonshire, Warwickshire, Leicestershire, Northamptonshire, Cambridgeshire, Norfolk, Suffolk, Bedfordshire, Buckinghamshire, Oxfordshire, Berkshire, Hampshire, Hertfordshire, Essex, Middlesex, Surrey, Kent and Sussex.
Black Country
  A term used to designate the manufacturing district south of Staffordshire, occupies radius about 10 miles round West Bromwich.
Cyfartha
  In northern vicinity of Merthyr Tydfil, Glamorgan, Wales; seat of iron works.
East Anglia
  Counties of Huntingdonshire, Cambridgeshire, Norfolk and Suffolk.
east midlands
  Counties of Derbyshire, Nottinghamshire, Lincolnshire (Kesteven & Holland divisions), Leicestershire, Rutland and Northamptonshire.
Forest of Dean
  WNW in Gloucestershire; forest supplied wood needed for charcoal in early iron making; largely deforested by 1800.
Highlands
  General region of Scotland beyond the Grampians; population primarily of Celtic heritage.
Home Counties
  Counties of Essex, Kent, London, Middlesex and Surrey; sometimes referred to as 'the Six Home Counties' including Hertfordshire with those above.
Lothians
  District on the south side of the Firth of Forth; included the Scottish counties of East Lothian, Midlothian and West Lothian.
midlands
  Counties of Derbyshire, Herefordshire, Leicestershire, South Lancashire, Northamptonshire, Nottinghamshire, Rutland, Shropshire, Staffordshire, Warwickshire, Worcestershire; divided into the east midlands and the west midlands.
north-east
  Counties of Northumberland, Durham and Yorkshire (North Riding).
North Wales
  Counties of Anglesey, Carnarvonshire, Denbighshire, Flintshire, Merioneth and Montgomeryshire.
north-west
  Counties of Cumberland, Westmorland and Lancashire (perhaps also including Cheshire).
pastoral zone
  Counties of Northumberland, Cumberland, Durham, Yorkshire (North & West Ridings), Westmorland, Lancashire, Cheshire, Derbyshire, Staffordshire, Shropshire, Worcestershire, Herefordshire, Monmouthshire (Wales), Gloucestershire, Wiltshire, Dorsetshire, Somersetshire, Devonshire and Cornwall.
Scottish Lowlands
  The Scottish mainland not included in the Highlands; generally applied to the counties south of the Firths of Clyde and Tay; 'eastern': East Lothian,

Midlothian, West Lothian, Peebles-shire, Selkirkshire and Roxburghshire;
'Western': Renfrewshire, Lanarkshire, Ayrshire, Wigtownshire, Kirkudbright-
shire and Dumfries-shire.

south-east
Counties of Bedfordshire, Buckinghamshire, Oxfordshire, Berkshire, Hampshire, Hertfordshire, Essex, (Greater London), Surrey, Kent and Sussex.

South Lancashire
Area in NE England; now Merseyside and Greater Manchester.

South Wales
'Formally' comprised of the counties: Brecknockshire, Cardiganshire, Car-
marthenshire, Glamorgan, Pembrokeshire and Radnorshire.

south-west
Counties of Gloucestershire, Wiltshire, Somerset, Dorset, Devon and Cornwall.

West Country
Counties of Cornwall, Devon, Somerset and parts of Wiltshire, Gloucestershire
and Dorset.

east midlands
Counties of Shropshire, Staffordshire, Warwickshire, Worcestershire and
Herefordshire.

PARISHES

Ash
In Derbyshire, 8 miles SW of Derby.

Banbury
In Oxfordshire, 22 miles N of Oxford.

Blackburn
In Lancashire; 11 miles E of Preston and 210 miles NW of London; one of the
principal locales of cotton manufactures.

Bottesford
In N Leicestershire, 7 miles NW of Grantham or in Lindsey, Lincolnshire, 7
miles W of Briggs.

Burslem
In Stoke-on-Trent, N Staffordshire; 20 miles NNW of Stafford by rail; most
notably the birthplace of Josiah Wedgwood (1730–95).

Dawlish
In E Devonshire.

Gedling
In Nottinghamshire, 3 miles NE of Nottingham.

Morchard Bishop
In Devonshire, N of Exeter.

Odiham
In NE Hampshire.

Shepshed
In Leicestershire, 4 miles W of Loughborough.

Winlaton
In Durham on river Tyne.

Ayr
River in Ayrshire, Scotland; flows 38 miles W to Firth of Clyde at city Ayr.
Bristol Channel
An expansion of the estuary of the river Severn; it is about 85 miles long and from 5 to 43 miles wide; rapid rising of the tide creates a *bore*, or sudden wave.
Boyne
River in Leinster (len'ster), south-eastern province of Ireland; flows 70 miles through countries of Kildare and Meath to the Irish Sea; 'Battle of the Boyne' found James II defeated by William III on 1 July 1690.
Channel Tunnel
Tunnel connecting Folkestone, England, and Calais, France; built beneath the English Channel; frequently beset by financial and political problems since the 1960s; formally termed 'the Eurotunnel', but nicknamed 'the Chunnel'.
Clyde
Scotland's most important river; 91 miles long; even the largest ships could navigate it to Glasgow; many shipbuilding enterprises built along its banks.
Culloden (Moor)
On the border of Nairnshire, a maritime co. of NE Scotland; site of the defeat of Prince Charles Edward and the Highlanders (the Jacobites) by the Duke of Cumberland which signalled the defeat of the Stuarts.
English Channel
Extension of the Atlantic Ocean between S England and N France; connected to the North Sea by the Strait of Dover; fishing grounds for mackerel and oysters; often simply 'the Channel'.
Humber
Estuary of the rivers Ouse and Trent; 38 miles long and 1 to $7\frac{1}{4}$ miles across.
Kentish Weald, *see* Weald
Mersey
North-western river formed by the confluence of rivers Goyt and Tame; empties into the Irish Sea; 70 miles in length; large ships could anchor there.
Thames
Britain's most important river; navigable by a great variety of vessels; vital to London's import/export trade; the Thames from London Bridge to Blackwall was known as the 'Port of London' and the section below London Bridge was known as 'The Pool'.
Wear
River in Durham; 65 miles long; barges could navigate it to Durham.
Weald
A landmark of physical geography covering parts of Kent, Surrey and Sussex counties; previously it was densely forested but was largely stripped of timber to make charcoal for early iron making; later it supported pasturelands, hop cultivation and orchards, particularly in Kent.

LONDON: AREA AND LANDMARKS

East End
Area of London generally associated with poverty and the poorer classes of labour; possibly so-named to contrast with the fashionable West End.

Euston Station
  Station built for the London & Birmingham railway; located N central London; recognised for its architecture prior to renovations made by British Rail in the 1960s.
Greater London
  1963 redesignation of the counties of London and Middlesex and parts of Surrey, Kent, Essex and Hertfordshire.
Heathrow
  Formally London (Heathrow) Airport; opened 31 May 1946 to connect the United States and the United Kingdom by direct air-service; to the W of Greater London.
Spitalfields
  Neighbourhood in London's East End; after 1865 French Protestants established silk weaving as an industry there.
Soho
  District in W London; centre for Victorian era entertainment, reputable and disreputable alike; also recognised as a neighbourhood of immigrants.
St Pancras Station
  London terminal for the midland railway; built in the centre of one of London's slum areas, Agar Town.
Sandown Park
  150 acre race course, $\frac{1}{2}$ mile N of Esher Station in Surrey.
Whitehall
  Formerly a royal residence; seat of the executive branch of the British government; a street between Trafalgar Square and Parliament Square, and a general designation for the area including the Prime Minister's residence, 10 Downing Street.

Index and glossary

Abel-Smith, B., 301
Abramovitz, M., 119, 135, 210, 339
absolute advantage
Greater efficiency than someone else. For example, Britain had an absolute advantage in both agriculture and manufacturing in the nineteenth century. Absolute advantage is irrelevant, however, to the question of what Britain should have specialised in doing: comparative advantage (q.v.) is relevant.
accelerator
The dependence of investment on consumption, as the building of petrol stations depends on the amount of petrol sold. The 'acceleration' refers to the speeding up of flow it causes in an underemployed economy: a rise in investment in one industry causes a rise in income earned in others by the 'multiplier' (q.v.), which then causes still more investment (to service the consumption out of the new income), accelerating the rise in income.
Ackrill, M., 142
Addison, P., 287
Afghanistan, 350
age-specific rate
The frequency of some event at a specific age. The age-specific death rate, for instance, is the deaths per 1,000 people of age one year; similar rates can be calculated for those aged two years, ten to fifteen years, etc. Marriage, birth and other rates are also used.
age structure
The proportion of people at each age. In a rapidly growing population, for example, there will be many more children than old people, and the age structure will look, if plotted on a graph, like a triangle with a large base; there

will be a high proportion at ages one year, two years, etc.
agricultural sector, 11–12
aircraft industry, 162–3
Albu, A., 147
Aldcroft, D. H., 202, 204, 309
Alexander, S. S., 228
Allen, R. G. D., 11, 19–20
Amalgamated Society of Engineers, 143
Amory, Heathcoat, 58, 238
Anglo-American Council on Productivity (AACP), 30, 212, 214
Anglo-American Financial Agreement (1945), 39–41, 231, 256–9, 347
appreciation
Of a currency; a rise in its value relative to other currencies. Cf. depreciation.
Armed Forces, 6, 22–4
Armstrong, H. W., 160, 202
Arndt, H. W., 264
Artis, M. J., 82, 240–1
Ashworth, W., 176
Associated Dairies, 128
Atkinson, A. B., 296, 301–2, 313, 315
Atomic Energy Authority, 164
attitudes, 109–11, 119–20
Attlee, Clement, 39, 221, 279, 289, 347
Australia, 20
Austria, 272
autarky, 19
Self-sufficiency, especially of a whole country. Autarky is the opposite of free trade.
autonomous spending, autonomous expenditure
Spending that is not affected by the size of income, but by other things, such as optimism about the future, government policy or purchases by foreigners. Part of investment, much of government spending, most of exports fall in this category. Its significance is that it is the

  (1) Commodities used to make other
commodities in future. Thus, bricks,
steel, lathes and mastery of the Latin
fourth declension are not valued in
themselves for direct consumption, but
are all used to make things in the future
that are: houses, motor cars, chairs,
Latin poetry.
  (2) The pile of existing capital, somehow
added together into one number. The
related but distinct idea is 'investment',
i.e. the additions to the stock. The flow
of water per minute into a bathtub
added up over the number of minutes it
has been flowing is the stock of water in
the bathtub. Likewise, investment added
up is the stock of capital.
  (3) In business, the financial resources
available for an enterprise; what is put
into a project (*see* capital market).

capital deepening
  Giving more machines to the same
number of men; or, producing a given
output with more capital. An assembly
line producing automobiles is a
deepening of capital relative to hand
methods. Cf. capital widening.
capital formation
  Investment (q.v.), i.e. using up resources
now to get a return in the future, such as
building a railway, educating the people,
making ships.
capital gains and losses
  Changes in the value of a long-lived
asset caused by a rise or fall in its price.
If the land tax is raised unexpectedly, for
example, land becomes suddenly less
desirable and landlords experience a
capital loss.

capital intensive
  Using much capital (long-lived goods
used to produce other goods) relative to
labour or land. Relative to a
blacksmith's forge, a fully automated
continuous processing mill is a capital-
intensive way to produce iron nails.
Hence, 'capital intensity' as a measure
of how much capital is used. Cf. capital
deepening; labour intensive.
capital market
  A market in which IOUs are bought and
sold, that is, in which 'capital' in the
financial sense is bought and sold. It
need not be in a single location, as is the
Stock Exchange. The bond market
(located wherever bonds are bought and
sold) and the banks, for example, are
capital markets, part of the unified
capital market of a developed economy.
  The ratio of the value of machinery,
buildings and the like to the value of
their output. It is a measure of the
capital intensity (q.v.) of an economy
and figures in the Harrod–Domar model
of economic growth (q.v.).
capital–output ratio, incremental
  The change in capital required to sustain
a given small rise in production. It is the
inverse of the marginal product of
capital (q.v.).
capital widening
  Increasing the number of men equipped
with a given amount of capital; or,
producing more output with a given
amount of capital. An expansion of
coastal shipping with no change in the
amount of capital per sailor or per ton
shipped would be capital widening (as
against deepening, q.v.).
cartel
  A group of firms organised into a
monopoly. Cartels are illegal under
English common law.
central bank
  The state's bank, such as the Bank of
England, or (in the USA) the Federal
Reserve Bank. A fashionable
circumlocution for central bank is 'the
monetary authority', i.e. the institution

corset, 245

cost, constant factor, *see* national income at factor cost

cost-benefit analysis

An assessment using economics of the desirability of some project, such as a railway. The railway has costs, smoke pollution as well as the conventional costs such as engines, that may require the use of economic methods. And it has benefits that may require their use as well: the total benefit, for example, is what consumers are willing to pay, not merely what they actually pay, and the method of demand curves must be used to assess the willingness to pay. Cf. consumers' surplus; social savings

cost curve, cost function

The expenditure to produce various different amounts of a good. What 'the' expenditure is depends on what definition one has in mind: of 'total' cost (all the expenditures to produce the amount produced), 'average' cost (total cost per unit produced) or 'marginal' cost (the increase in total cost from producing one more unit). The total cost of producing a million yards of cotton gray cloth might be 6 million shillings; this would imply an average cost of 6 shillings a yard. But if it were difficult to expand production the marginal cost might be higher, say 10 shillings a yard.

cost of living index

A measure of the prices of consumer goods, such as food, housing, health, cars, clothes and so forth.

cost-push inflation

A rise in prices caused by rises in costs, such as oil prices or trade union wages. The existence of such inflation is disputed among economists, as is its opposite, demand-pull inflation.

Cotton Board, 139–40

Cotton Industry Act (1959), 139

Cotton Spinning Industry Act (1948), 138–9

cotton textiles, 136–41

  firm size, 138–9

  government role, 138–40

  skilled labour, 137–8

  technology, 137–8

Coulter, F., 302, 313–15

Council for Prices, Productivity and Incomes (COPPI), 62

counterfactual

An event contrary to actual fact, though perhaps possible. 'British income would have been 10 per cent lower in 1865 had the railway never been invented' is a counterfactual: the railway was in actual fact invented, and the counterfactual makes an assertion about what the world would have been like if it had not. Statements of cause, such as that the railway caused 10 per cent of British national income in 1865, are said to entail counterfactuals. Consequently, analytical economic history of the sort pursued in this book, which wishes to make causal statements, uses counterfactuals.

country banks

Banks outside London, especially in the eighteenth and nineteenth centuries outside the local, legal monopoly of issuing money possessed by the Bank of England.

Courtaulds, 140, 329

Cousins, Frank, 213–14

Coutts, K., 322, 326, 331

covariance

A measure of how closely two things vary together. Over the nineteenth century, for example, British national income and exports have positive, large covariance, which is to say that when exports were high so was income. Like correlation, to which covariance is related mathematically, covariance does not imply the two things are causally connected, or causally connected in one direction.

Crafts, N. F. R., 135, 137, 146, 204, 207, 210, 212, 214, 218, 267, 322–5, 344

credit creation, credit multiplier, money multiplier

The lending of banks to businesses and so forth, especially the loans that banks make beyond the money they have in their vaults to back up the loans. Cf. bank credit.

Creedy, J., 312

Cripps, Stafford, 41, 49–50, 53, 74, 233

Crockett, A. D., 241

Crosland, C. A. R., 161, 173, 284, 297, 305

Cross, R., 203, 205

temporarily while moving from a job society does not now want to a job it does want. Identical to cyclical unemployment.

demand for labour
The number of people businesses wish to hire at some wage. The lower the wage the larger the number demanded.

demand management, 27–8, 32–3, 49, 55, 107, 156, 262
end of, 113–14
see also budgetary policy; fiscal policy; stop–go cycles
The government's attempt to keep the society's spending at the level of full employment (q.v.), neither too high nor too low, by manipulating its own expenditures. Since its expenditures are part of aggregate demand (q.v.), the attempt may theoretically achieve success.

demand-pull inflation
A rise in prices generally in the economy due to the society's desire to buy more than it has. Contrast cost-push inflation, cf. deflation.

demographic crisis, subsistence crisis
Overpopulation relative to the amount of land available for agriculture, and the misery that results.

demographic factors
labour force, 196–7
of unemployment, 204
of war, 29
welfare spending, 293–4

Denison, E. F., 30, 115, 265
Denmark, 118
Department of Economic Affairs (DEA), 73, 161, 264, 275, 278
Department of Scientific and Industrial Research, 164

dependency ratio
The ratio of those who do not work for money (i.e. normally children, old people and some married women) to those who do work for money.

deposits, deposit liabilities, demand deposits
Cheque-drawing privileges; your chequing account.

depreciation
Of a currency, a fall in its value relative to other currencies. Contrast appreciation, a rise in value, devaluation, which entails some intent.

depreciation, replacement investment
(1) The wearing-out of capital.
(2) Expenditure to replace the worn-out capital.
(3) The fund accumulated to allow for the expenditure to replace the worn-out capital.
The three need not be identical. Depreciation is subtracted from 'gross' income to get 'net' income because a fund used to maintain capital is not available for satisfying present wants.

deprivation, relative, 332, 340–3
deregulation, 252
devaluation
A fall in the value of a currency relative to another, with the connotation that the fall was intended and arranged (if not necessarily desired) by a nation's government. Contrast depreciation, which connotes an unintended fall in value.

Development Areas, 159–60
Development Councils, 161
deviation from trend, absolute and relative
Of a time series, i.e. a statistic for a series of years, cases in which the statistics are higher or lower than a trend, i.e. higher or lower than what might be expected from a line fitted through the points. A harvest failure in 1816, for example, would be a deviation from the trend of the wheat crop 1800 to 1820. The absolute deviation is the number of bushels below the 1800–20 trend that the crop fell; the relative deviation is the percentage fall.

Devons, E., 32
Diebold, W., 257
differentials
Usually in reference to wages, differences between wages from one job to another or from one place to another. If the higher wage is compensation for worse conditions or higher skills the differentials have no tendency to disappear, and are called 'compensating' or 'equalising'.

Digby, A., 285, 290, 301
Dilnot, A. W., 289–92, 303, 313–14
diminishing returns
The fall in the amount of additional output as additional doses of input are applied. The nation's agriculture is subject to diminishing returns as more

exponential growth
Growth at a constant percentage rate per year, in the manner of compound interest. A straight line upward sloping on an ordinary graph against time has a falling percentage rate of growth, because the constant absolute rise per year is applied to a larger and larger base. An exponential curve would have to be curving up steeper and steeper to maintain the same rate.

exports
growth of, 108
manufacturing and commerce, 126, 130–1

ex post
The realised value or from the point of view of after the event or attained. Cf. ex ante.

externalities, external effects, external economies or diseconomies
Effects you did not directly pay for, such as the pain of smoke in your eye from the local factory or the pleasure of the council's flower garden. The weeds that spread from your neighbour's ill-kept plot in the village fields to your plot is a 'negative' (i.e. bad) externality. The quickening of trade that spreads from the new railway to your business is a positive (i.e. good) externality. An alternative terminology is that external economies are good, external diseconomies bad. Whatever terminology is used, the key idea is the external nature of the event, that is, outside your own control and not directly affected by your activities. Contrast internal economies of scales.

extractive industry, 125

factor, factor of production
One of the inputs into making things, especially the tripartite division into the inputs, land, labour and capital.

factor endowments
The inputs a nation has at its disposal, including labour, machinery, buildings and skills as well as coal, climate and soil. Cf. classical vs. Hecksher–Ohlin.

factor income distribution
The incomes to each of the three classical 'factors' of productions, i.e. labour, land and capital. It is also called the functional distribution of income.

factor shares
The fractions of income going to labour, capital, land and other inputs.

Fairey, 187
Fair Trading Act (1973), 158
Falkingham, J., 313
Falklands, 320, 350
Family Allowance Act (1945), 287
Federation of British Industries, 161
Feinstein, C. H., 5, 8–9, 15, 25, 51, 62, 95–122, 126, 133, 199–200, 209, 229, 244, 326, 339, 350
Fender, J., 262
Ferranti, 165, 187, 276
Fforde, J. S., 233–6, 238–9, 270
Fiegehen, G. C., 301

final goods
Goods used for consumption, investment, government spending or exports, i.e. not used merely to make other goods. Contrast intermediate goods; compare aggregate demand.

financial constraints, wartime, 13–18
financial innovation, 249, 252

financial intermediation
Transferring money from ultimate savers (in trade union pension funds, insurance policies, railway bonds, personal IOUs, etc.). Banks, insurance companies and other financial institutions are engaged in intermediation: they borrow from the public, who get a secure place to put their funds and a reward in interest; and they loan to business, who get use of the funds.

firms
financial help for small firms, 165–6
nucleus firm, 10
size, 138–9, 158–9

First World War, 4, 7, 10, 14, 28, 135, 146, 198, 285, 322

fiscal policy, 225–6, 267–71
taxation, 269
see also budgetary policy; demand management
The plans by government for its own taxing and spending, which may achieve goals such as full employment, growth and stable prices. Cf. demand management; full employment surplus; monetary policy.

Fishbein, W. H., 272

fixed capital
Capital that cannot be varied in amount quickly to suit circumstances; opposite,

non-economist's notion that one
person's or one country's gain is
another's loss.
See consumers' surplus
Gaitskell, Hugh, 49, 53–4, 233–4
Gamble, A., 154, 156, 211
garden cities
A movement in Britain in the early
twentieth century to settle the population
in healthy new cities far removed from
the great conurbations. Result: Welwyn
Garden City.
Gardner, R. N., 256
Garside, W. R., 200, 202, 204
gas, 174
General Accident, 128
General Agreement on Tariffs and Trades
(GATT), 31, 108, 157, 208, 257, 347
Germany, 35–6, 42, 45–6, 65, 94, 319, 326,
335, 344
Blitzkrieg strategy, 8
economic growth, 108, 110, 115–16, 118,
121–2, 322, 339
industrial performance, 131, 133–6, 145,
148–9
Operation Barbarossa, 9
Second World War, 8–9, 12, 14, 26,
29–30
social welfare, 294, 300, 308–9
state ownership, 169, 179, 187, 189–90
Technische Hochschulen, 146
Trade Continuation Schools, 146–7
Gerschenkron, A., 119
Gillion, C., 341
gilt-edged market, 249
Glennerster, H., 293, 297, 310
Godley, W., 322, 326, 331
gold devices
The exploitation by the Bank of England
of details in the market for gold in order
to encourage or discourage the flow of
gold into Britain, especially in the late
nineteenth century. For instance, though
legally bound to pay out English gold
coins (sovereigns) for Bank of England
notes at a fixed rate, the Bank could pay
out foreign coins at whatever rate it
could get.
gold exchange standard
The system of valuing paper currencies
at fixed amounts of gold or of other
currencies whose value is fixed in terms
of gold. Thus, the currency of a small
country might be backed by reserve
holdings of gold or of sterling or dollars.

gold reserves
The holdings of gold by the Bank of
England available to maintain the gold
value of British paper money. Cf. official
reserves.
gold standard
The system of valuing paper currencies
(pounds, dollars, francs) at fixed
amounts of gold. Being fixed to gold
they are fixed (within limits of transport
cost called 'gold points') to each other.
The gold standard, then, amounted to a
system of fixed exchange rates. Britain
was on gold from 1819 to 1914 and from
1925 to 1931. From 1872 to 1931 or
1933 enough other countries were on
gold to justify calling it a system.
Goldthorpe, J. H., 110
Goodhart, C. A. E., 241, 243, 245, 249–50,
252–3
Goodin, R. E., 292
Goodman, G., 214
goodwill
The reputation, trademark, employee
morale, good collection of managers or
other distinctive features of a firm. As an
accounting idea it makes cost equal
revenue when revenue is high: if revenue
exceeds costs the excess can be called the
income of goodwill. As an economic idea
it serves a similar function, and is called
'entrepreneurial income'.
Gordon, R. J., 206
Gourvish, T. R., 176, 181
government debt
Bonds, or IOUs, issued by government.
Cf. budget deficit; Consols.
government expenditure
For purposes of reckoning the national
income, the purchases by the
government of goods and services valued
by consumers. Transfers of income that
are not purchases of goods are not part
of government spending in this sense:
allowances under the Poor Law are not
part of spending, nor under some
conventions are interest payments on
past government borrowings. Under
some conventions of measuring national
income, indeed, the provision of roads
and police are taken to be depreciation,
and are therefore not included in net
income.
government role, 32–4
cotton textiles, 138–40

reducing, 77–80, 86
see also industrial policy; national debt;
nationalisation; public expenditure
Gowing, M. M., 11, 22
Gowland, D., 243, 245–6, 248–50
Graham, A., 158
Grand Metropolitan, 127–8
Grant, W., 154, 276
Grassman, S., 257
Great Depression, 108, 208
(1) The business slump of the 1930s
which was in Britain a continuation of a
slump in the 1920s.
(2) In an obsolete and exploded but still
widely used sense, the slow growth of
1873–96 – which was not in fact slow
real growth but merely a fall in prices.
Great Universal Stores, 128
Gribbin, J. D., 207, 212, 214
Griffiths, B., 173
gross
In economic terminology, 'inclusive of
something', distinguished from 'net'.
Thus gross exports of shipping services
from Britain are all British sales of
shipping services to foreigners, whereas
net exports are all British sales to
foreigners minus sales by foreigners to
Britain.
gross barter terms of trade
The ratio of the amount of exports a
country gains from trade to the amount
of exports it must sacrifice to acquire the
imports. The concept was introduced by
the American economist Frank Taussig
(1859–1940) to allow for tribute payment
and immigrants' remittances home as an
element in trade. It has proven
unsuccessful, and most modern studies
focus attention on the net barter terms,
simply called *the* terms of trade
(q.v.).
gross domestic fixed capital formation
The expenditure to produce ('form') new
machinery, buildings and other slow-to-
adjust assets ('fixed capital') located at
home ('domestic', as opposed to
foreign), and including ('gross')
replacements of worn-out capital as well
as entirely new capital.
gross domestic product
The sum of the value of everything
produced in Britain, by contrast with
things produced by British capital or
labour abroad.

gross national income or gross national
product
Gross national income or (what amounts
to the same thing) product, or 'GNP',
includes as output of the economy the
costs of maintenance and replacement of
the machinery buildings, railways, etc.,
that make up the nation's capital. Net
national income or product subtracts out
these costs, as not available for
consumption or new investment. The
difference is usually small. Cf.
depreciation.
gross reproduction rate
A measure of how many children the
typical woman will have over her life. It
eliminates the effect of varying
proportions of women at various ages.
Group of Seven, 92
growth theory
A branch of economics dealing in an
abstract (usually mathematical) form
with certain of the causes of the wealth
of nations. Despite its encouraging
name, it is not empirically based, and is
not therefore a theory of any actually
achieved economic growth.
Grubb, D., 208, 217
Guardian, R. E., 128
Guillebaud Committe, 308
Gwyn, W. B., 331

Halewood, 144
Hall, P. A., 268, 280
Hall, Robert, 55, 154, 156, 233, 239
Halsey, A. H., 310
Ham, A., 279
Hammond, R. J., 11, 17
Hannah, L., 138, 150, 157, 168–94, 197,
207
Hansen, B., 269
Hare, P. G., 265
Hargreaves, E. L., 11
Harland, 162
Harris, J., 286–7
Harris, N., 264
Harrison, M., 5, 8–10, 25
Harrod–Domar model
The extension of Keynesian thinking to
the long run, named in honour of the
economists who developed it. The model
contemplates the possibility that the
'natural' growth of income necessary for
full employment (given the growth of
population) may be less or more than

merely the out-of-pocket expenses of the landlord. But if the improvement temporarily disrupts the farm or if the improvements makes impossible some other project (e.g. road widening), then more costs need to be counted to capture the full opportunity cost.

Organisation for European Economic Cooperation (OEEC), 42, 48, 66

outmigration, 92

output, 348
  declining growth of, 71
  industry and commerce, 128–9
  manufacturing, 97–9

output, full employment
  The goods made by an economy when all who wish to work do. Cf. full employment.

overhead, fixed costs
  Costs such as administration and plant that do not vary with output.

overseas new issues
  New lending to foreigners, especially in the form of IOUs. Thus, new issues are 'portfolio investment' by Englishmen in foreign bonds.

overvaluation
  A condition of a currency in which the price at which it is presently selling in terms of other currencies is for some reason too high. The pound sterling, for example, is said to have been overvalued when Britain returned to gold in 1925. The price of the pound ($4·86) did not fall, because the Treasury would buy up pounds to keep the price up. According to the traditional story, the price level in Britain had to fall to achieve equilibrium at the too high price of pounds.

Overy, R. J., 12, 26

Oxford, 188

Paige, D., 190

Paish, F. W., 107

Pakistan, 140, 347

Palestine, 36

P and O Navigation, 127

Papps, I., 182, 191

parameter shift
  A change, whether actual or hypothetical, in the value of something normally thought of as a constant. For example, if bankers suddenly revised their notion of how much they needed to hold in reserve against the chance of

someone demanding currency out of his chequing account, the change might be called a parameter shift.

Parker, H. M. D., 6

Parkin, J. M., 241

Parkin, M., 111

Parsons, D. W., 260, 275

partial equilibrium analysis
  Economic thinking that takes one small sector of the economy in isolation, on the argument (sometimes true, sometimes false) that the more remote consequences of a change in question by way of other parts of the economy are unimportant. The other member of the pair is 'general equilibrium analysis'.

participation rate, 6, 23, 196–9
  The percentage of a group who work in the market instead of at home. It is most commonly applied to women, whose rate has varied markedly from one time or social class to another.

patents, 145
  An exclusive right to use or sell one's invention.

Pathirane, L., 169

Pavitt, K., 145–6

Pay Board and Price Commission, 80

payment agreements, 41–2

payments, balance of, see balance of payments

Peacock, A. T., 292

Peck, M. J., 148–9

Peden, G. C., 15, 17, 28

Pelling, H., 289

Pennant-Rea, R., 279

pensions, old age, 289, 313

permanent income
  The income one can count on having, contrasted with 'transitory' income (which includes any unusual unexpected rise or fall in income). The 'permanent income hypothesis' is the notion that the amount people consume (i.e. the amount they do not save) is dependent on their permanent not their transitory income. Identical to expected lifetime income. Cf. relative income hypothesis, transitory/windfall income.

Persian Gulf, 350

Phelps, E., 205

Phillips, A. W., 205

Phillips curve
  An association of high unemployment with low inflation and low

directly to the investors in the project, by
contrast with the more comprehensive
returns that include any benefits
(subtracting any hurts) that come to
people other than those who invested.
The profits from a railway line, for
example, would be private returns; the
rise in the rent of my land when the
railway ran by it would have to be added
to measure 'social' returns (q.v.)

process innovation
The introduction of a new way of
making an old thing, as distinct from the
introduction of a new thing ('product'
innovation).
producers' surplus
The excess of what producers are
actually paid over what they would be
willing to accept at the least. The idea is
analogous, on the other side of the
market, to 'consumers' surplus' (q.v.). It
is identical to 'rent' (q.v.) and to profit.
product innovation
The introduction of a new thing as
distinct from a new way of making an
old thing ('process' innovation). The
word 'innovation' in both phrases
emphasises that it is not invention – i.e.
discovery – that is entailed, but bringing
into practical use.
production function
The relation between output and input.
productive potential
The most the society can make under
conditions of full employment (q.v.).
Output per man in some industry or
economy. Since it is per man, ignoring
other inputs (such as capital or raw

materials), it is not usually an
adequate measure of efficiency overall
in the use of resources.
The ratio of all output to a composite
of all inputs. If it rises it signifies a rise
in output relative to inputs, greater
'efficiency' in common parlance. It is
called 'total' (as distinct from
'partial') productivity because it is *not*
merely output per unit of labour
alone, or any one input alone. It is the
productivity of *all* 'factors' (i.e.
inputs) taken together. Other names
for it are 'the residual', 'technical
progress' or 'productivity change'.
Output per unit of input, conventionally
either of land, labour, capital or some
combination of these.
propensity to consume
The amount consumed out of the
average £ or (a slightly different notion)
the additional £ of income. Cf.
consumption function; marginal
propensity to import; multiplier.
psychic income
Satisfactions not paid for explicitly in
money, such as from the neighbour's
garden or from the company furniture in
one's office. Cf. externalities.
public good
A commodity from the benefits of which
no one in the public can be (or in some
definitions should be) excluded. National

regression analysis, regression equation, curve fitting

Techniques for fitting straight lines through a scatter of points. In finding the straight line that would best summarise the relationship during 1921–38 between consumption and income, for instance, one is said to 'regress consumption on income', i.e. fit a straight line through points on a graph of annual consumption and income for these years. The simplest and by far the most widely used of the techniques is called 'least squares' or 'ordinary least squares'. The result will be an equation for a straight line, such as: Consumption in £ million at 1938 prices equals £277 million plus 0·44 times income in £ million at 1938 prices. Symbolically, the equation is in general $C = a + bY$. The actual numerical result says that the line that best fits the scatter of combinations of consumption and income is a constant (£277 million) plus 44 per cent of whatever income happens to be. The 'slope' or 'slope coefficient' or 'regression coefficient' or 'beta' is in this case 0·44. Consumption here is called the 'dependent' variable, income the 'independent' variable, in accord with the notion that consumption is dependent on income. The technique generalises easily to more than one independent variable, in which case it is called 'multiple regression' and amounts to fitting a plane (rather than a line) through points in space (rather than through points on a plane surface). In multiple regression the coefficient 'on' (i.e. multiplying) each independent variable measures the way each by itself influences the dependent variable. The equation fitted in the case mentioned above was in fact Consumption = 277 + (0·44) Income + (0·47) Consumption Last Year, which is a multiple regression of this year's consumption on this year's income and last year's consumption. It says that for a given consumption last year each £ of income raised consumption by £0·44; and for a given income each £ of consumption last year raised

consumption this year by £0·47. The technique generalises with rather more difficulty to more than one dependent variable, in which case it is called 'simultaneous equation estimation'.

regressive taxes

Taxes whose burden falls on the poor, as taxes on food are said to be relative to 'progressive' taxes such as those on mink coats and yachts.

relative income hypothesis

The notion that one's consumption (as distinct from savings) depends on one's relative economic position, not absolute wealth. According to the hypothesis the poor will save little (i.e. consume virtually all their income) even though they are in absolute terms as wealthy as, say, the high-saving middle class of a much poorer country. Cf. permanent income.

relative price

As distinct from 'nominal' or 'money' or 'absolute' prices, the price of one good in terms of another good, rather than in terms of money. If farm labour earns 16 shillings a week when wheat sells for 8 shillings a bushel, then the price of a week of labour relative to a bushel of wheat is 2·0 bushels per week. Note the units: they are physical, not money, units. Relative prices are determined by the real effectiveness of the economy, whereas money prices are determined by relative prices and by the dearness of money.

rent, economic rent, pure rent

The return to specialised factors of production in an industry, i.e. those factors used in that industry alone. Agricultural land with no use outside of agriculture is the classic example. A coal seam is another. Economic rent need not correspond exactly to the amount earned in 'rent' in the ordinary sense of weekly rent for a flat, or even yearly rent for land. For definitions in slightly different terms, cf. economic rent; producers' surplus.

rentier

The receiver of rent, from French (and pronounced as French). Often with an unfavourable connotation, it means the

weighted average
The typical value of some measure, adjusted for the relative importance of various items. Thus, the unweighted average of city sizes would count Camberley and London each as cities; the weighted average would count London more times than Camberley, perhaps in proportion to their sizes. Such a procedure would give the size of city in which the typical person lived while the unweighted procedure would give the average population of a list of places called cities.
welfare benefits
changing value, 293–4
contributory and non-contributory, 287–8
means-tested, 290, 313
services and cash, 287–8
welfare state, 27, 284–317
change in coverage, 293–4
comprehensive, 288–9
demographic factors, 293–4
distributional effects, 300–5
economic impact of, 296–305
efficiency effects, 297–300, 315–16
equality, 315–17
failure to alleviate poverty, 316–17
funding for, 52–3
growth of, 292–6
origins of, 285–7
reduction in, 298
structure and finance, 287–92
Wells, J. R., 328
Westland, 162
Whiteman, J. C., 132
Whiting, A., 278
Wicks, M., 292, 311

Wiener, M. J., 124, 146, 154
Wildavsky, A., 296
Wilensky, H. L., 286
Wilkinson, F., 149
Wilks, S., 142, 154–5
Williams, F., 314
Williams, K., 283
Williams, P. M., 83
Wilson, D., 292
Wilson, Harold, 53, 163, 241
Wilson, T., 292
Winch, D., 211
Winter, D., 316
winter of discontent, 85–6
Winters, L. A., 208
Wiseman, J., 292
women, participation rate, 6, 23, 197–8
Wood, Kingsley, 15–16
work, hours of, 6, 80, 105, 199
working capital
The capital (q.v.) of a firm in the form of materials to be worked on, cash in hand, inventories of finished products and so forth that can be readily made into cash.
World Bank, 31
Wrigley, C., 152

X-efficiency, 186

Yamey, B. S., 207
Yarn Spinners' Association, 157
Yarrow, G., 184
York, 301
Yorkshire, 159

Zimbabwe, 349
Zweig, F., 213
Zysman, J., 330